EARTH'S EARLIEST AGES

EARTH'S EARLIEST AGES

AND THEIR

Connection with Modern Spiritualism and Theosophy

BY

G. H. PEMBER, M.A.,

AUTHOR OF "THE GREAT PROPHECIES," ETC

ISBN: 978-93-5128-956-2(PB)

First Published in 1884
Indian Reprint in 2017

Published by

Kalpaz Publications
C-30, Satyawati Nagar,
Delhi – 110052
E-mail: kalpaz@hotmail.com
Website: kalpazpublications.com
Ph.: +91-9212142040

PREFACE.

IN 1876 the author of the present volume published a smaller book, entitled "Earth's Earliest Ages and Their Lessons for Us," in which his object was twofold. He first attempted to remove some of the Geological and other difficulties usually associated with the commencing chapters of Genesis; and then endeavoured to show that the characteristic features of the Days of Noah were reappearing in Christendom, and, therefore, that the Days of the Son of Man could not be far distant.

For guidance in his efforts after the first of these aims, he adopted the following obvious principles—which, if they be admitted, render the interpretation easy and precise, and anticipate every possible Geological objection.

I. That the first chapter of Genesis, equally with those which follow it, is, in its primary meaning, neither vision nor allegory, but plain history, and must, therefore, be accepted as a literal statement of facts.

II. That care must, however, be taken to elicit the exact sense of the Hebrew text, which the English Authorised Version often fails to express.

III. That, to those who really believe in a Supreme

Being, the occurrence of supernatural interference, causing physical convulsions and changes, presents no difficulty, especially in connection with a world the moral condition of which was evidently out of course ages before the creation of our race.

In the latter half of the volume, it became necessary to investigate Spiritualism, because that strange movement was deemed to be an incipient revival of the last and greatest cause of corruption in the days of Noah. And possibly it may have been owing to this investigation, and its admission of the supernatural character of phenomena then generally ascribed to illusion or imposture, that the book lay for a while in comparative neglect. When, however, its surmises began to be verified by the spread and forcible intrusion upon public notice of Spiritualism, the speedy sale of the remaining copies, and the letters received by the author, testified to an awakening interest, and determined the reissue, in some form, of the work. It was, however, apparent that a mere reprint would be very inadequate, since, apart from the author's increased familiarity with the subject, Spiritualism itself had greatly developed, and two other waves of kindred thought, Theosophy and Buddhism, had followed it.

Not only, then, has the original work been revised with copious additions, but fresh chapters have also been added to deal with the later phases of that which, in spite of great diversities among its supporters, we must, nevertheless, regard as one threefold movement. And in no point, perhaps, is its real unity more easily discerned than in the main object of its teachings, which is, to set aside the salvation of the Lord Jesus, and to substitute the doctrine that sin must be gradually worn away by our own works and sufferings, either in the spirit-world or in a series of reincarnations upon earth.

The latter scheme, or spiritual evolution, preceded and, as it were, introduced by the physical evolutionary theories, is, under sundry disguises and with various modifications, insinuating itself in quarters where its rejection might have been deemed certain. But Christians, at least, ought to perceive that it is directly subversive of the Biblical cosmogony and plan of salvation; and that, by its very nature, it tends, more slowly, perhaps, but not less surely, to obliterate the great Creator Himself from the minds of His creatures.

Should any of our readers be predisposed in favour of such a theory, we would entreat them to consider its pedigree as given in our chapter on Theosophy; to note its avowed origin from "descending angels," who can be none other than those Nephilim which the Bible mentions as having already appeared twice upon earth; and to remember that its acknowledged depositaries and guardians have been, not the apostles and Church of the Lord Jesus, but the initiates of the Mysteries, the Brahman priests, and the followers of Buddha.

A solemn thought remains. It would seem to have been by means of this very doctrine that Satan effaced the primal revelation from the minds of the intellectual among men, and changed their faith in the only true God into that Pantheism which is ever found to be the basis of Pagan philosophy.

But many signs appear to testify that the hour of the Powers of Darkness is again approaching—that eclipse of faith which, it is foretold, shall precede the coming of the Son of Man. And "the thing that hath been, it is that which shall be."

CONTENTS.

CHAPTER IX.

CHAPTER X.

CHAPTER XI.

SPIRITUALISM. PART I.

CHAPTER XII.

SPIRITUALISM. PART II.

CHAPTER XIII.

SPIRITUALISM. PART III.

CHAPTER XIV.

CHAPTER XV.

CHAPTER XVI.

INTRODUCTION.

CHAPTER I.

INTRODUCTION.

BIBLICAL INTERPRETATION. IMPORTANCE OF THE PROPHETIC SCRIPTURES.

Modern objections to Christianity are often grounded upon the diversity of Biblical interpretation.

BEFORE we proceed to examine and attempt to explain an important subject of revelation, it will be well to offer a few general remarks on the interpretation of the Bible. For in our days Christianity is vehemently assailed with arguments based upon the diversities of opinion among its professors. Men point with sharp sarcasm to the many sects of Christendom, and to the numerous and serious disagreements of those sects, not merely in questions of Church government and discipline, but even upon vital points of doctrine. They impugn the Divine origin of writings which admit of such variety of interpretation, and can be made the basis of so many differing, and even conflicting, systems.

Nor is this sentiment confined to those who live in professedly Christian countries. It is beginning to spread even among the Heathen: it has already supplied them with a powerful weapon against the worshippers of the Triune Jehovah, and is presenting a new and formidable barrier to missionary success.

The charge of diversity is true; but its cause is to be sought in man, and not in the revelation vouchsafed to him.

Now the fact that there are countless diversities in the nominal Church cannot be denied. Nay, we must go still further, and confess that the mischief may be detected even among those who call upon the name of the Lord Jesus in sincerity, and march to meet the future with unfaltering step through faith in His once offered sacrifice for sin: for they, too, have differences of opinion and sundry opposing doctrines all claiming to be derived from the Word of God.

What, then, shall we reply to our assailants? Are the Scriptures really so inconsistent, or so vague, that a multitude of conflicting opinions and doctrines can be fairly deduced from them? Were they so, the fact would indeed be a strong argument against their Divine origin. But we are by no means forced upon such an admission: nay, as soon as we begin to consider the enigma an obvious and certain solution presents itself. For not the revelation of God, but the expounders of that revelation, are responsible for the diversities of Christendom: the fault rests with the fallen and corrupt nature of man, which so affects him that he cannot clearly discern truth even when it is set before his eyes.

Proof of this from the early history of the Church.

Do we doubt this? Let us, then, glance at the history of the first reception of the Gospel as recorded in the New Testament. Do we not find error mingling with truth from the very beginning? Does it not seem to have been the first anxiety of an apostle, after planting a Church, to check the simultaneous upgrowth of rank weeds which threatened soon to choke it? Need we instance Corinth, Galatia, Colossæ; the strange doctrines taught at Ephesus and Crete, which are mentioned in the letters to Timothy and Titus; the warnings against existing heresies in the Epistles of Peter, John, and Jude? And if we pass on to examine the uninspired writings of the early Church, we shall be still more impressed with the same sad fact, that, from the very first, there were counteracting influences which impaired the purity of the messages of God.

There were at least three classes of corruptors. The first consisted of, perhaps, sincere Christians, whose minds were not entirely freed from the influence of a Pagan education.

For men did not bring the tablets of their hearts smooth and unmarked to receive a first grand impression from the revealed will and purposes of their Creator; but came filled with myths, philosophies, and prejudices, which they could not altogether throw off, but retained, in part at least, and mingled—quite unwittingly, perhaps—with the truth of God. As time went on, the incongruity of this human admixture became more and more apparent; and yet men clung to it, because they felt that it softened the corrective severity of revelation, and forced it into some kind of sympathy with the lusts of fallen nature.

And so they soon found themselves constrained to devise a means of blunting the sword of the Spirit, lest its keen edge should be used to sever the spurious from the genuine. Those portions of Scripture which were most determinedly antagonistic to the hopes and feelings of men were allegorised, or, as by a sad misnomer it was called, "spiritualised," out of their literal and proper meaning; and, being thus deprived of the power which God had placed in them, were no longer able to present insurmountable obstacles to the entrance of false doctrine. And yet, so far, we are speaking only of the mischief done by those who may, perhaps, have been sincere Christians, but who corrupted the Word of God through short-sightedness and lack of wisdom, and, above all, through that inability to clear the mind of fixed ideas which is common to all mortals.

The second, of those who joined the Church from motives of self-interest.

But there was another class of corruptors described by Paul as "many unruly and vain talkers and deceivers. . . who subvert whole houses, teaching things which they ought not, for filthy lucre's sake":* men who, when they saw Christianity rapidly spreading, when they perceived the hold it had upon the minds of those who were affected by it, desired, for their own ambitious or covetous ends, to become leaders of a party which promised to be so influential, which bid so fair for power. These had no scruple in introducing such doctrines as suited themselves, and mightily helped to establish a practice which has been too common in all subsequent time, that use of the Bible which virtually regards it as a book by the aid of which one may justify one's own opinions.

The third, of those who became nominal Christians for the express purpose of corrupting Christianity.

And lastly; there was yet a third class of men devoted to the higher and more intellectual forms of Pagan worship, initiates of the mysteries—those secret societies which had then woven their nets over the whole of the civilized world. These crept into the fold unawares, as true wolves in sheep's clothing, with

* Titus i. 10, 11.

deliberate intent to worry and destroy the flock. For from the first, with an instinct of Satan, they marked the Christian as their mortal foe, and perceiving with ever increasing alarm the failure of persecution after persecution, from Nero to Galerius, to suppress the new sect, felt that it could not be exterminated by open warfare, and must, therefore, be seduced and corrupted by craft. This plan was far more successful than the violence of persecution. Where the sword of the World failed its flatteries were victorious. The astonished Church beheld the frown of her cruel oppressor softening into a friendly smile; was bewildered with offers of peace and union from those who had hitherto breathed out threatenings and slaughter; and, becoming elated with the sudden change, was not indisposed for compromise. And thus the World became nominally Christian, and vast crowds of idolaters passed within the pale of the visible Church, bringing with them their old gods and goddesses under new names, as well as their incessant sacrifices, their rites, their vestments, their incense, and all the paraphernalia of their impious worship. Nor did the philosophers fail to contribute their share to the perplexing confusion which speedily obscured every vital doctrine of Christianity. For, by skilfully blending their own systems with the truths of Scripture, they so bewildered the minds of the multitude that but few retained the power of distinguishing the revelation of God from the craftily interwoven teachings of men.

So complete, then, even in early times, was the corruption of the Word of God. Nor has the Church ever succeeded in freeing herself from it, though she did make a strenuous effort to do so at the epoch of the

Reformation. From the time when the Adversary first sowed them, the tares have been ever mingled with the wheat, as indeed they must continue to be until the harvest. And the result is that inconsistent and unsound interpretations have been handed down from generation to generation, and received as if they were integral parts of the Scriptures themselves; while any texts which seemed violently opposed were allegorised, spiritualised, or explained away, till they ceased to be troublesome, or, perchance, were even made subservient. From time to time, too, systems and sects were formed more or less pure than the main body, but into which the Adversary never failed to foist some error; and men, trained to look upon their own Church as the only perfect one, contended fiercely for its tenets, and freely, though often unconsciously, perverted Scripture in maintaining the struggle.

This early corruption, from which the nominal Church has never yet been purged, is a sufficient explanation of the diversity and inconsistency of Biblical interpretation.

Weighing, then, all these causes, we surely need not accuse the Bible of vagueness or inconsistency in order to explain the diversities of its interpretation. For, if we be observant and honest, we must often ourselves feel the difficulty of approaching the sacred writings without bias, seeing that we bring with us a number of stereotyped ideas, which we have received as absolutely certain, and never think of testing, but only seek to confirm. And yet, could we but fearlessly and impartially investigate, we might find that some of these ideas are not in the Bible at all, while others are plainly contradicted by it. For the tracks of many a popular doctrine may be followed through the long range of Church history, till at length we start with affright at the discovery that we have traced them back to the very entrance of the enemy's camp.

We must, therefore, be careful to study without prejudice, and with earnest prayer for the guidance of the Spirit.

We will not stay now to illustrate this fact, some proofs of which will come before us in the course of our subject. But it is a matter which every Christian should carefully test for himself, if he be really desirous to seek first, in preference to any other consideration, the Kingdom of God and His righteousness. For he need be in no perplexity as to the mode of procedure, and God will grant him the requisite wisdom if he ask it. Let him but believe that the Bible is the infallible word of the great Creator, and that all men are, and ever have been, prone to error, and he will readily see that to discover the truth of any doctrine he must first strive to divest himself of preconceived notions, of all that he has ever heard about it, and of all feeling either for or against it. And then, with earnest prayer for the Spirit's aid, let him examine every portion of Scripture which bears upon it, noting the simple and obvious teaching of each, and observing how the various texts interpret and corroborate one another. So will he by God's help arrive at the truth. But yet another precaution will be necessary; he must mark the degree of prominence assigned to it in the Bible, and give it, as nearly as possible, the same in his own teaching. For even true doctrines may sometimes be mischievous if unduly pressed to the exclusion of others, to which, as we may see by their more frequent mention, the Spirit of God attaches greater importance.

Were this course generally pursued, there would soon be an end of diversities in the real Church: the true followers of Christ would present an unbroken phalanx to the world; the greatest obstacle to the spread of the Gospel would be removed; and very different would be the result both of our preaching at home and of our missionary work abroad. For the sword of the Spirit, if drawn forth keen and glittering from its own scabbard, and not merely picked up from the ground where it has been left, blunted and dulled, perchance, by some former warrior, is irresistible, and pierces through body and soul to the inmost shrine of the God-conscious spirit.

Such a course, if generally adopted, would put an end to diversities, and restore its power to the Word of God.

We propose now to examine the testimony of the Divine oracles in regard to three deeply interesting subjects—the creation of our earth, the changes which appear to have taken place in it during ages preceding the Six Days—though our information concerning these stupendous events is very fragmentary and obscure—and the history of our own race until the terrific catastrophe of the Deluge. We shall then endeavour to ascertain whether such records of the past are able to throw any light upon predicted changes in the future; also what lessons we should learn from them, especially in regard to that already widespread and continually increasing intercourse with the other world which is now called Spiritualism, or, if it be of a more philosophic order, Theosophy or Occultism.

The subject proposed. Revived interest in the prophetic Scriptures.

And may the Holy Spirit guide us with a wisdom not our own; keep us from handling the Word of God deceitfully; enable us to consider it without bias, and to discern the meaning which He Who gave it would convey.

Now the latter part of our investigation will be concerned with prophecy, a subject to which, after more than fifteen centuries of neglect, the Spirit of God is again directing the minds of many of His people. For another long age is drawing to its close, the time to set seal to vision and prophet is at hand, and the Lord will not hide from His own what He is about to do.

The objection of a believer to the study of prophecy is unreasonable.

Still, however, there lingers in the minds of many Christians a strong objection to prophetic study, though surely a little honest consideration would convince them of their error. For more than a fourth part of the Bible is prophetic: and if God chooses to say so much, dare we refuse to listen? If He has bidden us attend to these truths, shall we turn away almost contemptuously, and say, "It profiteth not"? Certainly, if this be our course, we are setting up our own will in opposition to His, and would do well to inquire whether we really be in the faith or not. For "if any man have not the Spirit of Christ, he is none of His." * If, then, the Spirit loves to dwell on the future purposes of God, will not also the mind of every one that has that Spirit exhibit a similar desire? Must there not be identity of feeling? If the Spirit of God be really influencing us, should He not be accompanied in His testimony by our spirit?

That study involves three great blessings. First: the grace which always follows obedience.

In the commencement of the last of the sacred books we find a special blessing promised to him that readeth, and to them that hear the words of the prophecy. † This promise is not merely for him that readeth and is able to explain, nor only for them that hear and fully understand; but for all who read or hear with earnest

* Rom. viii. 9. † Rev. i. 3.

attention, whether they be able to penetrate into the depths of the meaning or not. Nor is it difficult to see some of the channels through which the blessing flows. We will mention three of them.

First, then, the study of prophecy is commanded,* and we know generally that the grace of God follows every act of direct obedience on our part. If we search out even the most minute commands of His law, and do them; if we show that we would not have a word uttered by Him fall to the ground, we testify both to ourselves and to others that we do in very deed, and not in word only, recognise Him as our God and our King, the Rightful Disposer of our every thought, word, and action.

Nor will He on His part be slow in acknowledging us as His subjects, as those who have a claim upon His aid and protection. He will give us grace to help in every time of need; His covering shield will be quickly interposed when the black air begins to hurtle with the darts of the enemy; His strength, by which the worlds are sustained, will uphold us when our flesh and our heart are failing; His almighty hand will clasp and guide us when the last impenetrable gloom begins to thicken around us, and a darkness that can indeed be felt veils the place on which we next must set our foot. Nor will His grasp slacken till He has drawn us through the night, and our eyes are dazzled as we behold that for which He had caused us to hope, the golden gates of the Paradise of God.

Secondly; if a man read and believe prophecy, though he may not altogether understand it, he cannot at least avoid a strong conviction of the transitoriness

* 2 Peter i. 19.

of the present order of things, and is thus mightily helped in his efforts to look beyond it. We are all by nature inclined to Positivism, and for the most part act practically, if we do not theoretically, upon the hypothesis that things always have been and always will be as they are; that no changes will ever take place, except such as may be brought about in an ordinary way by agencies already at work.

Secondly; prophecy teaches us the certain doom of the things that are seen; and so prepares us for a change, and aids us to fix our hopes on the World to Come.

And the fact that prophecy instantly dispels this false security is the secret reason why, when God draws back the curtain of the future, men either shudder and turn sullenly away, or else explain what they see as no literal picture of that which must shortly come to pass, but as a figurative foreshadowing of something which they are careful to show is by no means alarming, and indeed nothing more than a natural result of existing influences. For they find it difficult to conceive a violent change such as they themselves have never experienced. They are quite willing to talk of development: they love to speak of the time when preachers will be more successful, and somehow contrive to persuade the whole human race out of its pride, its selfishness, and its general ungodliness: they delight to increase the influence of their own particular sect—though in doing this they frequently confuse political power with the power of the Spirit, and are apt to forget who is the reigning Prince of this World and present dispenser of its brief glory.

Or, perhaps, they are cosmopolitan in their views, and affect to despise the narrow-minded restrictions of sect; while they altogether ignore the fact that they hold sufficiently defined opinions of their own, and are unyieldingly tenacious of them. And so, floating with the stream of a torrent which is now daily increasing in volume and impetuosity, they preach peace and good will towards all men from a beneficent God who has no idea of ever troubling us about sin, and predict a golden age of liberty, equality, and fraternity. And yet if you test in their own case the first absolutely indispensable condition of their Millennium, they will probably fail, in worse fashion than did the young lawyer, to prove that they love their neighbours as themselves, by going away not merely in sorrow but in wrath.

Such ideas, then, man will readily adopt: for they are all consistent with a continuance of the present order of things: they can all come to their perfection—so he imagines—without a violent shock, without any supernatural interference.

But he who with earnestness and faith looks down the great vista of futurity which God has opened is quickly penetrated by very different thoughts. He beholds the conflict between good and evil intensifying, until that which is good seems overcome and well nigh annihilated: then he feels the firm ground shaking and giving way beneath him: he looks, and, lo, all the cities of the nations are tottering in ruins upon the trembling earth: the sun is withdrawing its wonted light, the moon becomes as blood: the once solid objects around him wave and reel in confusion, like the breaking up and evanescence of a vivid dream. A sudden flash speeds through the gloom, and he sees the Son of Man coming in the clouds of heaven: he starts with affright as the red lightnings strike the earth: he gazes with awe upon the many slain of the Lord. And then at length a change passes over the scene: the thunders cease to roll, the flashing of the lightning is stayed; and forth from smoke and ruin comes the earth, purified and fair as the garden of Eden; the towers and pinnacles of a noble city appear at the foot of Mount Zion, and from the summit of the mountain rises majestically the wondrous temple described by Ezekiel, before which all flesh shall come to worship the Lord.

For by the outstretched hand, and by the strong arm of the Almighty, and not by preaching, will the world be taught to acknowledge her Creator, and at last find rest from her feverish toil. The preaching of the Gospel in this present time is but for the calling out of an election according to the purpose of God, and for a witness to the rest of mankind. It is only, as Isaiah tells us, when the judgments of the Lord are in the earth that the inhabitants of the world will learn righteousness.*

These outlines, at least, the devout reader of prophecy will be able to trace: and so, when the close of this present age comes like a snare upon all them that dwell upon the face of the whole earth,† it will find him prepared and undismayed.

Lastly; a knowledge of the revealed purposes of God tends to conform our will to His, and is profitable for sanctification.

Lastly; the study of prophecy reveals to us the mind and will of God. Seems this a light thing? Do we indeed despise the confidence of our Almighty Creator? Let us fear lest we so insult Him; lest, like swine, we trample on the pearls offered to us. And regarding them in this light, how great is the practical value of the prophetic Scriptures! For if we are already justified by Christ, we still have need of daily progress in sanctification, we should be ever becoming more and

* Isa. xxvi. 9.

† Luke xxi. 35.

more transformed to the image of God. And to that end what greater help could we have than a revelation of His mind and purposes in regard to ourselves, our fellow-creatures, and the earth in which we dwell; an estimate by Him of all temporal things, of those visible surroundings by which we are continually affected, and His declaration of their speedy judgment and destruction?

Is it not a duty to become minutely acquainted with all this; to meditate on it continually; to shape our wishes, hopes, and aspirations, from it; to bring our whole mind into accordance with it; to use our every endeavour to spread the knowledge of it among men; and so to prepare ourselves and others for that new order of things, into which we either must enter individually at the unknown time of death, or may enter simultaneously at any moment by the long-expected return of our Lord and Saviour?

THE CREATION.

CHAPTER II.

THE CREATION.

The popular error in regard to the Creation sprang from the Pagan doctrine of Chaos.

AT the very outset of our inquiry we have to encounter a deeply-rooted popular fallacy in regard to the creation of the world—a fallacy which can boast of long antiquity, and which seems originally to have sprung from a sort of compromise between revelation and the legends of Pagan cosmogony.

The ancient poet Hesiod tells us that the first thing in existence was Chaos; that is, according to its etymology, "the yawning and void receptacle for created matter." But the word soon lost its strict meaning, and was used for the crude and shapeless mass of material out of which the heavens and the earth were supposed to have been formed. Ovid thus describes it;—"There was but one appearance of nature throughout the whole world: this they called Chaos, an unformed and confused bulk."* And in his "Fasti" he makes Janus, whom he identifies with Chaos, speak as follows:—

"The ancients used to call me Chaos: for a primeval being am I. See of how remote an age I shall recount the events! This air, full of light, and the three remaining elements, fire, water, and earth, were a confused

* Metam. i. 6, 7.

heap. As soon as this mass was separated through the discord of its component parts, and had dissolved and passed away into new positions, the flame ascended upwards; a nearer place—that is, nearer to earth—received the air; the earth and the sea settled down to the bottom. Then I, who had been but a mass and shapeless bulk, passed into a form and limbs worthy of a god."*

Thus, according to the cosmogonies of Greece and Rome, the universe sprang from Chaos. Uranus, or Heaven, was supposed to have been the first supreme god. But he was driven from power by his son Cronos or Saturn, who afterwards received the same treatment at the hands of his son Zeus or Jupiter. Chaos was the first thing in existence, and the transient series of gods came subsequently into being.

Misleading influence of this doctrine upon the Christian world.

This doctrine, ancient and widespread as it was in the time of our Lord, did not fail to influence the real as well as the spurious Christians. Among the last mentioned, the important sects of the Gnostics believed in the eternity and intrinsic evil of matter; but, unlike the Heathen, they taught that the Supreme Being also existed from eternity. The orthodox Christians escaped the greater error altogether; but, nevertheless, gave clear testimony to the influence of the popular belief in their interpretation of the commencing chapter of Genesis. For they made the first verse signify the creation of a confused mass of elements, out of which the heavens and earth were formed during the six days, understanding the next sentence to be a description of this crude matter before God shaped it. And their opinion has descended to our days. But

* Fasti i. 103-112.

it does not appear to be substantiated by Scripture, as we shall presently see, and the guile of the serpent may be detected in its results. For how great a contest has it provoked between the Church and the World! How ready a handle do the geological difficulties involved in it present to the assailants of Scripture! With what perplexity do we behold earth gloomy with the shadow of pain and death ages before the sin of Adam! How many young minds have been turned aside by the absolute impossibility of defending what they have been taught to regard as Biblical statements! And lastly, in carrying on the dispute, how much precious time has been wasted by able servants of God, who would otherwise have been more profitably employed!

Examination of the Mosaic record. "In the beginning."

Let us, then, turn to the Mosaic account, and endeavour to elicit its plain and obvious meaning. "In the beginning," we read, "God created the heaven and the earth." * The beginning refers, of course, to the first existence of that with which the history is concerned, the heaven and the earth.† Here, then, is at once an end to speculation in regard to the eternity of matter: for God was before the things that are seen, and by His supreme volition called them into being. And again; this short sentence strikes a mortal blow at all pantheistic identification of God and nature. Nature is but one of His many creatures, one of the works of

* Gen. i. 1.

† Therefore the expression has in this case a sense very different from that which it bears in the first verse of John. Here it is used of the beginning of time; but there of the countless ages of eternity before time was. The third verse of John, "All things were made by Him," brings us down to the period of the first of Genesis.

His hands: her years can be numbered, the day of her birth is known; but from everlasting to everlasting He is God.

The earth and its surroundings are said to have been "created" in the beginning; while in the six days they were only "made." Meaning of the Hebrew words *bara*, *asah*, and *yatsar*.

Now, in the inspired description of what took place in the beginning, the heaven and earth are not said to have been moulded, fashioned, or made out of material, but to have been created. For, whatever may have been the original meaning of the word *bara*, it seems certain that in this and similar passages it is used of calling into being without the aid of pre-existing material. The Hebrew writers give it this sense, and Rabbi Nackman declares that there is no other word to express production out of nothing. But it is, of course, easy to understand that a language might not possess a verb originally confined to such a meaning: for the idea would scarcely have been conceived by men without the assistance of revelation. The development theories so popular in our days, coupled as they almost invariably are with more or less of scepticism, indicate the natural bent of human minds on this point: and the philosophic poet Lucretius was an exponent of it when he declared the first principle of nature to be, "Nothing is ever gotten out of nothing by Divine power." *

Hence we can readily understand that the word selected by the Holy Spirit to express creation may have previously signified the forming out of material. But its use is sufficiently defined in this and other similar passages. For we are told that in the beginning God *created* the heaven and the earth; but the Scriptures never affirm that He did this in the six days.

* De Rer. Nat. i. 150.

The work of those days was, as we shall presently see, quite a different thing from original creation: they were times of restoration, and the word *asah* is generally used in connection with them.

Now *asah* signifies to make, fashion, or prepare out of existing material; as, for instance, to build a ship erect a house, or prepare a meal.

There are, however, two acts of creation mentioned in the history of the six days. First; God is said to have created the inhabitants of the waters and the fowls of heaven: because these do not consist merely of the material mould of their bodies, but have a life principle within which could be conferred only by a direct act of creation.* Hence the change of word in this place is quite intelligible. Just in the same way man is said to have been created, though in the second chapter we are expressly told that his body was formed from the dust.† For the real man is the soul and spirit: the body, which is naturally changed every seven years, and must ultimately moulder in the grave, is regarded merely as the outward casing which gives him the power of dealing with his present surroundings, and the materials of which were appropriately taken from that earth in contact with which he was destined to live.

In the detailed account of man's origin, a third word is used to signify the forming of his body. This is *yatzar*, which means to shape, or mould, as a potter does the clay.‡

A passage in Isaiah well illustrates the meaning and connection of all three verbs;—"I have created him for My glory; I have formed him; yea, I have made

* Gen. i. 21. † Gen. i. 27; ii. 7.
‡ Gen. ii. 7.

him."* On this verse Kimchi remarks;—"I have created him, that is, produced him out of nothing; I have formed him, that is, caused him to exist in a shape or form appointed; I have made him, that is, made the final dispositions and arrangements respecting him."

God, then, in the beginning created the heaven and the earth, not merely the materials out of which they were afterwards formed. How this wonderful work was accomplished we are not told: but it may be that the creative power of God has a very dim analogy in the beings who were made after His image, an analogy which would well illustrate the distance between the creature and the Creator. We know that by force of imagination we can not only place before our eyes scenes in which we were long ago interested, spots which we would fain revisit in the body, departed forms dear to us as our own lives, but are even able to paint in fancy future events as we would wish them to be. The vision is, however, shadowy, fleeting, and alas! too often unholy. Somewhat, then, perhaps, as we produce this dim and quickly fading picture, the thoughts of God, issuing from the depths of His holiness and love, take instant shape, and become, not an unsubstantial and evanescent dream, but a beautiful reality, established for ever unless He choose to alter or remove it. Hence it may be that a great part, or, perhaps, the whole host of innumerable suns and planets which make up the universe, flashed into being simultaneously at His will, and, in a moment, illumined the black realm of space with their many-hued glories.

A faint reflection of the creative power of God may, perhaps, be detected in man.

* Isa. xliii. 7.

The heaven mentioned in the first verse of Genesis is the starry heaven, not the firmament immediately surrounding our earth:* and since its history is not further unfolded, it may, for aught we know, have remained, developing, perhaps, but without violent change from the time of its creation until now. Not so, however, the earth, as the next verse goes on to show: "And the earth was without form, and void; and darkness was upon the face of the deep."

The first verse of Genesis is not a summary of what follows, but a record of the first of a series of events.

Now the "and," according to Hebrew usage—as well as that of most other languages—proves that the first verse is not a compendium of what follows, but a statement of the first event in the record. For if it were a mere summary, the second verse would be the actual commencement of the history, and certainly would not begin with a copulative. A good illustration of this may be found in the fifth chapter of Genesis.† There the opening words, "This is the book of the generations of Adam," are a compendium of the chapter, and, consequently, the next sentence begins without a copulative. We have, therefore, in the second verse of Genesis no first detail of a general statement in the preceding sentence, but the record of an altogether distinct and subsequent event, which did not affect the sidereal heaven, but only the earth and its immediate surroundings. And what that event was we must now endeavour to discover.

* See remarks on the Fourth Day in Chap. IV., and also the exposition of Gen. ii. 4, in the latter part of the same chapter.

† Gen. v. 1.

The words translated, "And the earth was without form, and void," when rightly understood, describe a catastrophe which befell the earth some time after its creation.

According to our version, "the earth was without form, and void." This, however, is not the sense of the Hebrew, but a glaring illustration of the influence of the chaos-legend. Fuerst gives "ruin," or "desolation," as the proper meaning of the noun rendered "without form." The second word signifies "emptiness," then, "that which is empty"; so that in this case the authorised translation is admissible. Now these words are found together only in two other passages, in both of which they are clearly used to express the ruin caused by an outpouring of the wrath of God.

In a prophecy of Isaiah, after a fearful description of the fall of Idumea in the day of vengeance, we find the expression, "He shall stretch out upon it the line of confusion, and the stones—or, as it should be translated, the plummet—of emptiness."* Now "confusion" and "emptiness" are, in the Hebrew, the same words as those rendered "without form, and void." And the sense is, that just as the architect makes careful use of line and plummet in order to raise the building in perfection, so will the Lord to make the ruin complete.

There is, then, no possibility of mistaking the meaning of the words in this place, and the second passage is even more conclusive. For, in describing the devastation of Judah and Jerusalem, Jeremiah likens it to the preadamite destruction, and exclaims;—"I beheld the earth, and, lo, it was without form, and void; and the heavens, and they had no light. I beheld the mountains, and, lo, they trembled, and all the hills moved lightly. I beheld, and, lo, there was no man, and all the

* Isa. xxxiv. 11.

birds of the heavens were fled. I beheld, and, lo, the fruitful place was a wilderness, and all the cities thereof were broken down at the presence of the Lord, and by His fierce anger. For thus hath the Lord said, The whole land shall be desolate; yet will I not make a full end." *

We see, therefore, that the Hebrew word *tohu* signifies "desolation," or "that which is desolate"; and *bohu* "emptiness," or "that which is empty," probably with reference to the absence of all life ("I beheld, and, lo, there was no man," etc.). And again; the verb translated "was" is occasionally used with a simple accusative in the sense of "to be made," or "to become." An instance of this may be found in the history of Lot's wife, of whom we are told, that "she became a pillar of salt."† Such a meaning is by far the best for our context: we may therefore adopt it, and render, "And the earth became desolate and void; and darkness was upon the face of the deep."

But if any further evidence be needed to prove that our verse does not describe a chaotic mass which God first created and afterwards fashioned into shape, we have a direct and positive assertion to that effect in the forty-fifth chapter of Isaiah: for we are there told that God did not create the earth a *tohu*.‡ This word, therefore, whatever meaning be assigned to it, cannot at least be descriptive of the earliest condition of earth. But our translators have obscured the fact by rendering *tohu* "in vain": they can hardly have compared the passages in which it occurs, or they would surely have seen the propriety of translating it in Isaiah's

* Jer. iv. 23-27. † Gen. xix. 26. ‡ Isa. xlv. 18.

manifest reference to creation by the same word as in Genesis.

There is, therefore, ample space between the first and second verses of Genesis for all the geological ages, which are not, however, alluded to in Scripture. Reason of the omission.

It is thus clear that the second verse of Genesis describes the earth as a ruin; but there is no hint of the time which elapsed between creation and this ruin. Age after age may have rolled away, and it was probably during their course that the strata of the earth's crust were gradually developed. Hence we see that geological attacks upon the Scriptures are altogether wide of the mark, are a mere beating of the air. There is room for any length of time between the first and second verses of the Bible. And again; since we have no inspired account of the geological formations, we are at liberty to believe that they were developed just in the order in which we find them. The whole process took place in preadamite times, in connection, perhaps, with another race of beings, and, consequently, does not at present concern us.

And it is to be observed that God has never, since the fall of man, revealed anything to gratify a mere thirst for knowledge; but only such matters as may sufficiently illustrate His everlasting power and Godhead, our own fallen condition with its remedy of unfathomable love, and the promise of a speedy deliverance from sin, a complete restoration to His favour, and a never-ending life of perfect obedience and perfect joy.

In our present condition knowledge is a dangerous possession.

Knowledge in this life is a gift fraught with peril: for our great task here is to learn the lesson of absolute dependence upon God, and entire submission to His will. His dealings with us now are to the end that He may withdraw us from our own purpose, and hide pride from us.* But knowledge, unless it be accompanied by a mighty outpouring of grace, causes undue elation. It was the vision of knowledge which filled the breast of our first parent with impious aspirations, and made her listen to the Tempter when he bade her hope to be as God. And it is an ominous fact, that, after the fall, the first inventors of the arts and sciences were the descendants, not of the believing Seth, but of the deist and murderer Cain.

So in our own days the leaders of science are too often the leaders of infidelity, the despisers of God and of prayer. Except by special grace, man seems incapable of bearing the slightest weight of power upon his shoulders without losing his balance.

And hence the Scriptures take up just the attitude we should expect. They altogether, as in the verses before us, avoid contact with the science of men. God does not forbid us to search so far as we can into the laws of His universe; but He utterly refuses to aid or accelerate our studies by revelation. For the present He would have us rather attentive to the moral renovation of ourselves and our fellow-creatures: but after a short season He will open vast stores of His wisdom to those who love and trust Him, and delight their souls with the secrets of His creative power.

* Job xxxiii. 17.

THE INTERVAL

CHAPTER III.

THE INTERVAL.

Sin was the cause of the preadamite destruction.

WE see, then, that God created the heavens and the earth perfect and beautiful in their beginning, and that at some subsequent period, how remote we cannot tell, the earth had passed into a state of utter desolation, and was void of all life. Not merely had its fruitful places become a wilderness, and all its cities been broken down; but the very light of its sun had been withdrawn; all the moisture of its atmosphere had sunk upon its surface; and the vast deep, to which God has set bounds that are never transgressed save when wrath has gone forth from Him, had burst those limits; so that the ruined planet, covered above its very mountain tops with the black floods of destruction, was rolling through space in a horror of great darkness.

But what could have occasioned so terrific a catastrophe? Wherefore had God thus destroyed the work of His hands? If we may draw any inference from the history of our own race, sin must have been the cause of this hideous ruin: sin, too, which would seem to have been patiently borne with through long ages, until at length its cry increased to Heaven, and brought down utter destruction.

The fossil remains indicate preadamite ages of sin: for they may be proved to be the relics, not of the Six Days, but of far earlier creations.

For, as the fossil remains clearly show, not only were disease and death—inseparable companions of sin—then prevalent among the living creatures of the earth, but even ferocity and slaughter. And the fact proves that these remains have nothing to do with our world; since the Bible declares that all things made by God during the Six Days were very good, and that no evil was in them till Adam sinned. Through his fall the ground was cursed, and it was doubtless at the same time that the whole creation was subjected to that vanity of fruitless toil, of never-ceasing unrest, and of perpetual decay, in which it has since groaned and travailed in pain together until now.* When thorns and thistles sprang out of the earth, and its fertility was restrained, then a curse affected the animal kingdom also. There appeared in it a depraved and even savage nature which ultimately, though not perhaps in antediluvian times, reached its climax in a cruel thirst for blood, and completely changed the organization of some species at least. How this change was brought about, it is of course useless to speculate: for the hand of the Almighty wrought it. But that it did take place, and that the beasts of the earth were not always as they now are, we have proof in the following facts.

On the Sixth Day God pronounced every thing which He had made to be very good, a declaration which would seem altogether inconsistent with the present condition of the animal as well as the vegetable kingdom.† Again; He gave the green herb alone

* Rom. viii. 22. † Gen. i. 31.

for food "to every beast of the field, and to every fowl of the air, and to every thing that creepeth upon the earth." * There were, therefore, no carnivora in the sinless world.

Lastly; in a great prophecy of the times of restitution we read;—"The wolf also shall dwell with the lamb, and the leopard shall lie down with the kid; and the calf and the young lion and the fatling together; and a little child shall lead them. And the cow and the bear shall feed; their young ones shall lie down together; and the lion shall eat straw like the ox. And the sucking child shall play upon the hole of the asp, and the weaned child shall put his hand on the cockatrice's den. They shall not hurt nor destroy in all My holy mountain: for the earth shall be full of the knowledge of the Lord, as the waters cover the sea." † That is, that, when sin has been suppressed by the return of the second Adam, the curse shall lose its power, the savage nature of the beasts of the field shall disappear, the carnivora shall become graminivora, the poisonous shall lay aside their venom; all shall be restored to their first condition, and be again as when God pronounced the primal blessing. ‡

Since, then, the fossil remains are those of creatures anterior to Adam, and yet show evident tokens of disease, death, and mutual destruction, they must have belonged to another world, and have a sin-stained history of their own, a history which ended in the ruin of themselves and their habitation.

* Gen. i. 30.

† Isa. xi. 6-9.

‡ Except the serpent, who will lose his power to injure, but will still exhibit the sign of his degradation. See Isa. lxv. 25.

Probable existence of men in preadamite times. Satan seems to have been the first cause of sin and destruction. Vastness of the subject.

And since a lord and vicegerent was set over the animal kingdom of our world, through whose fall deterioration, disease and death obtained irresistible power over every living creature, so we should naturally conclude that superior beings inhabited and ruled that former world, and, like Adam, transgressed the laws of their Creator.

But who were these ancient possessors of the lands now given to us? Whence came they, and whither have they gone? What fearful sin caused their own disappearance, and involved in one confused ruin their earth and its aerial surroundings?

We have no records left to us: the numerous remains in primeval rocks are only those of the lower forms of creation. Yet, as we peer hopelessly into the night, a faint and unsteady gleam seems to emanate from the Scriptures in our hand, a very different light from that which they pour upon other subjects, scarcely more than sufficient to make darkness visible, but enough to reveal the outline of a shadowy form seated on high above the desolation, and looking sullenly down upon his ruined realm.

It is our own great enemy, the Prince of this World and of the Power of the Air.

Let us, then, consider the scanty hints which the Bible seems to offer in regard to this great mystery. But we must tread lightly and rapidly over the bridge which we shall attempt to throw across the foaming torrent: for we cannot be sure of its foundation: nay, in the darkness of the night there may also be serious defects in its construction. Yet the revelation to which we shall refer was given for our learning, and, like all

Scripture, is profitable, even if we fail to grasp the secret contained in it, provided we handle it with reverence and fear.* For the contemplation of such a theme gives us some idea of the ineffable magnitude of the events, past and future, by which time is bounded, and of the countless millions of actors concerned in them: it calls off our minds which are prone to dwell so complacently, and yet so irrationally, upon this present brief age and our still more insignificant selves: it strikes us with inconceivable awe: it makes us tremblingly anxious to be safe in the only refuge before the next great storm of God's wrath comes thundering over our doomed world: it urges us to fulfil our minute duty in the stupendous drama which the great Supreme is rapidly hastening to its close.

Sources of information.

Now there are, perhaps, two sources from which we may extract some information respecting the former condition of the earth. First, from any passage which seems to refer directly to it; and secondly, from the account given to us of "the times of restitution of all things," † the very name of which suggests that God's original purpose will not be frustrated by sin, but that everything will be restored even as it was before the earliest rebellion of the fallen angels.

The titles "Prince of this World," and "God of this Age."

If, then, we glance at the few particulars of Satan's history which have been revealed to us, we cannot fail to observe that, besides the actual power attributed to him, he manifestly holds the legitimate title of "Prince of this World"; or, in other words, that this dignity, together with the royal prerogatives which of right pertain to it,

* 2 Tim. iii. 16. † Acts iii. 21.

was conferred upon him by God Himself.* For there is no other way of explaining the fact that the Lord Jesus not only spoke of the Adversary by this title,† but plainly recognised his delegated authority in that He did not dispute his claim to the present disposal of the kingdoms of the world and their glory.‡

And it is only by recognising the legitimacy of that claim that we can understand a passage of Jude, in which the conduct of the archangel Michael towards Satan is adduced as an example of due respect for authority, even though it be in the hands of the wicked.§

The meaning of "World" is somewhat ambiguous: for while the signification of the Greek word may be confined to our earth and its inhabitants, it may also extend to the totality of the universe, and in the case before us possibly does comprehend all the spheres of our solar system. At least if there be truth in the accounts given by astronomers of the ruined condition of the moon, which is described as "an arid and lifeless wilderness," it would seem likely that Satan's power extends so far. And it may be also that the catastrophe in the sun, which was remedied on the Fourth Day, testifies to his connection with that glorious luminary.

In one passage Paul, according to our version, styles him "the God of this World."‖ There, however, the Greek for "World" is a different word, and should be translated "Age." Satan is indeed the legitimate

* Previously of course to his fall. See the exposition of Ezek. xxviii. 11-19, in the subsequent part of this chapter.

† John xiv. 30.

‡ Luke iv. 6-8.

§ Jude 9.

‖ 2 Cor. iv. 4.

Prince of this World; but it is only by abusing his power, and blinding the eyes of men, that he induces them to worship him as their god. At the close of the present age he will be deprived of his princedom; and, the basis of real power being thus removed, his impious superstructure will immediately fall to the ground.

But, even at the risk of interrupting the argument, we cannot refrain from pausing for a moment to glance at the solemn warning contained in the title "God of this Age." There is indeed reason to believe that the Devil has received far more directly personal worship than those who are not accustomed to investigate such matters would imagine. But it is to something more general that Paul refers. His own words in another place will best explain his meaning;—"Know ye not, that to whom ye yield yourselves servants to obey, his servants ye are to whom ye obey?" * There are two laws set before us, that of God and that of Satan; and whose law we keep, his servants and worshippers we are. Profession, however vehement, goes for nothing in the other world. We may profess the worship of the Supreme God, we may be very sedulous in the outward part of it; but if at the same time we are obeying the law of Satan, his subjects we are reckoned to be, and to him our prayers and praises ascend. And the law of Satan is this;—That we seek all our pleasures in, and fix all our heartfelt hopes upon, this present age over which he presides; and that we use our best endeavours—by means of various sensuous and intellectual occupations and delights, and countless ways of killing time which he has provided—to keep our thoughts from ever wandering into that age to

* Rom. vi. 16.

come, which will see him a fettered captive instead of a prince and a god.

The princedom of the Power of the Air.

But he is also called "the Prince of the Power of the Air."* This principality would seem to be the same as "the heavenly places"—our version incorrectly translates "high places"†—which, as Paul tells us, swarm with the spiritual hosts of wickedness. It is by no means necessary to restrict it to the eighty or a hundred miles of atmosphere supposed to surround the earth: for if Satan's power extends to the sun, as we suggested above, and so to the whole of our solar system, the kingdom of the air would include the immense space in which the planets of our centre revolve; and in such a case it seems not unlikely that the throne of its prince may be situated in the photosphere of the sun. We should thus find a deep underlying significance in the fact that idolatry has always commenced with, and in no small degree consisted of, the worship of the Sun-god, whether he be called San, Shamas, Bel, Ra, Baal, Moloch, Milcom, Hadad, Adrammelech and Anamelech, Mithras, Apollo, Sheikh Shems, or by any other of his innumerable names.‡

There is, perhaps, something suggestive in the word used to describe this kingdom: for it means thick and

* Eph. ii. 2. † Eph. vi. 12.

‡ May there not be great significance in the fact that the very name of Satan passes, through its Chaldaic form "Sheitan," into the Greek "Titan," which last word is used by Greek and Latin poets as a designation of the Sun-god?

Indeed it would almost seem as if this connection were understood in the dark ages: for Didron, in his *Christian Iconography*, describes three Byzantine miniatures of the tenth century, in which Satan is depicted with a nimbus, or circular glory, the recognized sign of the Sun-god in Pagan times.

As the Church became Paganized, the nimbus began to ap-

misty, in contrast to bright and clear, air. Hence it may have been selected to indicate the polluted and sin-defiled condition of Satan's heaven. And this view appears to be confirmed by a passage in the Epistle to the Hebrews, where we read;—"It was, therefore, necessary that the patterns of things in the heavens should be purified with these; but the heavenly things themselves with better sacrifices than these." * The purification of the latter will probably be accomplished at the return of the Lord, after that expulsion of Satan and his angels from heaven which is foretold in the twelfth chapter of the Apocalypse. And we may notice the beautiful agreement between this idea of the existing impurity of the first heaven and the prophecy of Isaiah, that, in the age to come, "the light of the moon shall be as the light of the sun, and the light of the sun shall be sevenfold, as the light of seven days." †

The spiritual powers of the world.

What, then, is the nature of the power indicated by these titles of Satan? To understand it we must glance at the general hints of Scripture concerning spiritual agencies. For, though unseen and little suspected by the rulers of earth, there are also spiritual powers,‡ all originally appointed by God, whether they be loyal to Him now or not. Rank above rank these watchers stand, each passing on his account to a superior until it reaches the Most High at the apex of the pyramid. So in Zechariah's first vision, those whom the Lord had sent to walk to and fro upon

pear in images and pictures of Christ and the saints. At the same time the Church was corrupted by the introduction of other customs—such as the circular tonsure, and the practice of turning to the East—which had been connected with sun-worship from hoar antiquity.

* Heb. ix. 23. † Isa. xxx. 26. ‡ Eccles. v. 8.

the earth are represented as delivering their report to the Angel of the Lord, who then appeals to the Almighty Himself.*

And hence we read of thrones, dominions, principalities, powers,† archangels,‡ and angels. Nor can we know much of Scripture without discovering that vast numbers of these invisible beings, who supervise the affairs of men and their world, are in open rebellion against the Almighty; that there are principalities, powers, and world-rulers, of darkness, with whom, as Paul tells us, we have to wage a fearful warfare.§ These all render account to Satan, their prince, who, in his reports to the Most High, makes use of their intelligence to accuse ourselves and our brethren before God day and night.‖

Interesting disclosures of the eighty-second Psalm respecting the injustice of their rule, God's controversy with them, and the sentence pronounced upon them.

If we would know something of the manner of their rule we may read God's own estimate of it in the eighty-second Psalm. That brief poem—one of the grandest of the revelations which raise the separating veil and permit a momentary glimpse of mysteries beyond our own sphere—is so important as an illustration of our subject, and also as affording a solution of many moral difficulties caused by the present condition of the world, that we subjoin an amended translation of it, together with a few words of comment.

* Zech. i. 11, 12. † Col. i. 16.

‡ But we ought not, perhaps, to speak of archangels in the plural; since Michael, called *the* archangel, is the only one mentioned in Scripture. Probably, however, there may be other beings of the same rank connected with other worlds. For Michael appears to bear the title because he is the appointed ruler of all faithful angels in the heaven of our earth. And hence we find him standing as the prince of God's chosen people and the great opponent of Satan (Dan. xii. 1; Rev. xii. 7; Jude 9).

§ Eph. vi. 12. ‖ Rev. xii. 10.

1\. "God standeth in the congregation of God:
In the midst of the gods doth He judge.
2\. 'How long will ye judge perversely,
And take the side of the wicked? (Selah.)
3\. Defend right for the wretched and fatherless:
Do justice to the afflicted and needy:
4\. Deliver the wretched and poor:
Rescue them from the hand of the wicked!'

5\. 'They know not, and they understand not;
In darkness they walk to and fro:
All the foundations of the earth are tottering.'

6\. 'I have said, Ye are gods,
And sons of the Most High are ye all.
7\. But ye shall die like men,
And shall fall like one of the princes.'

8\. Arise, O God, judge Thou the earth:
For Thou hast all the nations for Thine inheritance."

The Psalm thus falls into four paragraphs, the first of which represents the Almighty as standing among the angelic rulers of this world, and charging them with their folly. Apparently we have two examples of such an assembly in the beginning of the Book of Job, where the sons of God, and Satan among them, are described as coming to present themselves before the Lord. In each of these cases the council, so far as its purposes are revealed to us, had reference to an inhabitant of earth, and its decisions were of the gravest moment to him. The Book of Kings furnishes us with a third instance, in the celestial assize held to determine the fate of Ahab.* And just as Satan takes part in the deliberation respecting Job, so here we read of the presence of a lying spirit who receives permission to possess and inspire the false prophets for the destruction of those who trusted them.

The "gods" of the second line are angels—in this case, of course, fallen angels—so called as being the agents of God.† A similar use of the word אֱלֹהִים may be found in the ninety-seventh Psalm, in quoting from which Paul renders the clause, "Worship Him, all ye gods," by, "Let all the angels of God worship Him."‡

In the charge which follows, how graphically is the present state of the world portrayed! How plainly are we made to see that if lying, fraud, oppression, and violence are prospering; if the tears of the weak are flowing; if there is many a child of God whom,

> . . . "in this world's hard race
> O'erwearied and unblessed,
> A host of restless phantoms chase";

if there are multitudes who can say, No man cares for my soul—all this is because a Rebel is swaying his sceptre of iron over the groaning earth.

In the third and fourth verses we seem to discern a wondrous unveiling of the love of God. Not only over the fallen race of Adam has He yearned: nay, He has offered space for repentance, and would have shown grace, to the sinning angels also. We are reminded of those mysterious words which the Lord uttered, just after the voice from heaven had resounded

* 1 Kings xxii. 19-23.

† So our Lord explains;—"If He called them gods unto whom the word of God came" (John x. 35).

‡ Compare also Heb. ii. 9, with the Hebrew of Psalm viii. 5.

through the Temple—"Now is the judgment of this world: now shall the Prince of this World be cast out!" For it would seem as though the irrevocable decree, fixing the doom of "the world-rulers of this darkness," had only then gone forth, and the ears of the Lord had, as it were, caught the thunder of the closing gates of mercy, which up to that time had stood open even for Satan and the spiritual hosts of wickedness. Possibly it was their hostility to the incarnate Son of God which filled up the measure of their iniquity: so that to them, as well as to the Jews, the Parable of the Husbandmen might have been applied. They had refused to offer to the great Creator the fruits of His earth which had been committed to their care: they had rejected merciful pleadings, such as our Psalm discloses: and finally, as soon as they descried the Son entering their realms, they had destroyed whatever hope might have remained to them by crying;—"This is the Heir! Come, let us kill Him, that the inheritance may be ours!"

The fifth verse shows that God had already foreseen the end. He declares that His remonstrance is vain: the rebels will not listen. By breaking away from Him they have lost their wisdom, and can no longer understand; they have become shortsighted after the manner of men, if not in their degree. They can but move restlessly to and fro under the darkness into which they have wandered, striving by incessant activity to forget the Divine fulness of their former estate; while they exhibit the reckless madness of sin by stretching out their hand against God and strengthening themselves against the Almighty.

And terrible are the consequences of their condition

to the earth which groans beneath their sway. All its foundations are tottering: it is filled with flagrant abuses and crimes, the cry of which ascends to heaven: there is an anarchy of injustice and oppression. They must, then, be deposed: their power must be taken away: a fearful retribution must vindicate the justice of Him Who is King over all.

Accordingly their sentence follows, and its terms should have prevented that vague interpretation of the Psalm which has been content to refer it to merely human rulers. Not to those who are called into existence under mortal conditions are these words addressed, but to beings who from the earliest hour of their life have rejoiced in the immortality of the sons of God. Nevertheless, because they have sinned and fallen from their first estate, they also must come under the law of sin and death. Like the ephemeral children of Adam they shall perish, and fall like one of the short-lived princes of Earth.

This sentence has not yet been carried out: it will be so, apparently, when Satan is bound and cast for a thousand years into the abyss, or vast fiery deep in the centre of the earth, which, as we may gather from Scripture, is the prison-house of the lost dead.*

The Psalm closes with a prayer. While he contemplates the evils brought upon the world by its present Prince, the Psalmist is moved to long for the advent of the Righteous King, for the coming of Christ to depose the rebel powers, to inherit all nations, and to judge the earth.

* He thus suffers the first death during the Millennium, and is afterwards cast into the Lake of fire and brimstone, which is the second death. See Isa. xxiv. 21, 22; Rev. xx. 1-3; Rev. xx. 14.

It is then plainly revealed that spiritual as well as human powers are concerned in the administration of our earth. And these diverse agencies are mentioned as making up the totality of its government in a verse of Isaiah, where we are told that the Lord at His coming will depose and punish two distinct governing bodies, "the High Ones that are on high, and the Kings of the Earth upon the earth."* Of these, the former are manifestly identical with Satan and his angels; the latter with the antichristian world-powers.† Nor will Christ alter the form of government, though He change the rulers. For Himself and His Church will then take the place of the High Ones that are on high, while the first rank among the Kings of the Earth upon the earth will be given to the seed of Abraham according to the flesh.

The regular principalities of our earth appear, with one exception, to be under the sway of Satan.

It is, however, a startling fact that the present disposal of the regular spiritual powers of the world seems to be entirely in the hands of Satan. This is evident from the eighty-second Psalm, as well as from the verse of Isaiah; since in either passage the spiritual rulers are stigmatised without any reserve as rebels against God.

And, again, in the tenth chapter of Daniel we read of the Satanic Prince of Persia, and also of the Prince of Grecia: but the angel of the Lord who opposes the former does not take a similar title. Nay, from his own words we may see that his post is no permanency; he is merely sent down for a special purpose,

* Isa. xxiv. 21.

† That is, with the Gentile powers of Christendom. For after Israel's temporary rejection the dominion of earth was formally transferred to the Gentiles in the person of Nebuchadnezzar (Dan. ii. 37, 38).

and retires when it is accomplished, leaving the Prince of Grecia unassailed. And how deeply significant, how worthy of our most solemn thought, is his complaint that, upon his entrance into the heaven of our earth, he found, with a solitary exception, all its principalities either hostile or indifferent!* From the whole region of the vast rebel empire there came forth but one loyal prince of God to aid him in his conflict with the powers of darkness. This faithful archangel was Michael: nor is it difficult to account for his presence in the regions of air. For he is described to Daniel as "your prince," and afterwards as "the great prince which standeth for the children of thy people."† It appears, then, that he is the spiritual ruler of Israel; and so, that when God chose a people upon earth for Himself, He took them out of the jurisdiction (ἐξουσία‡) of Satan, and appointed one of His own princes to govern and protect them. Hence with fierce enmity the Prince of Darkness seems to have matched himself against Michael, and to have directed in person his desperate assaults upon the alienated principality. One of his victories is recorded in the Book of Chronicles, where we are told how he "stood up against Israel, and provoked David to number Israel."§

In the third chapter of Zechariah we seem to have

* Dan. x. 21. † Dan. x. 21; xii. 1.

‡ Acts xxvi. 18; Col. i. 13.

§ 1 Chron. xxi. 1. Dan. x. 13, 20, will show us that this was probably effected by a victory over Michael and the consequent suspension of the archangel's protecting influence. A remarkable hint of the spiritual conflicts which seem to be connected with every earthly event may also be found in 2 Kings vi. 16. For when the trembling servant of Elisha told his master that Dothan was surrounded by the Syrians, the prophet seems to have immediately glanced at the spiritual forces *on both sides*, and then, a typical representation of the whole conflict, with a glance at its final result. For the angel of the Lord, before whom Joshua the high priest is seen standing, would naturally be Michael, the protector of Israel; Satan himself is present to accuse; and the Lord is introduced as Judge, deciding against the Adversary, and in favour of Joshua and Jerusalem. But this sentence has not yet taken effect: for Satan, by the vigour and pertinacity of his attacks, afterwards caused the ruin and dispersion of the Jewish people, thus apparently defeating the purpose of God, and completely recovering his lost province. Michael's rule seems, therefore, for the present to be almost in abeyance; but, as we find from the prophetic Scriptures, he will shortly resume the battle, and gain a decisive and final victory.*

Therefore the Prince of Darkness still wields a mighty power: and hence the fearful reality of the Christian conflict.

From all this we may surely infer that, although Satan is a rebel, he has not yet been deprived either of his title or his power. He is still the great High One on high, who divides the world into different provinces according to its nationalities, appointing a powerful angel, assisted by countless subordinates, as viceroy over each kingdom, to direct its energies and bend them to his will. And so we get some idea of the terrible reality of Paul's meaning, when he affirms that our great conflict is not with flesh and blood, but has to be carried on against principalities,

satisfied with what he had seen, replied;—"Fear not; for *they that be with us* are more than *they that be with them.*" The subsequent blinding of the hostile army was doubtless effected at God's command by the fiery host which protected Elisha, and the miracle certainly seems to imply a previous defeat of those who were with the Syrians.

* Dan. xii. 1; Rev. xii. 7-9.

against powers, against the world-rulers of this age of darkness, against the spiritual hosts of wickedness in the heavenly places.*

But who is sufficient for these things? For the whole aerial surroundings of our planet are densely peopled with a hostile race of beings unutterably superior in wisdom and power to ourselves; having had during a vast number of years every conceivable experience of the weak points of humanity; possessing the incalculable advantage of being themselves invisible, though as spiritual intelligences they are probably able, not merely to judge of us by our words and outward expression of countenance, but even to read the innermost thoughts of our heart; co-operating with the most perfect and never-failing organization; and lastly, directed by a leader of consummate wisdom and skill, who is assisted by powerful princes, and finds his subjects so numerous, that, if we are to lay any stress on the word "legion" in the memorable narrative of Luke, he is able to spare some six thousand of them to guard one miserable captive.†

But the Lord is mindful of His own, and does not leave them unprotected.

Truly, with such facts as these before us, we might well faint for fear did we not know that there is a mightier Power above all the hosts of the Prince of Darkness, One Who regards us with feelings of wondrous love, Who is not only able, but yearning, to shield us from the destroyer now, and Who purposes shortly to deliver us altogether from the anxiety, the terror, and the danger, of his assaults. For although the Lord has not yet formally deposed the rebel, and arranged a new government, He does not leave the world entirely to

* Eph. vi. 12.

† Luke viii. 30.

Satan's mercy. Angels of God penetrate the realms of air, encamp round about them that fear Him, and protect them from the malignant foes to whom they would otherwise fall an easy prey.* Nor are their numbers insufficient: the servant of Elisha beheld the mountain full of horses and chariots of fire round about his master.† Angels of God are appointed to take the charge of whole churches, as we find from the first three chapters of the Apocalypse. Nay, the reins of government are sometimes wrested even from the hands of Satan's most powerful princes, and a great kingdom is for a while ruled by an angel of God. This, as we found just now, was the case with the empire of Persia when the Lord would have the world-power favourable to His exiled people.‡

The motions of the elements are probably directed by Satan.

It might also at first seem that the elements are not left altogether in the hands of the rebels. For the voice of the angel of the waters sounded not like that of an apostate, when John heard him saying;—"Thou art righteous, O Lord, Which art, and wast, and shalt be, because Thou hast judged thus. For they have shed the blood of saints and prophets, and Thou hast given them blood to drink; for they are worthy." § These are indeed the words of one who has long sighed and groaned for the wickedness which his eyes have seen, and at last recognises the righteous judgment that overtakes it. And again; the angel "which had power over fire" is evidently one of the princes of God.‖

But since these two, as well as those whom John saw holding the four winds of the earth,¶ are only

* Psalm xxxiv. 7.
† 2 Kings vi. 17.
‡ Dan. x. 13.
§ Rev. xvi. 5, 6.
‖ Rev. xiv. 18.
¶ Rev. vii. 1.

introduced in connection with the time of the end, it is probable that they are the appointed successors of Satan's ministers, who will hereafter take possession of the elements to use them in the execution of the wrath to come. For until the Devil be deposed from the throne of the air, it is likely that he will exercise control, to a great extent at least, over atmospheric phenomena. In the Book of Job we find him even wielding the lightning: for at his bidding the fire of God fell from heaven, and consumed both the flocks and servants of the patriarch.* And when, many centuries afterwards, our Lord arose from His sleep and "rebuked" the winds and the sea,† it cannot be supposed that He was chiding the mere rush of the blast, or the senseless waves; but rather, those malignant spirits of air and water which had combined to excite the storm.

General condition of the world owing to the present rebellion of its spiritual rulers and the partial interference of God.

Such, then, is the picture set before us in the Word of God—the whole earth divided into provinces by the Prince of this World, and systematically governed and administered under his direction by his viceroys with their officers and subordinates countless in number; this organisation, perfect in itself, but continually disturbed by interferences from a mightier Power for the protection of individuals, of churches, and occasionally of whole nations. And the product of these two influences gives us the exact state of the world as it is at present; a state generally and systematically evil and godless, but with many individual exceptions, and subject at times to partial changes on a more extensive scale, which we call

* Job i. 16. † Matt. viii. 26.

reformations or revivals; a thick darkness, illumined, however, here and there by burning and shining lamps; an arid desert, but not without its oases; an ever-restless sea, on the surface of which the broad stream of the spirit that now worketh in the children of disobedience is the prominent feature, but with some under-currents setting in an opposite direction.

Ezekiel's prophecy concerning the Prince and the King of Tyrus. These titles are not to be referred to the same person.

Let us now turn to the twenty-eighth chapter of Ezekiel, from which we may, perhaps, extract a little more information on this mysterious subject. The first nineteen verses of the chapter contain a very remarkable but somewhat obscure prophecy, consisting of two distinct parts, an address to the Prince of Tyrus, and a lamentation upon the King of Tyrus. Now there can be no doubt that these titles refer to two persons, and are not merely different appellations of the same. For in the address to the prince there is nothing which could not be said to a human potentate; but the king is manifestly superhuman. Of the prince it is said that he will be slain by the hand of strangers, and the word translated "slain" means "thrust through" with sword or spear: but the king is to be devoured by fire, and brought to ashes upon the earth.

Interpretation of the address to the Prince of Tyrus.

With regard, therefore, to the first ten verses, there is no reason why we should not apply them to the then reigning prince of Tyre, whose name, as we learn from Josephus, was Ittiobalus. Now Tyre was built on a rocky island about half a mile from the mainland, and was strongly fortified. Hence Ittiobalus is represented as exulting in the strength of his sea-girt city, and likening himself, in proud reliance upon his inaccessible dwelling, to the God that sitteth above the heavens: he is ironically told that he is wiser than Daniel, whose fame was evidently world-wide at the time: his presumption is ascribed to his wisdom, his success in commerce, and the vast riches he had acquired. But because he had set his heart as the heart of the Most High, therefore the terrible of the nations, that is, the Chaldeans, should come against him; and, when about to be slain by a man, he should at length discover that he was no god.

Thus far the prophecy is easily intelligible; and we know that a short time after its delivery Tyre was besieged by Nebuchadnezzar. It is curious, too, to find the Tyrians in later times flattering Herod by exclaiming that his voice was the voice of a god, and not of a man, and so bringing upon him a punishment far more signal than that which befell their own ancient prince.*

The remainder of the prophecy probably refers to Antichrist. Reasons for this supposition.

But the lamentation upon the King of Tyrus † does not so readily yield its meaning: for there are expressions in it which cannot be applied to any mortal. Now to adopt the too common plan of explaining these away as mere figures of speech, is to trifle with the Word of God. We have no right to use so dishonest a method of extricating ourselves from difficulties, a method which enables men to deduce almost any desired meaning from a passage, and makes the whole Bible an enigma instead of a disclosure. We must rather confess, if it be necessary, that we have no clue whatever to an interpretation.

But there is a kind of prophecy, especially frequent

* Acts xii. 20-23. † Ezek. xxviii. 11-19.

in the Psalms, in which the prophet, speaking first of a cotemporary matter, is then borne on by the Spirit to some stupendous event of the last times, of which the incident in his own days is a faint type. And if we apply this principle to the passage before us, we are at once struck, upon considering the type, by the similarity of the pretensions of Ittiobalus to those of Paul's Man of Sin, "who opposeth and exalteth himself above all that is called God, or that is worshipped; so that he as God sitteth in the Temple of God, showing himself that he is God." * Can, then, the King of Tyrus, as distinguished from his type the Prince, be the great final Antichrist? Let us try the key, and see if the wards fit.

And first; is there any reason why Antichrist should be called the King of Tyre? It would seem so. For Tyre is in Palestine, and in the second verse of this chapter is said to be "in the midst of the seas." Now if we turn to Daniel's prophecy of the Wilful King, we shall find it predicted of that destroyer, that he will enter into the glorious land, and plant the tabernacles of his palace "between the seas." † This in other words seems to mean that he will invade Palestine and fix his abode at Tyre.

But there is a significant change in the expression for Tyre. In Ezekiel's address to the Prince it is said to be "in the midst," or, more literally, "in the heart of the seas," that is, surrounded on all sides by water. ‡ And it is a well-known fact, that in former times, up to the date of Alexander's siege at least, Tyre was an island. But it is now a peninsula, and is, therefore, likely to be so in the still future days of Antichrist:

* 2 Thess. ii. 4. † Dan. xi. 41-45. ‡ Ezek. xxviii. 2.

hence the expression in the original of Daniel is merely, "between the seas." * And so, perhaps, we may explain the connection of Antichrist with Tyre.

Some expressions in the lamentation can, so far as we know, apply only to Satan. But Antichrist will be Satan incarnate.

But what shall we say of the lamentation itself? For there are assertions in it which could be true of no mortal, not even of Adam. Certainly our first father was in Eden, and in the garden of God; but we are not told that every precious stone was his covering: we know not how he could be called the Anointed Cherub: we do not hear that he was upon the Holy Mountain of God, and walked up and down in the midst of the Stones of Fire. Indeed, so far as we can see, there is but one being of whom some of the expressions in this passage could be used, and that is Satan: the whole of the remainder may be explained of Antichrist.

But why this strange confusion? Why should these two mysterious wonders be thus apostrophized as though the history and personality of both were merged in one being? It is not difficult to find an explanation. For it needs but little study of Scripture to learn that all human energy is raised and directed by spiritual influences. Upon the children of God comes the Spirit of God, and they are then able to do His will. But if they lose their feeling of dependence upon Him, and grow remiss in prayer, they are liable to be seized and misdirected by spirits of evil, and fearful consequences may ensue. So David was once moved by Satan to the cost of himself and his people,† though not to his final ruin; for the Devil cannot compass that even in the case of the weakest of God's saints. But the wicked

* Dan. xi. 45. † 1 Chron. xxi.

are altogether subject to the spirit that now worketh in the children of disobedience.*

Now while evil angels and demons are doubtless appointed for the ordinary work of influencing mankind, yet we can easily imagine that, whenever there is any transcendently mighty issue at stake, their great leader, who excels them all in wisdom and power, would himself undertake the more arduous labour. And, accordingly, at our Lord's first advent, when the hour of the Prince of Darkness had come, Satan himself entered into Judas, and directed him to his fearful crime.† So when that last great master-piece of the Adversary shall appear, the Antichrist, whose coming, as Paul tells us, is after the working of Satan,‡ and to whom the Dragon shall give his power, and his throne, and great authority,§ it is but reasonable to suppose that he will be possessed and energised by the Devil in person. And thus he will be a compound being, partly human, partly superhuman ; at once the king of Tyre and the Anointed Cherub that covereth ; a travesty by Satan of the incarnation of our Lord. Hence the great difficulties of this prophecy vanish : the tangled web of the lamentation is unravelled. For it is easily intelligible if understood to be spoken sometimes to the human, sometimes to the Satanic part of Antichrist.

Nor need this twofold address seem strange to us : for we have a similar one in connection with the very earliest mention of Satan in the Bible. At his first introduction to us we find him commencing his work of ruin through the medium of a serpent's body. And the just sentence of God, though nominally pronounced

* Eph. ii. 2.
† John xiii. 27.
‡ 2 Thess. ii. 9.
§ Rev. xiii. 2.

upon the serpent alone, comprises both the punishment of the beast energised and that of the Devil within it. Thus the parallelism with our passage is complete.

Details of the lamentation. Satan's eminence in wisdom and beauty.

With this general clue to the lamentation let us now proceed to its details. The first sentence seems to apply, primarily at least, to Satan, who is said to have sealed up the sum, being perfect in wisdom and beauty.* His vast empire is often alluded to in Scripture, and, as we have already seen, may not improbably comprehend the whole of our solar system. Certainly no other angelic power of greater or even equal dignity has been revealed to us. The archangel Michael himself is quoted by Jude as preserving towards the Prince of Darkness the respect due to a superior, however wicked he may be, until God has formally commanded his deposition.† If, then, he be a being of such high degree, he would also in God's perfect kingdom, where there are no anomalies as with us, excel his subordinates in wisdom and beauty as much as he does in rank.

He was placed in an Eden, which, however, bore no resemblance to the Eden of Adam; but rather to the New Jerusalem as described in the Apocalypse.

The next clause speaks of him as having been in Eden, the garden of God.‡ Now Satan was indeed in Adam's Eden: he did not, however, appear there as a minister of God, but as an apostate and malignant spirit eager for the ruin of the new creation. Hence the Eden of this passage must have been of a far earlier date. Nor did it at all resemble the garden in which Adam was placed. For we read nothing of trees pleasant to the sight and good for food: but the prominent feature is the covering, that is, probably, the pavilion or palace, of Satan, which is

* Ezek. xxviii. 12. † Jude 9. ‡ Ezek. xxviii. 13.

described as being made of gold and of every precious stone.

Yet, while this description does not in any way remind us of Paradise, we cannot but be struck by its resemblance to that of the New Jerusalem, with its buildings of pure gold as it were transparent glass, its foundations garnished with all manner of precious stones, its jasper wall, and its gates of pearl. And that city, be it remembered, seems to be the destined habitation of the Church of the Firstborn, who will then be spiritual beings of a higher order, equal to the angels,* and, with Christ at their head, will have succeeded to that same power which Satan and his angels are now so fearfully abusing.†

The remainder of the verse should be translated ;—

He was a mighty prince from the very day of his creation.

"The service of thy tabrets and of thy pipes was prepared with thee on the day when thou wast created."‡ Now music is one of the necessary attendants of royal state. In the third chapter of Daniel we have an enumeration of the various instruments which were to signal the time of the king's pleasure : § and in the fourteenth of Isaiah the pomp of the King of Babylon and the noise of his viols are said to be brought down to the grave with him.‖ Nay, the blast of a trnmpet accompanied the manifestation of God Himself upon Mount Sinai ;¶ and the trump of the archangel will sound at the return in glory of the King of the whole earth.

The meaning, then, of this clause seems to be that Satan was from the moment of his creation surrounded by the insignia of royalty ; that he awoke to conscious-

* Luke xx. 36.
† Rev. v. 10.
‡ Ezek. xxviii. 13.
§ Dan. iii. 5.
‖ Isa. xiv. 11.
¶ Exod. xix. 16.

ness to find the air filled with the rejoicing music of those whom God had appointed to stand before him.

He was also a priest of the Most High, and his place was at the footstool of the throne of God.

In the next verse we seem to pass from the royalty of Satan to his priestly dignity.* He is said to have been, by God's appointment, the Anointed Cherub that covereth. Anointed doubtless means consecrated by the oil of anointing; while the Cherubim appear to be the highest rank of heavenly beings, sitting nearest to the throne of God, and leading the worship of the universe.† Possibly they are identical with the thrones of which Paul speaks in the first chapter of his Epistle to the Colossians.‡ The words "that covereth" indicate an allusion to the Cherubim that overshadowed the ark; but we cannot, of course, define the precise nature of this office of Satan. The general idea seems to be that he directed and led the worship of his subjects.

He is also said to have been upon the Holy Mountain of God, and to have walked up and down in the midst of the Stones of Fire.§ The Mountain of God is the place of His presence in visible glory, where His High Priest would, of course, stand before Him to minister. The Stones of Fire may, perhaps, be explained as follows. We know that the station of the Cherubim is just beneath the glory at the footstool of the throne.‖ Now when Moses took Aaron, Nadab, Abihu, and seventy of the elders of Israel, up the mountain of Sinai to see the God of Israel, "there was under His feet as it were a paved work of a sapphire stone, and as it were the body of heaven in his clearness. . . . And the sight of the glory of the Lord was like devouring fire upon the top

* Ezek. xxviii. 14.
† Rev. iv. 9, 10; v. 11-14.
‡ Col. i. 16.
§ Ezek. xxviii. 14.
‖ Ezek. i. 26.

of the mount."* This paved work of sapphire glowing with devouring fire, is, perhaps, the same as the Stones of Fire: and if so, Satan's presence in the midst of them would indicate his enjoyment of the full Cherubic privilege of nearness to the throne of God.

At his creation Satan was perfect in all his ways.

The next verse shows that God is not the Author of evil.† For even the Prince of Darkness was by creation perfect in all his ways, and so continued, until iniquity was found in him and he fell.

Interpretation of the words "by the multitude of thy merchandise."

That which follows is more difficult. "By the multitude of thy merchandise they have filled the midst of thee with violence, and thou hast sinned: therefore I will cast thee as profane out of the Mountain of God: and I will destroy thee, O covering Cherub, out of the midst of the Stones of Fire."‡

The first clause of this verse may refer solely to the human aspect of Antichrist: for there are prophetic intimations that commerce will be a prominent feature in the perilous times of the end.§ In the past history of the world we have many instances of its demoralising effects upon nations wholly given to it, of the luxury, fraud, and violence, which ever seem to develop with its growth.

Proposed new rendering, and more probable interpretation.

Nevertheless, the clause may apply to Satan in some mysterious way which we cannot yet explain: for we are only able to discern the dimmest outlines of these spiritual matters. Certainly such an application seems to be required by the context, and if the authorised version seems obscure, an admissible change in the

* Exod. xxiv. 10, 17.
† Ezek. xxviii. 15.
‡ Ezek. xxviii. 16.
§ Rev. xviii. 11-19.

rendering will suggest a very suitable interpretation. For the word translated "merchandise" may also (as an investigation of the root will show) * signify "detraction" or "slander"; and we know that the very name "Devil" means "the slanderer," or "malignant accuser."

Now that Satan does carry to God slanderous reports of the actions and motives of men we learn from the Book of Job. And the life of the same patriarch also supplies us with an instance of the cruel violence which seems to follow these accusations so invariably that the whole princedom of Satan has become a realm of injustice, in which the servants of God suffer affliction, while the wicked, as a rule, flourish. For the present the Lord permits this state of things, because His own children need the furnace to purge away their dross; but hereafter He will assuredly require all their sorrows and all their tears at the hands of their malignant persecutor.

From the twelfth chapter of the Apocalypse we learn that He will at length put an end to the slanders of Satan by sending Michael to drive him down from his throne on high, and expel him altogether from the heavenly places. And at the instant of his fall from his aerial dominions a loud voice is heard saying in heaven;—"Now is come the salvation, and the strength, and the Kingdom of our God, and the authority of His Christ: for the accuser of our brethren is cast down, which accused them before our God day and night." †

* רָכַל to go about—(1) in order to traffic, (2) for the purpose of slandering. Hence רֹכֵל a merchant, and רָכִיל slander. רְכֻלָּה, the word used by Ezekiel, might, therefore, incline to either meaning.

† Rev. xii. 10.

This expulsion is probably identical with the one mentioned in our text. For, if we adopt the rendering "slander," or "malignant accusation," the cause assigned for the casting out in Ezekiel exactly corresponds to the proclaimed result of it in the Apocalypse.

The next verse presents no difficulty.* For that the heart of Satan was lifted up because of his beauty, and that he corrupted his wisdom by reason of his brightness, we may infer especially from Paul's warning;—"Not a novice, lest being lifted up with pride he fall into the condemnation of the Devil." †

Satan fell through pride.

Pride in his own superiority seems to have prompted this wondrous being to turn to himself that worship which it was his office to direct to his Almighty Creator. But already the ruin of God has fallen upon his realm: he finds his power checked and cut short by angels who are irresistible because they come in the strength of the Most High: he sees, perchance, the gathering armies of Michael preparing for the fatal onslaught which will drive him from heaven: and knows that they will be quickly followed by the Son of God, Who will hurl his blasted and helpless form from his last stronghold upon earth into the depths of the abyss. Then will he at length both feel and exhibit in his own person to the whole universe the ineffable distance between the loftiest, wisest and fairest of created beings and the great and ever blessed Creator, Who alone is worthy to receive glory and honour and power.

With the latter part of the prophecy, referring as it does to the joint downfall of Satan and Antichrist, we

* Ezek. xxviii. 17.

† 1 Tim. iii. 6.

have at present no concern, since we are just now occupied not with the future, but with the past.

Summary of the history which appears to be contained in the lamentation.

It, therefore, only remains to put together the information which, if our interpretation be correct, this passage contains. The outline will be somewhat as follows.

God created Satan the fairest and wisest of all His creatures in this part of His universe, and made him Prince of the World and of the Power of the Air. Since his wisdom would be chiefly used in expounding the will and ways of God, we can probably discern in its mention his office of prophet. He was placed in an Eden, or region of delight, which was both far anterior to the Eden of Genesis—for he was perfect in all his ways when he entered it—and also, apparently, of an altogether different and more substantial character, resembling the New Jerusalem as described in the Apocalypse.

In the scanty account given to us of this Eden we may, perhaps, trace the lineaments of the heavenly Tabernacle. For, from the second chapter of Genesis, we find that Eden was a district, and the garden an enclosure within it.* Following this analogy we discover in Satan's habitation three enclosures, Eden, the Garden of God, and the Holy Mountain of God, corresponding, possibly, to the Outer Court of the Tabernacle, the Holy Place, and the Holy of Holies, respectively. And this idea is strengthened by the fact that Satan is said to have been upon the Holy Mountain of God as the Anointed Cherub that covereth ; just as the images of the covering Cherubim were placed in the Holy of Holies.

* Gen. ii. 8.

He, therefore, appears to have been the great High Priest of his realm, dwelling in a splendid palace of gold and precious stones near to the place of God's presence; just as the Israelitish High Priest resided at Jerusalem in the vicinity of the temple.

He was also its King, having been placed upon this summit of honour at his creation, and not subsequently raised to it from a lower rank. Finally; he was perfect in all his ways, and apparently continued so for a length of time.

Now all this evidently took place before his fall and the preparation of the present world. And so we can only conclude that he is closely connected with our earth, and that a large portion of his history extends back into times far anterior to those of Adam.

It thus appears that Satan was appointed prophet, priest, and king, of the world: but he proved himself a rebel. Therefore the Lord Jesus came forth from the Godhead, to assume the abused dignities, and restore the confusion.

Now the analogy between Satan's office and that which our Lord has already taken upon Himself in part, and will shortly exercise in full, is so striking that it is not easy to avoid the following inference. That Satan abused his high office of prophet, priest, and king, and thus involved the whole of his province in sin, and the earthly part of it, at least, in a ruin to which allusion is made in the second verse of Genesis. That, when his return to obedience had been proved an impossibility—perhaps by his conduct towards the new creation, which may have been intended to give him an opportunity of repentance—and when no other created being could be found able to restore the confusion, the Lord Jesus Himself came forth from the Godhead, to take the misused power into His own hands, and to hold it until the rebellion be altogether suppressed, and every trace of it obliterated.

The offices of prophet and priest He is already exercising, but not that of king. For had He at once assumed the sceptre, the result would have been utter destruction to all living; since all have sinned, and whatsoever is sinful must be cast out of His kingdom into unquenchable fire. It was, therefore, necessary first to put away the iniquity of those who should be saved. This He came into the world to do by the sacrifice of Himself: and now, having given us instructions as to our conduct during His absence, and many exhortations to be ever watching for His return, He has departed with the blood into the heavenly Holy of Holies, there to appear in the presence of God for us. This done, He will come to earth a second time, to wrest the power from the hands of Satan, and, after destroying that which cannot be healed, bring back the residue of creation to purity and order.

Hence from the prophecies of the times of restitution we may conjecture the nature of Satan's preadamite kingdom.

Seeing, then, that the government which Christ will shortly take upon His shoulders appears to be exactly identical with that which was once committed to Satan, and that God's first arrangements were of necessity perfection, does it not seem likely that, when the times of restitution arrive, the original order of things will begin to be restored in Christ's Millennial kingdom?

If so, we can easily discover the outline of Satan's preadamite world. For in the Millennium, Christ and His Church, the members of which will then have been made like unto Himself, are to reign in the heavenly places over earth and its inhabitants. So, probably, in remote ages, before the first whisper of rebellion against God, Satan, as the great governing head and the viceroy of the Almighty, assisted by glorious beings of his own nature, ruled over the sinless dwellers upon earth. At the same time he directed the worship of his subjects, and expounded to them the oracles of the all-wise Creator.

But his weight of glory was more than he could bear: pride lifted up his heart, and he fell from his obedience. Then, doubtless, corruption appeared among his angels, and so descended to those who were in the flesh. How long God bore with this; what warnings and opportunities He gave; whether any availed themselves of His mercy, and are now holy angels who from time to time revisit the place of their ancient habitation—all such questions as these we can only answer by conjecture from the analogy of our own race. But the fact that we can ask them shows how rightly all our vaunted wisdom in this life is said to be at best but a knowledge in part, and how wonderful a supplement may, in the World to Come, be added to our present scanty information even in regard to the history of our own planet.

The two orders of Satan's subjects may be traced in the New Testament. Use and meaning of the name Devil.

We are, however, apparently able to discern in the New Testament clear traces of the two orders of Satan's subjects, the spiritual, and those who were in the flesh. For there are three distinctive terms applied to the dwellers in the Kingdom of Darkness.

The first is ὁ διάβολος, the Devil, a word which in this sense is never used in the plural, and is always a designation of Satan himself. Its literal meaning is "the one who sets at variance," "the slanderer," or "malignant accuser." And how apt a name is this for him who began to slander God to man when he corrupted our first parents, and has since continued to do so by the stream of hard thoughts and evil suggestions which he is ceaselessly pouring into human hearts! Nor does he stop at this: for in giving in his reports of the inhabitants of earth he also slanders man to God. So we find him declaring that self-interest was the sole motive of Job's righteousness:* so we hear him desiring to have Peter that he may sift him as wheat:† so we read that he accuses ourselves and our brethren before our God day and night.‡ The name Devil is, then, applied to Satan alone: for he appears to be the only evil power who reports the actions of men directly to God.

The angels of the Devil.

In the second place we find mention of the angels of Satan,§ who are doubtless the spiritual intelligences which God appointed to assist him in his government, and who chose to follow him into sin. These probably constitute the principalities, powers, and world-rulers of this darkness.‖

The demons, which are not angels, but disembodied spirits.

But another class of Satan's subjects is much more frequently brought before us, that of the δαιμόνια, or demons; and great confusion is introduced into our version by the erroneous translation "devils."¶ We may, however, in some measure avoid this confusion by remembering that the proper word for Devil has, as we have just said, no plural, and is only applied to Satan himself. Whenever, therefore, we meet the plural in the English Testament, we may be sure that the Greek is δαιμόνια, which ought to be rendered "demons."

* Job i. 9-11. † Luke xxii. 31. ‡ Rev. xii. 10.
§ Matt. xxv. 41. ‖ Eph. vi. 12.

¶ This mistake has been most unaccountably confirmed in the Revised Version, notwithstanding the protest of the American Committee.

Now these demons are the same as evil and unclean spirits, as we may see by the following passages. "When the even was come they brought unto him many that were possessed with *demons;* and He cast out the *spirits* with His word." * Again, in Luke's Gospel, we read;—"And the seventy returned again with joy, saying, Lord, even the *demons* are subject unto us through Thy name." To which the Lord responds;—"Notwithstanding in this rejoice not, that the *spirits* are subject unto you." † So in Matthew's account of the lunatic boy, the *demon* is said to come forth from him; ‡ but in Mark's Gospel this same *demon* is called a *foul spirit*, and also a *deaf and dumb spirit.* § And Luke gives us a list of "certain women which had been healed of *evil spirits* and infirmities," of whom the first mentioned is "Mary called Magdalene, out of whom went seven *demons.* ‖ Demons and evil spirits are, therefore, synonymous terms.

But they must be carefully distinguished from angels, bad as well as good. For angels are not mere disembodied spirits, but—as we may learn from our Lord's declaration that the children of the resurrection shall be equal to the angels—are clothed with spiritual bodies, such as are promised to us ¶ if we "shall be accounted worthy to obtain that age and the resurrection from the dead." **

This distinction was clearly understood by the Jews: for in the Acts of the Apostles we read that the

* Matt. viii. 16. † Luke x. 17, 20. ‡ Matt. xvii. 18.
§ Mark ix. 25. ‖ Luke viii. 2, 3.
¶ Compare Phil. iii. 21 and Luke xxiv. 39.
** Luke xx. 35. We must carefully distinguish between the resurrection from, or rather, out of (ἐκ), the dead and the resurrection of the dead. The latter is, of course, the final uprising, when all who are at the time in their graves shall hear the voice

Pharisees cried out concerning Paul;—"We find no evil in this man: but if a spirit or an angel hath spoken to him, let us not fight against God."* And in the preceding verse we are told of their opponents, the Sadducees, that they denied the existence of angels and spirits.

The classical meaning of the term "demon."

What then is the meaning of the term "demon"? Plato derives it from δαήμων, an adjective formed from δάω, and signifying "knowing" "intelligent"; most modern scholars refer it to δαίω, to divide, as though it meant a divider or distributor of destiny. We incline to Plato's opinion, which makes the word point to the superior knowledge believed to be possessed by disembodied spirits.

Its classical use is as follows. By Homer it is applied to the gods; but we must remember that Homer's gods are merely supernatural men. It was afterwards used of a sort of intermediate and inferior divinity. "The deity," says Plato, "has no intercourse with man; but all the intercourse and conversation between gods and men is carried on by the mediation of demons." And he further explains that "the demon is an interpreter and carrier, from men to gods and from gods to men, of the prayers and sacrifices of the one, and of the injunctions and rewards of sacrifices from the other."

If we inquire whence these demons came, we shall be told that they are the spirits of men of the golden age acting as tutelary deities—canonized heroes, pre-

of the Son of man, and shall come forth; the former expression refers to the calling of a privileged few out from the great company of the dead, and is applied only to the resurrection of Christ, or to the first resurrection of Rev. xx. 4-6. See Acts iii. 15; Luke xx. 35; Phil. iii. 11.

* Acts xxiii. 9.

cisely similar both in their origin and functions to the Romish saints. In Hesiod's curious description of the ages of the human race we find the following account.*

"First of all the immortals, who possess the mansions of Olympus, made a golden race of articulate-speaking men. These lived in the time of Cronos, when he ruled in heaven. Like gods they spent their lives, with hearts void of care, apart and altogether free from toils and trouble. Nor did miserable old age threaten them: but ever alike strong in hands and feet they rejoiced in festal pleasures far from the reach of all ills. And they died as if overcome by sleep. All blessings were theirs. And spontaneously the fruitful soil would bear crops great and abundant. And so they occupied their cultivated lands in tranquillity and peace with many goods, being rich in flocks and dear to the blessed gods. But after that earth had covered this generation, they indeed by the counsels of mighty Zeus became demons, kindly ones, haunting the earth, being guardians of mortal men. These I ween, shrouded in mist, and going to and fro everywhere upon the earth, watch both the decisions of justice and harsh deeds, and are dispensers of riches. Such a royal prerogative is theirs."

Now if we remember that according to Bible teaching the Heathen gods were really evil angels and demons who inspired oracles and received worship, we shall easily understand that the golden age of which ancient bards so rapturously sang was no reminiscence of Paradise, but of the times of that former world when Satan's power was still intact. A change in the heavenly dynasty, the expulsion of Cronos or Saturn, is always mentioned as having brought to a close this

* "Works and Days," 109-126.

age of unmingled joy. Nor need we be startled at the good influence attributed by Hesiod to demons. For in a Heathen poem we can only expect to learn what the Prince of this World may choose to say, and have no cause for wonder if he commend his own agents.

The incidents recorded by inspired writers seem to identify the New Testament meaning with the classical.

Such, then, are the demons of the classical writers. Nor does there appear to be any reason for changing the meaning of the term in the New Testament. For may not these demons be the spirits of those who trod this earth in the flesh before the ruin described in the second verse of Genesis, and who, at the time of that great destruction, were disembodied by God, and left still under the power, and ultimately to share the fate, of the leader in whose sin they acquiesced? Certainly one oft recorded fact seems to confirm such a theory: for we read that the demons are continually seizing upon the bodies of men, and endeavouring to use them as their own. And may not this propensity indicate a wearisome lack of ease, a wandering unrest, arising from a sense of incompleteness; a longing to escape the intolerable condition of being unclothed—for which they were not created—so intense that, if they can satisfy its cravings in no other way, they will even enter into the filthy bodies of swine? *

We find no such propensity on the part of Satan and his angels. They, doubtless, still retain their ethereal bodies—for otherwise how could they carry on their conflicts with the angels of God?—and would be likely to regard with high disdain the gross and unwieldy tabernacles of men. They may, indeed,

* Matt. viii. 31.

possibly enter human frames; not, however, from inclination, but only because such a course is absolutely necessary for the furtherance of some great conspiracy of evil.

Thus in the New Testament the spiritual subjects of Satan are plainly divided into two classes; nor would it be difficult to prove a similar distinction in the Old. Such angels as the princes of Persia and Grecia, of which we have already spoken, would of course belong to the first order; while the familiar spirits, and probably also the *Shedim*, *Seirim*, *Lilith*, *Tsiim*, and *Iim*, would be identical with the demons.

We may also distinguish the two classes of Satan's subjects in the Old Testament.

But here a question naturally arises. Why, if a preadamite race really existed upon earth in the flesh, do we not find some indications of it among the fossil remains? Certainly no human bones have been as yet detected in primeval rocks; though if any should be hereafter discovered, we need find no contradiction to Scripture in the fact.

The absence of human remains in the geological strata is no proof of the non-existence of preadamite men.

But the absence in the fossiliferous strata of any vestige of preadamite man is no real obstacle to the view we have taken. For we are totally unacquainted with the conditions of life in that pristine world, which may not have been, and indeed probably were not, the same as in our own. For Adam was created after, and apparently, as we shall presently see, in full view of a previous failure. Hence it may be that death did not touch those primeval men until the final destruction, and that the decaying and dying state of the animal and vegetable kingdoms was a warning ever before their eyes of the wrath that would at length reach their own persons except they repented. It may be that their bodies were resolved into primal elements, leaving the spirit naked, instead of the spirit departing and giving up the body to decay as with us. It may be that they were smitten with some consuming plague of the Lord which changed their comely forms into indistinguishable masses of corruption,* or reduced them in a moment to ashes upon the earth.† It may be that the earth opened her mouth, and swallowed them up, with all that appertained to them, so that they went down alive into the pit.‡ It may be that they all perished in what is now to us the deep, and that their remains are covered by the deposit at the bottom of ocean. Evidently our habitable land was once the floor of the sea, theirs may be now.

Either the depth of the sea, or a place of confinement immediately below it, appears to be a prison of demons.

Indeed we may find hints which perhaps add some little confirmation to the last conjecture, and tend to link these disembodied spirits with the locality which may have been the scene of their sins in the flesh, and of the just punishment by which they were finally overtaken. At least there is a prison mentioned in Scripture, which is either in the depths of the sea or is connected with them, and in which we may with probability infer that many demons are already confined, while fresh captives are from time to time placed under the same restraint whenever an outrage of more than ordinary daring calls forth the righteous indignation of God, and causes Him to bring the mischievous career of its perpetrators to a sudden and final close.

* Zech. xiv. 12. † Ezek. xxviii. 18; Mal. iv. 3.
‡ Numb. xvi. 30.

Certainly the knowledge of some such fact seems to have terrified the legion of spirits from which our Lord delivered the Gadarene; or, otherwise, what meaning can we assign to their agonizing entreaty that He would not command them to depart into the Abyss.* In Matthew's account their words are different, and they fear lest they should be tormented before the time.† But the latter expression probably conveys the same idea as the former; and we are thus made to understand that at a certain fixed, and to them well known, time all the demons who are still at liberty will be cast into the same prison. It is called "the Abyss";‡ and in some passages, such as the ninth chapter of the Apocalypse, this term is evidently applied to a fiery hollow in the centre of the earth: but it is also used for the depths of the sea, a meaning which accords well with its derivation. For instance, in the Septuagint version it is the deep over which darkness was brooding before the Six Days, and also the great deep, the fountains of which were broken up to inundate the earth. The connection may be merely the idea of depth in both significations: but it seems not unlikely that the Abyss in the centre of the earth was so called from the fact that the compartment which forms it lies immediately beneath, and is entered through, the deep sea by which it is probably secured.

Hence perhaps the reason why, after the last judgment, when all the prisoners of the Abyss will have

* Luke viii. 31. † Matt. viii. 29.

‡ *ἄβυσσος* is usually derived from *α* (the Greek Alpha) privative and *βύσσος*—akin to *βύθος, βένθος, βαθύς*—"depth," and especially the deep waters of the sea. But this would make it mean "the depthless," "the shallow," rather than "the bottomless." It is better, then, to derive it from *α* intensive and *βύσσος*, in which case it will signify "the great deep," "the abyss."

been cast into the lake of fire and brimstone, there will be no more sea in the renovated earth.

Possible meaning of the words, "And the sea gave up the dead which were in it."

And regarding the sea as the bar of the pit, or assuming that the Abyss may sometimes be called the sea, just as the deep sea is called the Abyss, we seem to be helped to the exposition of a passage which has not hitherto received an adequate interpretation. In the account of the last great judgment we read ;—"And the sea gave up the dead which were in it; and Death and Hades"—that is, "the unseen world"; for the translation "Hell" is incorrect—"delivered up the dead which were in them; and they were judged every man according to their works." * Now the sea is commonly supposed to be mentioned as giving up the bodily germs of those who have been drowned or buried in it. But if the meaning goes no further than that, why do we not also hear of earth giving up the far more numerous dead which lie beneath its sods? Instead, however, of sea being coupled with land, we find it mysteriously connected with Death and the unseen world: that is, it is mentioned in a list of places filled, not with the remains of material forms, but with disembodied spirits.

This is certainly a fatal objection to the common interpretation: but if the sea be the prison of demons, all difficulties vanish, and in that case we can well understand why it is the *first* to give up its dead. For every one will be judged in his order, and, therefore, these preadamite beings will have an awful precedence of the prisoners of Death and Hades, whose innumerable cells are, perhaps, filled exclusively with criminals from our present world.

* Rev. xx. 13.

Conclusion and practical application.

But we must now pass on from this stupendous subject: for enough has been said to exhibit the hints of Scripture in regard to former ages and the preadamite destruction. And since that which is set before us is but a shadowy form, we must not persuade ourselves that we see a sharply defined outline. To be wise above that which is written is to entangle oneself in a net of Satan from which it is all but impossible to escape.

Let us not, however, fail to learn one lesson from the wondrous things we have been contemplating. Rebellion is ruin, no matter how noble, or wise, or fair, its leader may be. For even Lucifer, the bright son of the morning, the loftiest of the angels of God, has fallen low from his high estate, and ere long, shorn of all his wisdom, and might, and beauty, will be plunged into the perpetual night of the Abyss. There is but one attitude natural or possible for a created being, and that is entire submission and unreserved obedience to the will of Him Who created and sustains him.

Let the proud of the earth consider this, those who madly turn against God the very abilities and advantages which they owe to His bounty, those wilful ones who walk defiantly in the ways of their own heart. But if any deny the law, destruction must follow, or the whole universe would soon be disintegrating in anarchy. For the sake of the remainder of His creation the mercy of God is restricted to a fixed limit; and except the rebel repent in time, deprived of all that lifted up his heart, and blasted by the thunderbolts of the Omnipotent, he must sink into the horrible silence of the everlasting darkness.*

* 1 Sam. ii. 9.

THE SIX DAYS.

CHAPTER IV.

THE SIX DAYS.

The destruction of the preadamite world seems to have been caused by tremendous convulsions, and also by a glacial period consequent on the extinction of the sun.

WE must now return to the ruined earth, the condition of which we can only conjecture from what we are told of the six days of restoration. Violent convulsions must have taken place upon it, for it was inundated with the ocean waters: its sun had been extinguished: the stars were no longer seen above it: its clouds and atmosphere, having no attractive force to keep them in suspension, had descended in moisture upon its surface: there was not a living being to be found in the whole planet.*

Now the withdrawal of the sun's influence had probably occasioned that glacial period the vestiges of which, as geologists tell us, are plainly distinguishable at the close of the Tertiary Age. And the same cause will also account for the mingling of the waters that were above the firmament with those that were below it. Both effects are well illustrated by the following extract from one of Herschel's "Familiar Lectures on Scientific Subjects."

"In three days from the extinction of the sun there

* Gen. ii. 5.

would, in all probability, not be a vestige of animal or vegetable life on the globe; unless it were among deep-sea fishes and the subterranean inhabitants of the great limestone caves. The first forty-eight hours would suffice to precipitate every atom of moisture from the air in deluges of rain and piles of snow, and from that moment would set in a universal frost such as Siberia or the highest peak of the Himalayas never felt—a temperature of between two and three hundred degrees below the zero of our thermometers. . . . No animal or vegetable could resist such a frost for an hour, any more than it could live for an hour in boiling water."

From this description we may form some idea of the ruin which befell the preadamite world. Of its main features there is a graphic portrayal in a grand passage of Job, in which the folly of contending with God is enforced by an obvious reference to Satan's rebellion and its consequences.

"The Wise in heart and Mighty in strength,
Who hath defied Him, and remained unhurt?
Who displaceth mountains, and they know not
That He has overturned them in His wrath;
Who maketh the earth to tremble out of her place,
So that her pillars rock to and fro;
Who commandeth the sun, and it riseth not,
And sealeth up the stars."

The terrific convulsions by which the earth was shattered and destroyed are almost placed before our eyes in this sublime description; while the suddenness of the catastrophe is vividly presented by the poetic conception that the mountains were overturned before they were aware of it. The extinction of the sun is plainly indicated, and also the veiling of the stars, so that the thick darkness was relieved not even by their scanty lights.*

How long the glacial period continued it is impossible even to conjecture; but in the scene which the second verse of Genesis places before us we must suppose the ice to have broken up—perhaps through some development of the earth's internal heat,† which in its

* Job ix. 4-7. In the following verses (8-10) the patriarch alludes to the reconstruction of the Six Days.

> " Who Alone spreadeth out the heavens,
> And treadeth upon the heights of the sea;
> Who maketh the Bear, Orion, and the Pleiades,
> And the chambers of the South;
> Who doeth great things past finding out,
> And marvellous things without number."

Here, since the spreading out of the heavens evidently refers to the work of the Second Day, it may be that "the heights of the sea" are the waters above the firmament. The mention of the constellations points to the reversal of God's previous action in sealing up the stars. In regard to the meaning of the Hebrew word *asah*—rendered "maketh"—see p. 23, and also the comment upon the work of the Fourth Day in this chapter.

† This conjecture may derive a little support from the following considerations.

The heat increases as we descend into the earth, and hence many scientific men have held that the interior of our globe is a reservoir of liquid fire. With this opinion the Scriptures are in accord: for, in Rev. ix. 2, when the well or shaft of the Abyss is opened, a smoke, like the smoke of a furnace, pours forth so copiously that the sun and air are darkened by it. Such a description inclines us also to prefer the translation of 2 Peter iii. 7, which makes the Apostle speak of the earth as "stored with fire." And perhaps the context of the expression suggests that, just as God broke up the fountains of the great deep to cause the Deluge, so will He command His stored fires to burst through the crust of the earth for its future destruction. A heat will then be developed so intense as to fuse the very elements, or materials of which the crust is composed. Nor will this be a new thing: the condition of the non-fossiliferous strata seems to point to the occurrence of a similar catastrophe in former ages.

May we not then conceive some development of these internal

convulsive struggles may also have displaced the bed of ocean. Thus the whole globe was covered with water, on the surface of which the Spirit of God was already brooding.

The First Day of restoration. God creates light, which did not, however, spring from the sun; but was, possibly, magnetic, like the terrestrial light of the Aurora Borealis.

Then, startling the deep silence, and pealing over the black floods of ruin, was heard the thunder of the voice of the Almighty, and the command went forth "Light be." Instantly it flashed from the womb of darkness, and illumined the rolling globe; but only to reveal an overspreading waste of waters.

This "light" of the First Day must be carefully distinguished from the "light-holders" of the Fourth, since the word used conveys in itself no idea of concentration or locality. Nevertheless the light must have been confined to one side of the planet, for we are told that God at once divided between the light and the darkness, and that the alternation of day and night immediately commenced.

In past times infidels have scoffed at the idea of light being called into existence independently of the sun. And certainly it does seem difficult to conceive that Moses could have anticipated science by so many centuries except upon the one supposition that he was instructed by the Spirit of God, Who is not circumscribed by the limits of human knowledge. But now science also has discovered that the sun is not the only

fires, comparatively slight, but sufficient to melt the ice with which the earth was covered? In some localities of volcanic Italy the soil is found to be quite warm; and a short time ago the newspapers were giving accounts of a tract of land in Germany which had become so heated by subterranean fire that tropical plants were growing upon it.

source of light; but that the earth itself, and at least one other planet in our system, may under certain conditions become self-luminous.

The light of the first day may, possibly, have been magnetic, like the Aurora Borealis, which seems to be powerful only when the sun is weak: for its most brilliant displays are restricted to the long nights of the cold north. In more southern climes its appearance is rare, and its development comparatively incomplete: but it is more frequent and vivid at those periods, recurring every eleventh year, when the spots on the sun are larger and more numerous, and the solar power is consequently diminished. It would thus almost seem that the sun absorbs this light and afterwards diffuses it in a modified form. On the purely terrestrial origin of the Aurora Borealis Humboldt makes the following interesting remarks:—

"This phenomenon derives the greater part of its importance from the fact that the earth becomes self-luminous, and that as a planet, besides the light which it receives from the central body, the sun, it shows itself capable in itself of developing light. The intensity of the terrestrial light, or rather the luminosity which is diffused, exceeds, in cases of the brightest coloured radiation towards the zenith, the light of the moon in its first quarter. Occasionally, as on the 7th of January, 1831, printed characters could be read without difficulty. This almost uninterrupted development of light in the earth leads us by analogy to the remarkable process exhibited in Venus. The portion of this planet which is not illumined by the sun often shines with a phosphorescent light of its own. It is not improbable that the moon, Jupiter, and the comets, shine with an independent light, besides the reflected solar light visible through the polariscope. Without speaking of the problematical but yet ordinary mode in which the sky is illuminated, when a low cloud may be seen to shine with an uninterrupted flickering light for many minutes together, we still meet with other instances of terrestrial development of light in our atmosphere. In this category we may reckon the celebrated luminous mists seen in 1783 and 1831; the steady luminous appearance exhibited without any flickering in great clouds observed by Rozier and Beccaria; and lastly, as Arago well remarks, the faint diffused light which guides the steps of the traveller in cloudy, starless, and moonless nights in autumn and winter, even when there is no snow on the ground."

The record of the existence of light apart from the sun is a proof of the Divine origin of the Scriptures. Memorable anticipation of science in the book of Job.

The fact, then, that, at a time when terrestrial luminosity was probably unknown, Moses spoke of the existence of light without the sun, is a strong proof of the Divine source of his knowledge. For though the Bible gives no information by which science is likely to be advanced, yet it does here and there drop mysterious utterances, the truth of one after another of which is discovered as scientific men become better acquainted with the laws of the universe.

Perhaps the most memorable instance of this is the familiar passage in which God demands of the patriarch, "Canst thou bind the sweet influences of Pleiades?"* Through the long lapse of centuries since the writing of the Book of Job, which probably dates back into the past as far as three thousand three hundred years,

* Job xxxviii. 31.

no adequate sense was found for these words. But now a meaning seems to be assuming shape, and gradually becoming more defined and vivid, a meaning worthy of the great God Whose lips first uttered the mysterious sentence. For in 1748 the astronomer Bradley gave a hint, which others have subsequently developed and confirmed, that our solar system, together with the whole of the sidereal heavens within range of our vision and telescopes, is but a portion of an inconceivably vast circle of stars revolving around one centre. And that centre, the pivot of the universe, is now supposed to be among the Pleiades. If this be the case, wonderful indeed are "the sweet influences of Pleiades" which keep the whole of the starry heavens in orderly motion.

The Six Days were not ages, but literal days of twenty-four hours.

We are next told that God called the light day and the darkness night, and that the evening and the morning were the First Day. Now in order to verify certain systems of interpretation attempts have been made to show that in this chapter a day must be understood to signify an age.

And doubtless the word "day" is sometimes used of prolonged periods, as in the expression "the day of temptation in the wilderness," and many others. But whenever a numeral is connected with it, the meaning is at once restricted thereby, and it can only be used in its literal acceptation of the time which the earth takes to make one revolution upon its axis. It is, therefore, clear that we must understand the Six Days to be six periods of twenty-four hours each.

But still further; these days are mentioned as comprising an evening and a morning, as being made up of day and night. Here, then, is another warning against the figurative interpretation, which we must carefully avoid lest we expose ourselves to such attacks as the following :—

"It is evident that the bare theory that a day means an age or immense geological period might be made to yield some rather strange results. What becomes of the evening and morning of which each day is said to have consisted? Was each geologic age divided into two long intervals, one all darkness, the other all light? And if so, what became of the plants and trees created in the third day or period, when the evening of the fourth day—the evenings, be it observed, precede the mornings—set in? They must have passed through half a seculum of total darkness, not even cheered by that dim light which the sun, not yet completely manifested, supplied on the morning of the third day. Such an ordeal would have completely destroyed the whole vegetable creation, and yet we find that it survived, and was appointed on the sixth day as the food of man and animals. In fact, we need only substitute the word period for day in the Mosaic narrative to make it very apparent that the writer at least had no such meaning, nor could he have conveyed any such meaning to those who first heard his account read." *

Now the justice of these remarks cannot be denied, and the lesson to be learnt from them is this: that, if believers would but keep to the plain statements of the Bible, there would be very little for infidels to cavil at; but that as soon as they begin to form theories, and twist revelation into agreement with them, they expose themselves, and, still worse, the Scriptures, to ridicule.

* "Essays and Reviews," p. 240.

On the next day a second command went forth, and in obedience to it a movement commenced among the waters. At the word of God the firmament, or atmosphere which we breathe, was formed: and by its insertion the waters which float above the earth were again raised to their own place, and separated from those which are upon the earth.

Second Day. The firmament placed between the waters, but not pronounced good.

There is, however, in the account of this day's work an omission which is probably significant: for the usual conclusion, "And God saw that it was good," is in this case left out. And since the reasons ordinarily given for the omission are unsatisfactory, we venture to suggest the following explanation. May not the withholding of God's approval be a hint of the immediate occupation of the firmament by demons, those, indeed, which are its present inhabitants? Since they were concerned in the fall of man, they must have speedily appeared in the newly-formed atmosphere. May they not, therefore, have been imprisoned in the deep, and having found some way of escape at the lifting up of the waters, have swarmed into the dominion of the air, of which their leader is Prince? In this case the firmament might have been teeming with them before the close of the Second Day, and we need not wonder that God refused to pronounce their kingdom good.

In twenty-four hours the firmament was completed, and then the voice of the Lord was again heard, and in quick response the whole planet resounded with the roar of rushing floods as they hastened from the dry land into the receptacles prepared for them, and revealed the moun-

Third Day. The waters upon the earth retire to their bounds: the dry land is again seen, and brings forth grass, herbs, and trees. Grand description in the Book of Psalms.

tains and valleys of the earth. This grand movement is thus described in the hundred-and-fourth Psalm.*

5. "He established the earth upon the foundations thereof,
That it should not be moved for ever and ever.
6. With the deep as with a garment Thou didst cover it,
Above the mountains did the waters stand.
7. At Thy rebuke they fled,
At the voice of Thy thunder they hasted away—
8. The mountains rose, the valleys sank—
To the place which Thou hadst established for them.
9. Thou hast set them a bound which they cannot pass,
That they turn not again to cover the earth."

In this passage we may remark a strong confirmation of the view we have adopted. For while the deep is represented as spread over everything, the mountains, together, of course, with all their fossil inclosures, are mentioned as already existing beneath it. They had evidently been formed long before the Third Day. And in strict accordance with this fact is God's command, "Let the dry land appear," or more literally, "be seen"; not, "Let it come into existence." The words, "The mountains rose, the valleys sank," are a parenthesis, and describe, of course—or they would conflict with the statement in the sixth verse—the general effect of the scene to a spectator as the waters subsided to their proper level.

On the same day the word of God went forth a

* Psalm civ. 5-9.

second time, and the now liberated soil began to cover itself with a garment of vegetation, the fresh verdure of which was diversified with the hues of countless flowers.

Fourth Day. Preparation of the light-holders. *Or* and *Maor.*

Thus the earth itself was completely restored, and again fitted for the support and enjoyment of life: it only remained to establish its relations with the heavenly bodies. This God did upon the Fourth Day by concentrating the light-material, which He had previously created, into light-holders. For the word used of the light of the First Day is *Or*, and of that of the Fourth *Maor*. And this last is the same as the first, but with a locative prefix which makes it signify a place where light is stored, or a light-holder.

Now we must carefully observe that God is not said to have created these light-holders on the Fourth Day, but merely to have made or prepared them. They were created, as we have seen, in the beginning: and, since the sun appears to be a dark body enveloped by luminous clouds, it was doubtless around its mass that the earth was revolving from the first. Probably, too, the great luminary of our world was also the light of the preadamites: but its lamp had been extinguished, and on the Fourth Day God gave or restored to it the capacity of attracting and diffusing the light-material, by the exercise of which power its photosphere was quickly formed.

And so the solar rays, as they hastened through space, struck upon the moon, and lighted up its silver orb in the firmament of night.

We are next told that God made or prepared—not created—the stars also; that is, apparently, so altered or modified the firmament, perhaps by the concentration of light into the sun, that the stars then first appeared, or re-appeared, in it. For that they had been previously created we have positive proof. At the close of the Third Day earth was finished and ready for the reception of life, while the stars are not mentioned till the Fourth Day. But in a passage of Job we are told that the morning stars were admiring witnesses when God laid the foundation stone of the earth, and sang together for joy at its completion.* They must, therefore, have been pre-existent. And so God's preparation of them on the Fourth Day must have had reference only to their appearance in our firmament, to the purpose which they were to serve in regard to our earth.

Appearance of the stars in the heaven of our earth.

Thus the Fourth Day came to its close: all was now ready; the work of restoration was finished, and the habitation prepared. Then the creative power of God was put forth, and the waters, which had hitherto been void of living beings, were commanded to swarm with the creature that hath life. Our version, "Let the waters bring forth," is incorrect: the literal rendering is, "Let the waters swarm with swarms, with living creatures"; but the text does not tell us that these creatures were produced from the waters.

Fifth Day. Creation of fish and birds. Confusing mistake in our version.

The following clause is still more grievously mistranslated, since the English is made to imply that even birds were formed from the same element. This would be a direct contradiction of the nineteenth verse of the second chapter, where they are said to have been moulded of earth. But the contradiction does

* Job xxxviii. 4-7.

not exist in the Hebrew, the exact sense of which is, "And let fowl fly above the earth in the face of the firmament of heaven." Hence in this verse both fish and fowl are merely commanded to appear in their respective elements without any hint as to their origin.

Sixth Day. Creation of cattle, creeping things, and beasts of the field, all of which were graminivorous.

Sea and air were thus filled with life. Then, last of all, on the Sixth Day, God proceeded to people the earth, which was commanded to bring forth—and here the translation is correct—three classes of living creatures—cattle or domesticated animals, creeping things or land reptiles, insects and worms, and beasts of the field or wild roaming animals.

But, as was shown above, all these creatures were graminivorous: for in the thirtieth verse the green herb alone is given them for meat. Nor, of course, was man allowed to feed upon animal flesh: in the twenty-ninth verse his diet also is restricted to the seed-bearing herb and the fruit of trees. The present state of things, in which animal food is allowed and necessary to man, and carnivorous beasts, birds and fishes abound, testifies to a wofully disorganised and unnatural condition; such a one as would be impossible save in a world at variance with the God of order, peace, love, and perfection.

Further proof that the history of the Six Days is not a record of geological ages.

We have before seen that neither the plants of the Third nor the creatures of the Fifth and Sixth days have anything to do with the fossilised remains found in the earth's crust; because that crust is assumed to have been formed before the great preadamite catastrophe. For the mountains with all their contents are described as already existing beneath the floods of the deep, and as having appeared, without need of creation or preparation, as soon as the waters retreated to their bounds. We are now able to add other cogent reasons in confirmation of this view.

During the Six Days there were three distinct acts of creative power, by which vegetation, fish and birds, and land animals and man, were successively produced. And we are clearly given to understand that all the plants of our world were created on the third day, while no moving creature that has life was called into being until the fifth day. If, then, the theory which makes each day a geological period were correct, the remains of plants only would be found in the lowest fossiliferous strata. These would fill the formations of their own and the following age; after which they would be mingled with fossil birds and fishes: then, in the rocks of a yet later period, the remains of land animals would also appear. And such a sequence would form the only possible agreement with the account in Genesis.

But what is the result of an examination of the strata? The lowest fossiliferous system is the Silurian: do we find in it nothing but vegetable petrifactions? Quite the contrary. The lower and middle Silurian rocks contain a few seaweeds indeed, but no land plants whatever. Yet they abound in creatures belonging to three of the four sections of the animal kingdom, in mollusca, articulata, and radiata. It is only when we get to the highest strata of the upper Silurian rocks that land plants begin to appear, and together with them some specimens of vertebrata, the remaining section of the animal kingdom. If, then, in this oldest fossiliferous system we find plants rare and yet every division of the animal kingdom represented, how can we attempt to force such a fact into accordance with the Mosaic narrative!

Again; the history of Genesis mentions, as we have seen, but three distinct creations—of plants, of birds and fish, and of land animals. But in the eight classifications of strata, from the Tertiary down to the Silurian, there would appear to have been at least as many creations as there are systems, each creation including a very large proportion of animals and plants peculiar to itself. Agassiz goes still further, as the following quotation will show:—

"I hold it to be demonstrated that the totality of organic beings was renewed, not only in the intervals of those great periods which we designate as formations, but also in the stratification of each separate division of every formation. Nor do I believe in the genetic descent of the living species from the different tertiary divisions which have been regarded as identical, but which I hold to be specifically different; so that I cannot adopt the idea of a transformation of the species of one formation into that of another. In enunciating these conclusions, let it be understood that they are not inductions derived from the study of one particular class of animals—such as fishes—and applied to other classes, but the results of direct comparison of very considerable collections of petrifactions of different formations and classes of animals."

Thus the crust of our earth appears to be a vast mound which God has heaped over the remains of many creations. And geology shows us that the creatures of these ancient worlds either perished by painful disease and mutual destruction, or were overwhelmed in an instant by the most terrific convulsions of nature.

Lastly; it is recorded* that all the living creatures and plants created during the Six Days were given to man. It is reasonable, therefore, to suppose that they were intended to remain with him throughout the whole course of his world. And hence, again, the certainty that the fossil plants and animals, nearly all of which were extinct before the creation of Adam, have nothing to do with the creatures of the Third, Fifth, and Sixth days.

Creation of man. God pronounces every thing to be very good, and rests on the Seventh Day.

The creation of the humbler inhabitants of earth having been thus accomplished, but one other work remained to be done. All was ready for the introduction of those who were to be set over the world as the vicegerents of the Almighty. Accordingly God proceeded to make them in His own image and after His likeness. But in the first chapter of Genesis the calling into being of man, male and female, is simply mentioned to signify his place in creation. Further details are reserved for the present, and the history goes on to say that God saw all He had made that it was very good.

For no evil ever came from His hands. Let this truth be fixed in our hearts: and whenever we are troubled with the thorn or the thistle, with the poisonous or useless weed, with the noxious beast, with the extreme of heat or cold, or with any of the other countless inconveniences and pains of our present condition; whenever we feel ready to faint by reason of fightings without and fears within, let us remember that God

* Gen. i. 26, 29.

made all things good, and avoiding hard thoughts of Him, say, An enemy hath done this.

Then follows the institution of the Sabbath on the Seventh Day: and the fact of its introduction in this connection is sufficient to show that it was no special ordinance for the Israelite, but a law of God for all the dwellers upon earth from the days of Adam till time shall cease.

Summary and introduction to the next section of the history. Different meanings of the expressions "the heaven and the earth" and "the earth and the heaven."

And so the first section of this wondrous history closes with a summary of the subject and an introduction to the next part in the words;—"These are the generations of the heavens and the earth when they were created, in the day that the Lord God made the earth and the heavens, and every plant of the field before it was in the earth, and every herb of the field before it grew: for the Lord God had not caused it to rain upon the earth, and there was not a man to till the ground. But there went up a mist from the earth, and watered the whole face of the ground."

Here the creation of the heavens and earth, that is, of the whole universe, refers, of course, to the creation in the beginning. But the making or preparing of the earth and the heavens points to the Six Days of restoration. And this is indicated not only by the change in the verb, but also by the inverted order, "the earth and the heavens," which is only found in one other passage, and is plainly significant. For the Hebrew word for "heavens" has no singular, and it was thus impossible to make in the Old Testament a distinction such as we often find in the New, where the singular of the Greek word is generally used for the first heaven or firmament of our earth, while the plural comprises the starry realms and the heaven of heavens. Hence some other device was necessary, and the fact that "the heavens" in the second clause of this verse mean the firmament of earth is indicated by the inverted order. And this order is also the historical one: for the firmament was not made perfect, so that sun, moon, and stars could be seen in it, until after the entire restoration of the earth. The same sequence in the hundred and forty-eighth Psalm is explained by the seventh verse, "Praise the Lord from the earth." For this Psalm is divided into two parts: in the first six verses praise to God is invoked from the starry vault and the heaven of heavens, in the last eight from the earth and its atmosphere. Hence in the thirteenth verse the glory of the Lord is appropriately said to be above "the earth and the heaven," earth being first mentioned because here also by heaven is meant the firmament which belongs and is, therefore, subordinate to it.

The plants and herbs of our world were newly introduced by God on the third day, and did not spring up from the relics of a former creation.

In the next verse, if we retain the Authorised Version, which follows the Septuagint, we must of course understand the verb "make" or "prepare" as applying not only to earth and heaven, but also to "every plant of the field," etc. The sense will then be that God prepared the seeds and placed them in the ground; so that the plants and herbs of our world did not spring from the relics of former creations or grow up spontaneously, but were newly introduced by God at that time. And this is corroborated by the fact that since the withdrawal of the salt and barren waters of the deep He had not as yet caused it to rain upon the earth, nor was there any preadamite spared from the previous destruction to cultivate the soil. All our verdure and plants grew up, therefore, from new germs placed in the ground by God and afterwards developed and nourished by a mist which went up from the earth.

Such appears to be the meaning of the passage, and this special allusion to the work of the Third Day seems to be inserted as an introduction to the following account of Eden and its garden.

There is no real discrepancy between the narratives in the first and second chapters of Genesis.

In closing our remarks on the continuous history of the Six Days, we may observe that many discrepancies have been alleged to exist between the first and second chapters of Genesis. Some of these we have already explained: none of them have any real foundation. We have only to bear in mind the different objects of the two records and all difficulty will vanish: for while the one chapter gives a continuous history of the week of restoration, the other is evidently a supplement, adding details of man's creation that we may better understand his nature and his fall. Hence in this second account reference is made to other works of the Six Days only when they happen to be immediately connected with the main subject, and without any regard to the order in which they were performed.

THE CREATION OF MAN.

CHAPTER V.

THE CREATION OF MAN.

THE detailed account of the creation of man which now presents itself for our consideration is a subject of the deepest interest: for it forms the only possible basis of true doctrine in regard to the origin and nature of our race. We must, therefore, carefully examine it: but the labour will not be tedious, for the whole revelation is contained in the following brief record;—"And the Lord God formed man of the dust of the ground, and breathed into his nostrils the breath of life; and man became a living soul." * We have thus three points to consider; the formation of the body, the infusion of the breath of life, and the result that man awoke to consciousness a living soul.

Supplementary history of the creation of man.

First, then, we are told that the Lord God formed man, that is, moulded his bodily shape as the potter does the clay. Indeed the meaning of the Hebrew verb is so decided that its present participle, used as a substantive, is the ordinary word for a potter. To this first act of God Job refers when he says, "Remember, I beseech Thee, that Thou

The moulding of the body.

* Gen. ii. 7.

hast made me as the clay; and wilt Thou bring me into dust again?"* For the material moulded was the dust of the ground which had just been moistened by a mist: and hence it is afterwards said, "Dust thou art, and unto dust shalt thou return."†

The word translated "ground" is *adamah*, which properly means red earth, and from which the name Adam seems to be derived. This corresponds to the natural colour of human skin, which is red on white, and in accordance with which Solomon's description of ideal beauty begins with the words, "My beloved is white and ruddy."‡

The infusion of the spirit.

The spirit of man had nothing to do with the formation of its sheath. God first moulded the senseless frame, and then breathed into it "the breath of lives"; for the original of the last word is in the plural. We have not, however, previously noticed this, because it may be nothing more than the well known Hebrew plural of excellence: the word, which is the common term for life, is rarely found in the singular. But if we wish to give significance to the number, it may refer to the fact that the inbreathing of God produced a twofold life, sensual and spiritual, the distinct existence of each part of which we may often detect within ourselves by their antagonism.

This breath of lives became the spirit of man, the principle of life within him—for, as the Lord tells us, "it is the spirit that quickeneth"—and by the manner of its introduction we are taught that it was a direct emanation from the Creator. We must, of course, carefully avoid confusing it with the Spirit of God, from Whom the Scriptures plainly distinguish it, and Who

* Job x. 9. † Gen. iii. 19. ‡ Cant. v. 10.

is represented as bearing witness with our spirit.* But, as we are told in the Book of Proverbs,† it is the candle of the Lord, capable of being lighted by His Spirit, and given by Him as a means whereby man may search into the chambers of his heart and know himself.

The origin of the soul.

Man was thus made up of only two independent elements, the corporeal and the spiritual: but when God placed the spirit within the casing of earth, the combination of these produced a third part, and man became a living soul.‡ For direct communication between spirit and flesh is impossible: their intercourse can be carried on only by means of a medium, and the instant production of one was the result of their contact in Adam.

He became a living soul in the sense that spirit and body were completely merged in this third part; so that in his unfallen state he knew nothing of those ceaseless strivings of spirit and flesh which are matters of daily experience to us. There was a perfect blending of his three natures into one, and the soul as the uniting medium became the cause of his individuality, of his existence as a distinct being. It was also to serve the spirit as a covering, and as a means of using the body; nor does Tertullian seem to have erred when he affirmed that the flesh is the body of the soul, the soul that of the spirit.

But it is interesting to notice that, while the soul is the meeting-point of the elements of our being in this

* Rom. viii. 16. † Prov. xx. 27.

‡ Hence, possibly, the meaning of the plural in the expression "breath of lives." The inbreathing of God became the spirit, and at the same time, by its action upon the body, produced the soul. It was thus the cause both of the spiritual and sensual life.

present life, the spirit will be the ruling power in our resurrection state. For the first man Adam was made a living soul, but the last Adam a quickening Spirit;* and that which is sown a psychic body is raised a spiritual body.†

The doctrine of man's threefold nature is, with one or two exceptions, much obscured by the inadequacy of our version.

Thus in the very beginning of Scripture we are warned against the popular phraseology of soul and body, which has long sustained an erroneous belief that man consists of but two parts. This idea has, indeed, taken such firm root among us that it has caused a deficiency in our language. For though we possess the nouns "spirit" and "soul"—which are, however, too commonly treated as synonyms—we have no adjective derived from the latter, and are thus unable to express connection with soul except by a paraphrase. Certainly an attempt is being made to Anglicize the Greek "psychic"; but the unwonted form and sound of the word seem likely to prevent its adoption into ordinary language. Yet the need of such an adjective has almost concealed the doctrine of man's tripartite nature in our version of the Scriptures: and English readers are carried away from the sense by inadequate translations of a Greek word which signifies "pertaining to the soul," but is sometimes rendered "natural," sometimes "sensual."‡

There are, however, one or two passages in which a reference to the threefold composition of our being could not be obscured. Such is the very remarkable verse in the Epistle to the Hebrews;—"For the Word of God is quick, and powerful, and sharper than any

* 1 Cor. xv. 45. † 1 Cor. xv. 44.
‡ 1 Cor. ii. 14; James iii. 15; Jude 19.

two-edged sword, piercing even to the dividing asunder of soul and spirit, and of the joints and marrow, and is a discerner of the thoughts and intents of the heart." * Here Paul plainly speaks of the immaterial part of man as consisting of two separable elements, soul and spirit; while he describes the material portion as made up of joints and marrow, organs of motion and sensation. Hence he claims for the Word of God the power of separating, and, as it were, taking to pieces the whole being of man, spiritual, psychic, and corporeal, even as the priest flayed and divided limb from limb the animal for the burnt offering, in order to lay bare every part, and discover if there were any hidden spot or blemish.

Another obvious passage is the well known intercession of Paul for the Thessalonians;—"And I pray God your whole spirit and soul and body be preserved blameless unto the coming of our Lord Jesus Christ." †

Respective functions of body, soul, and spirit.

Now the body we may term the sense-consciousness, the soul the self-consciousness, and the spirit the God-consciousness. For the body gives us the use of the five senses; the soul comprises the intellect which aids us in the present state of existence, and the emotions which proceed from the senses; while the spirit is our noblest part, which came directly from God, and by which alone we are able to apprehend and worship Him.

This last, as we remarked above, can only act upon the body through the medium of the soul: and we have a good illustration of the fact in the words of Mary;—"My soul doth magnify the Lord, and my spirit hath rejoiced in God my Saviour."‡ Here the change in tense shows that the spirit first conceived joy in God,

* Heb. iv. 12. † 1 Thess. v. 23. ‡ Luke i. 46, 47.

and then, communicating with the soul, roused it to give expression to the feeling by means of the bodily organs.

But the spirit of the unconverted is steeped in a deathlike slumber, save when it is roused to a momentary sense of responsibility by that Spirit of the Lord, Who convinces even the world of sin, of righteousness, and of judgment. Such men are unable to hold intercourse with God: the soul, manifested sometimes in intellectuality, sometimes in sensuality, often in both, reigns over them with undisputed sway. This is what Jude wishes to set forth in his nineteenth verse, which should be rendered, "These be they who separate, men governed by soul, not having spirit." * And even in the case of the converted the powers of the spirit are at present in great part suppressed, their place being supplied, though most inadequately, by the faculties of soul and body.

How inadequately which of us does not feel? For when at length we awake from the dream of this world; when our eyes are opened to a contemplation of realities, and a startling conviction of the ever decaying and quickly passing nature of all that is visible flashes upon our mind, from that moment we are possessed by one absorbing desire, that of attaining to life eternal. But to this end what guidance can we expect from the

* ψυχικοί, πνεῦμα μὴ ἔχοντες. Scarcely, "the Spirit." The preceding ψυχικοί makes the contrast between the human soul and spirit so obvious and natural that, if Jude had meant the Holy Spirit, he would surely have guarded his meaning by prefixing the article to πνεῦμα. However, it does not seem necessary to press the sense further than to understand that, in the men described, the God-consciousness is stifled by sensuousness. Even in their case the spirit may still be a potentiality, though as regards present influence it is as good as dead.

bodily senses, whose ceaseless march is ever to the grave? Nay, even the soul, however intelligent, however diligent in its search, cannot by any pains find out the path of wisdom. Often indeed it essays to do so: but how absolutely untrustworthy its conclusions are we may see in the difficulty of discovering even two men of the highest order of intellect with an identity of opinion. Reason is but an uncertain and deceitful instrument at the best, and the blinding pride of man makes matters still worse. For when one has set his heart upon an idea—which is, perhaps, nothing but the creation of his own fancy, as unsubstantial as the castle of a dream—his powers are thenceforth used for the single purpose of making the picture of his imagination stand out as vividly and as like reality as possible.

Reason is fallible and often dangerous; but the power of the spirit is an instinctive and unerring perception of truth.

And thus we may easily see that intellect is not merely fallible, but the most dangerous of all gifts, unless it be guided by the Spirit of God. For it can call evil good, and good evil: it can put darkness for light, and light for darkness; bitter for sweet, and sweet for bitter. Nay, the wave of its magic wand can fill not only this life, but even the region beyond the river of death, with sunny landscapes and fair scenes, to all of which it is able to give the semblance of firm reality, until the fatal moment which separates spirit and body, when in an instant the brilliant vista is blotted out for ever by the fiery darkness of the lost.

And even in the case of those who have been born again, who have received power to become sons of God, the intellectual faculty is still so incompetent that, though they possess truth in the Divine revelation, they are nevertheless, as Paul tells us, only able for the present to know and understand it in part. But when hereafter the spirit, our real life, shall be released and restored to its throne, we shall immediately become conscious of powers which we can now neither apprehend nor even imagine; we shall no longer people darkness with the phantoms of reason's dim and ever-changing dreams, but find ourselves in a world where there is no night, and endowed with a piercing and unerring vision which God shall give to all His redeemed. In the place of the uncertain and deceptive logic of the soul, we shall be gifted with that instinctive perception of truth which is the prerogative of untainted spirits.

Adam is placed in the garden of Eden, and the first trial of man commences.

Thus, then, the Lord created man in His own image; and we can picture the joy with which Adam awoke to consciousness in the midst of the beautiful world prepared for his habitation and possession. But fair as earth then was, the inexhaustible kindness of his Creator would still further ravish his heart by arranging for his abode a scene of pre-eminent beauty and superabounding delights. Eastward in Eden the Lord God planted a garden, and enriched it with every tree which is pleasant to the sight and good for food, including among them the tree of life and that of the knowledge of good and evil. He then took the man whom He had made, and put him into this Paradise to dress, and, as our version reads, to keep it. But the Hebrew of the latter verb also suggests the idea of watching over or guarding, and seems to point to an enemy and possible assailant.

And now commenced the first age or dispensation of our world, man's first trial to determine whether when in possession of innocence he is able to retain it.

Earth by the work of the Six Days was filled with unmingled blessings, all that it contained was very good; supreme dominion was given to Adam, and he was a pure and sinless being. Moreover, there was but one commandment; and, therefore, sin was circumscribed, and but one transgression possible. Of all the numerous trees of the garden man might freely eat, even the tree of life was open to him: but he was commanded to do homage to the great God Who had given him all things, to pay a tithe in acknowledgment of the exhaustless bounty bestowed upon him, by abstaining from one tree, that of the knowledge of good and evil. Of this he was not to eat, or he would prove himself a rebel, and lose his kingdom and his life.

In regard to the hostile denizens of the air he seems to have received no distinct warning, but only that which was implied in the injunction to dress and watch over the garden. And he needed nothing more: for knowing well the single prohibition of his God, he could at once detect a foe in any being who should tempt him to disobey it.

The two names Elohim and Jehovah.

There is no mention of this covenant with Adam in the first chapter of Genesis: for there we have merely a record of creation and restoration, while in the supplementary account we are concerned with the moral responsibility of man. And hence a change in the appellation of God, Who when regarded only as the Creator and Ruler is called Elohim or the Mighty One, but Who takes the title of Jehovah—usually translated "the Lord" in our version—as soon as He appears in covenant relation with man. At its first introduction the name Jehovah is joined with Elóhim, to obviate all doubt as to the identity of the Being designated by both words.

Now it is evident that, while either of these names will suit some passages, there must, nevertheless, be many cases in which the one would be appropriate and the other not. Of this the sacred writers are always mindful, and we shall presently meet with other instances of their careful discrimination. It thus appears that the very fact adduced by rationalists as a proof that the Scriptures are a clumsy compilation of diverse and incongruous documents, which they call Elohistic and Jehovistic—that this very fact beautifully exhibits the unity and consistency of the whole volume.

Adam gives names to animals, and must, therefore, have been gifted with speech from the day of his creation.

Yet another and crowning joy was in store for Adam. His benign Creator, knowing that it was not good for him to be alone, determined to bestow upon him a companion and partner of his joy. But first He brought to him the beasts of the field and the fowls of the air, to see what he would call them: that is, to see if he would claim any of them as bone of his bones and flesh of his flesh. Adam gave names to all, but to none that of woman; a result which had, of course, been anticipated by God. Indeed it seems not improbable that He made the trial to stimulate in His creature a desire which He intended to gratify.

And if the first man was able on the very day of his creation to give names—founded, doubtless, on their peculiarities—to beasts and fowls, it is evident that language was a gift bestowed upon him by God at the time when the breath of lives was breathed into his nostrils. Christians, therefore, cannot countenance the speculations of modern philosophers in regard to the gradual development of speech.

By naming the animal kingdom Adam took possession of his dominion before the appearance of the woman; so that she shared his lordship over creation, not in her own right, but as being bone of his bones and flesh of his flesh. And herein we may discern an evident type of the second Adam and His bride. For the Church, though all things are hers, will possess them through no merit or right of her own, but only as the bride of Him Who is the Heir of all things.*

Creation of woman. Adam and Eve a type of Christ and His Church.

In the history of the creation of woman we should observe the close connection between male and female, and the responsibilities of mutual love which it involves; the protection due on the one side, the subjection on the other. Each particular is so suggestive of the great mystery of Christ and His Church that it will be well to notice some of the points of comparison.

First, then, the Lord began His final work by casting Adam into a deep sleep. And so did the second Adam lie three days in the sleep of death before the creation of His bride could be commenced.

A consideration of some of the details of the type.

While the first Adam slept, God opened his side and took out the rib wherewith He made the woman. So while the second Adam slept in death upon the cross, a soldier pierced His side, so that there came forth blood and water; and by means of that blood, without the shedding of which there could never have been remission of sins, the Church is now in process

* 1 Cor. iii. 21-23.

of formation. Thou "didst purchase unto God by Thy blood men of every tribe, and tongue, and people, and nation,"* is the cry of the elders when the time has at length come to sing the new song.

After the rib had been withdrawn God closed up the flesh instead thereof. No second rib was to be taken: only one woman was made for Adam, though many were afterwards born of him. So also will it be with the second Adam: He, too, will have but one heavenly bride, the Church of the First-born, they that are His at His coming.† This body will be completed during His presence in the air, or first heaven, and His marriage will take place just before the terrible destruction which is to precede the Millennial reign, as may be seen by the order of events given in the nineteenth and twentieth chapters of the Apocalypse. Multitudes will be afterwards saved by Him: kings' daughters will be among His honourable women; but upon His right hand will stand the queen in gold of Ophir.‡

We next read;—"The rib which the Lord God had taken from man made He a woman." But the last words are by no means an adequate rendering of the original, which should be translated "builded He into a woman." And there is a remarkable coincidence in the use of such a term, and the frequent application of the words "build" and "edify" to the Church in the New Testament.

When God had made the woman He brought her unto Adam. So is God now bringing the elect in spirit to the heavenly Bridegroom, and no man can come

* Rev. v. 9.

† Or rather, "presence." See the chapter on the Presence and the Appearing in the author's work "The Great Prophecies."

‡ Psalm xlv. 9.

unto Christ except the Father draw him.* And so will He presently bring the completed bride in person to the second Adam, and at length answer that prayer ;—Father, I will that they also, whom Thou hast given Me, be with Me where I am; that they may behold My glory, which Thou hast given Me."†

Upon receiving his wife Adam exclaimed ;—"This is now bone of my bones, and flesh of my flesh." So the second Adam tells us that He is the vine and we are the branches ;‡ while His apostle still more plainly affirms ;—"For we are members of His body, of His flesh, and of His bones." §

Adam then proceeds, "She shall be called woman, because she was taken out of man." *Ish* is the Hebrew for man, *isha* for woman. She partook of Adam's nature, therefore she should be called after his name. And at His coming Christ, having changed the bodies of His waiting people into the likeness of His glorious body and made them partakers of His nature, will then fulfil His promise to the overcomer ;—"I will write upon him My new name." ‖

Lastly; the words, "Therefore shall a man leave his father and his mother, and shall cleave unto his wife: and they shall be one flesh," are, in their application to the woman, paralleled by the Lord's saying, "He that loveth father or mother more than Me is not worthy of Me." ¶ And yet again by the exhortation to the mystic bride ;—"Hearken, O daughter, and consider, and incline thine ear; forget also thine own people and thy father's house; so shall the King greatly desire thy beauty: for He is thy Lord; and

* John vi. 44.
† John xvii. 24.
‡ John xv. 5.
§ Eph. v. 30.
‖ Rev. iii. 12.
¶ Matt. x. 37.

worship thou Him."* These words have far greater force if we remember that those who are saved by Christ but do not belong to the Church of the first-born will probably inhabit the earth from which they sprang, and not be called away from their ancient dwelling into the heavenly places.

We may thus see how evidently the history of Adam and Eve foreshadows wondrous things to come, and sets forth the mystery of marriage in its reference to Christ and His Church.

* Psalm xlv. 10, 11.

THE FALL OF MAN.

CHAPTER VI.

THE FALL OF MAN.

The mercy of God seems to have predetermined the fall to remove pride from the heart of man, that he might be afterwards restored to an immortal purity and a more excellent power and glory.

THUS the man and the woman were created on the same day; so that Adam could only have been in existence a few hours before his wife. Nothing was wanting to complete their joy save the certainty that it would be lasting; and on this point they probably felt no fear. For what suspicion had they of the power of evil: how could they read in all that surrounded them the destruction of mightier creations? They knew not the secrets of the ground on which they trod: they rejoiced in the flowery verdure, and saw not the ruins of world beneath world reaching far into the bowels of the earth. They dreamt not that the blue sea was rippling over a vast prison-house of sin; that the very atmosphere above them was swarming with fallen angels and the disembodied spirits of those who had rebelled against the Most High.

And they, too, were destined to be overcome of evil: they were soon to experience the meaning of that awful word, death, which the lips of their Creator had uttered; to feel the terrors of His wrath, the desolation of ruin, the horrors of corruption. For the all-wise

God well knew the great obstacle to perfection in the creature, and that, until it could be removed, He was unable to show forth His love and pour out His bounty to the full. He could not endow men with great power and wisdom; He could not make them excellent in majesty and glorious in might, swift as the winds or the lightning to do His will, until they had passed the danger of abusing His gifts, and so falling as the sinful angels had done before them.

Therefore they should not be perfect from the day of their creation; but, by a painful yet most salutary experience, should learn their own creature weakness: they should be imprisoned in bodies of humiliation: * they should be left to try what their own strength could do, to endeavour to save themselves by their own arm amid the hostile powers of darkness, which should not, therefore, be at once consigned to the doom of the obstinately rebellious: they should fall, but by the merciful pre-arrangement of God not an eternally fatal, not a hopeless fall: they should know what it is to abide in sin, and so to be consumed by His anger, to be troubled by His wrath, to be subjected to vanity, wasting, and decay: with shuddering awe they should enter into the thickening darkness which enshrouds the dread portals of death: all their beauty should turn to corruption, their bodies, however majestic or fair, become repulsive and loathsome.

And through and out of all this they should be saved by a power not their own: benighted, helpless, distraught, not knowing whither to turn, they should be led by the hand of Another: their sin, which they would be utterly unable to expiate, should be punished

* Phil. iii. 21.

in the person of a Substitute; the only begotten Son of their loving Creator should die in their stead. Thus should they be taught the absolute dependence of the creature upon the love and power of the Almighty God.

And if they could humble themselves under His almighty hand; if they could trust Him in the time of their darkness; believe that He was causing all things to work together for their good; and thankfully accept His way of peace and salvation—then, after a little space, the days of their mourning should be ended. He would wash away every stain of sin or tears: instead of the garment of corruption He would invest them with the robes of immortality: He would place the crown of life upon their head: everlasting joy should break forth upon them without the possibility of an intervening cloud: nay, many of them, gifted by His favour with a more complete submission, with a stronger faith, should even be exalted to sit down upon the throne of His Son, and, under Him, to rule in glory over that very earth which had been the scene of their hopes and fears, of their gloomy and toilsome wanderings, while they bore about with them the body of this present condition of death.*

Satan was created in glory and fell: man is born into a state of weakness and misery, and does not attain to his perfection till the resurrection of the just.

Such seems to be an outline of God's purposes in regard to man, as indicated in the Scriptures: such the reason of our sojourn here in weakness, continual liability to misery, and certain progress to decay. Satan first awoke to consciousness in the dazzling light of God's glory, to find himself a mighty prince, perfect in wisdom and beauty.† But, having known no other condition, he thought that

* Rom. vii. 24. † Ezek. xxviii. 12-15.

his power and his splendour proceeded from himself, lost his sense of dependence, and fell without hope. In our case God's foresight and mercy prevented this irremediable ruin.

Therefore our being begins in darkness, far from the light and joy of His presence: we are no princes, but slaves to those horrible despots sin and corruption: our beauty is faulty and evanescent: our wisdom is foolishness: our purposes are continually broken off: our bodies date their tendency to dissolution from the day of our birth. Yet there is a hand stretched out to lead us through the night: and if we grasp it, giving up our own ideas of the right way, it will guide us along a road, rough, toilsome and perilous indeed, but which will at length bring us safely to the home of our Father.

And then, when this corruptible shall have put on incorruption, and this mortal shall have put on immortality: when, after having borne the image of the earthly, we shall also bear the image of the heavenly: when we shall rest,. no longer in hope, but in abundant and never failing satisfaction after awaking in God's likeness: then at length shall we have attained the goal of our being, the position for which He created us, nay, to which He ordained us before the foundation of the world. Then shall we know why He bade us consider ourselves strangers and pilgrims upon earth: then shall we feel His meaning when He told us that while in the flesh we are but in a state of death, our real life being hid with Christ in God: * then, when the heavenly treasure is unlocked before our wondering gaze, shall we under-

* Rom. vii. 24: Col. iii. 3.

stand to the full His dark saying ;—"And if ye have not been faithful in that which is Another's, who shall give you that which is your own?" *

A powerful effect must needs be wrought in us when we glance backward upon this life after we have left it.

Nor, after having been thus led through darkness and perils to God, shall we feel any wish to stray out into the night again. With such a retrospect we shall not be tempted to think that our glory and beauty are an inseparable part of ourselves. And not only shall we have learnt by a fearful experience the dependence of creatures, but our whole being will be penetrated with a burning and unquenchable love of our Creator.

For even in this life how great do His mercies seem! But when once we find ourselves safe in the Paradise of God, freed for ever from the assaults of the world, the flesh and the devil, the first backward glance at the dangers we have just escaped will, perhaps, act upon us with greater power than the whole course of discipline through which we may have previously passed. For we shall then see our fearful accumulation of sin, understand its appalling nature, and be lost in amazement at the love which bore with us while we went on day after day repeating and multiplying transgression. We shall look back upon the many thousand perils out of which we were from time to time delivered, and only a very few of which we had even suspected. We shall behold the horrid and innumerable hosts of darkness, from whose malignant power we were defended for so many years, and at length finally rescued, by a Mightier than they. We shall gaze upon the pit prepared for them, into which we also must needs have descended had not a

* Luke xvi. 12.

ransom been found, even the most precious blood of the Lord Jesus.

And as we turn away from these dark and painful scenes—during the whole time of our connection with which there is but a step betwixt us and death—to the bright smile of our reconciled God, to the glory given to us, to the golden city prepared for our habitation, to the eternity of ever deepening joy before us, shall we not, emptied at last of pride and self-will, and overpowered with humble gratitude, cry aloud, with a strength of love and devotion unknown to this world, "Blessing, and honour, and glory, and power, be unto Him that sitteth upon the throne, and unto the Lamb for ever and ever!"

And with such thoughts as these should we comfort one another whenever we are in sorrow and heaviness during our present brief season of trial.

Probable reason of the hostility of the fallen angels. Their cunning.

We must now return to Adam and Eve, whom we left enjoying in innocence the pleasures which God had provided for them. But short, indeed, was their time of happiness: for the powers of evil were already setting the fatal snare. And they were, perhaps, stimulated to their fell purpose, not only by pure malignity and the wish to oppose God whenever they could do so indirectly, but also by a desire to prolong their own reign. For, knowing themselves to be rebels, they were probably well aware that the Almighty never intended sinless man to be subject to them, and that in Adam He was raising up a seed, not merely to inhabit the earth, but also to take possession of the realms of air. Hence we can easily understand their anxiety to retard, at least, the counsel of God by reducing the new creation to their own level of sin and ruin. And, perchance, they may have known from experience that the result would be a delay of long ages, during which the mercy of the Supreme would grant His creatures time for repentance and recovery.

The plan of Satan showed that God had not yet deprived him of his wisdom; though, alas! it had been changed by his fall from the noble power of a prince of the Most High to the cunning of a deceitful intriguer! He would not make his assault with power and terror: for that would drive the assailed into the arms of their Protector instead of drawing them away from Him, and their earnest cries for help would quickly call down hot lightnings upon their daring foe. But he would present himself in the form of an inferior and subject animal, from which they would never suspect harm. For, like all his children of this world, Satan, though proud even to destruction, can yet degrade himself to the very dust in order to carry out his purposes.

Reasons which seem to have determined Satan to make his first assault upon Eve.

He would not essay the man and the woman together: for combined they might uphold one another in the obedience and love of God. And he well knew that, if he were once detected and baffled, a second attempt would be attended with far more serious difficulties; nay, might by some appeal of Adam to God be rendered altogether impracticable.

Again; two reasons seem to have deterred him from tempting Adam alone. For had he commenced by overcoming the man, and then through him worked the fall of the woman, her ruin would have been incomplete: she would not have been wholly without excuse before God, since she would have acted under the orders or influence of the one whom He had set over her.

And secondly; man, as we have before seen, consists of three parts, spirit, soul, and body; and of these the soul is predominant in consequence of its power over the body. Now it is just in this point that the weakness of man lies, in the fact that his body is psychic and not spiritual. But Adam was created directly from the image of God, Eve only mediately so. If, then, the man was an imperfect image through the predominance of his soul, this defect would naturally be increased in the woman, who would, therefore, be the more susceptible of outward form and beauty, and of all emotions connected with the sense- and self-consciousness, while the influence of her spirit would be proportionally diminished. On this second account also Satan would seem to have chosen her as the fittest object for his first attack.

Eve is enticed to the locality of the forbidden tree.

Influenced, then, by some such considerations as these, the powers of evil either watched till Adam was absent, or, perhaps, by that mysterious power which we often feel but cannot explain, drew him away from his wife, and, when she was left alone, enticed her through the garden towards the tree in its midst. It may be that their suggestions set her musing on the strangeness of God's prohibition. Wherefore did He plant the tree in their garden if they were not to enjoy it? What so great difference could there be between it and the other trees of which they might eat at pleasure? And then, perhaps, a foolish curiosity may have moved her to examine the forbidden object, in order to see if she could detect its peculiarity.

But, however it happened, she at any rate suffered herself to be allured to the fatal spot, and so gave opportunity to the Devil. For we should keep as far as possible from that which is prohibited, nor ever tempt God by unnecessarily approaching it, either through curiosity or any other impelling cause. Had Eve avoided the vicinity of the tree, she could never have cast upon it that look which ruined herself and the world. And how many of her descendants have worked their own woe in the same way, by lingering on the borders of wrong, by too curiously examining, by wishing to understand too well, that which they knew to be evil!

The Tempter appears in the form of a serpent, which at that time was probably the most attractive, as well as the most intelligent, of the beasts of the field.

While Eve was standing near the tree a serpent approached and addressed her. The fact that she was not startled by such an occurrence seems to point to the existence of an intelligent communication between man and the inferior creatures before the fall. But we must not, of course, think of the serpent as the repulsive and venomous reptile to which we now feel an instinctive antipathy. For it had not then been cursed, but held itself upright, the most intelligent and, probably, the most beautiful of all the beasts of the field. It is an interesting fact that in that remarkable sculpture—the oldest surviving representation of the fall—which was found in the temple of Osiris at Phylæ, Eve is seen offering the fruit to Adam, the tree is between them, and the serpent stands by in an erect posture. Perhaps it sustained itself by wings; and indeed the epithet "flying" is applied to the *saraph* or fiery species in a passage of Isaiah.* The creature was, then, free from venom, and not improbably winged, while its scales glittered in the sun like burnished gold. Perhaps, too, it was recognized by Eve as the most intelligent and most companionable of all animals; and thus in every way it would be the most fitted for pleasing her eye and attracting her attention.

Little did she suspect that a powerful enemy lurked beneath that beautiful and apparently innocent form: as little as did the disciples imagine that their own and their Master's bitter foe was sitting at meat with them in the body of Judas Iscariot. Nor can we at any time be sure of our safety from similar ambuscades. But there is one test always possible, which, like Ithuriel's spear, compels Satan to assume his true form, and which might have saved Eve. We should surmise the worst, and act accordingly, as soon as we hear one suggestion opposed to God's will and laws: and we should be so much the more on our guard in proportion as it comes from an unlikely source, and is craftily mingled with truth.

The first words of Satan to Eve.

"Can it be true that God has forbidden you to eat of any tree of the garden?" began the serpent. Perhaps the fact that Eve was casting a longing eye upon the tree and yet abstained from touching it suggested this crafty question. Simple as it may at first appear, it was wondrously full of fascinating guile, marvellously adapted to the purpose of disturbing the moral being of Eve, and so preparing the way for its complete subversion. The tempter

* Isa. xiv. 29.

affects to think that she abstains because God has harshly forbidden herself and her husband to touch any of the beautiful fruit around them. And so by his brief, but most skilful, interrogation he begins to envelop her in the mists of error from at least five outspringing suggestions. First; he throws her off her guard by his assumed ignorance. Secondly; he stirs up vanity from the depths of her self-consciousness by giving her an opportunity to correct and instruct him. Thirdly; he uses the term Elohim, and not the covenant name Jehovah, to represent the Creator as far distant, and as having but little concern with His creatures. Fourthly; he puts in a doubt as to whether God had uttered the prohibition, and hints at the possibility of a mistake. And lastly; he insinuates the blasphemous thought that harshness and caprice on God's part are not inconceivable, but may sometimes be expected.

Her answer shows that she is beginning to doubt, and is already caught in the snare.

The blinding effects of this question are immediately evident in Eve's answer. She replies that they may eat of the other trees of the garden, and are only warned off from the one in its midst. Of this alone God had said, "Ye shall not eat of it, neither shall ye touch it, lest ye die." But God had not prohibited them to touch it: and hence we seem to see in the exaggeration of this added clause a secret discontent and an inclination to set the command of the Almighty in as harsh a light as possible.

Nor is this all: not only does she increase the stringency of the law, but she also weakens the penalty. God had said, "Thou shalt surely die," which she alters into, "lest ye die." Doubt was already doing its work in her mind, she was now prepared to hear the truth of God openly denied.

And yet again she follows Satan's lead into the dark, and speaks of her Creator and Benefactor as Elohim—the Power, mighty indeed, but to men vague, distant, and almost unknown—instead of Jehovah, the God in covenant with her husband and herself. Satan wished to banish from her heart all thought of a near and closely connected God, and she accepts his suggestion and co-operates with him. For the image of Jehovah is rapidly fading from her mind, and self and sin are beginning to take its place.

Solemn is the warning which the analysis of her thoughts affords to her descendants, to the offspring by whom her own sad path is ceaselessly trodden. For how often, when we are perfectly aware of some direct command of God which we do not wish to obey, are we seduced into an exaggeration of its magnitude and its inconvenience, till at length, by the continual play of evil imaginings, we almost arrive at its impossibility. At the same time we strive to diminish its importance, and the penalty which its neglect is likely to involve, not perceiving that, while we are thus working out our own will in defiance of the will of God, His Holy Spirit is gradually withdrawing from us, and that our God-consciousness—or, as it would be ordinarily termed, religious feeling—is becoming weaker and weaker. Not so, however, the sin within us, which is proportionally growing and acquiring strength; till at last, when our eyes are again opened, we find it like some horrible tumour, which, loathsome and painful as it is to bear, has been so long neglected that it will scarce leave life in us if it be removed.

Satan quickly perceived the state of Eve's mind: his plan was succeeding: she had begun to doubt. He instantly pressed on his attack by a bold lie combined with a truth, indeed, so far as it went, but one presented in characteristically Satanic fashion, so that the woman might miss its real import, and interpret it in accordance with her own rising vanity. "Ye shall not surely die," said this liar from the beginning, thus daring to place his own assertion in opposition to the Almighty.

Satan follows up his advantage by a daring accusation of God, and an appeal to Eve's vanity.

And Eve believed him; believed this beast of the field, as she supposed him to be, rather than the great Creator of all things! Earth laden with her countless tombs is ever sighing for the credulity: Ocean, as his chasing waves roll over the bones of multitudes lying amid their unheeded treasures, moans in response: and Hades, while his vast realms are being daily peopled by fresh colonies of unclothed spirits, solemnly proclaims that God is true.

"For God doth know," pursued the Tempter, "that in the day ye eat thereof, then your eyes shall be opened, and ye shall be as God"—for so we ought to translate—"knowing good and evil." Truly Jehovah did know this: but why did it not occur to Eve that He must also have known more; that this opening of their eyes would be no addition to their happiness, but harmful and destructive? Could she not by a moment's reflection perceive the fearful responsibility which the knowledge of evil would necessarily involve, and bless the Lord Who had spared her from its perils? Or could she not, at least, trust Him Who had called her into being, and of Whose hands from that time she had received nothing but good, and turn with horror from the blasphemous impiety which suggested to her the possibility of in any way raising herself to His height? She could not, for she was deceived: her reason was perverted by desire; the vision of self-exaltation had intoxicated her. There was no error in Satan's judgment: he had detected the weakest point when he appealed to her vanity and suggested to her the idea of becoming as God.

Does not the readiness with which she received the daring thought show the necessity of our present state of weakness? Does it not sufficiently explain the fact that a broken and a contrite heart is the first indispensable condition of entering into the Kingdom of the Heavens?* And do we not continually perceive, both in ourselves and others, the workings of that feeling upon which Satan played in the case of our first parent? Does it not appear in self-will, which is the determination to be obeyed as God instead of obeying? Is it not evident in pride and conceit, whether arising from birth, ability, beauty, wealth, or any other source? May it not be traced in that boundless self-confidence which puts forth its own wisdom and opinions as alone worthy of notice, and expects them to be received with gratitude and deferred to by all? And, perhaps, its very worst aspect is seen in the complacency with which men listen to reproof and correction richly deserved by themselves, but which they forthwith apply only to others.

The temptation of Eve compared with that of our Lord.

Carried away, then, by the new feeling aroused in her, Eve turned and gazed upon the tree, while Satan plied her with the three temptations which from that time he has ever employed to ruin the human race—the

* Matt. v. 3.

lust of the flesh, the lust of the eyes, and the pride of life.

She saw that the tree was good for food. That was the lust of the flesh, and corresponded to the Lord's temptation to turn stones into bread. But how different the circumstances and the result! Eve was surrounded with plenty, every other tree in the garden was hers; yet she must needs cast a longing eye upon that which had not been given; her pride and self-will make that one seem more desirable than all the rest. The Lord was in the midst of a desert and faint from hunger: yet He would not break through the limits of his manhood, but submissively waited till His Father sent relief.

Again; Eve saw that the tree was pleasant to the eye. That was the lust of the eyes, and corresponded to the offer of all the kingdoms of this world and their glory to Christ. And though the whole garden was filled with objects of beauty on which she might have gazed with lawful pleasure, Eve, nevertheless, discarded them all for that which God had forbidden. The Lord, on the other hand, as man possessed nothing, and yet refused with indignation the accumulated beauties glories and pleasures of the whole world spread out in one view before His gaze.

Lastly; Eve saw that the tree was a tree to be desired to make one wise. That was the pride of life, and corresponded to our Lord's temptation to throw Himself from the pinnacle of the temple. Eve wished to raise her condition, and yet there was none greater than herself upon earth save her husband. But the Lord, though despised and rejected of men, and known only as the carpenter's son of Nazareth, refused to descend from the pinnacle of the temple, and be at once hailed by the assembled multitude below as the long expected sign from heaven, as the royal Messiah.

Triumph of the Tempter. Adam was not deceived, but sinned deliberately.

Eve had thus first given way to doubt, afterwards submitted to hear direct contradiction of God, and lastly turned to gaze upon the forbidden tree. Then the torrent of her desire rose with such impetuous violence that it carried away every barrier; and without waiting to consult her husband, without pausing to think of her God, she put forth her hand, and in a moment the fatal deed, which nearly six thousand years have not sufficed to obliterate, was accomplished. The days of Eve's innocence were ended: and shortly afterwards, upon the arrival of her husband, she afforded another sad instance of that selfishness of sin, of that insatiable and reckless desire on the part of the fallen to involve others in their own miserable ruin, which had been previously exhibited by Satan. For the tempted immediately became the tempter.

Now Paul expressly tells us that Adam was not deceived, but only the woman.* For she, when Satan made known to her the qualities of the fruit, at once admitted as the only possible explanation of God's prohibition that He was either ungracious or feared rivals. But Adam probably saw both the impiety and the utter folly of such an imagination, knew that the command was undoubtedly given in God's wisdom for their good, and was, perhaps, not a little confirmed in this view by the condition in which he found his wife. We seem, therefore, to be driven upon the supposition that excessive love bent him to her entreaties, and made him

* 1 Tim. ii. 14.

determine to share her fate. And herein we see his unfitness to receive such a gift from God; for though he had done well to love her better than himself, he was hopelessly entangled in the snare of folly when he so idolised her as to transgress for her sake the law of her Creator.

Thus did the Prince of this World prevail. The new creation had been seduced to rebellion; there was no longer any bar to the resumption of his dominion. Forth from the ground he rose triumphant, and expanded his shadowy wings over the recovered territory, impeding the pure rays of God's sun, and dropping thick the poisonous mists of sin, under which earth's flowers faded, her fruits withered, her plenty was restrained, and she brought forth evil as well as good.

THE TRIAL AND SENTENCE.

CHAPTER VII.

THE TRIAL AND SENTENCE.

The nature of the covering of glory which our first parents lost.

THE sin was irrevocably committed: the Tempter had triumphed. But what of the affirmation, "Your eyes shall be opened, and ye shall be as God, knowing good and evil"? Alas! it had indeed proved true; but in a fashion widely differing from Eve's expectation. For in the impetuosity of her pride she had not tarried to reflect that the knowledge of God must needs be fraught with destructive peril to those who have neither the wisdom nor the power of God. Her eyes and those of her husband were indeed opened; but only to see themselves, to behold their own sad condition of nakedness and shame. For now they became suddenly conscious of the vileness of that flesh which had been the medium of their transgression; they were bewildered with the painful sense of a fall from the eminence on which God had placed them, of their resemblance to the brutes around them, nay, even of their unfitness to be seen.

And these feelings seem to have been intensified in no small degree by an instant and visible change in their outward appearance. For while they remained in obedience, the spirit which God had breathed into them retained its full power and vigour. Its pervading influence defended their whole being from the inroads of corruption and death; while at the same time its brightness, shining through the covering of flesh, shed a lustrous halo around them; so that the grosser element of their bodies was concealed within a veil of radiant glory.* And thus, as the rulers of creation, they were strikingly distinguished from all the creatures which were placed under them.

But their sin was only made possible by a league of soul and body which destroyed the balance of their being. The overborne spirit was reduced to the condition of a powerless and almost silent prisoner; and, consequently, its light faded and disappeared. Its influence was gone: it could no longer either preserve their bodies from decay, or clothe them in its glory as with a garment. The threat of God was an accomplished fact; the reign of death had commenced.

At the coming of Christ the sons of God will be manifested by the restoration of the lost covering.

Nor is it difficult to prove that the recovery of a visible glory will be the instant result of the restoration of spirit soul and body to perfect order and harmony, the sign of our manifestation as the sons of God. But it will then shine with far more intense brilliancy than it did in Adam: for, as we have before seen, the body of unfallen man was not a spiritual body. The spirit did indeed exercise a mighty and vigorous influence, but the soul was the ruling power, even as it continues to be: for the first man became a living soul.† But when the resurrection, or the change

* Compare the description of God in Psalm civ. 2;—"Who coverest Thyself with light as with a garment."

† 1 Cor. xv. 45.

consequent upon our Lord's return, takes place, our bodies will become spiritual:* the God-consciousness will be supreme in us, holding both soul and body in absolute control, and shedding forth the full power of its glory without let or hindrance.

Hence in speaking of that time Daniel says;—"And they that be wise shall shine as the brightness of the firmament; and they that turn many to righteousness as the stars for ever and ever."† So, too, the Lord Himself declares;—"Then shall the righteous shine forth as the sun in the kingdom of their Father."‡

And yet again; both John and Paul tell us that, when we are summoned into the presence of the Lord Jesus, we shall be like Him, that He will change the body of our humiliation into the likeness of the body of His glory.§ Nor are we left in ignorance as regards the nature of the body of His glory; for upon the mount of transfiguration He permitted the chosen three to behold the Son of Man as He will appear when He comes in His kingdom. Then His Spirit, ever restrained and hidden during His earthly sojourn, was suddenly freed, and in an instant His whole person was beaming with splendour; so that His face did shine as the sun, and His raiment was white as the light.‖

Attempt of Adam and Eve to supply themselves with a covering by artificial means.

The man and his wife were ashamed; and that fact was the one gleam of hope in their horizon. For had they been dead to the shame of guilt, they would have differed in nothing from evil spirits: their salvation would have been impossible. But the existence of this feeling showed that the God-consciousness within them,

* 1 Cor. xv. 44. † Dan. xii. 3. ‡ Matt. xiii. 43.
§ 1 John iii. 2; Phil. iii. 21. ‖ Matt. xvii. 2.

though overwhelmed, was not altogether extinguished. The blaze had dimmed, but the flax was still smoking, and might even yet be fanned into flame again by the Spirit of God.

Bewildered by their altered condition they immediately tried to supply the lost covering artificially, even as their descendants have ever since been doing. For every living creature, whether of earth, air, or sea, has its own proper covering, not put on from without, but developed naturally from within; man alone is destitute and compelled to have recourse to artificial aids, because through sin he has lost his natural power of shedding forth a most glorious raiment of light. And hence we may see why our Lord preferred the robe of the humble lily to all the magnificence of Solomon.* For the splendid array of the Israelitish king was foreign, and put on from without; whereas the beauty of the lily is developed from within, and is the simple result of its natural growth.

Scarcely had the fallen pair arranged their miserable

The inquisition.

garments when they heard the voice of the Lord God, that voice which had hitherto been their greatest joy. But how different did it now seem, though its tones were as yet unaltered! They fled in terror to the shrubs of the garden, and endeavoured to hide themselves. Vain attempt! While we are committing sin we may, perhaps, succeed in putting away all thought of God, and persuade ourselves that, because we have forgotten Him, therefore He neither sees nor regards us. But when He comes forth for judgment this delusion is no longer possible: there is no escape: there may not even be delay: we must, however

* Matt. vi. 29.

unprepared, meet Him face to face. At the call of God Adam is forced to leave his hiding place. With trembling steps he creeps into the presence of his Maker, and is first constrained to acknowledge that he had fled through shame, and then that the shame arose from his transgression of the only commandment imposed upon him. But his confession is not a frank one, and he gives a miserable proof of his fallen condition, of the loss of all the royalty of his original nature, in his attempt to cast the blame upon his wife, nay, even to censure God Himself. "The woman," he says, "whom Thou gavest to be with me, she gave me of the tree, and I did eat."

Nor, when the Lord turns to her, is the answer of Eve more satisfactory than that of her husband. For she does not plead guilty, and throw herself upon God's mercy; but would lay all the fault upon the serpent, as though she were not a responsible agent.

The judgment of the serpent, and the curse upon all cattle.

The Lord hears what the two culprits have to say, and patiently gives them every opportunity of defending themselves: but when He turns to the serpent His manner changes. He asks the Tempter no questions, gives him no chance of defence; but, treating him as already condemned, immediately pronounces sentence. What deep thoughts are suggested by this change of procedure; what fearful antecedents of rebellion seem to float like spectres in the gloom of this instant and hopeless judgment!

"Because thou hast done this." There is to be no mistake as to the reason of the curse: it is no accident, no merely natural misfortune; but the deeply-burnt brand which testifies to God's abhorrence of him who brought sin into the new world. The first part of the sentence has immediate and literal reference to the serpent which co-operated with Satan; but there is in it a wondrous type of the degradation of the Son of the Morning himself.

The words, "Thou art cursed above all cattle," seem to imply a general curse upon the animal kingdom which is not elsewhere mentioned. Possibly it fell upon that part of creation, not through Adam's sin, but because the serpent, the head and representative of the beasts of the field, yielded itself as an instrument of evil. And that the curse should thus extend to every animal is not more marvellous than the transmission of sin through Adam to the whole human race. The cause of the fact in either case has not been revealed to us: the secret is one of those deep things which we cannot know now, but may understand hereafter when the mystery of God shall be finished.

Certainly, however, there is some strange bond connecting together the creatures of our world, so that all are mysteriously affected by, and in a measure responsible for, the conduct of each. This seems to be a great law of creation, and is, perhaps, intended, in part at least, as a means of preserving unity. At any rate Paul, when treating of its application to the Church, puts forth as its object, "that there should be no schism in the body."* And how welcome will be its fulfilment when, just as we have been born into sin through the transgression of Adam, we shall all be made the righteousness of God in Christ.

From the first clause of the sentence upon the serpent it is clear that the creature did not originally

* 1 Cor. xii. 25.

crawl upon its belly. Its structure must, therefore, have been entirely changed, and one who is not biassed by any wish to prove the inspiration of Scripture remarks;—

The original form of the serpent was altogether changed by the curse.

"It is agreed that the organism of the serpents is one of extreme degradation; their bodies are lengthened out by the mere vegetative repetitions of the vertebræ; like the worms, they advance only by the ring-like scutes of the abdomen, without fore or hinder limbs; though they belong to the latest creatures of the animal kingdom, they represent a decided retrogression in the scale of beings." *

By the words, "Dust shalt thou eat," we are not, perhaps, to understand that dust should be the serpent's only food; but that having no organs wherewith to handle its prey, it would be compelled to eat it from the ground, and so to swallow dust with it. "All its food has the flavour of dust," says a Jewish commentary.

Signification of the words, "Dust shalt thou eat."

And since in undergoing this visible punishment the serpent is a type of Satan, with whom it directly co-operated, its condition is hopeless, and will not be improved when the remainder of creation is delivered from the bondage of corruption. Even in Millennial times dust will still be the serpent's meat, and then, perhaps, its only food. † The sight of its degradation, and the more frightful spectacle of the carcases in the valley of Jehoshaphat, ‡ will serve as warnings against sin during the Millennial age.

* Kalisch's "Genesis," p. 125.
† Isa. lxv. 25.
‡ Isa. lxvi. 24.

The enmity between the serpent and the woman.

So far the sentence seems to have no more than a typical reference to Satan. But in the following clauses the serpent begins to recede from view, and the great Adversary, who had been concealed within it, is dragged forth to judgment, and hears of the frustration of his hopes, of the brevity of his triumph, and of his terrible and inevitable doom. Wonderfully pregnant with meaning are the few words of this first of prophecies: for they contain the germ of all that has since been revealed, and afford a remarkable proof of the consistency of God's purposes, of His perfect knowledge of the end from the beginning.

Satan had deluded Eve into an alliance with himself against the Creator; but God would break up the confederation: the covenant with Death should be disannulled: the agreement with Hell should not stand. "I will put enmity between thee and the woman," were His almighty words to the abashed and speechless serpent. Nor was it difficult for Satan to divine the meaning of this separation: he was cast out to perdition, but Eve the Lord would save.

Henceforth, therefore, deprived of her beautiful home, driven into the accursed and uncultivated earth, and subjected to toil, pain, and a gradual decay which should at last terminate in complete dissolution, she should know that her false friend was the cause of all her misery, and so regard him as her bitterest foe.

On the other hand, the mere fact that the woman would no longer be willing to subserve his purposes would have sufficed to provoke the anger of the fallen angel. Yet God presently gave him a far sharper incentive to hatred, when He declared that the seed of the deceived woman should ultimately destroy her deceiver.

For the enmity should not be confined to the serpent and the woman, but should also extend to their seed. Who, then, are the seed of the serpent? They are those who manifest that spirit of independent pride by which their father the Devil fell: those who will not acknowledge their own hopeless condition, and submit to be saved by the merits of the Son of God; but will either themselves do what is to be done, or else proudly deny the necessity of any doing at all, and clamour against God—if they have any belief in His existence—because He does not at once gratify all their wishes without any reference to His broken law. For blinded and maddened by self-conceit they believe the lie of the serpent, and, considering themselves as God, have, consequently, no reverence for Him, nor hesitate to defy His will if their own inclination prompts them to do so. Such are the serpent's seed, distinguished by the spirit which animates their father and federal head, and doomed at last to share with him the Lake of Fire.

The seed of the serpent.

Nor was it long before this seed appeared in the person of Cain, "who," as the apostle tells us, "was of that Wicked One, and slew his brother." * Very significant is the remark which John adds to this declaration;—"And wherefore slew he him? Because his own works were evil, and his brother's righteous." In other words the predicted enmity was the sole cause of the murder.

Our Lord when on earth did not fail to recognise the seed of the serpent in those sinners whose contra-

* 1 John iii. 12.

diction He endured. "O generation of vipers," * He cries, using a phrase which had already issued from the lips of His forerunner, "how can ye, being evil, speak good things?" By these words He clearly designates the Pharisees as a brood of "that old serpent, called the Devil and Satan, which deceiveth the whole world." † Yet again He exclaims;—"Ye serpents, ye generation of vipers, how can ye escape the damnation of Hell?" ‡ For being the serpent's seed they must share the serpent's fate.

The reference in both passages is obvious: but, if there could be any doubt, it would be entirely dispelled by a third utterance, in which, throwing aside all figure, the Lord plainly says;—"Ye are of your father the Devil, and the lusts of your father ye will do." §

The seed of the woman is the Lord Jesus, Who was born of a virgin.

Thus far there is no difficulty; but the significance of the term, "seed of the woman," is not so immediately apparent. The whole human race cannot be meant, as the previous remarks show. Nor would mankind in general be called the seed of the woman, but of the man; and God is here speaking of the seed of the woman exclusively. For she first sinned, and was the cause of sin to her husband and ruin to the world. Therefore she had a double punishment: but lest the blame should rest too heavily upon her, lest she should be swallowed up by over-much sorrow, she was by God's mercy appointed to be the sole human agent in bringing the Deliverer into the world.

Nor is it difficult to discover that Deliverer: for there is none but Christ who could in a strictly literal

* Matt. xii. 34.
† Rev. xii. 9.
‡ Matt. xxiii. 33.
§ John viii. 44.

sense be called the seed of the woman. Here, then, we have a wonderful example of the consistency of Scripture; since in this primeval prophecy, uttered four thousand years before its accomplishment, we find it declared that the Lord Jesus should be born of a virgin. Had our translators perceived this they might have avoided a mistake. For in the well-known prediction of Isaiah,* as also in the quotation from it in the first chapter of Matthew,† they have adopted the rendering, "a virgin," in defiance of the original which has "the virgin" in both passages. They did not understand the meaning of the definite article, and, therefore, cut the knot of the difficulty by omitting it from their version. But Isaiah is evidently referring to the sentence passed upon the serpent, and speaks of the particular virgin who should be chosen as the human instrument for the fulfilment of God's purpose.

The predicted enmity between the seeds is being manifested in the ceaseless conflict of the Church and the World.

Thus Christ is the literal seed of the woman. But just as all those who wilfully deny the truth in ungodliness are the seed of the serpent, so there is also a seed that serves the Lord,‡ is accounted to Him for a generation, and reckoned as one with Him. He and His Church are one, He is the Head and they are the body: He and they together make up the mystical Christ.

And hence we see the enmity of which God spoke in the long vista of estrangement and bitter conflict between the Church and the World. We behold on the one side the alternations of malignant persecution and treacherous flattery; on the other a patient endurance, and a rendering of blessing for cursing. Yet

* Isa. vii. 14. † Matt. i. 23. ‡ Psalm xxii. 30.

the part of the Church is not altogether confined to suffering, but is also continually aggressive. For the children of light are first found wandering among those that dwell in darkness: the lost sheep are ever straying into the midst of the wolves, and must be boldly sought and led out of danger by those who have been themselves rescued from similar perils.

The issue of the conflict. The two advents.

But was there no hope: should the painful and ever-varying struggle go on for ever? No, it should find its end at last: it should be decided after many years by a deadly conflict between the seed of the woman and the old serpent himself. Christ should bruise the serpent's head, should deal a mortal blow: not, however, before the serpent had bruised His heel, had wounded Him sore, but not fatally, not in a vital part.

Here, then, we have the germ of all prophecy respecting the two advents of Christ. In the bruising of the heel we recognise His first coming to suffer what appeared to be an utter defeat; to find that His own would not receive Him; to endure the contradiction and insults of the serpent's seed; to be rejected of His generation; and finally, to lay down His life and pass for a short season under the dominion of him that hath the power of death. And the bruising of the serpent's head is in after prophecies developed into the second coming of Christ, with power and great glory, to drive the false king from air and earth, and cast him bound into the abyss. Nay, it even looks beyond this and the post-Millennial rebellion to the final destruction of Satan and his consignment for ever to the Lake of Fire and Brimstone.

So far as God's words to the serpent are concerned

the two great events which they foreshadow might have been almost simultaneous. And, indeed, throughout the Old Testament the advents are generally treated as if there were no interval between them. The Israelitish prophets beheld them in the remote future just as we might look upon some far-off mountain peaks, each more distant than the other, which from our first standpoint seem, indeed, to be very near together, but disclose as we journey on an ever-widening breadth of valley between them.

Such was the curse pronounced upon the serpent.

The judgment of the serpent was the first outlet of God's mercy to fallen man.

And here we cannot but pause in amazement, and render thanks for the great mercy vouchsafed to the fallen parents of our race. God could not, indeed, give Adam a direct promise at a time when the man was waiting as a condemned criminal to receive sentence. Therefore His lovingkindness devised the plan of first pronouncing judgment upon the serpent, and therein implying that the fallen should not sink hopelessly to the condition of their deceiver, but be set in sharp opposition to him; until, after a painful struggle, the woman's conquering seed should bruise him under their feet, and make both the death from which they shrank, but must now undergo, and Hades the dread place of unclothed spirits, to pass away for ever.* And so a bright ray of hope broke in through their despair, and they were strengthened to hear their own doom of woe.

Having thus passed sentence upon the Tempter the

The sentence upon the woman.

Lord next turned to the woman, who was the first to yield to temptation. For the general sin she was judged in her husband as

* Rev. xx. 14.

being one with him; but, because she enticed him to transgress, she was to bear a special curse superadded to that which affected the whole human race. This is signified in the words, "I will greatly multiply *thy* sorrow"; the force of which will be seen if we notice that Adam also is afterwards doomed to sorrow, the same Hebrew word being used in both cases.

The sentence upon the man.

Lastly; the Lord decrees the punishment of the man. Adam had excused himself on the ground that Eve was his tempter; and God begins by showing that this very fact increased the heinousness of his guilt. Had Eve sinned through the influence of her husband she would not have been without a plea; for God had made her subject to him. But that Adam, whose duty as appointed head was to watch over, to restrain, to guide, and to rule, his wife —that he should so far forget his responsibilities as to follow her sinful suggestion, to obey her voice rather than God's, was a serious aggravation of his offence. Therefore the reason of the curse is, "Because thou hast hearkened unto the voice of thy wife, and hast eaten of the tree, of which I commanded thee, saying, Thou shalt not eat of it."

The sentence itself is not in the main a direct one, as in the case of the serpent, but strikes Adam through his surroundings. The earth, his dominion, is cursed; and in that fact we see a refutation of all those theories respecting the inherent evil of matter which figure so prominently in the early history of the nominal Church, and are now being revived by the sects of so-called Spiritualists. Evil proceeded, not from matter to spirit, but from spirit to matter. Adam was not cursed on account of the earth, which God had declared to be in itself very good; but the earth was cursed because of the sin of Adam, which again originated in the spirit of the Evil One. As a punishment for man's transgression the soil should be henceforth comparatively barren. It should no longer yield spontaneous abundance, but he should be compelled to force out of it, with heavy toil and in the sweat of his face, even the bare necessaries of life.

Thorns and thistles. They seem to have resulted naturally from the curse of barrenness.

Nor would this be the end of the trouble. Earth should now be the parent of evil as well as good, and, teeming with thorns and thistles, should baffle and protract the labour of its tillers.

These noxious plants probably existed, though in very different condition, before the curse was pronounced; and then, owing to the sterility of the blighted earth, were no longer able to attain to their proper development and luxuriance, and so became what they are now found to be, abortions. The following remarks of Professor Balfour will illustrate this.

"In looking at the vegetable world in a scientific point of view, we see many evidences of the great plan upon which the all-wise Creator seems to have formed that portion of His works. At the same time there are many marks of what we may call, with reverence, incompleteness. Thus we see that there is in all plants a tendency to a spiral arrangement of leaves and branches, etc., but we rarely see this carried out fully, in consequence of numerous interruptions to growth and abnormalities in development. When branches are arrested in growth they often appear in the form of thorns or spines, and thus thorns may be taken as an indication of an imperfection in the branch.

"The curse which has been pronounced on the vegetable creation may thus be seen in the production of thorns in place of branches — thorns which, while they are leafless, are at the same time the cause of injury to man. That thorns are abortive branches is well seen in cases where, by cultivation, they disappear. In such cases they are transformed into branches. The wild apple is a thorny plant, but on cultivation it is not so. These changes are the result of a constant high state of cultivation, and may show us what might take place were the curse removed.

"Again; thistles are troublesome and injurious in consequence of the pappus and hairs appended to their fruit, which waft it about in all directions, and injure the work of man so far as agricultural operations are concerned. Now it is interesting to remark that this pappus is shown to be an abortive state of the calyx, which is not developed as in ordinary instances, but becomes changed into hairs. Here, then, we see an alteration in the calyx which makes the thistle a source of labour and trouble to man. We could conceive the calyx otherwise developed, and thus preventing the injurious consequences which result to the fields from the presence of thistles.

"I have thus very hurriedly stated to you what occurred to my mind as to the curse of thorns and thistles, and I have endeavoured to show that the spines and hairs are abortive, and, so to speak, imperfect portions of plants. The parts are not developed in full perfection like what may have been the case in Eden, and like what will take place when the curse is removed."

Fit objects, then, are the thorn and the thistle to

remind man of the curse. And keeping their origin in view we can see a deep significance in that awful scene when our Lord suffered Himself to be crowned with thorns, so that even His enemies set Him forth as the great Curse-bearer; when He wore on His bleeding brow that which owed its very existence to, and was the sign of, the sin which He had come to expiate.

Man must return unto the dust from whence he came.

Lastly; man should no longer eat of the fruits of Paradise, but should henceforth find the staff of his fleeting life in the bread-producing herbs of the field, till he himself descended into that dust out of which he obtained his food: for dust he was, and unto dust he should return.

How did the impious vision raised by Satan vanish into blackness at these last words of terror, words which have sunk deeply into the heart of man, and ever rise to the surface when he finds himself in the presence of his God, or when he is brought low and his hopes perish! "Behold now," says Abraham, "I have taken upon me to speak unto the Lord, which am but dust and ashes." *

Hence, doubtless, the custom of bowing to the earth, and the feeling which prompted the casting of dust on the head, in time of bitter affliction, as a sign of broken pride and humble acknowledgment of the truth of the Creator's words. So Jeremiah says of the man who bears the yoke in his youth that "he putteth his mouth in the dust, if so be there may be hope." † And in regard to the actual return to the dust, Job mournfully declares of his hopes;—"They shall go down to the

* Gen. xviii. 27. † Lam. iii. 29.

bars of the pit, when our rest together is in the dust." * Yet again he says of the prosperous and the miserable; —"They shall lie down alike in the dust, and the worms shall cover them." †

But as it is to the dust that we go down at death, so it is from the dust that we arise at the resurrection. "Thy dead men shall live," is the wondrous proclamation by Isaiah, "together with My dead body shall they arise. Awake and sing, ye that dwell in the dust: for thy dew is as the dew of herbs, and the earth shall cast out the dead." ‡ And Daniel also tells us that, at the first resurrection, "many of them that sleep in the dust of the earth shall awake." § So, then, even the dust is a resting-place of hope for the people of God.

The beginning of the night.

Thus was sentence pronounced. Upon the serpent the judgment was eternal; while the man and his wife were doomed to degradation and anguish, but not for ever. God then seems to have departed, the serpent probably slunk away, and Adam and Eve were left alone, like those who have just awakened from a dream of peace to find themselves pressed down and overwhelmed by every kind of misery and fear.

All around them, beyond the precincts of the garden at least, was changing. Earth was reeling under the first stroke of the curse: its flowers were fading, its fruits were blighted; the former luxuriance of its vegetation could not be supported by the now sterile soil and vitiated atmosphere; the living creatures that passed by no longer did homage to their appointed lord, but wore in their eyes the wild look of incipient

* Job xvii. 16.
† Job xxi. 26.
‡ Isa. xxvi. 19.
§ Dan. xii. 2.

savagery. Nay, the very sun—as we may, perhaps, infer from a previously quoted passage of Isaiah *—seems to have withdrawn six-sevenths of its light; so that, although its beams may still have been as bright as ever they are to us, the distraught pair must have felt that the shadow of death had fallen upon their sickening world.

The darkness, literal and spiritual, of which Scripture so often speaks had set in; that dread season during which the principalities and powers of evil are the world-rulers: that gross darkness which is only illumined by a few light-holders placed here and there in the gloom, whose spirits have been kindled by the Holy Spirit, so that they have become lamps of the Lord: that night of blackness and horror during which weeping must endure, till joy return with the morning: that night in regard to which Paul cheered those of his time with the assurance that it was even then far spent, the four thousand years which had already elapsed being much the greater part of it: that night into the breaking dawn of which the wise and faithful servants are now earnestly gazing in expectation of the appearing of their Lord as the bright and morning Star, before He rises in all His glory as the Sun of righteousness, and restores light and life to the beclouded and death-stricken earth.

Bewildered by these new sensations the fallen ones remained, perhaps, for a while mute in the torpor of deep and overwhelming sorrow. But at length the light of faith began to steal over the softening countenance of Adam: he had laid hold of the implied promise: he

The faith of Adam as displayed in the name which he gave to his wife.

* Isa. xxx. 26.

had perceived God's mercy mingled with His judgment, had caught a glimpse of light beyond the darkness, and felt that there was yet hope in his end.

And so, taking up again the function of naming which God had bestowed upon him, he called his wife Eve, that is, Life; because without cavil or doubt he frankly took God at His word, and believed that by the promised seed of the woman he and his posterity should be delivered from the death to which they had become liable, and live for ever. Thus, if any feeling of estrangement had arisen between the man and his wife, it was now removed; and being through the marvellous ways of the great Peacemaker again united in heart, they were better prepared to face the troubles before them.

The coats of skins; which typified the righteousness of Christ offered, after His sacrificial death, to sinners for a covering.

Adam had professed a simple trust in God's promise, though he had but a dim apprehension of its meaning, and immediately we find the Lord returning to the mourners, and rewarding their faith by further mercy and further knowledge. He took away their coverings of fig leaves, and clothed them with coats of skins. Most significant was the action: for by it He testified that their shame was not groundless, that there was need of a covering, but that the best the sinners could make for themselves was of no avail. They were as yet unacquainted with corruption and decay, and knew not that the fig leaves would quickly wither and fall off, an apt emblem of every device which man has ever contrived to cover his shame and fit himself for the presence of his Maker. And beyond this, they must learn that only by life can life be redeemed; that if the sinner die not, there must be a Substitute; that the Most High is holiness and justice as well as love, and can by no means clear the guilty.

Now sacrifice as an expiation must have been ordained by God Himself. Man could never have thought of such a thing, or have dared in his worship to take the life of one of God's creatures, unless he had been commanded to do so. Probably, then, it was at this most appropriate time that the Lord instituted the rite as a type of the great sacrifice to come. He slew the victims, and as He shed their life-blood Adam and Eve for the first time gazed upon death with affrighted eyes. Then He showed them how to lay the carcases upon the altar, that they might be an offering made by fire unto the Lord. Finally He took the skins of the slain beasts, and made of them the coats with which He clothed the trembling pair.

Thus the Gospel was preached from the beginning: the Lamb of God slain from the foundation of the world was revealed as soon as sin had made His death necessary: the robe of His righteousness, which may be put on by every sinner for whom He has died, was shown to be the only garment which will effectually cover the shame of fallen man. And, by comparing the promise of the woman's Seed and the bruising of His heel with the slain sacrifice and the coats made from the skins of the victims, Adam may have been at once able to discern the outline of the great plan of salvation.

Adam and Eve are expelled from the Garden of Delight.

But a precaution was now necessary. Man had obtained the knowledge of good and evil without the power of resisting evil. Therefore he must no longer remain in the beautiful garden, lest he should put forth his hand, take of the tree of life, and so render his state of sin everlasting. For to be immortal in his fallen condition would be the greatest of all calamities; to continue in sin for ever would be nothing less than the second death. And it was only by passing through the first death that man could be restored to spotless innocence again.

Hence, after another solemn consultation of the Blessed Trinity, the sorrowful, but no longer hopeless, pair were expelled from the garden of beauty, and driven into the cold world to seek another home. With heavy hearts they wended their way amid the towering pyramids of green brilliant with ruddy fruit or sprinkled with thick blossom, through the bright maze of flowers and verdure, until they had passed the great gate, which immediately closed behind them.

They stood without, exiled from their home, under a comparatively chilling climate, looking upon a vegetation which to them must have seemed stunted and deformed, no longer expecting their food directly from the bounteous hand of God, but doomed to labour for it with wearisome care and toil. Nor was there any hope of deliverance until they had returned to the dust from whence they came, until they had rendered up their spirits unto Him Who gave them, and left their mortal frames motionless and inanimate, even as the slain victims upon whose carcases they had lately gazed with shuddering awe.

And now the Garden of Eden disappears from view, and is scarcely ever mentioned again until we come to the last of the books of revelation. But in the Apocalypse it rises before us once more in all its pristine beauty, and we see the sons of Adam walking on the banks of the crystal stream, and no longer excluded from the tree of life.

How this happy restoration shall be effected is the subject of the whole Bible, which treats—as the significant fact just noticed indicates—of the dealings by which God conducts men round the painful circle from Paradise lost to Paradise regained.

THE AGE OF FREEDOM.

CHAPTER VIII.

THE AGE OF FREEDOM.

THUS the first dispensation ended in failure, yielding as its result a mournful proof that man is a being too weak to retain his innocence even in the most favourable circumstances. It now remained to be seen whether after the experience of the fall, after tasting the bitter consequences of sin, he could recover his position and become again obedient and holy. Of this God made trial in several ways.

In the second age men were restrained neither by government nor law.

And first, in what we may term the age of freedom, during the lapse of which He left Adam and his descendants almost entirely to their own devices. Marriage had indeed been instituted: and they were instructed to approach God by means of typical sacrifices, and commanded to toil for their bread by tilling the earth. But beyond this God would neither Himself issue laws nor suffer men to do so. The sword of the magistrate might not be used for the repression of crime: even the murderer should be unpunished, as we may see by the case of Cain. No government was permitted: every man should go in his own way, and do that which was right in his own eyes.

Thus the fitness of man for a condition of extreme liberty, and the worth of a trust in the innate justice supposed to lie at the bottom of the human heart, have been already tested by the great Creator. Modern philosophers are urging a repetition of the experiment; but the history of the times of old proves the fallacy of their views. For the wickedness of man became great: all flesh corrupted its way upon the earth, and the earth was filled with violence. And as it was in the days of Noah, so shall it be also in the days of the Son of Man.*

Hence a consideration of the second age should be peculiarly interesting to us: for it will help us to understand our own times, and, by the course of events before the Deluge, give us some idea of what may be expected in the present dispensation, the closing scenes of which seem to be already projecting their dark shadows before them.

The stages of our journey to God are prefigured in Eden, and also in the Tabernacle.

After the expulsion of Adam from Paradise God does not appear to have removed the beautiful garden: but its gates were inexorably closed, and at the east end of it were placed the Cherubim, and the flaming sword which turned itself to and fro and guarded every access to the tree of life. And so we seem to find here also the rudiments of a Tabernacle, just as we found them in the Eden of Satan. The tree of life, with the Cherubim underneath it and the Shechinah or glory around it, is the Holy of Holies; Paradise the Holy Place; and Eden, the district in which the garden was planted, the Court of the Tabernacle.

And both in Paradise and in the Tabernacle we may, perhaps, discern an outline of our way to God. For as the district of Eden was to Adam, so to us is

* Luke xvii. 26.

this earth, which was once, like Eden, a realm of delight, but is now blasted with the curse of sin. The fallen Adam prayed and offered up sacrifices before the closed gates of Paradise, in sight of the tree of life and the glory: and so do we with the eye of faith behold the throne of grace beyond the limits of this present world, and casting ourselves before it plead the once offered sacrifice of Christ.

But at death the Paradise of God will be thrown open to us: for the very word is used in the New Testament of the place in which we abide during the intermediate state. "To day shalt thou be with Me in Paradise," * said our Lord to the dying thief.

Now the word is of Persian origin, and had a well-defined meaning, which the Saviour surely intended to suggest when He used it. For the Persian kings and nobles were accustomed to surround their palaces with parks of vast magnitude, planted with beautiful trees and shrubs, and stocked with beasts wild and tame. Some suppose these parks to have been reminiscences of a tradition of Eden: at any rate a place of the sort was called a paradise. And so, by adopting the word, Christ appears to indicate that at death we pass, as it were, into the wondrous garden that surrounds the Father's house, but not into the house itself.

For He declared to His disciples that He was going to prepare abodes for them in that glorious palace, and would shortly return to fetch them; † return, as angels subsequently announced, in like manner as He went up,‡ in actual bodily presence. At death, therefore, we shall enter into the garden: but only at the return of Christ and the resurrection can we obtain access to

* Luke xxiii. 43. † John xiv. 2, 3. ‡ Acts i. 11.

the tree of life which is in the midst of the Paradise of God,* and which seems to correspond to the actual place of the presence.

So also the Court of the Tabernacle seems to represent this present world, during our stay in which we must offer up the slain victim on the brazen altar by thankfully believing in the sacrifice of Christ, and must afterwards be cleansed and sanctified in the laver with the washing of water by the word.†

Then, being clad in the white robes of Christ's righteousness, we shall, in the intermediate state, enter into the Holy Place, where the implements of our service will be no longer of the baser metals—which are continually subject to the rust of sin—but only of pure gold.

Lastly; at the resurrection we shall be admitted into the Holy of Holies, the dwelling-place of the glory, into the mansions prepared for us in the Father's house.

The Cherubim.

Of the Cherubim we must speak as briefly as possible; but the subject is very important, since these glorious beings appear to be closely connected with the redemption of creation. In mentioning them for the first time, the Hebrew original nevertheless styles them "*the* Cherubim," from which we may infer that their forms were familiar to the Israelites of Moses' time; and, therefore, that they were the same as those of the Cherubim represented in the Tabernacle. Indeed, the words by which they are introduced, if literally rendered, are, "And He caused the Cherubim to tabernacle at the east of the Garden of Eden." The most detailed account of their appear-

* Rev. ii. 7. † Eph. v. 26.

ance is that which is contained in the first chapter of Ezekiel, which we will now examine.

Ezekiel's description of them.

The prophet tells us that he was among the Hebrew captives on the banks of the Chebar, when the heavens were opened to him, and he beheld visions of God. He saw a storm coming from the north, a mighty cloud having an infolding fire within it and a flashing brightness round about it. In the midst of the fire there was, as it were, the glancing of furbished brass: and as he gazed upon this glittering splendour with its terrific surroundings, it drew nearer to him, and he began to distinguish glorious forms. There were four living creatures, each standing beside a wheel dreadful in height. Stretched over the heads of these wondrous beings was the likeness of the firmament, of the colour of the terrible crystal. Above the firmament was a sapphire throne, and upon the throne the likeness of a man radiant with heavenly glory and surrounded with the appearance of a rainbow. It was the chariot of the Lord: it was Jehovah borne upon the Cherubim, and coming forth to judgment.

Each Cherub was in the form of a man, that is, displayed the body and upright position of a man. But every one had four faces: the first face was that of a man, the second that of a lion, the third that of an ox, and the fourth that of an eagle. Now the lion, the ox, and the eagle, are the representatives of the beasts of the field, of cattle, and of the fowls of the air. Hence from this vision arose the Jewish saying;—"Four are the highest in creation: the lion among the beasts, the ox among cattle, the eagle among the fowls, and man above these; but God is the highest of all."

In the temple of Ezekiel* the Cherubim are associated with palm trees, in that of Solomon† with palm trees and flowers. Now, the palm was considered to be the king of trees. Humboldt calls it "the noblest of plants, to which the nations ever assign the prize of beauty." And the flower is the glory of the herb of the field.

Thus the Cherubim and the accessories with which they were surrounded seem to have been made up of the highest forms of the animal and vegetable kingdoms, and to have been representatives of creature life in its perfection, and in obedience to and union with its Creator.

Each Cherub had also four sides, and, apparently, six wings, though four only are mentioned at first.‡ Of these we are told that two were spread out and joined to the wings of those on either side, while with another pair the Cherubim covered their bodies in reverence. But it quickly becomes evident that in the commencement of the description Ezekiel is speaking only of their appearance from one point of view: for a little later he tells us that "every one had two (wings), which covered on this side, and every one had two, which covered on that side, their bodies."§ Underneath their wings were the hands of a man, and their feet were straight feet, sparkling like the colour of burnished brass, and the soles of their feet were as the sole of a calf's foot. Lastly; their whole body, their backs, their hands, and their wings, as well as the wheels beside which they stood, were full of eyes, indicative, perhaps, of intense vigilance and intelligence.

* Ezek. xli. 18-20.
† 1 Kings vi. 29.
‡ Ezek. i. 6.
§ Ezek. i. 23.

Description and possible significance of the wheels.

Each of the wheels was, as it were, a wheel within a wheel, that is, one wheel passing transversely through the centre of another, so that the chariot might go in the direction of either of the four faces without turning. In appearance the wheels were like to the colour of beryl, or rather of chrysolite: their rings, or felloes, were full of eyes: and the spirit of life, or, perhaps, of the living creature, was in them. Wherever the Spirit of God willed to go, thither would the chariot of the Cherubim speed and return as the flashing of lightning.

Since the Cherubim appear to be symbols of creature life, it is not improbable that the wheels represent the forces of nature;—"Fire, and hail; snow, and vapours; stormy wind fulfilling His word."*

The Cherubim are identical with the living creatures in the Apocalypse.

Such were the Cherubim as seen by Ezekiel. And though there are some differences of detail—owing, probably, to differences in the circumstances†—there can be no doubt that they are identical with the living creatures which John saw at the foot of the throne.‡ The word used in the Apocalypse is a literal translation of Ezekiel's "living creature," being indeed the very word by which the Hebrew is rendered in that passage of the Septuagint. But, unfortunately, in our version of the New Testament it is translated "beast," though it

* Psalm cxlviii. 8.

† For instance, in Ezekiel each Cherub has four faces, which is not the case in the Apocalypse. The reason of the difference seems to be that in the former passage, where the Cherubim are in attendance upon the chariot of the Lord, their four faces and four sides correspond to the wheel passing transversely through the centre of the other, and enable them to move in any direction without the necessity of turning. But in the Apocalypse they are before the Throne, and movement is not required.

‡ Rev. iv. 6.

simply means a living being. It is quite a different term from that used of the ten-horned, and also of the two-horned, beast of the later chapters.

And probably also with the Seraphim of Isaiah.

Again; the six-winged Seraphim of Isaiah* seem also to be the same as the Cherubim. For the number of their wings corresponds, and they hold the same position in the glory, just beneath the throne. And again; their cry, "Holy, holy, holy, is the Lord of hosts," is similar to that of the living creatures which John saw.

The word Seraphim appears to signify the "burning ones," and perhaps the Cherubim were so called from the fervour of their worship. Or it may be that the change of name indicates a different function. For the Cherubim are represented as taking up coals of fire for the execution of the wrath of God:† but a Seraph brings a live coal from the altar, and by applying it to Isaiah's lips purifies him from his iniquity and sin.‡ Thus it may be that the former name is used when the Lord appears as a consuming fire, the latter when His glory is acting as a purifying flame.

They are not angels, nor do they wield the flaming sword.

The Cherubim are evidently not angels; for if they were, their connection with the animal and vegetable kingdoms would be without a parallel in Scripture. Moreover, they are distinguished from angels in two passages of the Apocalypse, in the first of which we read of "many angels," and in the second of "all the angels," standing round about the Throne, and the Living Creatures, and the Elders.§ Wherever, therefore, they appear in Scripture, whether in the Garden of Eden, upon the Ark of

* Isa. vi. 2.
† Ezek. x. 7.
‡ Isa. vi. 6, 7.
§ Rev. v. 11; vii. 11.

the Covenant, or before the Throne, we must remember that they always retain their own peculiar forms.

Nor did they, according to the popular conception, handle the fiery sword which forbade approach to the Tree of Life. The Hebrew expressly states that the sword turned itself, that is, was a revolving flame, corresponding to the glory which appeared above the Cherubim in the Tabernacle.

Probable significance of their number.

In the number of the Cherubim we may, perhaps, discern another proof of their connection with the earth, since four is in Scripture, and especially in the Apocalypse, the number of terrestrial creation. Thus, among other instances, we read of "the four quarters of the earth,"* "the four corners of the earth," and "the four winds of the earth."† Again; created beings are described as "every creature which is in the heaven, and on the earth, and under the earth, and such as are in the sea":‡ the human race is summed up as "every tribe, and tongue, and people, and nation";§ and there are "four sore judgments" for creation—"the sword, and the famine, and the noisome beast, and the pestilence."‖ So, too, the destined earth-rulers were directed, when marching through the wilderness, to pitch their tents in four camps, turned towards the four cardinal points.¶ And lastly, the visions of Daniel disclose four world-empires, and the breaking into their number by the fifth changes the dispensation, and causes the glad cry to go forth, "The kingdom of the world is become the kingdom of our God and of His Christ."

* Rev. xx. 8.
† Rev. vii. 1.
‡ Rev. v. 13.
§ Rev. v. 9.
‖ Ezek. xiv. 21.
¶ Numb. ii.

Passing, then, from these preliminary considerations, we proceed to inquire into the real significance of the Cherubim, the clue to which seems to lie in the terms of the Noachian covenant.

They appear to stand before God as representatives of the four earth-tribes to which the promises of the Noachian covenant were made.

We have already seen that during the Six Days God created six tribes of living creatures to inhabit the earth—the fish, the fowls of the air, the cattle, the creeping things, the beasts of the earth, and man. Of these, the first five were placed under the dominion of man; but three of them were subsequently distinguished from the others on two memorable occasions.

When God brought the living creatures to the father of our race, "Adam gave names to all cattle, and to the fowl of the air, and to every beast of the field":* but he is not said to have done so in the case of the fish and of the creeping things.

And again, there is a similar omission in the Noachian covenant, which is expressed in the following terms;—"And I, behold, I establish My covenant with you, and with your seed after you, and with every living creature that is with you, of the fowl, of the cattle, and of every beast of the earth with you."†

Now if we observe that the four tribes specially included in the covenant—man, the fowls, the cattle, and the beasts of the earth—are also those which are indicated by the forms of the Cherubim, we shall readily perceive the meaning of the latter. They stand before God as the representatives of the four great earth-tribes with which He has made a covenant that He will never again destroy them utterly from the face of the earth.

* Gen. ii. 20. † Gen. ix. 9. 10.

Their representative character appears to be still further set forth by their Hebrew name כְּרֻבִים, the obvious derivation of which is obtained by separating it into כְּ־רִבִּים, that is, "as the many."

And their connection with the Noachian covenant would seem to be demonstrated by the additional fact that, in two of the three subsequent passages in which their forms are minutely described, the great sign of that covenant, the rainbow, is seen above them.* In the third passage, the tenth chapter of Ezekiel, it is not actually mentioned; nevertheless there also its presence is implied, since the prophet observes that the glory of the God of Israel appeared on this occasion, just as he had previously seen it in the plain.†

The reason why the tribes of fish and creeping things are neither mentioned nor represented in the covenant is uncertain.

What is signified by the omission of the two tribes, or at least of any special mention of them, in the lists of those which are said to have been named by Adam, and to have been included in the Noachian covenant, and why they are not represented in the symbolism of the Cherubim, it is difficult to conjecture. If we also remember that sin entered into our world through the medium of the serpent, and that in the renewed earth there will be no more sea, we may be led to infer that the tribes of creeping things and fish will ultimately disappear. On the other hand, it is possible that they may be included in the higher forms of life. Still, however this may be, it does not interfere with the fact that the Cherubim represent all the creatures which God is pledged to save.

* Ezek. i. 28; Rev. iv. 3.
† Ezek. viii. 4.

God's covenant with the four earth-tribes involves also a promise of their redemption.

But if the great Creator has entered into a covenant that He will never destroy the four earth-tribes, there is also of necessity much more involved in such a promise. Other Scriptures, in drawing back the curtain of futurity, disclose the glad truth that times of refreshing and restitution are approaching, when earth will be freed from the curse, and its inhabitants once more restored to innocence and peace. Since, therefore, the four tribes are to be preserved through this glorious age, they must also participate in its conditions, or, in other words, be redeemed from the consequences of sin.

And such a destiny is certainly implied by the position in which we find the Cherubim on the Ark. For there, each of them displaying the four heads as described by Ezekiel,* they appear in close proximity to the awful Shechinah; while the violated law beneath them is covered by the golden Mercy-seat upon which they rest in security. They thus set forth in wondrous symbol the redemption and reconciliation of man and beast through the merits and death of the Lord Jesus.

But a significant feature of this symbol shows us how exclusively its prophetic fulness looks forward to the future, to the great changes of a coming dispensation. The Cherubim stand in the immediate presence of the Almighty, and yet two of the living beings repre-

* It is scarcely necessary to remark that there is no authority whatever for the conventional pictures of the Ark in which the Cherubim appear as angels. We have no right to represent them in any forms save those which are attributed to them in Scripture. And since the four heads are evidently necessary to the symbolism, while there were but two Cherubim on the Ark, we must not in this case take our pattern from the description given in the Apocalypse, but must understand each Cherub to have had four heads as in the vision of Ezekiel.

sented by the heads are unclean. But God shall presently cleanse them, and they will then be no longer common or unclean. They are also creatures of prey; but when the age of rest has come, "the lion shall eat straw like the ox,"* and the eagle shall cease to behold the prey from afar, nor shall it any more be said of her that "where the slain are, there is she."† For, to quote the glowing words of the apostle, "the creation itself also," which is now groaning and travailing in pain together, "shall be delivered from the bondage of corruption into the liberty of the glory of the children of God."‡

Standing, then, in the presence of God as memorials of His promise, the Cherubim also act as the ministers of His will.

Thus the Cherubim stand before the Lord for a purpose similar to that of the Book of Remembrance of which Malachi speaks, as memorials of those earth-tribes which He has pledged Himself to save. Their special office appears to be attendance upon the Lord when He is engaged in the government of the world: they co-operate with Him in all that tends to its redemption: they act as His higher executive, calling forth the powers which inflict His judgments, and furnishing angels with the means of carrying out His will.

Thus, at the successive breaking of the first four seals, each of the Living Creatures in turn cries, "Come!" and instantly the horses and their riders appear.§ Our version has "Come and see," as though the cry were addressed to John: but it is now generally admitted that the words "and see" are a gloss entirely destructive of the sense. Again, in Ezekiel's vision of

* Isa. xi. 7.
† Job xxxix. 29, 30.
‡ Rom. viii. 21.
§ Rev. vi. 1-8.

the departure of the glory from the Temple, one of the Cherubim gives to the man clothed in linen coals of fire to scatter over Jerusalem.* Lastly, it is one of the Living Creatures who brings to the seven angels the seven golden bowls full of the wrath of God.†

Significance of the Cherubim to Adam.

It will now be seen that the appearance of the Cherubim in Paradise was a glorious prophecy of hope to the banished Adam. For it told him that although the crown had fallen from his head, and himself and all creation were now subjected to decay and corruption, yet the time would come when he should again have access to the Tree of Life, again draw near to God, and be reinstated in his sovereignty over the world, which should also be brought back to its original perfection and beauty. Thus did the mercy of God support him in his present trouble by glimpses of future restoration.

The flaming sword.

But, though the emblems of hope were ever before him, there was also a revolving sword of flame, ceaselessly turning with lightning flashes to guard the tree of immortality, a fiery circle which kept him from his God and from life. For Jehovah is a consuming fire to those who are in sin; He dwells in the light unto which no fallen man can approach.‡

That the sword was connected with the Shechinah we can see from its counterpart, the fire infolding itself, in Ezekiel's vision of the glory. Its destructive power was shown when, at the consecration of the tabernacle, it flashed forth and consumed the burnt-offering upon the altar; § and when its lightning flame smote Nadab and Abihu, so that they died before the Lord.‖

* Ezek. x. 6, 7. † Rev. xv. 7. ‡ 1 Tim. vi. 16.
§ Lev. ix. 24. ‖ Lev. x. 2.

Henceforth, therefore, man's whole attention was to be concentrated upon the means provided by God for the removal of the flaming barrier, that he might at length regain his natural position and be at rest.

Birth of Cain and Abel. Significance of their names.

Adam now commenced his labour of tilling the ground, the toil of which, owing to the want of implements and experience, must have been doubly distressing. But after a while the first infant was born into the world: and we can imagine the joy of Eve at the thought that the promise was now realised, that the delivering Seed had appeared. In happy exultation she called his name Cain—that is, "acquisition," or "possession," exclaiming, "I have gotten a man with the aid of Jehovah!" The grammar of this sentence admits the rendering, "I have gotten a man, even Jehovah!" but it is, to say the least, uncertain whether this could have been Eve's meaning. For we have no intimation that the great mystery of godliness, God manifest in the flesh, had as yet been revealed. She believed, however, that the promise, as she understood it, had been fulfilled: she thought she had gotten the Deliverer: she would call her son the possession of that which was promised.

Alas! how little did she know of the bitter disappointments, the heart-sickening succession of hopes deferred, which were henceforth to be the lot of herself and of all her descendants. For she was not merely mistaken in supposing Cain to be the Deliverer: nay, the son whom she loved, of whom she hoped so much, was actually the first of the serpent's hostile seed, the first link of a chain which would end, not in Christ, but in Antichrist. By the time of her second son's birth she seems to have had some apprehension of the truth: for her joy had then given way to depression, and she called his name Abel—that is, "a breath," or "that which passes as a breath"—thus showing her consciousness of the speedy mortality of her offspring and the fall of all her high hopes.

Their wives.

Now since the birth of Seth must have followed quickly upon the death of Abel, and we are told that Seth was born when Adam was a hundred and thirty years old,* there was, probably, a lapse of some hundred and twenty-nine years between the birth of Cain and the death of Abel. During this time Adam doubtless had many other sons and daughters, and Cain and Abel seem to have been directed to take them wives of their sisters. Such marriages could not be avoided in the beginning of man's history, since the whole race was to be united in descent from a single pair; and it must be remembered that the children of Adam were not merely a family, but the whole human family. As soon, however, as the necessity had disappeared, such connections were discountenanced, and afterwards rigorously prohibited.†

Their pursuits.

As they grew to manhood the brothers adopted different pursuits. Cain became a tiller of the ground, and, therefore, had reason to feel the curse in all its bitterness: but Abel was a keeper of sheep. And, since men were not, at that time, allowed to touch animal food, these sheep must have been kept for sacrificial purposes and for the manufacture of garments. Hence Cain assisted in the production of food for the primeval family, while Abel's duties were concerned with their religious services and clothing.

* Gen. v. 3. † Lev. xviii. 9

Their sacrifices. Reason of Cain's rejection.

In process of time the brothers brought each an offering unto the Lord, presenting it, probably, at the gate of Paradise. And God had respect unto Abel and to his offering; but unto Cain and to his offering He had not respect.

The reason of this difference is fraught with the deepest interest to us: for there are many in these latter days who, according to the prophecy of Jude,* have gone in the way of Cain: the theology of the first murderer is that of a large and perpetually increasing school of our times. He neither denied the existence of God, nor refused to worship Him. Nay, he recognised Him as the Giver of all good things, and brought an offering of the fruits of the ground as an acknowledgment of His bounty. But he went no further than this; and, therefore, though he may have passed among those with whom he dwelt as a good and religious man, he failed to satisfy God. For being yet in his sins he presumed to approach the Holy One without the shedding of blood: he was willing to take the place of a dependent creature, but would not confess himself a sinner guilty of death, who could be saved only by the sacrifice of a Substitute.

He is a type of the many in these times who will descant upon the benevolence and love of the Creator, and are ever ready to laud Him for those attributes, and claim the benefit of them, without any reference to their own unworthiness and sinful condition, without a thought of that perfect holiness and justice which are as much elements of the mind of God as love itself. But the Most High did not accept the sacrifice of Cain; for none may approach to worship Him except through

* Jude 11.

the shedding of blood, even the blood of the Lamb which He has provided: the sin-offering must come first, then the thank-offering: we can enter into the Holy of Holies, and cast ourselves before the Mercy-seat, only by passing through the rent veil of Christ's flesh.

Abel knew something of this, and confessed it: therefore he brought of the firstlings of his flock, and poured out their life-blood in humble avowal of his own deserts. And God at once accepted his offering; perhaps—as many have thought—by sending forth fire from the Shechinah to consume it, and thus showing in a type that His wrath in regard to Abel would be satiated upon a Substitute.

God's unavailing remonstrance with Cain. The murder.

At the sight of this Cain's countenance fell, and he was angry: he committed the appalling sin of judging his Creator, and stirring up human wrath at His just dealings. Nevertheless God would not at once abandon the sinner to his fate. He patiently reasoned with Cain, as with a wilful child: He sought to bring him back to a right mind, pointing out his evil condition, and that a dire sin was crouching at his door ready to spring upon him like some ravenous beast upon its prey. Nor did He cease without promising that, if the offender would repent and do well, he also should be accepted, and preserve that ascendency over his brother to which, as being chosen by his Creator for the position of firstborn, he was lawfully entitled.

But the gracious expostulation was wasted: Cain took his opportunity, and the germ of sin which had been planted in Adam ripened into murder in his eldest son.

It was not long before God made inquisition for blood. "Where," He asked of Cain, "is Abel thy brother?" And so again, as in the case of Adam, He inquired, though He had full knowledge, to give the transgressor an opportunity of judging himself and confessing his guilt. Had Cain done so he would yet have found hope. But he branded himself a second time with the mark of the serpent by adding lying to murder. "I know not," he replied; "am I my brother's keeper?" So hardened had he become that he would fain deny the truth even in the presence of the omniscient God. Therefore he was instantly dragged forth to judgment: his covering of lies was torn away, and his crime in all its blackness laid bare by the piercing words, "What hast thou done? The voice of thy brother's blood crieth unto Me from the ground."

The conviction and the sentence.

Cain was speechless: he could offer neither defence nor excuse, and God went on to pronounce sentence. The earth, which had drunk up his brother's blood, should be laid under a second curse, and should no longer yield its strength, even in response to the severest toil. Nor should the murderer remain with his parents in Eden: he should be banished from the presence of the Lord, from the sight of the Cherubim and the glory, and go forth as a fugitive and wanderer upon the earth. But no human hand should touch him. Neither the other members of his family nor the descendants of Abel, if there were any, might avenge the crime upon pain of a sevenfold punishment: for magisterial power was not yet entrusted to man.

Thus were our first parents deprived of both their sons in one day. How appalled must they now have been with the progress of the mischief which their transgression had brought into the world! But the God of all consolation was merciful, and about this time gave them another son, whom Eve called Seth, that is, "appointed." "For God," she said, "hath appointed me another seed instead of Abel whom Cain slew." It is curious to notice that she here attributes the gift to Elohim and not to Jehovah, which is probably an indication that her hope had given place to despondency. After expecting the promised Seed for a hundred and thirty years she had at length lapsed into despair, and, seeing in Seth nothing more than a natural son, pours forth her thanks to Elohim, and not to the covenant-keeping Jehovah. But she was again mistaken. Long and weary had been the time of waiting and bitter the disappointments, but she had at last obtained the first link of the chain that was to end in the promised Seed: from the line of Seth Christ was to spring.

Adam and Eve are comforted by the birth of Seth.

Henceforth we find a twofold development in the human race: the Sethites and the banished Cainites remain separated for a while, and represent the Church and the World. The Cainites, with the restlessness of men alienated from God, were ever striving to make the land of their exile a pleasant land; to reproduce Paradise artificially, instead of longing for the real Garden of Delight; were ceaselessly trying by every means to palliate the curse, instead of patiently following God's directions for getting rid of it altogether. Cain himself, who had been condemned to wander, was the first to build a city, which he called Enoch, after

Characteristics of the Cainites. The city of Enoch.

the name of his son; the first to attempt to settle comfortably upon the blasted earth.

Some have wondered where he found inhabitants for his city. But they forget that, for aught we know, he may have built it centuries after his flight from Eden, and do not take into account the prodigious increase of population in an age when an ordinary life extended through eight or nine hundred years, and a man was contemporary with seven or eight generations of his descendants. Besides which, the city of Cain may have been at first nothing more than a fixed and substantial habitation for himself and his family.

Lamech and his sons. Mention of women among the descendants of Cain.

Beyond a mere enumeration of names, we have no further record of Cain's posterity till we come to his descendant of the fifth generation. But the few particulars concerning Lamech and his family present a vivid picture of human corruption, of the way of the children of this world. We see it beginning in a sensuous life that involves the loss of the God-consciousness, and of all fear of breaking the Divine laws: we trace it as it goes on to make present circumstances as comfortable and as indulgent as possible, substituting arts sciences and intellectual pursuits for spiritual aspirations, and, with the aid of divers amusements and pleasures, banishing thought by excitement: and at last we find it ending in a thorough concentration upon self, and a hardened defiance of God.

Lamech broke the primeval law of marriage, and was the first polygamist, thus giving proof of the utter godlessness into which the Cainites had lapsed. The mention and names of his wives are perhaps suggestive of the state of society in his circle. Adah signifies "ornament," or "beauty"; while Zillah means "shade," in reference, probably, to her rich and, as it were, overshadowing tresses. His daughter also was called Naamah, that is, "lovely." Now in the genealogy of Seth's family there is no mention by name of either wives or daughters. Here, therefore, we, perhaps, have an intimation that the women among the Cainites were unduly prominent, and that personal beauty and sensuous attractions were the only valued qualities.

Of the sons of Lamech, Jabal was remarkable as being the first man who accumulated cattle in large numbers and led a nomad life. Probably, in defiance of God's injunction, he introduced animal flesh and milk as food, with the view of escaping the labour of tilling the accursed ground. Jubal invented music, and Tubal-cain the mechanical arts.

Lamech's address to his wives.

The last piece of information which we possess concerning Lamech is contained in his address to his wives. This appears to be a kind of song, which may have been popular among the antediluvians. But it breathes a boasting spirit of self-reliance—arising, perhaps, from the weapons which Tubal-cain had forged—and of proud revenge, which quite prepares us to hear that the earth was shortly afterwards filled with violence. Literally translated it runs as follows;—

> "Adah and Zillah, hear my voice;
> Ye wives of Lamech, hearken unto my speech:
> For I have slain a man in return for my wound,
> And a young man in return for my bruise.
> For sevenfold shall Cain be avenged,
> But Lamech seventy and sevenfold."

The meaning of which appears to be that he had quarrelled with a young man, and, having been wounded and bruised by him, had slain him in revenge. That God chose to proclaim a sevenfold vengeance upon the one who should kill Cain: but let all know that, if any one injure Lamech, the vengeance will be seventy and sevenfold: if any one merely wound or bruise him, he will surely take his life as a recompense.

And this is the last we hear of the family of Cain as separated from the rest of the world. Its first ancestor was a murderer: and it disappeared in the person of a polygamist, murderer, and open worshipper of the god of forces.

Characteristics of the Sethites.

But when we turn to Seth's posterity the scene changes. Envyings, strifes, and deeds of license and violence, are no longer before us: our ears cease to be assailed with the lowing of herds, the strains of soft music used for the soothing of uneasy consciences, the clatter of the anvil, the vauntings of proud boasters, and all the mingled din which arises from a world living without God and struggling to overpower His curse.

But we see a people poor and afflicted; toiling day after day to procure food from the ungenial soil, according to their God's appointment; patiently waiting till He should be gracious, and humbly acknowledging His chastening hand upon them. They have no share in earth's history: that is entirely made up by the Cainites. As strangers and pilgrims in the world they abstain from fleshly lusts: they build no cities: they invent no arts: they devise no amusements. For they are not mindful of the country in which they live, but seek a better, that is, a heavenly. Lastly; as we may see by the allusion to it in the name of Noah,* they

* Gen. v. 29.

keep the curse which God laid upon the earth continually before them.

Meaning of the expression "to call upon the name of Jehovah."

In contrast to the boastings of the Cainite Lamech, Seth named his first son Enos, that is, "weakness"—a humble confession of the feebleness and helplessness of man, which is naturally followed by the next sentence, "Then began men to call upon the name of Jehovah."

But in what sense are we to understand this phrase, which is henceforth frequently used in Scripture? Jehovah, as we have previously seen, is the name by which God has revealed Himself to those with whom He has made a covenant, to whom He has given promises. When Moses asks what answer he shall return to the Israelites if they inquire the name of the God Who sent him, the Lord replies;—"I AM THAT I AM": "Thus shalt thou say unto the children of Israel, I AM hath sent me unto you."* Now in the Hebrew, not the present, but the future of the verb "to be" is used; and from the future the name Jehovah is derived. But the Hebrew future has a peculiar signification: it is often used to express a permanent state, that which exists and always will exist. Hence the words rendered "I AM THAT I AM" might be more intelligently translated "I EVER SHALL BE THAT WHICH I AM." And thus "Jehovah" signifies the immutable God, the Same yesterday, to-day, and for ever, Whose purpose no circumstances can affect, Whose promises can in no wise fail.

Whenever, therefore, we read of Abraham pitching his tent in some new place, rearing an altar there, and calling upon the name of Jehovah,† we must regard

* Exod. iii. 14.

† Gen. xii. 8.

him as appealing to God for protection and aid in his apparently aimless wanderings on the ground of the promises made to him.

Again: "What," asks the Psalmist, "shall I render unto Jehovah for all His benefits toward me?"* And the answer is;—"I will take the cup of salvation, and call upon the name of Jehovah." That is, I will thankfully accept the deliverance which God has wrought for me, and, calling upon Him by His name Jehovah, will thereby glorify Him as the immutable One Who never fails to redeem His promises.

Lastly; Joel tells us that in the dread time, immediately before the appearing of Christ and His Church in glory, when the world is affrighted with signs in the heavens and on the earth, blood, and fire, and pillars of smoke; when the sun is withdrawing its light, and the silver moon is reddening to a bloody hue—that, in that awful hour, whosoever shall call upon the name of Jehovah shall be saved.† The reference, as the context plainly shows, is to the Jewish remnant; and the meaning, that if any man warned by the fearful sights around him shall bethink himself of the promises to Israel, and appeal to his Maker by the covenant name on the ground of those promises, he shall be saved.

It is easy, therefore, to see the meaning of the phrase as applied to the Sethites. The descendants of Cain, worshipping nothing more than the creating and ruling Elohim, and, consequently, having no promises on which to rest, settled themselves as well as they could in the world, and used their best endeavours to do away with the inconveniences of the curse. The

* Psalm cxvi. 12, 13.

† Joel ii. 32.

Sethites, on the other hand, made no attempt to kick against the pricks, or to avoid the chastisement of God, but looked to Him for relief, relied upon His prediction of the delivering Seed, and began to address Him by His covenant name Jehovah, to keep alive their hope, and to express their trust in His promise.

Hence they seem to have shown somewhat of the spirit which, many centuries later, actuated the Thessalonian Christians:* they made no idols for themselves upon earth, but served the living and true God, and waited for His Son from heaven.

Enoch the first of the prophets.

A curious coincidence strikes us here. In the account of the Cainites, after a few particulars of Cain's history, just intimating the direction in which he guided his posterity, there follows a mere list of names till we come to Lamech, the seventh from Adam. Then we have a momentary glimpse of the first murderer's city, and find lawlessness and violence developing in it, while its inhabitants are making strenuous efforts to attain to happiness without God.

In the same manner we hear of Seth's humble confession of weakness, and that his community then began to call upon the name of Jehovah. And this is followed by a bare register of births and deaths till we come to Enoch, the seventh from Adam in Seth's line. Then the chronicle halts for a moment, and in a few words records an event of surpassing importance.

As evil had culminated in Lamech, so had godliness in Enoch: for he walked with God, and had this testimony, that he pleased Him.† But the dark shadow of the end was already beginning to fall upon the world.

* 1 Thess. i. 9, 10. † Heb. xi. 5.

Wickedness had increased to such an extent that not only was the inability of man to recover himself demonstrated, but even the necessity of bringing the trial to a speedy close. The Lord, therefore, bestowed a new power upon Enoch, and sent him forth as the first prophet to testify against the sin of the world, and to proclaim that the times of forbearance would soon have run their course.

Filled with the Spirit of God he moved among men preaching of righteousness, temperance, and judgment to come, and doubtless caused many to tremble. But there was very little permanent result: none save the prophet himself was thought worthy to escape the things which were coming on the earth. He alone was caught up to heaven before the perilous times of the great antediluvian tribulation commenced, being taken out of the world about six hundred and sixty-nine years before the flood. And although so many intervening centuries may seem a long respite, we must remember that, owing to the length of life in those days, the time would not be equivalent to more than fifty or sixty years with us.

The single extant specimen of Enoch's prophecy is concerned with a yet future event.

The only utterance of this primeval seer which has come down to us is preserved in the Epistle of Jude. It runs as follows;—

"Behold, the Lord cometh* with ten thousand of His saints, to execute judgment upon all, and to convince all that are ungodly among them of all their ungodly deeds which they have ungodly committed,

* In the Greek ἦλθε, that is, literally, "came." But the prophecy is evidently describing a vision of the future which passed before the eyes of Enoch; and, consequently, the present tense "cometh" sets the meaning of the quotation in a clearer light for the ordinary reader.

and of all their hard speeches which ungodly sinners have spoken against Him."*

These words do not refer, finally at least, to the Deluge, but concern our times, and point to the appearing of our Lord in glory with His Church. Had the prophecy descended to us without an inspired comment, it would doubtless have been made subservient to the "spiritualising" theory. An exclusive reference to the flood would have been assumed, and we should have been admonished to observe that the coming of the Lord is merely a figurative expression for a mighty judgment, and does not signify a personal advent. But such a perversion of meaning is impossible; for Jude tells us that in his time, after the ascension of Christ to the Father, the prediction was still awaiting its fulfilment. Hence, therefore, the reason of its preservation, because it refers to the personal appearing of the Saviour to close the present age. And Enoch's knowledge of this appearing, some five thousand years before it was to take place, shows us that the secrets of God are ever with them that fear Him; while at the same time it testifies to the vast importance of that event, the first stage of which we should now be hourly expecting.

Doubtless, too, the prophecy was fraught with peculiar consolation to the godly part of Seth's posterity, toiling as they were beneath the curse, and longing for the promised deliverance. For it is at the Lord's appearing that the battle shall at last be turned to the disaster of the serpent and his seed: it is then that the redemption of all creation from sin and death—the price of which was paid to the full upon the cross—

* Jude 14, 15.

shall be at length commenced after all the weary centuries of delay.

Enoch's translation is a type of the future rapture of the Church to meet the Lord in the air.

Enoch, then, continued walking with God, and testifying to the world, until his three hundred and sixty-fifth year, when he suddenly vanished: he was not: he had gone, and none could find him. For he had been caught up to the throne of the Most High, a first hint of the great secret that, although God made the earth for men, and intends them to inhabit it for ever, He, nevertheless, purposes to exalt an election from among them to a higher destiny, even to dwell with Christ in the heavenly places.

And in this translation of Enoch before the terrible times of Noah we have a type of the manner in which the waiting Church will be presently summoned to meet Christ in the air, and so to be ever with Him, before the corruption of the world comes to its worst, before the judgments of the day of the Lord commence. For the world heard no sound of a trumpet, saw no lightning flash, when Enoch was suddenly removed: he merely disappeared, and his companions, perhaps, knew not at first whither he had gone. Nay, it may be that they vainly sought him, even as the sons of the prophets sought Elijah for three days amid the mountains and valleys of Jericho. And so, probably, will it be at the translation of the Church; the Saviour will come unexpectedly, as a thief in the night, and steal away His own from the unsuspecting world. Their beds will be found vacant in the morning, or they will vanish from their customary places in the day; there will be no farewells to those whom they love, but have been unable to entice into their own paths: all that may be recorded of their end will be as the record of Enoch's departure, They were not: for God took them.

This view appears to be confirmed by the testimony of Scripture.

Perhaps it may be objected to this parallel that, in Paul's description of the rapture of the Church, the Lord is said to descend from the high heavens with a shout, with the voice of the archangel, and with the trump of God.* This, at first sight, seems to intimate that there will be at least a momentary proclamation of what is going on. But we must remember that Paul is writing, not to mankind in general, but only to the waiting Church. It does not, therefore, follow that the whole earth will be disturbed by the summons; but only, of necessity, that those who are concerned will hear.

That this will be the case among the dead is certain; for our Lord Himself tells us that, when He gives the signal for the first resurrection, all those who hear shall live.† But the rest of the dead will not hear, and, therefore, will not live until the thousand years of the Millennium are ended. And as with the dead, so will it probably be with the living. For although there is ample Scriptural proof that the Church will be removed from earth before the close of the age, there is, nevertheless, no trace in prophetic passages of the world being suddenly alarmed at that time by the voice of Christ and the trump of God. The Lord's own declarations that, although unmistakable signs and wonders shall herald His glorious appearing to the world, He will come for His own as unexpectedly and noiselessly as a thief in the night, evidently point in the same

* 1 Thess. iv. 16. † John v. 25.

direction. So does the fact that the details of the Church's translation seem to correspond to those of Enoch, of Elijah, and of the Lord Himself; neither of which events was seen by, or in any way immediately affected, the world.

It may be that those who are believers in Christ, and, therefore, a part of His redeemed; who have offered up the sacrifice on the brazen altar, but have not yet been sufficiently cleansed and sanctified in the laver, and are thus not ready to pass into the heavenly Tabernacle—it may be that these will have some intimation of the summons, only to feel their own inability to obey it for the present. They may be as Elisha witnessing the departure of Elijah: or as the disciples on the mount of Olives when they beheld the cloud receiving their Master out of their sight, but were not yet prepared to follow Him.

Real meaning of κέλευσμα, which our translators have inadequately rendered "a shout."

It is, however, worth while, before we pass on, to notice that the shout, with which Paul describes the Lord as descending, is no mere sound uttered to be heard generally. For the Greek word κέλευσμα properly means a "bidding," and was then used technically for the word of command given by either a naval or military officer.

The idea, therefore, to be conveyed is, that the Church resembles an army, the soldiers of which have already received orders to prepare for marching, have already been bidden to fall into rank, and to stand with girded loins and attentive ears ready to move simultaneously the instant the word of command is uttered by its great Leader. But there are some who, although they belong to the host, have neglected the first orders to be ready and watch, and are not expecting the second. These will be thrown into confusion by the sudden signal to march, and, being unable to follow at once, will have to rejoin their comrades by a circuitous and perilous route, the greater part of which will be disputed by powerful bands of the then assembled and doubly malignant foe.

The prophecy of Lamech and its fulfilment.

The first prophet thus passed away in a moment from the toils of life into the presence of God, and left behind him his son Methuselah and his grandson Lamech, which last was the father of Noah. The name Noah signifies "rest," and Lamech bestowed it upon his son with the words; —"This same shall comfort us concerning our work and toil of our hands, because of the ground which the Lord hath cursed."* Now this utterance cannot be a mere vague expression of joy at the birth of the child: for if so, it would scarcely have been recorded. But we know that Lamech's grandfather and son were prophets; and, perhaps, the gift, when once bestowed, was transmitted to each head of the family, so that Enoch, Methuselah, Lamech, and Noah, were a line of witnesses appointed by God to testify against the wickedness of the world, and to declare His purpose of judgment.

Hence the words of Lamech were probably prophetic, and found their accomplishment in some alleviation of the curse after the flood. For from the blessing of God when He accepted Noah's sacrifice we may, perhaps, infer that the condition of earth before the Deluge was worse than at any subsequent time.† The seasons would seem to have been irregular and

* Gen. v 29. † Gen. viii 21, 22.

altogether uncertain; there was no rain, and the mists, by which the earth was watered, may have been scanty and infrequent, so that the antediluvians often spent their strength in vain: their land did not yield its increase; neither did the trees yield their fruit. Dense fogs, too, or other unknown causes, may have interfered with the alternations of day and night. The curse was fresh and in full vigour: or, perhaps, these disasters arose from premonitory disturbances of nature similar to those which will precede the great judgment of our own age.

But when, after Noah's sacrifice, the Lord smelled a sweet savour, He said;—"I will not again curse the ground any more for man's sake . . . While the earth remaineth, seedtime and harvest, and cold and heat, and summer and winter, and day and night, shall not cease."* Man should still toil and struggle against many difficulties; but God would henceforth give him fixed seasons, would allow him, as a rule, to be always sure of some fruit of his labours. And it is not unlikely that the gift of rain contributed still further to mitigate the intense hardship of the curse; while the permission to eat animal food provided an altogether easier way of obtaining a large portion of the necessary sustenance.

* Gen. viii 21, 22

THE DAYS OF NOAH.

CHAPTER IX.

THE DAYS OF NOAH.

The history of Noah's times is a subject of great practical importance to us.

THE sixth chapter of Genesis contains an account of the days of Noah, a description of momentous interest to us: for our Lord has declared that a similar epoch of worldliness will at length exhaust the forbearance of God towards the present dwellers upon earth, and cause Him to come with fire, and with His chariots like a whirlwind, to render His anger with fury, and His rebuke with flames of fire; to plead with all flesh by fire and by His sword.*

It becomes, therefore, an obvious duty to consider the progress of wickedness and corruption among the antediluvians, so far as it has pleased God to inform us of it: to acquaint ourselves, not merely with the sowing, but also with the watering, the growth, and the ripening, of that hideous crop against which the gleaming sickle of the Almighty at length flashed forth from heaven; to note the various incentives to evil as they successively appeared, and to observe the particular influence of each upon the rapidly decomposing masses of society. For by so doing we shall arm ourselves against the errors and temptations which are daily

* Isa. lxvi. 15, 16.

multiplying around us, and be enabled to discern the threatening signs of our own times.

Now the first mentioned characteristic of those former days of wickedness and peril is the rapid increase of population;* a circumstance which in itself has ever tended, not merely to diffuse, but at the same time to intensify sin. For every form of evil which exists in thinly populated countries, will also be found where men have multiplied; while there are countless vices peculiar to crowded districts. And, if they are numerous, men support each other in rebellion, and are prone to become far more daring and defiant of God. Among ourselves, the strongholds of rationalism and atheism are always to be found in large cities.

The characteristics of those times. Increase of population.

But while the families of the earth were thus increasing in number, they were at the same time making vast progress in civilization and knowledge. Cain had taught them to settle in communities and build cities;† and the sons of Lamech—speedily followed, no doubt, by many others—had introduced the mechanical and fine arts, and had devised unlawful means of evading the labour imposed by the curse.‡ And in that age, when, instead of being cut off at three score and ten or four score, men lived on for nearly a thousand years, their immense accumulation of knowledge, experience, and skill, must have advanced science, art, and the invention and manufacture of all the appliances of a luxurious civilization, with a rapidity to us almost inconceivable.

Rapid advance in civilization, art, and science.

The one recorded specimen of antediluvian industry, the ark, was built by a Sethite; and yet it equalled in

* Gen. vi. 1. † Gen. iv. 17. ‡ Gen. iv. 20-22.

size the Great Eastern, the ship which but a few years ago afforded such marvel to ourselves, and which has not since been surpassed.

And doubtless many of the mighty labours accomplished by the earlier descendants of Noah may be considered to have sprung from reminiscences of pristine grandeur, and fragments of lore, handed down by forefathers who had passed a portion of their existence in the previous age of human glory and depravity. Such may have been the daring conception of a literally cloud-capped tower; the stupendous and splendidly decorated edifices of Babylon and Nineveh; and the wondrous structure of the first pyramid, involving, as it apparently does, an accurate knowledge of astronomical truth which would seem to have been at least on a level with the vaunted advances of modern science. For all these great efforts, be it remembered, were in progress during the lifetime of Shem, and probably in that of his brothers also.

Nor must we forget recent discoveries in regard to the primeval civilization of the Accadians, "the stunted and oblique-eyed people of ancient Babylonia," whose very existence was unknown to us fifty years ago. Their language was dying out, and had become a learned dialect, like the Latin of the Middle Ages, in the seventeenth century before Christ. And yet so great had been their intellectual power that the famous library of Agané, founded at that time by Sargon I., was stocked with books "which were either translated from Accadian originals, or else based on Accadian texts, and filled with technical words which belonged to the old language." A catalogue of the astronomical department, which has been preserved, contains a direction to the reader to write down the number of the tablet or book which he requires, and apply for it to the librarian. "The arrangement," says Sayce, "adopted by Sargon's librarians must have been the product of generations of former experience." Could we have a stronger proof "of the development of literature and education, *and of the existence of a considerable number of reading people in this remote antiquity*"?

According to Berosus there was an antediluvian "Town of Books" in Babylonia; and Sisuthrus, the Chaldean Noah, "is made to bury his books at Sippara before the Deluge, and to disentomb them after the descent from the Ark." But, apart from tradition, we have evidence that in very early times there were well-known libraries at Erech, Ur, Cutha, and Larsa, to which observatories and universities were attached.*

If, then, we give but their fair weight to these considerations, we seem compelled to admit that the antediluvians may have attained to a perfection in civilization and high culture which has scarcely yet been recovered, much as we pride ourselves upon our own times.

Union of the families of Cain and Seth.

Since we have no further mention of the Cainites as a separate tribe, and since of the Sethites—who must also have increased in numbers—but one person was translated to God from the evil to come, and only eight were saved through that evil, it is clear that the two families had at length mingled and intermarried. Seduced, probably, by the intellectual pursuits, the gay society, and the easy life, of the wicked, the Sethites first found a pleasure in their company, their luxuries, and their many skilful

* See Sayce's "Babylonian Literature."

and ingenious inventions; were then enticed to yoke themselves unequally with unbelievers; and, so, being drawn into the vortex of sin, disappeared as a separate people.

Sad and instructive was the result of this amalgamation: for when the time of dividing came, no true worshippers of Jehovah were to be found save in the single family of Noah. Men seem to have so prized their own wisdom, to have thought so little of God, that their religion had dwindled to a mere hero-worship of their own famous leaders,* those who, Prometheus-like, brought to them by their inventions the necessaries and comforts of life, and so enabled them for the time to foil the purposes of the Supreme Power.

Irruption of fallen angels into the world of men.

Then a new and startling event burst upon the world, and fearfully accelerated the already rapid progress of evil. "The sons of God saw the daughters of men that they were fair; and they took them wives of all which they chose."† These words are often explained to signify nothing more than the intermarriage of the descendants of Cain and Seth; but a careful examination of the passage will elicit a far deeper meaning.

When *men*, we are told, began to multiply on the face of the earth, and daughters were born unto them, the sons of God saw the daughters of *men*.‡ Now by "men" in each case the whole human race is evidently signified, the descendants of Cain and Seth alike. Hence the "sons of God" are plainly distinguished from the generation of Adam.

* Gen. vi. 4. † Gen. vi. 2.
‡ Gen. vi. 1, 2.

The "sons of God" are angelic beings.

Again; the expression "sons of God (Elohim)" occurs but four times in other parts of the Old Testament, and is in each of these cases indisputably used of angelic beings.

Twice in the beginning of the Book of Job we read of the sons of God presenting themselves before Him at stated times, and Satan also comes with them as being himself a son of God, though a fallen and rebellious one.*

For the term sons of Elohim, the mighty Creator, seems to be confined to those who were directly created by the Divine hand, and not born of other beings of their own order. Hence, in Luke's genealogy of our Lord, Adam is called a son of God.† And so also Christ is said to give to them that receive Him power to become the sons of God.‡ For these are born again of the Spirit of God as to their inner man even in the present life. And at the resurrection they will be clothed with a spiritual body, a building of God;§ so that they will then be in every respect equal to the angels, being altogether a new creation.‖

The third repetition of the phrase occurs in a later chapter of Job, where the morning stars are represented as singing together, and the sons of God as shouting for joy, over the creation of our earth.¶

And lastly; the same expression is found in the Book of Daniel;** but in the singular number, and with the necessary difference that *bar* is the word used for son instead of *ben*, the singular of the latter being unknown in Chaldee. Nebuchadnezzar exclaims that

* Job i. 6; ii. 1.
† Luke iii. 38.
‡ John i. 12.
§ 2 Cor. v. 1.
‖ Luke xx. 36.
¶ Job xxxviii. 7.
** Dan. iii. 25.

he sees four men walking in the midst of the fire, and that the form of the fourth is like a son of God,* by which he evidently means a supernatural or angelic being, distinct as such from the others.

It appears, therefore, that in the Old Testament the title "sons of God" is restricted to angels.† Several passages are indeed adduced to prove its application to men: but upon examination they will all be found wide of the mark, the words of the original being in every case different, and sometimes signifying sons of Jehovah. This last, as we have already seen,‡ is a very different expression, and would probably have been used by the inspired historian in the verse under our consideration if he had wished to distinguish the godly descendants of Seth from the Cainites. For, while it forms a true description of all saints upon earth, it would have been in this place peculiarly appropriate to the Sethites just after the mention of the fact that they had been

* There is no definite article in the original.

† This is the view taken by Josephus, Philo Judæus, and the authors of "The Book of Enoch" and "The Testament of the Twelve Patriarchs"; indeed, it was generally accepted by learned Jews in the early centuries of the Christian era. In regard to the Septuagint, all MSS. render the Hebrew "sons of God" by "angels of God" in Job i. 6, and ii. 1, and by "My angels" in Job xxxviii. 7—passages in which there was no dogmatic reason for tampering with the text. In Gen. vi. 2, 4, the *Codex Alexandrinus* and three later MSS. exhibit the same rendering, while others have "sons of God." Augustine, however, admits that in his time the greater number of copies read "angels of God" in the latter passage also (*De Civit. Dei*, xv. 23). It seems, therefore, extremely probable that this was the original reading; and certainly the interpretation which it involves was adopted by the majority of the earlier Christian writers. Those who would pursue this subject further can do so in a recent and exhaustive treatise by the Rev. John Fleming, entitled, "The Fallen Angels and the Heroes of Mythology."

‡ Pp. 188-90.

wont from the birth of Enos to call upon the name of Jehovah.

They are identical with the sinning angels mentioned by Peter and Jude.

It thus appears that the sons of God are angelic beings: and the mysterious statement respecting them in the sixth chapter of Genesis seems to refer to a second and deeper apostacy on the part of some of the High Ones on high. But these more daring rebels are not found among the spirits of darkness which now haunt the air. They no longer retain their position as principalities and powers of the world, or even their liberty; but may be identified with the imprisoned criminals of whom Peter tells us that, after they had sinned, God spared them not, "but cast them down to Hell, and delivered them into chains of darkness, to be reserved unto judgment."* Jude also mentions their present condition in similar terms,† and the context of either passage indicates with sufficient clearness the nature of their sin. They chose to leave their own world, and, having broken through God's limits into another, to go after strange flesh; therefore He dashed them down at once to His lowest dungeons as an instant punishment

* 2 Peter ii. 4. We have given the words of the Authorized Version, but the following would be a more literal rendering of the original. "For if God spared not angels when they had sinned, but cast them down to Tartarus, and committed them to pits of darkness, to be reserved unto judgment." Tartarus appears to be a place of imprisonment more terrible than Hades, but it cannot be the Lake of Fire and Brimstone, the flames of which are to be kindled specially for the Beast and False Prophet, the first who will be cast into it. Compare Isa. xxx. 33 with Rev. xix. 20. In the Greek mythology, Tartarus was a dark abode of woe, as far beneath Hades as Earth is below Heaven (Hom. Il. viii. 16)—a description which fairly corresponds to Peter's "pits of darkness." Very significant, too, is the fact that it was thought to be the prison of Cronos and the rebel Titans.

† Jude 6.

of their impious outrage, and to deprive them for ever of the power of producing further confusion.

The verse following the announcement of the angels' sin is a parenthesis of solemn import:* the scene is for a moment shifted from the fearfully increasing wickedness of earth, and transferred to the Heaven of heavens. There the invisible God sits enthroned, and, looking down upon the rebellion and sin beneath Him, pronounces sentence of doom upon the unconscious world. The end must come: His spirit shall not always strive with men, seeing that they are irrecoverably overpowered by the desires of the flesh: yet they shall have a further respite of one hundred and twenty years.

The Lord looks down upon the world.

Then the history is resumed with a brief hint at the cause which led to intermarriages between the sons of God and the daughters of men, both before and after the flood.† Our translators have again omitted a definite article in the beginning of this verse, which should be rendered, "The Nephilim—or fallen ones—were on the earth in those days, and also afterwards, when the sons of God came in unto the daughters of men."

Meaning of the word Nephilim.

Through a misapprehension of the Septuagint, which we will presently explain, the English version renders *Nephilim* by "giants." But the form of the Hebrew word indicates a verbal adjective or noun, of passive or neuter signification, from *Naphal*, to fall: hence it must mean "the fallen ones," that is, probably, the fallen angels. Afterwards, however, the term seems to have been transferred to their offspring, as we may gather from the only other passage in which it occurs. In

* Gen. vi. 3. † Gen. vi. 4.

the evil report which the ten spies give of the land of Canaan, we find them saying ;—"All the people which we saw in it were men of great stature. And there we saw the Nephilim, the sons of Anak, descended from the Nephilim: and we seemed to ourselves as grasshoppers, and so we did to them." *

It was doubtless the mention of the great stature of these men, together with the Septuagint rendering γίγαντες, that suggested our translation "giants." The roots of the Greek γίγας have, however, no reference to great stature, but point to something very different. The word is merely another form of γηγενής: it signifies "earth-born," and was used of the Titans, or sons of Heaven and Earth—Cœlus and Terra—because, though superior to the human race, they were, nevertheless, of partly terrestrial origin. The meaning of "giants," in our sense of the term, is altogether secondary, and arose from the fact that these beings of mixed birth were said to have displayed a monstrous growth and strength of body. It will, therefore, be apparent that the rendering of the Septuagint correctly expresses the idea which was in the mind of the translator, since he appears to have taken *Nephilim* in each case to signify the offspring of the sons of God and the daughters of men. We, however, as we have explained above, prefer understanding the word primarily of the fallen angels themselves.

The residence of the fallen angels upon earth was the immediate cause of their alliances with the daughters of men.

Now, in speaking of the sin of some of these, Jude† tells us that, despising the position of dignity and responsibility in which God had placed them, they voluntarily left their own home in the

* Numb. xiii. 32, 33.

† Jude 6.

Kingdom of the Air, prompted it would seem by earthward desires, and began to exercise an unlawful influence over the human race. And, perhaps, as punishment, their return was prohibited; they were banished altogether from heaven, and confined to the limits of earth; just as Satan and the remainder of his angels will be hereafter, a short time before the appearing of Christ to cast them into the still lower abyss.

But, however this may be, they were from some cause dwelling upon earth at the time, and the fact is apparently mentioned to account for their intermarriages with the daughters of men. If, then, their continued residence below was voluntary, they soon passed on to a far more frightful sin: if, on the contrary, it was penal, instead of humbling themselves under the mighty hand of God, and patiently enduring until He remitted His just punishment, they did not hesitate to defy Him still more daringly, and to violate the law of their being.*

The assertion of a similar occurrence after the Deluge agrees with the passage in Numbers where the sons of Anak are said to have been Nephilim, or of the Nephilim; † and seems also to account for God's command that the whole race of the Canaanites should be extirpated. For immediately after the commission of the antediluvian sin, the doom of the world was pronounced: and prophecy intimates that the future confinement of the angels of darkness to earth will be the proximate cause of the great rebellion which

* This they did, not merely by consorting with beings of a different order, but also by the very act of marriage itself; since our Lord tells us that, in their normal condition, angels "neither marry, nor are given in marriage" (Matt. xxii. 30).

† Numb. xiii. 33.

will call forth the Lord Jesus in flaming fire to take vengeance.*

The children of these unlawful connections before the flood were the renowned heroes of old: the subsequent repetition of the crime doubtless gave rise to the countless legends of the loves of the gods, and explains the numerous passages in the Classics, as well as in the ancient literature of other languages, in which human families are traced to a half Divine origin.

Before passing on, we should, perhaps, notice the most common objection to our interpretation, which is, that angels, as spiritual beings, *could* not take wives of the daughters of men. We are, however, unable to recognise the cogency of such an argument, because those who advance it lay claim to a more intimate acquaintance with angelic nature than we can concede as possible. On this point, therefore, we will merely quote a passage from Augustine—an opponent of the angel-theory—containing an admission which has been made by many other writers of various ages and climes, and which, absurd as it may have seemed to ourselves some years ago, is now rendered more probable by the disclosures of modern Spiritualism.

After citing the hundred and fourteenth Psalm to prove that angels are spirits, the great theologian proceeds as follows†:—

"However, that angels have appeared to men in bodies of such a nature that they could not only be seen but even touched, the same most true Scripture declares. Moreover, there is a very general rumour that Silvans and Fauns, who are commonly termed incubi, improbos sæpe exstitisse mulieribus, et earum

* Rev. xii.; xiii.

† *De Civit Dei*, xv. 23.

appetisse ac peregisse concubitum. Many trustworthy persons assert that they have had personal experience of this, or that they have been informed by those who have experienced it. And that certain demons, whom the Gauls call Dusii, are continually attempting and effecting the crime is so generally affirmed that it would seem impudent to deny it."*

So Augustine. And that Paul had some such thought in his mind when he bade the woman to worship with covered head "on account of the angels,"† is, to say the least, within the limits of possibility.

The earth becomes corrupt and filled with violence. Simultaneous progress of luxury and refinement. Historical parallels.

The foundations of established order being thus destroyed by the irruption of the fallen angels, the whole world became corrupt, and its morals were inverted. Men no longer recognised a God to Whom personally all obedience and worship is first due, and Whose equal relation to all men as their Creator imperatively demands from each a love for his neighbour as great as that which he bears to himself. But they judged that whatsoever was pleasant to any man was also right for him; and after thus bursting the bands of God asunder and casting His cords from them, it was not long before they went on to believe that the attainment of a desired end justified every means, that the coveted possession must be secured even if it were necessary to use deceit or violence. Blinded by the

* To the prevalence of this idea we have no slight testimony in the fact that the name of the demons is one of the Celtic words which have survived in our language. It is the origin of the English Deuse, or Deuce, which is still used in exclamatory or interjectional phrases.

† 1 Cor. xi. 10.

selfishness of the flesh, which can see nothing beyond itself, they pursued their several objects without consideration or even thought of their fellows, except when any either stood in the way or might be made subservient. And hence there sprang up a thick crop of frauds and assassinations, of open quarrels and violence, till the whole earth was filled with corruption and bloodshed.

And yet all this seems to have existed side by side with luxury, a refined culture, and a love of art and music. Such minglings of things apparently incongruous have not been infrequent in postdiluvial times. The profligacy, immorality, and sensuous intellectuality of Athens is an example.

A parallel might also be sought in the descriptions given by Tacitus, Juvenal, and others, of the times of the Cæsars. For then the whole body of society was corrupted, and even the streets of Rome were accustomed to violence. And yet the worst of vices, the most absolute immorality, the most profligate gluttony, the most wanton cruelty, prevailed in company with a splendid magnificence, a high appreciation of music, sculpture, and art generally, and a taste for literature, and especially for poetry, so great that recitations and readings were a common amusement. A very characteristic production of this age was the philosopher Seneca, who has been lately termed a seeker after God, on account of his books on morals, but who did not find the writing of beautiful sentiments any hindrance to a life of shocking depravity, and who presented to the world, as the fruit of his combined teaching and example, the proverbial monster Nero.

Nor were the times of Leo the Tenth without

resemblance to the days of Noah; when that famous Pontiff, seated amid every possible sensuous and intellectual refinement, and surrounded by the most brilliant cluster of stars that has ever adorned the firmament of art, exclaimed;—"This Christianity! how profitable a farce it has proved to us!" When, in a time which produced paintings, sculpture, and architecture, still marvels to the world, the sun as it rose day by day would expose the floating corpses of the assassinated in the Tiber; and infidelity and lawlessness kept such rapid pace with the culture of the beautiful that even Machiavelli, who will not be accused of too tender a conscience, declared that Italy had lost all principles of piety, and all religious feeling; that the Italians had become a nation of impious cut-throats.

God looks down a second and a third time, and then reveals to Noah His purpose to destroy all flesh.

Such, though on a far greater scale, was the wickedness of the antediluvian world. But the end was approaching. God looked down a second time upon the spreading demoralization beneath Him,* and saw that it would be necessary, at the close of the years of respite, to sweep man and beast, creeping thing and fowl, from the face of the earth.

Yet a third time the Creator beheld, and lo! evil had made such fearful progress that all flesh had corrupted its way upon earth.† Then He foretold the impending ruin to Noah, who alone found grace in His sight, and instructed him how he might avoid the universal doom. The commands laid upon the patriarch were a strong trial of his faith. He was to proclaim the speedy coming of a catastrophe which to unbelievers would

* Gen. vi. 5-7. † Gen. vi. 12-21.

appear simply irrational, of an overwhelming flood which should sweep away all life from the face of the whole earth.

Unavailing preaching of Noah.

It may be that men felt a momentary uneasiness at the first utterance of this prophecy of woe. Discussions may have taken place similar to those among ourselves, when the conjectured possibility of a collision between the earth and Donati's comet caused a brief anxiety to those who believed in it. But, this qualm over, we can readily picture to ourselves the contempt and derision which must have been poured upon the prophet. Our own times will teach us how the men of science soon proved that such a thing as a universal flood was an absolute impossibility, contrary to all the known laws of nature. And since Noah persisted, the world doubtless settled down into a belief that he was a weak-minded fanatic, void of intellect, and altogether unworthy of notice.

Noah builds the ark, and is commanded to enter into it. God closes the door behind him.

But Noah was not only directed to foretell the approaching doom: he was also bidden to make open preparations for avoiding it, preparations, too, of vast magnitude, and such as must have attracted general attention. And a grievous burden it undoubtedly was to endure the scoffs and deridings with which he must have been continually assailed while building his immense ship on the dry land, far, it may be, from any water; but by faith he persevered, and at last the days of his trial drew on to their close.

None had listened to his warnings: not one beyond the inner circle of his own family was accounted worthy to be saved. But the ark was now completed, and he was instructed to enter it with his wife, his sons and their wives, and all the creatures which were impelled by God to go with him. He was at no loss to understand the significance of the command; he knew well that the wrath of God was being restrained only till those which should be saved had been taken out of the way; and we can imagine his feelings as he watched the long procession slowly filing into the ark, and at length followed in its rear, leaving the unconscious world, friends and foes alike, in the inexorable grasp of destruction.

It may be that after entering he returned to the door, appalled at the thought of what was about to happen, and moved to make one more effort, one last impassioned appeal, if perchance he might constrain some few, at least, to flee to the shelter. But, if he did, he found the entrance to the ark closed: God had shut it: there was none that could open. Affrighted crowds might gather around imploring admittance; but Noah had no longer the power to aid them: the separation had been made: eight persons were safe within the ark, and the whole remainder of mankind was shut out for judgment: the acceptable year had passed by, the days of vengeance were come.

The world continues unconscious to the last.

And yet, as our Lord Himself tells us, the doomed multitudes knew it not. They had often heard, but had refused to listen: the voice of the prophet had seemed to them as the voice of one that mocked. Even on the morning of the fatal day, earth resounded with the noise of revelry and merriment: men were eating and drinking, marrying and giving in marriage: they were absorbed in the pleasures of the moment, and discerned not the slowly rising spectre of Death amid the gathering clouds, the destroyer, with uplifted scythe, about to mow down all flesh at one fell stroke.

God withdraws His restraints from the element of water, and the flood ensues.

But their dream of security was at length rudely dispelled : the shouts of riotous joy and laughter were first softened into whispers of breathless anxiety, and then exchanged for shrieks of despair. On the day in which Noah entered into the ark the windows of heaven were opened, and the waters that were above the firmament began to descend. The world wondered ; and then, remembering the words of Noah, trembled at the fast falling raindrops, the first they had ever beheld.*

Nor was this all. A fearful roaring from the sea announced that some mighty convulsion, equally beyond the calculation of the scientific men of the day, had commenced in the great deep. All its sealed fountains were bursting up : God had removed the bounds of ocean : its proud waves were no longer stayed, but were rising with prodigious tumult, and beginning to advance again upon the dry land.

What scenes of horror must have been presented beneath the dismal rainfall at this awful time ! What affrighted groups ! What countenances of dismay ! What shrieks of terror ! What faintings for fear !

*In Gen. ii. 5, 6, we are told that the Lord God had not caused it to rain, but that a mist went up from the earth, and watered the whole face of the ground. Probably this state of things continued until the flood, when the windows of heaven were for the first time opened. The rainbow must have been a new phenomenon when it was givenas a token to Noah: the words of God imply as much. Besides which, had the bow been seen before the flood, its subsequent reappearance could never have suggested security. But if there was no rainbow, there could scarcely have been rain.

What headlong flights to any place which appeared to offer safety for the moment!

Yet the mercy of God seems even then to have been mingled with His judgment. Ordinary means had failed with these sinners. They had received warning after warning; but their eyes were so immovably fixed upon the world and its amusements that they could not be induced to look off to God. Therefore He was compelled to destroy the life which they were abusing: He was constrained to overwhelm before their eyes all their palaces and fair gardens and places of delight, and to hurry the rebels themselves into the prison of disembodied spirits. Yet His mercy devised a doom which, though inexorable and complete, was, nevertheless, not instantaneous, but gave time for repentance before death, that by the destruction of the flesh the spirits of many might be saved.

Mercy mingled with judgment.

The waters continued to increase: the ark was upborne upon them: and it may be that for a time its inmates ever and anon heard, mingling with the roar of the elements, the cries and prayers of some still surviving crowd of miserable ones who had taken refuge upon a height near to which they were floating. But this was soon over, and earth was again almost as it had been before the six days of restoration, covered above its highest mountain tops with a shoreless ocean, on the surface of which were drifting the dead bodies of the men who had transgressed against God, and the carcases of the beasts and creeping things and fowls which had been involved in their ruin.

Earth is again covered with the waters of destruction.

Woful was the proof that man, if unrestrained, if left

to his own devices, is not merely incapable of recovering his innocence, but will rush madly down the steep of sensuousness and impious self-will until he finds himself engulphed in the abyss of perdition. The trial of freedom had failed: the second of the ages was ended.

"*AS IT WAS IN THE DAYS OF NOAH.*"

CHAPTER X.

"AS IT WAS IN THE DAYS OF NOAH.'

Retrospect

WE have thus endeavoured to trace the flow of history from its source to the great catastrophe which swept corruption and violence from the earth. We have seen its clear spring proceeding from the throne of the Everlasting God, and have then lost sight of it as it wound its way through vast regions that may not be trodden by mortal foot. Once or twice we have climbed an accessible height, and from the far distance gazed with strained eyes upon something which sparkled in the rays of God's Word, and which we supposed to be the waters of the river we were seeking: but we could obtain no certain knowledge of the mysterious stream, until we saw its turbid and foaming torrent emerging in fearful cataract from between the dark mountains which concealed its previous course.

We have followed it into a land of delight, in which it gradually calmed and brightened again, while its banks teemed with all that is beautiful and lovely: we have traced it as it passed the limits of that joyous realm, and hurried through dry and barren tracts, with ever increasing volume and rapidity, till at length its agitated waters were violently engulphed in the great ocean of the flood.

The warning of Christ. Does it apply to our times?

We must not, however, dismiss the story of doom which we have just been considering without some reflections on the solemn warning drawn from it by the Saviour. "But as the days of Noah were," is His awful declaration, "so shall also the coming of the Son of Man be. For as in the days that were before the flood they were eating and drinking, marrying and giving in marriage, until the day that Noah entered into the ark, and knew not until the flood came, and took them all away; so shall also the coming of the Son of Man be."* Thus the closing scenes of this present age will be a reproduction of the days of Noah: the same intense worldliness, and at last positive inability to care for the things of God, which was displayed by the antediluvians, will also be characteristic of our world when Christ begins the judgments that will quickly culminate in the glory of His appearing.

It seems fair, then, to infer that this second manifestation of the spirit that worked in them which were disobedient before the flood will be effected by a conjunction of causes similar to that which formerly produced it. And hence, as we have already remarked, it becomes a matter of the greatest practical importance to comprehend those causes: for whenever they are again found to be simultaneously affecting the masses of the world's population, the fact will afford a strong presumption that we are drifting rapidly to the great consummation of wickedness; that the avenging glory of the Lord is about to be revealed, so that all flesh shall see it together.

* Matt. xxiv. 37-39.

For us, therefore, the great question is, Are these fatal influences now in operation? Are they more universally characteristic of this epoch than of any other? Mature consideration has impelled many to return an affirmative answer: let us see whether facts warrant us in holding the same view. It is impossible to exaggerate our interest in the investigation. If the present times are only beginning to take the complexion of those of Noah, they send forth a piercing cry of warning, admonishing us to stand with our loins girded about and our lamps burning, waiting for the summons of the Lord. For He will remove His Church, as He removed Enoch, before the wickedness of man has come to its worst. He will take away that which He Himself has called the salt of the earth, and then the corruption of all flesh will go on unchecked, and the world speedily ripen for its doom.

The seven causes of antediluvian corruption. Are they all in present operation?

The seven great causes of the antediluvian apostacy have been already noticed, and may be summed up as follows.

I. A tendency to worship God as Elohim, that is, merely as the Creator and Benefactor, and not as Jehovah the covenant God of mercy, dealing with transgressors who are appointed to destruction, and finding a ransom for them.

II. An undue prominence of the female sex, and a disregard of the primal law of marriage.

III. A rapid progress in the mechanical arts, and the consequent invention of many devices whereby the hardships of the curse were mitigated, and life was rendered more easy and indulgent. Also a proficiency in the fine arts, which captivated the minds of men, and helped to induce an entire oblivion of God.

IV. An alliance between the nominal Church and the World, which speedily resulted in a complete amalgamation.

V. A vast increase of population.

VI. The rejection of the preaching of Enoch, whose warnings thus became a savour of death unto the world, and hardened men beyond recovery.

VII. The appearance upon earth of beings from the Principality of the Air, and their unlawful intercourse with the human race.

These causes concurred to envelope the world in a sensuous mist which no ray of truth could penetrate. They brought about a total forgetfulness of God and disregard of His will; and thus, by removing the great Centre Whc alone is able to attract men from themselves, rendered the dwellers upon earth so selfish and unscrupulous that the world was presently filled with lewdness, injustice, oppression, and bloodshed. It remains, therefore, for us to consider whether similar influences are now acting upon society.

The first cause may be detected in the universal spread of Deism.

And certainly we cannot but confess that the first mentioned cause is eminently characteristic of our times. For in all the professing Churches of Christendom, as well as among Jews, Mahometans, and Pagans, there are countless and ever-increasing multitudes who go in the way of Cain,* acknowledging the Supreme Being, but not recognising His holiness and their own depravity, and so denying all necessity of a Mediator between God and man. Many of these are willing to

* Jude 11.

look upon Christ as some great one, and will talk of His wise philosophy and exemplary life: but they neither confess Him to be the Only Begotten Son of the Father, nor feel the need of His atonement. Consequently, they reject His revelation, as an absolute authority at least, trusting rather to the darkness within them which they call light; and thus, closing their eyes to the true relations of man with his Creator, form their own conceptions both of the Deity and of themselves. This involves nothing less than a claim on their part to supreme wisdom and authority: it is moulding an idol out of their own imagination before which to fall down and worship. Nor need we wonder that it leads to a virtual deification of men of transcendent intellect or great renown. Who has not detected the working of this leaven in his own circle? Who has not observed this "pure Theism," as it is called, rising to the surface in all the sects of Christendom?

Second cause. Change in the relation of the sexes, and violation of the law of marriage.

If the second cause be rightly inferred from the scanty hints given to us, it is also in operation at the present time: for the female sex has certainly commenced a migration into a new sphere and more prominent position. And the looseness in regard to the marriage tie, which has long obtained on the continent, is now spreading in England also, as we may see from the records of our recently established divorce courts. Nay, there are not wanting those who, instead of fearing to put asunder that which God has joined, openly affirm that wedlock should be a contract, not for life, but only for so long a time as may be agreeable to the contracting parties.

At the close of the previous dispensation the same

sin was frequent among the Pharisees, who held that divorce is permissible for any reason; even, as Rabbi Akibah shamelessly says, "if a man sees a woman handsomer than his own wife." Hence the Lord's continual mention of adultery in His denunciations of the Pharisees: for the marriage after divorce which they legalized, He declared to be criminal. In the wonderful sermon contained in the fifteenth sixteenth and seventeenth chapters of Luke, He brings it forward with a startling abruptness, as a most open and undeniable sin, which would at once convict His hearers of having proved as disobedient to the Law and the Prophets as they were to the Gospel.* We know the punishment which quickly overtook them for this and their many other transgressions. In a few short years their lusts were extinguished in their blood: the fair walls and streets of their city were levelled with the ground: their beautiful temple in which they trusted perished in the flames, and the idolatrous shrine of Jupiter rose insultingly upon its ruins.

The third cause. Science, art, and luxury.

Of the third cause, the spread of science, art, and luxury, it is unnecessary to speak: for none will deny that this is a great characteristic of our days: nay, the fact is a common subject of boasting. And alas! how many instances have we of the self-deifying arrogance which frequently arises from a little knowledge of the laws of nature, or a marked success in those arts sciences and philosophies which are the delight of cultivated and refined intellects!† With what confidence, too, and carelessness

* Luke xvi. 18.

† For let it not be supposed that these remarks are directed absolutely against the pursuit of science and art. They are only intended to refer to the insubordinate and atheistical spirit which seems too commonly to arise from it.

do men settle themselves amid the comforts and indulgences of this luxurious age! Seeing good only in the present life, how little thought do they give to God, how deaf are they to any mention of the World to Come! How incredulous, even if their mouths be not filled with mocking, when they hear but a whisper of that tempest of God's fury which will shortly burst upon the apathetic world, and hurry multitudes away from all that they love into the dungeons of His wrath!

"For the day of the Lord of Hosts shall be upon every one that is proud and lofty, and upon every one that is lifted up, and he shall be brought low; and upon all the cedars of Lebanon, that are high and lifted up, and upon all the oaks of Bashan, and upon all the high mountains, and upon all the hills that are lifted up, and upon every high tower, and upon every fenced wall, and upon all the ships of Tarshish, and upon all pleasant pictures. And the loftiness of man shall be bowed down, and the haughtiness of men shall be made low: and the Lord alone shall be exalted in that day."* "Tremble, ye women that are at ease; be troubled, ye careless ones: strip you, and make you bare, and gird sackcloth upon your loins."† "I will send a fire on Magog, and among them that dwell carelessly in the isles: and they shall know that I am the Lord."‡

The fourth cause. Fraternization of the nominal Church and the World.

To reproduce the fourth cause the Prince of this World has long been striving, and certainly now seems near to his victory. It is the natural result of the first error, the denial of our position as sinners before God, as doomed to destruction unless a ransom be found. Let the Church surrender that truth, and what

* Isa. ii. 12-17. † Isa. xxxii. 11. ‡ Ezek. xxxix. 6.

hinders her from living in perfect accord with the World? If the practical teaching of religion be that God is fairly satisfied with our conduct, troubles but little about our sins, highly appreciates our works of virtue, even though pride be their mainspring, and looks with pleasure upon bold deeds and intellectual displays, why should such a theology clash with the cravings of fallen men? How could they hate a deity so like to themselves?

And have we not been describing the creed of vast numbers in the professing Church? Are not the walls of the city of God thus continually broken down before our eyes, so that the stranger may enter at will? Men do indeed frequent their churches and chapels in crowds: they excite a feeling, which they term religious, by grand buildings, by painted windows, by splendid vestments, by gorgeous ceremonies, by beautiful music, by sentimental or intellectual discourses, and by strong sectarian or political convictions. But if they clothe themselves with the semblance of devotion in their worship, they altogether lose this outward distinction in the world, and bewilder those who are honestly asking what they shall do to be saved by plunging into all the gaieties, frivolities, pursuits, and business, of this life, as if they were to remain among them for ever. They act as though God had promised that they at least should not be hurried out of the world as so many of their fellows are, but should have due warning and ample space and *inclination* for repentance.* They seem to be assured that they will never be unexpectedly startled by the dread sentence, "Thou fool, this night shall thy soul be required of thee"; † nor suddenly

* John vi. 44. † Luke xii. 20.

appalled by the blast of the archangel's trumpet, and the thunder of the voice of God. They have conceded that it is rational to seek contentment and pleasure in an existence of awful brevity, which was only granted to them for the decision of one stupendous question, whether it shall be followed by everlasting life, or by shame and everlasting contempt. The powers of the World to Come have lost their hold upon them, they are even as other men: so many points have been yielded, amusements permitted, and vices condoned, that it is almost impossible to distinguish them from non-professors unless they recite their creed. Nay, some would appear to be holding a doctrine of the ancient Gnostics who, denying the resurrection, affirmed that, their spirits being saved, they were at liberty to do what they would with the body, inasmuch as after death they would have no further concern either with it or its deeds. And although many are ready to confess that the Christian must take up his cross, yet being thoroughly satisfied that in these modern times the unwearied zeal of Christ and His apostles would be quite out of place, they can by no means find a cross to bear. If, however, God in His anger smite them with sickness, bereavement, disappointment, or loss, they talk of their trials, and comfort themselves with the thought that they are imitating the Lord by enduring troubles which they cannot in any way avoid.

Oh that those who are thus blinded by Satan would consider while there is yet time; would earnestly and prayerfully meditate upon the words of the Lord Jesus, and interpret them by His most holy life! Then would they see the inconsistency of their position, and keenly feel that they have been fulfilling to the letter the prophecy of the last times, that men should have a form of godliness, but deny the power thereof.* For the world will allow the mere statement of any doctrine, provided no attempt be made to put it into practice. It is only when faith begins to produce works that the Christian is confronted with bitter antagonism; when he feels that he must redeem the time because the days are evil; when, being conscious of a dispensation committed to him, he is impelled to preach the Word in season and out of season, to speak as a dying man to dying men; when he can no longer take part in frivolous gaieties or time-killing pleasures, knowing that such things are but as a painted curtain used by the foul fiend to hide from men the brink of death on which they are walking, until the time comes to tear it away and thrust them over the precipice.

If any be thus earnestly minded, they will have no difficulty in regard to the line of separation: they will quickly find the cross they have to bear: they will feel that, like their Master, they are not of this world, and will indeed have tribulation in it. But let them be of good cheer: for He is at hand, and great will be their joy at His coming.

Nor are the concessions of the nominal Church in point of doctrine less deplorable than those which concern conduct. We have before seen that men were ever prone to soften and corrupt those parts of God's Word which oppose their own thoughts and aspirations. But a strange and impious idea now prevalent is destroying the last vestiges of Biblical authority, and sweeping away every remaining barrier to peace between the professing Church and the World. This

* 2 Tim. iii. 5.

is a rapidly growing objection to what is called dogma. Now did the objection apply only to the too positive assertion by men of their own opinions, the sentiment would be wholesome: but upon inquiry we discover that "dogma" is practically a conventional term for the revelations and commandments of the Most High God. And many who profess a belief in the Bible, instead of strengthening "the things which remain, that are ready to die,"* are never weary of admonishing us to be charitable in regard to those who reject every vital doctrine of Scripture, and even deny the Lord Who bought them. We are told that, provided men be "honest," all will be well with them at last: that we must not be narrow minded: that there are other entrances into the fold besides the door:† that those are not necessarily thieves and robbers who climb over the wall; but, it may be, bolder and more manly spirits than their fellows.

It is easy to see that by such a line of reasoning all power is extracted from the Scriptures. Instead of being recognized as the living Word of Him Who shall hereafter judge the quick and the dead by the things which are written in them, they are regarded merely as an ordinary volume of advice to man, who, in assuming the right to accept or reject them at will, arrogantly places the crown of Deity upon his own head. And thus the great means which God has appointed for the separation of His Church from the World is destroyed: the light which reveals the continual peril and the fearful termination of the broad road is put out, and men go heedlessly on, amused with the trifles of the moment, until they fall headlong into the jaws of the pit.

* Rev. iii. 2. † John x. 7.

Upon the fifth cause there is no need to enlarge.

The fifth cause. Increase of the world's population.

For, without troubling the census papers, almost every Englishman could speak of the rapid growth of his own neighbourhood. Nor has the world ever previously beheld so vast an aggregation of human life as that which our metropolis now exhibits. Yet at the same time crowds of emigrants are leaving the country, and filling the solitary places of the earth. And statistics show that the population of almost every part of the world is also increasing.

But, in addition to this, there is a phenomenon of gloomy portent. For, while they multiply, men are also beginning to exhibit impatience of restraint: and, since they are learning to act together, and seem to be growing inflated with reliance on their fancied power, they will probably soon go on to deeds of impious daring. Large organizations, which are no longer confined to the frontiers of one people, forbode a second rebellion of Babel. The time of the shaking of all nations is approaching, and the hearts of many are already failing them for fear, and for looking after those things which are coming on the earth. Let believers consider their ways: for the Lord will shortly descend to see what the children of men are doing.

Whenever the Word of God is faithfully preached it

The sixth cause. Increased callousness of the world consequent upon the rejection of Enoch's testimony.

cannot return unto Him void: it will accomplish that which He pleases, and prosper in the thing whereto He sent it:* some effect it must produce upon all who hear. It separates the wheat from the chaff: it either draws men nearer to God, or renders them more

* Isa. lv. 11.

callous than before, and prepares them for speedy judgment. "For we are unto God," says Paul, "a sweet savour of Christ, in them that are being saved, and in them that are perishing. To the one we are the savour of death unto death; and to the other the savour of life unto life." *

And so the powerful appeals of Enoch, his loud calls to repentance and threatenings of judgment to come, since they were slighted by the world, must have mightily hardened the hearts of men, and caused the Spirit of God to cease striving with them. Very probably many were at first impressed and alarmed: but after a while, when they saw day following day without any sign of the predicted vengeance, they lost their fear: they went back to their favourite sins, as the dog to his vomit: they could no longer be roused as before: they began to be scoffers, and mocked at the most solemn warnings: the demon, who had been for a brief space expelled, returned with seven others more wicked than himself: so that their last state was worse than the first.†

In this case also history appears to be repeating itself. For some fifty years God has supplied an unbroken stream of evangelical testimony which has been gradually increasing in power; and there is now sounding forth such a proclamation of the Gospel as the world has never, perhaps, heard since the days of the apostles. The Spirit has fallen upon the Church with Pentecostal vigour: revivals, missions at home and abroad, and the efforts of many individuals, have caused the conversion of thousands. Those who are really Christ's, seem to be strenuously urged by a sense

* 2 Cor. ii. 15, 16. † Luke xi. 24-26.

of their responsibilities: they are going out into the streets and lanes, into the highways and hedges, constraining men to come in: the wedding-hall is rapidly filling with guests.

And amid the calls to repentance and offers of grace, amid the mutual exhortations to walk as children of the light, there peals forth, waxing ever louder and louder, the solemn cry, "Behold, the Bridegroom cometh, go ye out to meet Him";* while the testimony of the faithful to the world is assuming its last form;—"Fear God, and give glory to Him, for the hour of His judgment is come."† Indications of this new epoch have been growing more and more apparent for some years, and many papers and periodicals have been devoted to the resuscitation of the long neglected truth so prominently set forth by our Lord and His apostles. Hundreds of books and pamphlets have been written on the same subject; while the majority of the later revival preachers, and a daily increasing number of other witnesses, have promulgated it to such an extent that it would now be difficult to find a moderately intelligent Christian who is ignorant of the great hope, even if he does not accept it as his own.

There is also a significant change passing over this testimony, and rendering it far more consistent and powerful. For although but a short time has elapsed since the disagreement of prophetic writers was almost proverbial, the great body of them are now beginning to exhibit a wonderful harmony on all main points, and to proclaim that the solemn event which all should be awaiting is the command that will summon the Church into the presence of her Lord. We may, therefore, in

* Matt. xxv. 6.

† Rev. xiv. 7.

several particulars find a remarkable analogy between the preaching of God's people in the present time and the prophesying of Enoch before the days of Noah.

But the masses of the world are again rejecting God's more urgent appeals, and, as a natural consequence, His Spirit is ceasing to strive with them: infidelity and superstition are beginning to overshadow even the most favoured countries of Christendom. In our own land, how great an excitement was caused some twenty years ago by the publication of "Essays and Reviews": but that book, though hailed with such delight by those who were unwilling to submit to the Divine revelation, has now been swept out of memory by the flood of more daring infidel literature which has since been continually issuing from the press. How few of our newspapers, reviews, and periodicals, have escaped the contagion! How great a multitude of propagating secularists does our country contain, from the bold blasphemer coarsely inveighing against the Word of God, and either denying His existence or charging Him with injustice, to the refined and subtle reasoner who would fain make the ineffable light of his Creator pale before the flickering lamp of human intellect! It is, however, needless to enlarge on so obvious a matter, or to waste time in proving the simultaneous spread of Ritualism and Popery, which is now sufficiently evident even to the most careless observer; while in regard to the prevalence of sorcery we shall have more to say anon.

Have we not, then, reason to infer both from these apostacies, and from the general resemblance of our days to the perilous times of the end as described by

Paul,* that Christendom, as the inevitable punishment of a general rejection of the Gospel, is being judicially blinded and irremediably hardened?

The seventh cause. Unlawful intercourse with the denizens of the air.

The seventh and most fearful characteristic of the days of Noah was the unlawful appearance among men of beings from another sphere. This, many would quickly reply, is certainly an event which has not yet startled our age, strange as our experiences may be: we have still something at least to wait for before the completion of that fatal circle of influences which ruined the old world. But a diligent comparison of Scripture with the things that are now taking place among us will give a very different impression, and induce a strong conviction that the advanced posts of this last terrible foe have already crossed our borders. For it is no longer possible to deny the supernatural character of the apostacy called Spiritualism, which is spreading through the world with unexampled rapidity, and which attracts its votaries, and retains them within its grasp, solely by continual exhibitions of the miraculous. It is vain to speak of that power as mere jugglery which has convinced some of the *élite* of the literary world, which has caught in its meshes many scientific men, who at first only troubled to investigate for the purpose of refutation. Nor indeed can anything be more dangerous than utter incredulity: for the wholly incredulous, if suddenly brought face to face with the supernatural, is of all men the most likely to yield entire submission to the priests of the new wonder. Better far is it to prayerfully inquire whether these things are possible, and if so, in what light the

* 2 Tim. iii. 1-9.

Bible teaches us to regard them. We shall thus be armed against all the wiles of the Devil.

But an exposition of the nature and history of Spiritualism of sufficient length to exhibit its apparent identity with the antediluvian sin is a serious matter, and must not be commenced at the end of a chapter.

SPIRITUALISM. PART I.

THE TESTIMONY OF THE BIBLE.

CHAPTER XI.

SPIRITUALISM. PART I.

THE TESTIMONY OF THE BIBLE.

The open interference of evil spirits with our world might be reasonably expected.

THE mere mention of the supernatural is often received with a smile of incredulous contempt. And there are not a few professing Christians who manifest great anxiety to limit the number and extent of past miracles, and to obscure the possibility of their recurrence in the present time, though they do not venture upon an absolute denial of God's power to suspend or change His own laws. But that Satan can work wonders they will never allow: nay, in many cases they even refuse him a personal existence.

Surely such a state of mind must proceed either from ignorance or unbelief. For does not Paul speak of the working of Satan as being with all power and signs and wonders wrought in support of a lie?* And the simple assertion of Scripture, that the air which envelops our earth swarms with rebellious spirits, ought at least to prepare us for their occasional manifestation and open interference. Undoubtedly God has forbidden them

* 2 Thess. ii. 9.

eitherto communicate directly with man or to influence him for evil. Yet, since they are disobedient, and are not at present restrained by force, it is reasonable to believe that they sometimes break the former commandment even as they are continually defying the latter. And this supposition is confirmed by Scripture: for we find numerous allusions to dealings between men and demons in the Old Testament, while in the New witchcraft is treated as one of the manifest works of the flesh.*

The Mosaic laws against witchcraft referred to no mere imposture, but to an actual connection with fallen spirits.

"Thou shalt not suffer a witch to live,"† was the injunction of the Lord by Moses. And that this law is not concerned with mere superstition or deception, but points to a wilful fellowship with the powers of evil, we may learn from the severity of the punishment. Yet many would persuade us that the numerous Biblical terms applied to the practisers of forbidden arts are merely intended to indicate different forms of imposture. One example will suffice to prove the folly of such an opinion.

In the twentieth chapter of Leviticus we find the following enactment;—"A man also or woman that hath a familiar spirit, or that is a wizard, shall surely be put to death: they shall stone them with stones: their blood shall be upon them."‡ How, then, could an Israelitish judge decide in the case of a person arraigned under this law? Would not the whole issue depend upon the proof that the accused really had an attendant spirit? And is not the law an express declaration, not merely of the possibility, but also of the actual occurrence of such connections?

* Gal. v. 20. † Exod. xxii. 18. ‡ Lev. xx. 27.

Indeed the Bible, as we have already seen, mentions many things which have no place in modern philosophies, and, among them, one which is of the utmost importance to our subject. For it plainly recognises spiritual existences behind the idols of Heathenism, and affirms that these existences are demons. An attempt has been made to disprove this statement on the ground that two Hebrew words, the one signifying "nothings" and the other "vanities," are used as appellations of the Pagan gods, and that by such terms their non-existence is necessarily implied. But the fallacy of this inference may be exposed by a glance at the same words in other connections,

Scripture never denies the actual existence of the Heathen gods.

"Woe to the shepherd of nothing that forsaketh the flock!"* exclaims Zechariah. And certainly he does not speak of a purely imaginary shepherd, but of a worthless one, who is not what he pretends to be. Similarly Job, when he calls his friends "physicians of nothing,"† does not mean to tell them that they are non-existent, but merely, as our version has expressed it, that they are "physicians of no value." The Jewish idea of the word as applied to Heathen deities may be seen in the Septuagint version of the ninety-sixth Psalm, where it is rendered by *δαιμόνια*. Hence the fifth verse is made to mean, "For all the gods of the nations are demons; but the Lord made the heavens."‡

Again; the singular of the word for "vanities" is *Abel*, the name which Eve gave to her second son. But she had no intention of thereby denying the reality of his being. Nor when the preacher cries, "Vanity of

* Zech. xi. 17. † Job xiii. 4.
‡ Psalm xcvi. 5.

vanities; all is vanity,"* can we understand him to be affirming the non-existence of the universe.

It is, therefore, evident that these terms when applied to the Heathen gods do not dispute the fact of their being, but the truth of their pretensions. Real powers they are, but only finite ones; and hence they have no just claim to the title of gods.

On the contrary, the Old Testament treats them as real potencies.

Scripture, then, contains nothing to disprove the existence of false gods, but, on the contrary, asserts and assumes it as a fact. For instance, when foretelling the death of the first-born of both man and beast, the Lord signified His intention of also punishing the gods of Egypt.† And, in reference to the same event, Moses subsequently wrote;—"For the Egyptians buried all their first-born, which the Lord had smitten among them: upon their gods also the Lord executed judgments."‡

Again; in the tenth chapter of Deuteronomy we have the expression, "For Jehovah your God is the God of gods and the Lord of lords."§ And numerous are the Scriptural assertions that Jehovah is highly exalted above all gods, to be feared above all gods, and so on.

If, then, He executed judgment upon the gods of Egypt, they must have been living beings: if He is contrasted with other gods, they must be real existences.

And plainly indicates that they are demons. The *seirim* and *shedim*.

Nor does the Old Testament omit to hint at the nature of these so-called deities, as the following verses will show.

"And they shall no more offer their sacrifices unto

* Eccles. i. 2.
† Exod. xii. 12.
‡ Numb. xxxiii. 4.
§ Deut. x. 17.

demons (Heb. *seirim*), after whom they have gone a whoring."*

"They sacrificed unto demons (Heb. *shedim*), not to God; to gods whom they knew not, to new gods that came newly up, whom your fathers feared not."†

"And he ordained him priests for the high places, and for the demons (Heb. *seirim*), and for the calves which he had made." ‡

"Yea, they sacrificed their sons and their daughters unto demons (Heb. *shedim*)." §

In the place of the word *seirim*—which originally signified goats, and was afterwards used of wood-demons or satyrs—the Septuagint has τοῖς ματαίοις, that is, "vanities": but in two passages of Isaiah it translates the same noun by δαιμόνια, "demons." ‖ And this latter rendering is authoritatively confirmed in the New Testament by the passage in the eighteenth chapter of the Apocalypse which is parallel to that in the thirteenth chapter of Isaiah. ¶ *Shedim*—literally "mighty ones," "lords"—is invariably interpreted in the Septuagint by δαιμόνια. Thus, of the two words, the first appears to have been applied either to the Heathen idols or to the spiritual powers behind them, the second only to the demons themselves.

The teaching of the New Testament is to the same effect. Examination of two remarkable passages.

The testimony of the Greek Scriptures is to the same effect as that of the Hebrew, and we cannot better illustrate this than by examining two statements in the First Epistle to the Corinthians. In the eighth chapter we read as follows;—"We know

* Lev. xvii. 7.
† Deut. xxxii. 17.
‡ 2 Chron. xi. 15.
§ Psalm cvi. 37.
‖ Isa. xiii. 21; xxxiv. 14
¶ Rev. xviii. 2.

that there is no idol in the world, and that there is none other God but One. For though there be beings called gods, whether in heaven or upon earth—as there actually (ὥσπερ) are gods many and lords many—yet to us there is one God the Father, of Whom are all things, and we for Him; and one Lord Jesus Christ, by Whom are all things, and we by Him."*

Now the word idol (εἴδωλον) signifies a creation of the fancy, an idea of the mind. Therefore, by the words, "there is no idol in the world," Paul means that there are no such beings as Jupiter, Mars, or Venus, exactly as they are represented in Heathen mythology: such are not to be found in the universe, but are merely the creatures of man's imagination. Yet, he goes on to say, the gods whom the Heathen worship do exist, and are, moreover, real potencies, though differing altogether in their attributes and characteristics from the ideals of men. But they are falsely called gods: they are not uncreated and self-existent beings: † their power, though often great, is finite and subordinate: and, however they may delude the Heathen, we at least know that there is only one God.

The second passage is in the tenth chapter. "What, then, am I to say? That a thing sacrificed to an idol is anything—that is, any real sacrifice—or that an idol is anything? Nay, but that the things which the Gentiles sacrifice, they sacrifice to demons, and not to God: and I do not wish you to have communion with demons. Ye cannot drink the cup of the Lord, and

* 1 Cor. viii. 4-6.

† Nor have they any right to the title in a secondary sense, as being the delegates of the Supreme, those to whom the word of God has come (John x. 35); for their action is against His word.

the cup of demons: ye cannot partake of the table of the Lord, and of the table of demons." *

This quotation involves the same doctrine. An idol, the creation of man's fancy, is nothing; but it is not possible that men could be moved to worship nothing: there is a real power behind. The Heathen think that they are sacrificing to Deity; but their offerings ascend to demons, and by their sacrificial feasts they establish a fellowship with unclean spirits similar to that which exists between Christ and His Church.

Conclusion of the argument from Scripture.

It is plain, therefore, that the disembodied spirits which haunt the air are the beings whom the Heathen worship, the inspirers of oracles and soothsayers, the originators of all idolatry, whether Pagan or Popish, the powers that are ever striving by divers means to subjugate the human race to their sway.

Hence we may obtain the important deduction that Paganism, from its most intellectual phase down to the lowest fetichism, is not the mere worship of stocks and stones, but the cultus, whether conscious or unconscious, whether direct or through various mediums, of rebellious spirits. Nor can the converse of the proposition be denied, that the cultus of any such spirits is pure Paganism.

The great aim of Satan is not the spread of absolute scepticism, but the subjugation of the world to demoniacal power.

Now all idolatrous worship is inseparably connected with magic and the exercise of supernatural power. For it is only by a continual display of such power, or at least by a fixed belief in it, that the human race can be held in the grievous bondage of demon-service. The instant a man loses

* 1 Cor. x. 19-21.

faith in the possibility of the supernatural, he becomes, in spite of any vague ideas of Divine rule, a virtual sceptic. In the opinion of many such a result would satisfy every desire of the Evil One: but the following considerations deter us from assenting to their conclusion.

Whenever Scripture lifts the veil, and allows us a momentary glimpse of the Kingdom of Darkness, we behold a community, malignant indeed, but perfect in order and government, and thirsting for the subjugation of the human race. For the empire of Satan cannot be completely organized till men be as obedient to demons as demons are to the rebel principalities and powers, and these last again to their great prince. And so, the denizens of the air are not merely stirring up an aimless revolt against God, but would fain annex the whole of our world to their own orderly dominion.

Therefore, although for the present Satan will allure men from God by any bait which pleases them, he, nevertheless, fosters absolute scepticism only as Jesuitical emissaries are said to encourage revolution and anarchy in order to break down the barriers which withstand the advance of their own system. His real plan must be sought in the various false religions, by comparing which the thoughtful student may detect many strange and unsuspected points of contact. Differences indeed they have, arising from peculiarities of race or disposition: they resemble the fragments of a marble block, some of which display more of one coloured vein, some of another: but if the pieces be fitted together again, line meets line, and the variegated pattern appears perfect. Originally they all issued from one centre—Babylon has been the golden cup to make every nation drunken *

* Jer. li. 7.

—and around one centre will they be reunited when the time for its revelation arrives.

The grand aim, then, of Satanic miracles is to bring men under the influence of demons. The Devil would by no means destroy, but rather increase, a belief in the supernatural; he would, however, point out Satan, and not Christ, as the head of thrones, dominions, principalities, and powers, and hasten the time when one shall sit as God in the temple of God, showing himself that he is God.* To this end is all the teaching of his signs and wonders directed, however carefully they may be disguised, and whether they be appearances of aerial forms, visions, oracles—which seldom afford real help, and often lure men on to destruction by the ambiguity of their response, sooth-sayings—sometimes strikingly verified, but never reliable, spirit-writing, voices of the unseen, magnetic healings, or any other exhibition of his power. Nor can we examine the many superstitions confirmed by these miracles without astonishment at the skill with which they are adapted to the purpose of enthralling mankind. For is not this the obvious intent of spirit-communications, auguries, omens, tokens, lucky and unlucky days and seasons, purifications, holy water, spells, potions, amulets, charms, fetiches, relics, images, pictures, crosses, crucifixes, and all the countless prescriptions of demoniacal systems?

There are two ways by which men can acquire superhuman power. The first by an unlawful excitation of their own dormant faculties.

Now the false signs are usually exhibited through human mediums selected by the demons, who perceive, it may be, some affinity to themselves in the objects of their choice. And it appears that there are two methods by which men can acquire

* 2 Thess. ii. 4.

unlawful power and knowledge, and gain admittance to a prohibited intercourse.

He who would follow the first—but comparatively few have hitherto been able—must "so bring his body under the control of his own soul that he can project his soul and spirit, and, while living on this earth, act as if he were a disembodied spirit." The man who attains to this power is called an adept; and, according to a late President of the British Theosophical Society, "can consciously see the minds of others. He can act by his soul-force on external spirits. He can accelerate the growth of plants and quench fire; and, like Daniel, subdue ferocious wild beasts. He can send his soul to a distance, and there not only read the thoughts of others, but speak to and touch these distant objects; and not only so, but he can exhibit to his distant friends his spiritual body in the exact likeness of that of the flesh. Moreover, since the adept acts by the power of his spirit, he can, as a unitive force, create out of the surrounding multiplex atmosphere the likeness of any physical object, or he can command physical objects to come into his presence." *

The powers of such men are defined by the author of "Isis Unveiled" as "mediatorship, not mediumship." They may be exaggerated, but the existence, in all times of the world's history, of persons with abnormal faculties, initiates of the great mysteries, and depositaries of the secrets of antiquity, has been affirmed by a testimony far too universal and persistent to admit of denial.

The development of these faculties is, doubtless, possible but to few, and even in their case can only be

* Wild's "Spiritual Dynamics."

compassed by a long and severe course of training, the object of which is, to break down the body to a complete subjection, and to produce a perfect apathy in regard to all the pleasures, pains, and emotions, of this life, so that no disturbing elements may ruffle the calm of the aspirant's mind and hinder his progress. And two initial rules, laid down as indispensable to the discipline, are—abstinence from flesh and alcohol, and absolute chastity. In other words, he who would be an adept must conform to the teaching of those demons, predicted leaders of the last apostacy, who forbid to marry, and command to abstain from meats.

Thus, but doubtless not without the aid and instruction of evil spirits as well as of already perfected adepts, those latent powers are educed, which certainly exist in all men, but are as certainly forbidden by God to be used, or even sought out, in this life. For it is every man's duty, for the present, to preserve a clear and undisturbed consciousness of the world in which he is placed, of those material surroundings by dealing with which, in accordance with the Divine laws, it is appointed that he shall find the discipline needful to his sanctification. And for this reason our spiritual independence of time and space, and superhuman power of knowing doing and influencing, are suppressed by the nature of our bodies. Man is a spirit in prison, and so he must be content to abide, until God unlocks the door of his cell. But if he will have instant enjoyment by a premature excitation of potentialities which are reserved for future development, he can only do so by feloniously breaking through his dungeon bars, and thus shattering the harmony of his present nature.

The second, by a passive submission to the control of other spirits.

The second method is by a passive submission to the control of foreign intelligences, who, either by the direct action of their own power, or by guiding the application of certain means, will draw out the spirit of their subject and free it from the body. If this process be effected by demons,* the patient is termed a medium; but he must be a person whose spirit can be easily detached from the body, either because the latter is weak and diseased, or from causes which are not obvious. In such a manner he is brought into intelligent communication with spirits of the Air, and can receive any knowledge which they possess, or any false impressions which they may choose to impart. By practice the facility of this intercourse becomes much greater; and as the fellowship progresses, and men become more enamoured of their aerial visitants, the demons seem permitted to do various wonders at their request, and, finally, to reveal themselves to sight, hearing, and touch. Since, however, the spirits of some persons seem by their very nature to possess powers akin to those of the trained adept, it is at times difficult to decide in which way such phenomena are produced.

As we before remarked, the escape of the medium's spirit may be effected by the unassisted action of the demons. But it is often necessary to supplement that action by various aids—such as the *Sukra* and *Manti* of the Hindu Soma-mystery; or a cup of poisonous drugs similar to that which enabled the Chaldean initiate to behold the glittering form of the great

* For it may be done by a spirit still in the flesh, that is, by a magnetizer or mesmerist, in which case the patient is a mesmeric sensitive.

goddess passing by at the top of the cave; or a mephitic vapour, like that of the Delphic oracle; or the whirling dance of the dervish; or the long fasting and watching of the Ojibbeway Indian; or the gazing fixedly upon a metal plate or crystal held in the hand; or that fascinating power of a fellow-creature which in modern times is called mesmerism.

By such and other means the activity of the outward senses is diminished or altogether checked, and the consciousness passes into another sphere, where the spirit gazes upon wondrous visions; is able to hold intercourse with supernatural beings, to reveal secrets, and in some degree to foretell; can travel in a moment to any part of the world, and accurately describe places, houses, and the condition and actions of those who are living in them; has the power of seeing the internal mechanism of its own body or those of others; and will give a diagnosis of disease and prescribe for it. Indeed the spirit seems to leave the body just as at death—save that some silver cord is not yet snapped—and often, as in the case of trance-mediums, another spirit enters it, and speaks with a different voice and with different knowledge.

All spirits which hold intercourse with men in either of these two ways are evil spirits, from whose influence, if a communication be once opened, it is difficult to escape.

But since all such proceedings as these are a transgression of the limits of humanity as laid down by the Creator, it follows that all supernatural beings who sanction them and hold intercourse with the transgressor must be spirits of evil. And the unlawful confusion brings its own immediate punishment, in addition to the fearful judgment to come. For our body appears to be not only a prison, but also a fortress, and is, not improbably, devised for the very purpose of sheltering us in some degree from the corrupting influence of demons. In its normal condition it effectually repels their more open and violent assaults: but if we once suffer the fence to be broken down, we are no longer able to restore it, and are henceforth exposed to the attacks of malignant enemies.

It is but seldom that a person can be mesmerised for the first time without his own consent; and when such cases do occur they are probably to be referred to some special weakness, which may not infrequently be traced to a special sin. But if submission be once yielded, it is hard to withdraw it: and every fresh exercise of the power upon the same patient increases its influence.

So, in the case of fellowship with demons, there are but few who can become mediums without perseverance: but when a communication has been once established, the spirits are loth to relinquish it, and are wont to persecute those who, having become conscious of their sin, are determined by the grace of God to transgress no more.

Examination of Old Testament words applied to sorcerers.

We will now proceed to examine the Scriptural terms used to describe those who practise supernatural arts, giving in each case the Hebrew word with an attempted explanation.

Chartummim (חַרְטֻמִּים). "The sacred scribes."* This is a name given to the magicians of Egypt in the times of Joseph and Moses,† and also to those of Babylon in the days of Daniel. The word seems to be connected with the Hebrew *cheret* (חֶרֶט), a style or pen, and to signify those members of the priestly caste, who,

* Gen. xli. 8. † Exod. vii. 11.

although they also practised other kinds of magic, were mainly concerned with writing. Perhaps they were identical with the writing mediums of our days, who, according to the author of "Glimpses of a Brighter Land," are divided into five classes as follows. Those whose passive hand is moved by the demon without any mental volition on their own part: those into whose mind each word is separately insinuated instantaneously with its automatic inscription on the paper: those who write from the dictation of spirit-voices: those who copy words and sentences which they are made to see written upon the air, or upon some suitable object, in letters of light: and, lastly, those in whose presence spirit-hands, sometimes visible, sometimes invisible, will take up the pen and write the communication.

Chakhamim (חֲכָמִים). "Wise men."* But since this word is joined to *chartummim*, and since it appears that the *chakhamim* turned their rods into serpents, it follows that they were so called, not as mere philosophers or men of experience, but as having intercourse with supernatural beings, by whose assistance they displayed a greater than human wisdom, and could exhibit miraculous power. We may compare our own term "wizard," which originally meant a wise man, or sage.

In the eighteenth chapter of Deuteronomy there is a remarkable passage which in the English version reads as follows;—"There shall not be found among you any one that maketh his son or his daughter to pass through the fire, or that useth divination, or an observer of times, or an enchanter, or a witch, or a charmer, or a consulter with familiar spirits, or a wizard, or a necromancer.

* Exod. vii. 11.

For all that do these things are an abomination unto the Lord."*

This list of abominations begins with him "that maketh his son or his daughter to pass through the fire," a phrase which must not be understood of the burning of children as a sacrifice to Moloch, but of a sort of purification by fire, or fire-baptism, by which they were consecrated to the god, and supposed to be freed from the fear of a violent death.† This, as being a kind of charm or spell, is of course classed among sorceries. We will now examine the remaining terms in the order in which they stand.

Qosem (קֹסֵם). A diviner, one who discovers the hidden things of past present or future time by supernatural means. This appears to be a comprehensive term, being used of a diviner by omens and tokens or by direct spirit-communication.

Meonen (מְעוֹנֵן) is derived by some from a root which would supply a choice of significations: for the word might either mean a practiser of hidden arts, or a diviner by clouds. But a connection with *ayin* (עַיִן), the eye, is much more probable; and we may then deduce the meaning of a fascinator with the eyes, or, in modern

* Deut. xviii. 10-12.

† That this practice is still kept up in many parts of Christendom by the midsummer fires of St. John's Eve is a fact too well known to need illustration. We may, however, mention that a copy of the *Hereford Times* is now before us, containing a report of a lecture on "Home Heathenism," delivered at Wolverhampton by Mr. Gibson, a Wesleyan minister, in which the following statement occurs. "They had heard of the fire-worshippers of Persia, little thinking, perhaps, that they had fire-worshippers within a distance of sixty or seventy miles. At Midsummer, on many of the hills of Herefordshire, fires were burning while the peasantry danced around them, and the ceremony was not completed until some of the young people had passed through the fire."

language, a mesmerist, who throwing another into a magnetic sleep obtains oracular sayings from him. Many, however, prefer the signification of an "observer," that is, one who makes minute inspection of the entrails so as to deduce the omens, in contradistinction to the augur who divined by tokens requiring the use of the ear as well as that of the eye.

Menachesh (מְנַחֵשׁ). This word is connected with *nachash* (נָחָשׁ), a serpent, and is usually explained to mean a hisser or whisperer, and then a mutterer of enchantments. But the use of the verb of which it is the Piel participle seems to point in a different direction. In the thirteenth chapter of Genesis, Laban entreats Jacob to stay with him: "for," says he, "I divine—or, more literally, perceive by observation—that the Lord hath blessed me for thy sake."* And again; when to the pleading of Ben-hadad's servants Ahab replied, "Is he yet alive?† He is my brother," we are told that the men "divined," "took an omen," from what he had said. Hence the verb seems to have been used primarily of drawing an inference from rapid observation, and then of divining. From the first meaning comes *nachash*, a serpent, on account of its quick intelligence: from the second *menachesh*, an augur, one who divines by observing signs and tokens, such as the singing and flight of birds, aerial phenomena, and other sights and sounds.

Mekhashsheph (מְכַשֵּׁף). The root of this word signifies "to pray," but only to false gods or demons. Hence it is, perhaps, applied to those who use incantations or magical formulæ.

Chobher chebher (חֹבֵר חָבֶר). Literally, a binder of a band or spell. That is, either a fabricator of material

* Gen. xxx. 27. † 1 Kings xx. 32, 33.

charms and amulets; or, much more probably, one who by incantations and spells brings demons into association with himself, so as to obtain aid or information from them. It is a common practice to open a modern *seance* by chanting or singing hymns to invoke the presence of spirits.

Shoel obh (שׁאֵל אוֹב). A consulter of demons. That is, one who has established such a fellowship that he can communicate with them directly, and neither needs to do so mediately by means of signs or omens, nor even requires the aid of spells to draw them to himself.

An *obh* is a soothsaying demon: but by an earlier use the word is also applied to the person connected with such a demon. Originally it signified a skin bottle, and its transition from this first meaning to its second may be clearly detected in the following exclamation of Elihu;—"For I am full of matter, the spirit within me constraineth me. Behold, my belly is as wine which hath no vent; it is ready to burst like new bottles."* The word appears, then, to have been used of those into whom an unclean spirit had entered, because demons, when about to deliver oracular responses, caused the bodies of the possessed to grow tumid and inflated. We may, perhaps, compare Virgil's description of the soothsaying Sybil:† for he tells us that her breast began to swell with frenzy, and her stature appeared to increase, as the spirit of the god drew nearer. According to some, however, the medium was called an *obh* merely as being the vessel or sheath of the spirit: but in either case the term was afterwards applied to the demon itself.

* Job xxxii. 18, 19. † *Æn*. vi. 48-51.

That the spirit actually dwells within the person who divines by it, we may see from a previously quoted passage of Leviticus, the literal rendering of which is, "A man or a woman when a demon is in them," etc.* And in strict accordance with this is the account of the Philippian damsel who had a Pythonic spirit.† For Paul compelled the spirit to come out of her, and she instantly lost all her supernatural power.

From the stories of mediæval witches, and from what we hear of modern mediums, it seems likely that a connection with an *obh* is frequently, if not always, the result of a compact, whereby the spirit in return for its services enjoys the use of the medium's body. Indeed there is reason to believe that a medium differs from a demoniac, in the ordinary sense of the term, merely because in the one case a covenant exists between the demon and the possessed; whereas the frightful duality and confusion in the other arise from the refusal of the human spirit to yield a passive submission and acquiesce in a league with the intruder.

And let us not suppose that the age of demoniacs is past: the lapse of a few centuries has not reconciled demons to the disembodied state, they are still as eager as ever to clothe themselves with bodies. In the course of an interesting conversation which the writer had with the late Dr. Forbes Winslow, the latter expressed his conviction that a large proportion of the patients in our lunatic asylums are cases of possession, and not of madness. He distinguished the demoniac by a strange duality, and by the fact that, when temporarily released

* Lev. xx. 27.

† The reason for this deviation from our version will be found in a note towards the close of the chapter.

from the oppression of the demon, he is often able to describe the force which seizes upon his limbs, and compels him to acts or words of shame against his will.

Yidoni (יִדְּעֹנִי). A knowing one: that is, a person who is able to supply required information by means of the spirits with which he is associated.

Doresh el hammethim (דֹּרֵשׁ אֶל הַמֵּתִים). A seeker unto the dead, a necromancer, one who consults the dead for advice or information. The familiar was supposed to summon the spirit required, just as in modern Spiritualism; but, as we shall presently see, in many cases at least, and possibly in all, it is probable that the *obh* itself personated the dead.

Such, then, are the abominations mentioned in the eighteenth chapter of Deuteronomy; but there are yet other terms in Scripture applied to the practisers of similar or kindred arts.

Ittim (אִטִּים). This word occurs in Isaiah *: it seems to mean whisperers or mutterers, that is, those who repeat spells or charms.

In Isaiah's description of the downfall of Babylon, the city so famed for its astrologers, we find mention of *Hobhre Shamayim* (הֹבְרֵי שָׁמַיִם),† that is, dividers of the heavens, astrologers who divide the heavens into houses for the convenience of their prognostications.

The same persons are then described as *Chozim bakkokhabhim* (חֹזִים בַּכּוֹכָבִים), star-gazers, those who study the stars for the purpose of taking horoscopes.

Lastly; they are said to be *Modiim lechodashim* (מוֹדִיעִים לֶחֳדָשִׁים), deliverers of monthly predictions from their observations.

* Isa. xix. 3. † Isa. xlvii. 13.

In Daniel we have two other terms applied to those who were conversant with forbidden arts.

Ashshaph (אַשָּׁף).* A sorcerer. Properly a practiser of hidden arts: for the word is connected with *ashpah* (אַשְׁפָּה), a quiver, that in which arrows are hidden.

Gazrin (גָּזְרִין).† Deciders, determiners, practisers of the art of casting nativities. Used of astrologers who, from a knowledge of the hour of birth, determined the fate of men by the position of the stars, and by various arts of computation and divining.

Remarks on words expressive of sorcery in the New Testament.

In the New Testament the following names, all of which appear to be comprehensive and general, are applied to those who deal with the powers of darkness.

Μάγοι. Originally the Magi were a Persian religious caste; but their influence was subsequently extended to many countries. They acted as priests, prescribed sacrifices, were soothsayers, and interpreted dreams and omens. Origen‡ affirms that they were in communication with evil spirits, and could consequently do whatever lay within the power of their invisible allies. Certainly —if we may trust the statements of early Christian writers—they were well acquainted with mesmerism and every practice of modern Spiritualism.

Φαρμακεύς. One who uses drugs, whether for the purpose of poisoning, or for magic potions or spells—significations which are carefully distinguished by Plato in his *De Legibus*. In the *Nubes* of Aristophanes, Strepsiades suggests the hiring of a Thessalian witch (φαρμακίς) to draw the moon down; and the verb φαρμακεύειν is used by Herodotus in reference to the

* Dan. i. 20. † Dan. ii. 27.
‡ *Contra Celsum*, I. 60.

sacrifice of white horses whereby the Magi sought to charm the Strymon. Again; *φαρμακεία* is employed in the Septuagint to express those arts by which the magicians of Egypt imitated the miracles of Moses. These examples are sufficient to show that the word soon became a general term for a sorcerer; and, in tracing its meaning, we must not forget that drugs were often administered by the ancients for the purpose of producing an effect similar to that of mesmerism.

Twice in the New Testament sorcery (*φαρμακεία*) and idolatry are coupled together: * and in commenting upon the first passage Lightfoot well remarks that idolatry signifies the open recognition of false gods, and sorcery the secret tampering with the powers of evil.

οἱ τὰ περίεργα πράξαντες.† Those who had practised curious—that is, magical—arts. Perhaps, among other things, they trafficked in the celebrated amulets called Ephesian letters, which were said to be copies of the mystic words inscribed on the image of Artemis, and to have the property of preserving their wearers from all harm. The books which they destroyed may have contained astrological computations, the "Babylonios numeros" of Horace.

The practices of sorcery may be divided into three classes.

From this list of terms it will be observed that demoniacal arts fall readily into three classes. The first comprises all kinds of divination by omens, tokens, and forbidden sciences; the second the uses of spells and incantations as a means of accomplishing what is desired: and the third every method of direct and intelligent communication and co-operation with demons.

With regard to the first class, the signs and omens

* Gal. v. 20; Rev. xxi. 8. † Acts xix. 19.

were doubtless arranged by demons, who, after inducing a belief in their reliability by presenting them before the occurrence of certain events, could thenceforth easily act upon human minds, and, by simple appearances, either deter men from their purpose, or urge them on to enormities of evil.

As to forbidden sciences, since it is probable that everything in nature affects us, there may be a foundation of truth in them—indeed Scripture seems to hint that there is in the case of astrology. But such lore is for the present positively interdicted by God: nor is it difficult to discover reasons for His prohibition. For the mind of man is altogether unable to grasp and handle knowledge so profound and so complicated: with his present powers he would waste a whole life, and gain nothing but a miserably imperfect and altogether unreliable acquaintance with the mysterious law. Nor in his fallen condition could he be trusted with such tremendous secrets, even if he could comprehend them. His pride and independence would swell, nothing would be withheld from him, and his wickedness would devise crimes which can now scarcely find place even in his fancy.

The spells and incantations may either be mere arrangements of the demons, who, by bringing about the desired effect when they could, have established a faith in them: or, perhaps, they are in some cases grounded upon a real potency in the means employed, which has thus been unlawfully disclosed by rebellious spirits.

Direct communication with demons, whether by writing, clairvoyance, clairaudience, or in other ways, is now becoming universally prevalent. It is sustained by what is called mediumistic power, a faculty which, as we have before remarked, some seem to develop instinctively, but which in many cases can only be obtained by a sedulous and persevering use of the means prescribed.*

Historical notices of Spiritualism in the Bible. The Teraphim.

Having thus examined the Scriptural terms applied to dealers with demons, let us now glance at the historical facts illustrative of the subject. Upon the antediluvian sin we have already commented, and observed that its repetition in postdiluvian times seems to have originated all Heathen systems and mythology. We will, therefore, now proceed to the next indication of Demonism, which appears in the mention of teraphim.

The derivation of this word has caused much trouble: but the conjecture of R. S. Poole, in Smith's "Dictionary of the Bible," is worth consideration, and brings the teraphim into very close connection with Spiritualism. Their use appears to have commenced in Chaldea; but the affinity between that country and ancient Egypt in language as well as religion is well known, and hence Mr. Poole traces the name to an Egyptian root, and explains it as follows:—

"The Egyptian word *ter* signifies 'a shape, type, transformation,' and has for its determinative a mummy:

* In a case which came under the observation of the writer, it was only after a perseverance of three months that the aspirant to demon-intercourse compassed his desire. But it was not long before he began to perceive the diabolical nature of the fellowship into which he had entered, and resolved to abjure it. That which had been difficult to acquire was, however, far more difficult to renounce; and for some considerable time he was so incessantly tormented by the spirits, to whose influence he had yielded himself, that he well nigh lost his life, or at least his reason.

it is used in the Ritual, where the various transformations of the deceased in Hades are described. The small mummy-shaped figure, *Shebtee*, usually made of baked clay covered with a blue vitreous varnish, representing the Egyptian as deceased, is of a nature connecting it with magic, since it was made with the idea that it secured benefits in Hades; and it is connected with the word *ter*, for it represents a mummy, the determinative of that word, and was considered to be of use in the state in which the deceased passed through transformations, *teru*. The difficulty which forbids our doing more than conjecture a relation between *ter* and teraphim is the want in the former of the third radical of the latter; and in our present state of ignorance respecting the ancient Egyptian and the primitive language of Chaldea in their *verbal* relations to the Semitic family it is impossible to say whether it is likely to be explained. The possible connection with the Egyptian religious magic is, however, not to be slighted, especially as it is not improbable that the household idolatry of the Hebrews was ancestral worship, and the *Shebtee* was the image of a deceased man or woman, as a mummy, and therefore as an Osiris, bearing the insignia of that divinity, and so in a manner as a deified dead person, although we do not know that it was used in the ancestral worship of the Egyptians."

If there be any truth in this idea, the use of teraphim was precisely analogous to the consultation of the dead by modern Spiritualists. And, whatever be the derivation of the word, the fact at least remains, that the images signified by it were kept for the unlawful purpose of divination. But this fact is sometimes obscured in our version by the substitution of "idols," or "idolatry," for "teraphim." The well-known words of Samuel to Saul should be rendered ;—" For rebellion is as the sin of divination, and stubbornness is as idolatry and teraphim."* And Zechariah should be made to say ;—" For the teraphim have spoken vanity, and the diviners have seen a lie, and have told false dreams."†

But those who used teraphim, though they broke the law of Jehovah by seeking unto the dead and establishing a fellowship with demons, do not seem to have openly denied Him. This we may see by the cases of Laban, Michal the wife of David, and the heretical Israelites of later times. And herein we may discover another point of resemblance between the less advanced of modern Spiritualists and the ancient diviners by teraphim.

The cup which was found in Benjamin's sack.

We have already noticed the appearance of dream-interpreting mediums in Joseph's time. An incident of the same period discloses the prevalence of another supernatural art. For the steward, when he accused Joseph's brethren of stealing his master's cup, exclaimed ;—" Is not this it in which my lord drinketh, and whereby indeed he divineth ? "‡ Now we are not for a moment to suppose that Joseph followed the magical practices of Egypt: the words were merely devised by the steward, in reference to a universal custom of the country, to enhance the value of the cup. For when interpreting the dreams of the chief butler and chief baker, as well as when summoned into the presence of Pharaoh, Joseph disclaimed all intercourse with demons, and declared that the revelation he was about

* 1 Sam. xv. 23. † Zech. x. 2. ‡ Gen. xliv. 5.

to make had come directly from God. When, therefore, he afterwards says to his brethren, "Wot ye not that such a man as I can certainly divine?"* we must understand him to be disguising himself by an affectation of the customs of Egypt. He is not, however, referring to the previous words of the steward: for he could not have divined by a cup which was not at the time in his possession.

The practice to which the steward alluded was probably the same as that which is still in vogue among Egyptian magicians, and consists in pouring something into a cup, by gazing fixedly at which a person is mesmerised and enabled to see in the fluid whatever may be desired. Lane, in his "Modern Egyptians," gives a remarkable and well-known account of a sheikh who divined in this way: but with the immaterial difference that the boy who was to be mesmerised looked into a black liquid poured upon his hand.

Conflict of the Egyptian magicians with Moses.

When Moses began to exhibit the marvels of God before Pharaoh, the Egyptian mediums† were immediately summoned, as being themselves also accustomed to work wonders. And up to a certain point they did succeed in imitating the Hebrew prophet, though they were utterly unable to counteract his miracles and give relief to their countrymen. They caused their rods to become serpents: they turned water into blood: they brought frogs out of the river Nile: but there the power of their lord ceased, for, great as it was, it was finite. All their efforts to imitate the next miracle were in vain: they were compelled to fall back, and confess that they could no longer contend with the Almighty.

* Gen. xliv. 15.

† Or, adepts.

Reason of the frequent denunciation of sorcery in the law. The mediums destroyed by Saul.

We may now understand the frequent reference in the law of Sinai to practisers of all kinds of sorcery. It was necessary both to destroy the influence of the Egyptian magicians, and to prepare the people of God for the, perhaps, worse dangers which awaited them in the Land of Promise. For Canaan contained many descendants of the Nephilim,* and consequently teemed with mediums, through whose influence, since the law was not put in force against them, the Israelites were seduced to idolatry and involved in bitter troubles.

Saul, probably at the instigation of Samuel, destroyed these evil doers with such vigour that the few who survived could only practise their wicked arts in secret, and a long time elapsed before sorcerers and false prophets recovered their power in Judah.

Yet, after a while, the destroyer himself appealed for help to one who had escaped the edge of his sword, and verified the prophet's warning that rebellion is as the sin of divination, and that stubborn self-will is as idolatry and teraphim.† For when Samuel uttered those words, Saul had already been guilty of rebellion and stubbornness: he was, therefore, also capable of the crimes of divination, idolatry, and the consultation of teraphim, heinous as they at the time appeared to him. Let our heart but be estranged from God, and there is no sin so great, so outrageous, as to be impossible to us. The close of Saul's history is a mournful proof of this, and shows how easy a prey man becomes to the Powers of Evil when the multitude of his provocations has at length caused the Spirit of the Most

* Numb. xiii. 33. † 1 Sam. xv. 23.

High to depart from him, and he stands alone amid the ruins of his broken purposes, while the gathering of his fears portends a pitiless storm upon his unsheltered head.

The history of Saul and the witch of En-dor.

The dark shadow of approaching death was beginning to steal over the wayward king: he saw the glittering helms and spears of the invading army, and his heart trembled with gloomy forebodings.* The Spirit of the Lord no longer came upon him as in the day when he sent forth the bloody tokens, and indignantly summoned all Israel to march with him to Jabesh-Gilead.† Nay, the phantoms of past sins, and, perchance, the gory forms of the slaughtered priests,‡ floated continually before his eyes, and took away all rest, all stedfastness of purpose. The prophet who had so long borne with him, so often entreated for him, was dead. He essayed to pray, but found that if any regard iniquity in his heart the Lord will not hear him. For Jehovah, Who had pleaded with him so patiently, forgiven him so many times, had at last turned away, and would answer him no more, neither by dreams, nor by Urim, nor by prophets. The gates of salvation, which had remained open all the day in vain, were suddenly closed at nightfall, and there was neither form seen nor voice heard in response to his now despairing cry.

Then he yielded to an evil thought: he remembered the dealers with familiar spirits and the wizards whom, in obedience to the law, he had destroyed from the land: he knew that they were reputed able to call up the dead; and, perhaps, stifling his conscience with the plea that it was a prophet of the Lord with whom he

* 1 Sam. xxviii. † 1 Sam. xi. 7. ‡ 1 Sam. xxii. 18.

would converse, determined, since God would not hear him, to appeal to the Powers of Darkness.

Had he but said with Job, "Though He slay me, yet will I trust in Him,"* he might have found mercy even at the last. But faith is rarely given at the close of life to those who have spurned repeated offers of grace: experience teaches the general rule that, as a man lives, so does he die; and thus it was with Saul. Turning to his companions he asked if they knew of any surviving dealer with demons. The question must have filled them with astonishment: for could Saul, who had so mercilessly destroyed the mediums in the name of the Lord, be about to stultify himself by inquiring of them! But the king was evidently in earnest, and sore troubled: they, therefore, told him of a witch † who was at that time concealed in one of the caves of En-dor, not more than seven or eight miles from the camp. En-dor! There seemed to be a good omen in the name: for was it not there that two great enemies of Israel, Jabin and Sisera, perished, and became as dung for the earth? ‡

Saul waited for the shelter of night, and then, with two companions, went forth to fill up the measure of his iniquities. He arrived at the north-eastern slope of the Little Hermon, and the dexterity with which his attendants found out the witch's cave in the darkness, and amid the numerous perforations of the mountain, seems to prove their frequent habit of resorting to it. Passing into the recess of the cavern, dimly lighted, perhaps, by a fire of wood, the king accosted the

* Job xiii. 15.

† Or, if we render the Hebrew literally, "a woman who was mistress of a demon."

‡ Psalm lxxxiii. 9, 10.

woman with words which show the absolute identity of her craft with that of the modern medium. "I pray thee," he said, "divine unto me by the familiar spirit, and bring me him up whom I shall name unto thee." The witch was at first suspicious: but Saul reassured her by a strange oath, and swore by the name of Jehovah that no harm should befall her for breaking the law of Jehovah. Thereupon she inquired with what spirit he would communicate, and being requested to call up Samuel commenced her preparations.

Now the *obh* was supposed to have the power of summoning the dead; but, since we cannot admit that this power extended to the spirits of the just, the familiar must, in many cases at least, have personated the spirit required. Any necessary information could, of course, have been procured with lightning speed from the demons who had watched the life of the person invoked.* And so the woman's familiar would doubtless have presented itself as Samuel, and, perhaps, have uttered soothing words to the king. But the usual procedure was cut short by a sudden interference, and the medium shrieked with terror as she perceived, probably through her familiar, that the inquirer was her

* This seems the most probable way of accounting for that accurate knowledge of the past which is often displayed by mediums: but how shall we explain their still more wonderful, though altogether unreliable, predictions of the future? Perhaps somewhat as follows. The dealings of God with man, and the different stages of human probation, are doubtless both systematic and consequential; and, therefore, evil spirits, acquainted, it may be, with laws hidden to us, and taught by an experience of six thousand years, would be likely to have a general prescience of coming events. But they are by no means able to penetrate the deep counsels of the Almighty, and hence their calculations must be often baffled by an unexpected fiat of His will. We may thus understand why their predictions are often strikingly verified, while at times they as signally fail.

great enemy king Saul, and, still worse, that all her powers were held in abeyance, and her Satanic accomplice paralysed, by the apparition of a being with whom she felt that she had neither part nor lot. For since Saul would seek unto the dead, God had in anger sent up the real Samuel as the bearer of a fearful message of doom.

We need follow the history no further: the dread utterance of Samuel, the despair of Saul, his return to the camp, and his miserable end on the next day, are matters with which we are not at present concerned. We have only to remark that the woman was evidently well known to the officers of Saul; that she was assisted by an attendant spirit; that she was confident in her power of producing a supernatural voice, as well as an apparition which she, at least, could see and describe; that she recognised Saul by supernatural information; and that she was terrified at the appearance of the real Samuel in the place of the counterfeit one whom she had expected. Lastly; we are expressly told that the crime of consulting a medium sealed the doom of the first king of Israel.*

Spiritualism in the history of Judah.

From this time there is no mention of mediums in the history of Judah until the days of Isaiah. Then the streams of wickedness were returning upon the land from the surrounding Heathen nations, and idolatry and sorcery were rapidly overspreading it. And accordingly the prophet exclaims;—"Thou hast forsaken Thy people, the House of Jacob, because they are replenished from the East, and are mesmerisers like the Philistines, and abound with the children of strangers."† It is clear from this

* 1 Chron. x. 13.

† Isa. ii. 6.

verse that Demonism was again beginning to prevail, and strong are the words of Isaiah against it, and especially against those practices which have now reappeared in modern Spiritualism.*

Upon the accession of Manasseh, the wicked son of Hezekiah, the revolt was openly headed by the king: for of him we are told that he did evil in the sight of the Lord after the abominations of the Heathen, whom the Lord cast out before the children of Israel.† It will be instructive to mark the details of that evil as showing the connection of Spiritualism with Idolatry, and, therefore, with Romanism, which, owing to the discoveries of Layard, Rawlinson, and others, now stands clearly convicted of descent from the system of Babylon, and the Baal-worship of old. For the following is the explanation of the term "abominations of the Heathen";‡ "He built up again the high places which Hezekiah his father had destroyed; and he reared up altars for Baal, and made an Ashtaroth-symbol, as did Ahab king of Israel; and worshipped all the host of heaven, and served them. And he built altars in the house of the Lord, of which the Lord said, In Jerusalem will I put My name. And he built altars for all the host of heaven in the two courts of the house of the Lord. And he made his son pass through the fire, and divined by mesmerism and augury, and set in office one who had a familiar spirit and wizards: he wrought much wickedness in the sight of the Lord, to provoke Him to anger."

The consequence of these abominable practices was a fearful threatening of woe.‖ Jehovah would send a

* Isa. viii. 19; xix. 3; xxix. 4; xlvii. 12-14. † 2 Kings xxi. 2.
‡ 2 Kings xxi. 3-6. ‖ 2 Kings xxi. 12, 13.

judgment so terrible that both the ears of him who heard of it should tingle: He would level Jerusalem with the ground, even as He had destroyed Samaria: He would treat the Holy City as a man does a dish, when, after wiping away the moisture, he turns it over lest a single drop should remain.

The next king, Josiah, did indeed put away the abominations and remove the mediums from the land; but they soon returned, as we may see by the complaints and denunciations of Jeremiah. To the very last the infatuated nation trusted in them, and turned away from the servant of Jehovah when he cried;—"Hearken not ye to your prophets, nor to your diviners, nor to your dreamers, nor to your mesmerisers, nor to your enchanters, which speak unto you, saying, Ye shall not serve the king of Babylon: for they prophesy a lie unto you, to remove you far from your land; and that I should drive you out, and ye should perish." *

Thus the effects of Josiah's reformation were transient, and, therefore, the threatened judgment and overthrow of Jerusalem quickly followed. And this is the third instance which has presented itself to us of speedy destruction consequent on a more open and general intercourse with the rebel inhabitants of the air.

Traces of Spiritualism in the history of Israel.

In the kingdom of Israel, the spread of sorcery was, of course, a natural result of Baal-worship. The false prophets, as well as those who were active in the last days of the kingdom of Judah, were doubtless mediums inspired by the agents of Satan. And awful, yet instructive, is the scene in which a lying spirit receives permission to

* Jer. xxvii. 9, 10.

enter into the prophets of Baal, the mediums of the royal household, in order that by their influence the miserable Ahab may be led away to meet his death.*

A little later we have an unmistakable hint of the prevalence of mesmerism in Syria. For when Naaman heard the message of Elisha, he was indignant that the prophet did not appear, and angrily exclaimed;—"Behold, I thought, He will surely come out to me, and stand, and call on the name of the Lord his God, and move his hand up and down over the place, and recover the leper." † It will be observed that we have adopted the marginal rendering, which alone expresses the correct meaning of *nuph* in the Hiphil. For that verb signifies to wave up and down, and is the root of *tenuphah*, the wave offering.

Now Naaman well knew the mode of mesmeric healing as practised by the priests of Rimmon and the false prophets of his own land, and, therefore, expected Elisha to make passes over him in the same way. Hence we can understand the treatment he received. For had Elisha himself come forth and lifted his hand over the leprous spots, Naaman would doubtless have ascribed his recovery to the mesmeric influence of the prophet, who was, therefore, directed not to see him, but to send him to wash in the waters of Jordan.

"What peace, so long as the whoredoms of thy mother Jezebel and her witchcrafts are so many?" was the indignant reply of Jehu to Jehoram.‡ And the teachings of some modern Spiritualists seem likely to remind us of the close connection of the two crimes.

* 1 Kings xxii. 21-23.
† 2 Kings v. 11.
‡ 2 Kings ix. 22.

Of the references to mediums in the prophetical books we have already noticed so many that we will only further mention a remarkable promise by the mouth of Zechariah.

A prophecy of Zechariah.

"And it shall come to pass in that day, saith the Lord of hosts, that I will cut off the names of the idols out of the land, and they shall no more be remembered: and also I will cause the prophets and the unclean spirit to pass out of the land."* A consideration of this passage with its context makes it apparent that Spiritualism will be prevalent among the Jews when they return in unbelief to their own land: but that, upon the advent of their King, they will be for ever freed from that curse which was the cause of their former expulsion.

In the New Testament there are hints of the same sin, and the later inspired writers take the same view of it. We have already mentioned the Philippian damsel who had a Pythonic spirit, by which we are, probably, to understand that her familiar was a subordinate of the great power worshipped under the name of Apollo, the Sun-god, and the inspirer of the Delphic oracle.† But this inference

Spiritualism in the New Testament.

* Zech. xiii. 2.

† Such would certainly be the idea conveyed to the mind of a Greek or Roman by the significant adoption of this Pagan term. Python was originally the name of the great soothsaying serpent of Delphi, which was slain by Apollo. Hence the god took his title of Pythius, and became the inspirer of oracles and soothsayers. His priestess at Delphi was called Pythia or Pythonissa; and latterly the term Python was transferred to any soothsaying demon which gave responses in the name of Apollo.

In Acts xvi. 16, the reading Πύθωνα is preferable to Πύθωνος, and the literal rendering will be "a spirit a Python," that is, a Pythonic spirit.

Tertullian (*De Anim.* xxviii.) divides the demons who are connected with magic into three classes: (1) parabolic spirits

is entirely obscured in our version by the inaccurate substitution of "a spirit of divination" for "a Pythonic spirit": and, consequently, the hint that the being called Apollo really had to some extent the attributes assigned to him is veiled to English readers. Such should, however, be no longer the case: for the authoritative connection of Spiritualism with the ancient gods is of peculiar importance at a time when Apollo is reappearing as a mighty angelic existence in poems which claim to be demoniacally inspired.

We have also previously noticed Paul's inclusion of witchcraft among the manifest works of the flesh, and the conversion at Ephesus of those who had practised magical arts, and will only add that sorcerers are twice mentioned in the closing chapters of the Apocalypse. They are found in the catalogue of those who shall have their part in the lake that burneth with fire and brimstone,* and are warned that they shall never walk in the streets of the golden city.† The prophetical passage in the First Epistle to Timothy we designedly pass by for the present.

Thus the testimony of the Bible is everywhere consistent: nor could it be better expressed than in the emphatic words of Moses, that all practisers of demoniacal arts "are an abomination unto the Lord."‡

which throw men on the ground; (2) paredral spirits which keep ever at their side; and (3) Pythonic spirits which cast them into trances. If this be a true classification, the Philippian damsel must have been a clairvoyant or trance-medium.

* Rev. xxi. 8. † Rev. xxii. 15. ‡ Deut. xviii. 12.

SPIRITUALISM. PART II.

THE TESTIMONY OF HISTORY.

CHAPTER XII.

SPIRITUALISM. PART II.

THE TESTIMONY OF HISTORY.

Introduction. Repetitions of the antediluvian sin in postdiluvian times.

IN passing from the infallible utterances of inspired writers to the countless multitudes who, by floating their stored knowledge down the stream of time, have united to furnish us with records of the past, we must premise that we are far from attempting an exhaustive treatise. We shall merely adduce a few plain indications of the existence in ancient times of what is now called Spiritualism, and leave further investigation to the curious, whose task, if they are competent to examine the monuments of antiquity, will be sufficiently easy.

Nor do we wish to dwell upon the fearful culmination of sorcery, by which it is identified with the sin of the antediluvians. Such a matter is no subject for ordinary discussion. But, seeing that the danger is again threatening Christendom, it is well that the leaders of religious opinion should consider that which has been, that they may be stimulated to check with all the strength of their influence the first symptoms of its return.

Let, then, those whose duty it is ponder the statement of Herodotus in regard to the chamber on the summit of the tower of Belus, with its richly-adorned couch, its golden table, and its solitary inmate,*—let them, by the light of modern Spiritualism, consider whether the assertion of the Chaldean priests, that the god visited this chamber, may not have been something more than a mere myth or figure.† Let them weigh the fact that such things were said to take place at other temples also, as, for instance, at that of the Theban Jupiter, and at the Patarean oracle of Apollo. Let them read the strange history of Paulina, as narrated by Josephus,‡ and say if the priests of Isis must not have felt themselves supported by an ancient and universally recognised custom when they ventured to demand a chaste and noble Roman matron from her husband for the god Anubis. Let them reflect upon the story of Cassandra, and other similar tales of classical mythology, and upon the numerous claims to descent from the gods put forth by the heroes of Greece and Rome. To this let them add the many legends of the same kind which may be found in the ancient records of almost every nation, the case of the incubi and succubæ, the price reported to have been paid by mediæval witches for their supernatural power. And then, if with these hints of past time they compare the information which may be gathered from current Spiritualistic literature, they will not fail to find grave matter for thought.

But we hasten to examples of the more avowed practices of Spiritualism. Nor are they difficult to

* Herod. i. 181. † Herod. i. 182.
‡ Joseph. *Antiq*. xviii. 3, 4.

discover: for demons, Pythonesses, sybils, nymphs, augurs, and soothsaying men and women, are continually before us in the secular annals of early history.

Astrologers and oracles.

The astrologers of ancient nations, and above all those of the Chaldeans, are too well known to need more than a simple mention:* nor can the impartial student fail to recognise a superhuman foresight and wisdom in many answers of the famous oracles. This is especially true of those said to have been inspired by Apollo, whose ability to confer powers of divination is, as we have just seen, distinctly asserted in Scripture.† We will adduce one instance as a specimen, the celebrated history of Crœsus and the Delphic oracle, as related by Herodotus.‡ For, unless we absolutely refuse credence to the supernatural, there is no reason for disbelieving the story, and the splendid presents of Crœsus were to be seen at Delphi in the days of the historian.

A little more than five centuries and a half before

* Through the discoveries at Nineveh the whole subject of Chaldean Spiritualism has now been laid open to us; and, among many sources of information, some fragments of a vast work on magic, found by Mr. Layard in the royal library at Kouyunjik, are the most important. The treatise of which they form a part originally comprised not less than two hundred tablets, each of which was inscribed with from three to four hundred lines of writing. It is divided into three books, the first of which is entitled "The Wicked Spirits"; the second appears to be made up of formulæ and incantations for the cure of maladies; while the third is a collection of magical hymns to certain gods, to the chanting of which a mysterious power was attributed.

The identity of many of the doctrines in this work with those of modern Spiritualism is very striking.

† Acts xvi. 16.

‡ Herod. i. 46-51.

Christ, the king of Lydia, becoming alarmed at the spread of Persian power, was considering how to check the growth of the rival state. Naturally his mind turned to the oracles as the only sources of Divine guidance: but to which of them should he give the preference? For the world was filled with soothsaying shrines, all of which claimed to be inspired. He determined to make trial of those that were in highest repute, and to let the result decide his choice. Accordingly he sent out messengers in different directions; some to Abæ in Phocis; some to the speaking oaks and doves of Jupiter at Dodona; some to test the wondrous prophetic dreams which, after due purification, might be experienced at the tomb of the deified Amphiaraus; some to the dread cave of Trophonius, into which whosoever entered came forth pale and trembling with affright; some to Branchidæ in Milesia; some to the famous temple of Jupiter Ammon, which stood in solitary grandeur amid the desert wastes of Libya.

The famous test applied by Crœsus king of Lydia to the oracle at Delphi.

But we are at present concerned only with one of these embassies, that which was despatched to the great oracle of Apollo, and which was thus instructed. The messengers were to reckon a hundred days from the date of their departure, and were then to inquire of the god what Crœsus the son of Alyàttes, king of Lydia, was doing at that moment.

At the appointed time, after due preparation, they bound their heads with the mystic bay, and entered the precincts of the sanctuary. Then, as soon as the customary sacrifice had been offered and the lots drawn, they moved forward, gazing in wonder at the monuments and sculptures which lined the road, until they came to the steps of the noble shrine itself. But what followed, and the awe-inspiring circumstances of consultation, could not be better described than in the subjoined extract from the Arnold Prize Essay for 1859.

"And now the jubilant trumpets of the priests pealed out, with notes that rang round the valley, and up among the windings of the Hyampeian cliff. Awed into silence by the sound, he crossed the garlanded threshold: he sprinkled on his head the holy water from the fonts of gold, and entered the outer court. New statues, fresh fonts, craters, and goblets, the gifts of many an Eastern king, met his eye: walls emblazoned with dark sayings rose about him as he crossed towards the inner adytum. Then the music grew more loud: the interest deepened: his heart beat faster. With a sound as of many thunders, that penetrated to the crowd without, the subterranean door rolled back: the earth trembled: the laurels nodded: smoke and vapour broke commingled forth: and, railed below within a hollow of the rock, perchance he caught one glimpse of the marble effigies of Zeus and the dread Sisters; one gleam of sacred arms; for one moment saw a steaming chasm, a shaking tripod, above all, a Figure with fever on her cheek and foam upon her lips, who, fixing a wild eye upon space, tossed her arms aloft in the agony of her soul, and, with a shriek that never left his ear for days, chanted high and quick the dark utterances of the will of Heaven."

When the ambassadors of Crœsus approached the shrine, the Pythoness gave them no time to put their question, but immediately accosted them as follows;—

"I can count the sands, and know the measures of
ocean:
I understand the dumb, and hear him that speaketh
not.
On my sense there stole the savour of a strong-
shelled tortoise
Boiling in a cauldron with the flesh of a lamb:
Brass is the couch underneath it, and brass the
robe laid upon it."

They hastened to convey the strange response to Sardis, and the king, when he heard it, performed an act of adoration, and declared that the Delphic oracle was indeed worthy of confidence. For on the appointed day, wishing to do a most inconceivable thing, he had with his own hands cut to pieces a tortoise and a lamb, and boiled them together in a brazen cauldron covered with a lid of the same metal. Crœsus sent magnificent presents to Delphi, and was thenceforth completely under the influence of the oracle, which shortly afterwards, by an ambiguously worded response, lured him on to destruction.* O that those who are now giving heed to wandering spirits and teachings of demons would accept the warning afforded by his fate!

Egyptian Spiritualism.

Mesmerism was evidently practised in Egypt from the earliest times, as we may see by the pictures of priests making passes and patients under manipulation which are found among

* When he sent to consult the Pythoness in regard to his projected invasion of Persia, she gave the dubious response;—"Crœsus, if he crosses the Halys, will destroy a great empire." Naturally concluding that Persia was the empire indicated, Crœsus passed the boundary stream, was quickly defeated, and perceived too late that the oracle was being fulfilled in the destruction of his own power.

the temple-paintings. There are also many historical hints of the same fact, some of which have been already mentioned in the previous chapter. We may now add the strange history of Rhampsinitus, the predecessor of Cheops, as narrated by Herodotus.* That king is said to have descended alive into Hades, and, after playing at dice with Demeter, to have returned unhurt—a story which is, probably, to be explained as describing the experience of a mesmeric trance.

Indeed all the mysterious wisdom of Egypt appears to have been connected with forbidden arts, and how continually her priests were employed in practising them we may further infer from their diet, which was such as mesmerists and clairvoyants find necessary. For Clement of Alexandria tells us that they were not permitted to feed on flesh.†

Cures effected at the temples of Isis and Serapis.

The shrines of Isis and Serapis had a world-wide reputation for the magnetic cures performed in them, and for prescriptions which appear to have been dictated by clairvoyants precisely as they are in our days. And the frequently mentioned temple-sleep was undoubtedly a mesmeric trance, induced sometimes by making passes, sometimes by the fumes of a particular kind of incense accompanied by the music of the lyre.

Strabo ‡ mentions the temple of Serapis at Canopus as affording such startling instances of supernatural cures that the most famous men believed in them, and were willing to be entranced either for their own benefit or for that of others. Persons were appointed to keep a register of the cures effected, and also of the oracular answers which had proved true. But what struck the

* Herod. ii. 122. † Clem. *Strom.* vii. 6. ‡ Strab. xvii. 1.

geographer most of all was the vast number of pilgrims who kept coming to the shrine by the canal from Alexandria, and made the air resound with the noise of their flute-playing and dancing as they floated by.

Pilgrimages and processions of the Egyptians.

Herodotus* supposes that "pilgrimages, processions, and introductions (προσαγωγάς)," originated with the Egyptians. The technical meaning of the last of the three terms is uncertain: but it probably refers to the admission of pilgrims into a sanctuary where some sacred relic, or the statue itself of the deity, was exhibited by the hierophant.†

The historian goes on to mention five annual pilgrimages of the Egyptians to various shrines,‡ and gives a vivid account of the one to Bubastis, describing the long train of boats crowded with men and women, some of whom were piping and striking castanets, while the others sang and clapped their hands. The natives affirmed that about seven hundred thousand persons, exclusive of children, were usually present at this festival.

Another place of great resort was the temple of Isis at Busiris; § where the pilgrims, both male and female, were wont, after offering a strange sacrifice, to beat themselves before the shrine. The marvellous popularity of this goddess is partly explained by the following extract from Diodorus Siculus.

* Herod. ii. 58.

† It would not be difficult to apply these terms to modern pilgrimages. The first would express the journey to the locality of a shrine; the second, the processional march from the railway station to the sacred place; and the third, the admission into the church or grotto.

‡ Herod. ii. 59, 60.

§ Herod. ii. 61.

Account of the healing power and apparition of Isis, by Diodorus Siculus.

"Now the Egyptians say that Isis was the discoverer of many potions for the preservation of health, and is very skilful in the art of medicine; and that, having by this means attained to immortality, her greatest pleasure is to heal mortals. For to those who beg her help she dictates remedies during sleep, openly manifesting both her own apparition and her beneficence toward her suppliants. And they add that they offer in proof of this no fables, such as the Greeks tell, but self-evident facts. For almost the whole world supports their testimony by the zeal with which men worship Isis because of her visible appearance when she is performing cures. For she stands over the sick in their sleep, and prescribes remedies for their diseases: and those who obey her directions are most unaccountably healed. Numbers are thus cured after they have, through the malignancy of their disease, been given up by physicians; and many persons who have been absolutely deprived of sight, or disabled in any other part of the body, are restored to their previous soundness as soon as they have recourse to this goddess." *

We see, then, that the dictation of prescriptions by clairvoyants is not peculiar to the modern phase of Spiritualism. And it is difficult to read of the apparition of Isis and the pilgrimages to her shrines without being reminded of what is now said and done in connection with the "Holy Mountain" of La Salette, Lourdes, and other places.

The influence of Isis afterwards spread to Rome, where, in the depraved times of the early emperors, the goddess became the favourite deity. But the

* Diod. Sic. i. 25.

abominable impurity which characterised her worship provoked several attempts to abolish it, and caused repeated destructions of her temples: indeed, upon one occasion, Tiberius went so far as to crucify the priests and throw the statues of the goddess into the river. All, however, was in vain: Isis retained her power in the great city until, as time went on, it was deemed advisable to change her name and worship her, with some modifications, under the title of the Virgin Mary.

Vespasian and the temple of Serapis at Alexandria.

We will add but one more instance of Spiritualism in Egypt, the well-known story of Vespasian's visit to the temple of Serapis in Alexandria. It is recorded in the histories of Tacitus and Suetonius, and affords an early example of what is now said to be of frequent occurrence, the apparition of a living person at a great distance from the place of his bodily presence.

Tacitus * relates that two men, the one blind and the other suffering from a diseased hand, were directed by the oracle of Serapis to apply to Vespasian, who was then in Alexandria. They were promised that, if the Roman consul would consent to anoint the eyes of the one with saliva, and to step upon the hand of the other, both of them should be restored. Vespasian at first hesitated to comply with their strange requests: but at length, yielding to the importunity of the sufferers and the persuasion of his courtiers, he did what was required in the presence of a great multitude. Immediately the blind man recovered his sight, and the diseased hand was healed.

After remarking that these cures were well attested by eye-witnesses, who could have no object in support-

* Tacit., *Hist.* iv. 81.

ing a lie, seeing that the family of Vespasian was then extinct, Tacitus proceeds as follows * ;—

"These miracles strongly inclined Vespasian to visit the shrine, and consult the god in regard to the fortunes of the empire. Accordingly he ordered the temple to be cleared, and entered it alone. Then, while he was worshipping the deity, he saw standing behind him one of the nobles of Egypt named Basilides, whom he knew to be at that moment detained by sickness at a distance of some days' journey from Alexandria. He inquired of the priests whether Basilides had entered the temple that day: he asked those whom he met if the man had been seen in the city. Lastly; by despatching some horsemen, he ascertained that, at the moment when he had seen the apparition, the invalid was eighty miles distant from Alexandria. Then he concluded that the vision was divine, and inferred the answer conveyed by it from the name Basilides."

That is to say, that, since the word Basilides signifies "royal," Vespasian regarded the apparition as a prophecy of his succession to the throne of the world. And Suetonius, † in his version of the story, adds that shortly afterwards letters arrived announcing the ruin and death of Vitellius.

Mesmerism alluded to by Plautus. The tractatores.

The subjoined sentence from the *Amphitryon* of Plautus appears to be an allusion to mesmerism, and since it is introduced incidentally bears the stronger testimony to the prevalence of the art about two centuries before the Christian era.

"Quid si ego illum tractim tangam ut dormiat?"

"What if I stroke him to put him to sleep?" ‡

* Tacit., *Hist.* iv. 82. † Suet., *Vesp.* vii. ‡ Plaut., *Amph.* I. i. 160.

Probably, too, the well-known *tractatores* exercised a kind of mesmeric power. And they have many modern imitators: for the advertisements of "Curative Mesmerists and Rubbers," as well as of "Medical Clairvoyants," may be seen in almost every Spiritualistic periodical.

But the specimens we have given are sufficient to show that the classical authors abound with allusions to Spiritualism; we must therefore now descend to later writers.

Remarkable passages in the writings ascribed to the Roman Clement.

And first we will glance at the *Recognitions* of Clement and the Clementine Homilies, works which at any rate do not seem to have appeared later than the third century, and may be of an earlier date, and which contain many passages worthy of consideration. In the beginning of each book the author tells us that, while a Heathen, he was much perplexed with doubts respecting the immortality of the soul. How he proposed to resolve those doubts we will leave him to describe in his own words.

"What, then, should I do, but this? I will go to Egypt, and cultivate the friendship of the hierophants and prophets of the shrines. Then I will inquire for a magician, and, when I have found one, induce him by the offer of a large sum of money to call up a soul from Hades, by the art which is termed necromancy, as though I wished to consult it upon some ordinary matter. But my inquiry shall be to learn whether the soul is immortal. And I shall not care to know the reply of the soul, that it is immortal, from its speaking or my own hearing, but simply by its becoming visible; that, after seeing it with my very eyes, I may have a sufficient and reliable proof of its existence from the mere fact of its appearing. And so the doubtful words which the ears hear will no longer be able to overturn that which the eyes have made their own." *

This proposition strangely corresponds with the oft-repeated argument of Spiritualists, that the existence of another world is best proved by intercourse with the demons which are living in it. Shortly afterwards Simon Magus is introduced, and relates a story closely resembling the countless narrations of spirit-help which crowd the literature of the new religion. †

"Once when my mother Rachel ordered me to go to the field to reap, and I saw a sickle lying, I ordered it to go and reap; and it reaped ten times more than the others." ‡

List of Simon's miracles from the Clementine Homilies.

The following enumeration of Simon's wonders may be found in the second of the Clementine Homilies.

"And they told me that he makes

* Clem., *Hom.* i. 5.

† As a specimen take the following statements made at one of the meetings of the British National Association of Spiritualists.

"Mr. Morse said he had been informed that miners had manifestations in their pit-workings, and that a little boy, employed in a coal mine near Glasgow, was in the habit when tired of calling upon a spirit to help him to push his truck, which it generally did. On one occasion the spirit, it was said, used such violence as to damage the truck considerably."

"Mr. Latham mentioned an instance in which spirits had manufactured pills that were afterwards taken, with marked benefit, by a lady of his acquaintance."

Dr. Gully said that "in his house it was no uncommon thing for spirits to appear to members of the family, to remove articles from one room to another while all the doors were locked, to make his bed at night, and to walk up and down the stairs with a tread as heavy as that of an ordinary man."

‡ Clem., *Recogn.* ii. 9. It would appear that Simon was an adept.

statues walk about; rolls himself upon fire, and is not burnt; and that sometimes he even flies. And he turns stones into loaves: he becomes a serpent; changes himself into a goat; becomes two-faced; and transforms himself into gold. He opens fastened doors, melts iron, and at banquets produces phantoms of every conceivable shape. And lastly; he causes the vessels in his house to be seen moving about, as if spontaneously, to wait upon him, those who are bearing them not being visible. I wondered to hear them speak thus; but they assured me that they had seen many such things done in their presence."*

If we may believe Spiritualists, some of these wonders are now matters of daily occurrence. They are possibly exaggerated; but we may, nevertheless, infer from the mere mention of them that powerful mediums were not unknown at the time when the Clementines were written.

Another reported deed of Simon bears a striking resemblance to modern practices.

Story which appears to prove Simon's skill in mesmerism and the production of spirit-forms.

"And he even began to commit murder, as he himself revealed to us while we were yet friends. For by abominable incantations he separated the soul of a child from its own body, that it might become his assistant for the production of whatever apparition he might require. And he drew a likeness of the boy, and keeps it set up in the inner chamber where he sleeps, affirming that he once formed him of air by transformations such as the gods cause, and, after painting his likeness, gave him back again to the air. And he explains what he did in the following manner. He affirms that, in the first place, the spirit of a man,

* Clem., *Hom.* ii. 32.

after it had been changed into a hot condition, drew to itself and sucked in the surrounding air, just like a gourd; and that he thereupon converted this air, after it was enclosed in the form of the spirit, into water. And he added that, since, owing to the consistency of the spirit, this enclosed air could not escape, he changed it into the nature of blood; and that he afterwards solidified the blood, and made flesh of it. Then that, the flesh being thus solidified, he exhibited a man made, not of earth, but of air. And so, when he had thus convinced himself of his power to produce a new kind of man, he said that he reversed the changes, and restored him to the air."*

By the light of the nineteenth century we may interpret this passage without much difficulty. It would seem that by mesmerism Simon had drawn out the spirit of a boy into the higher magnetic state, and then omitted to recall it, so that the spirit had been finally separated from the body: and that he had done this for the purpose of procuring a familiar. The latter part of the passage, which describes the production of a temporary spirit-form, exactly accords, in its results at least, with the practices of modern mediums. This we shall show in the next chapter. And Simon may, perhaps, have denied the murder of the boy by asserting that he had merely resolved a spirit-form which he had himself produced.

Remarkable description of Simon's "levitation" found in the "Apostolical Constitutions."

We will add one more story of this renowned magician, taken from the "Apostolical Constitutions." It proves that what is now called "levitation" is no new thing; but has been a conception of

* Clem., *Hom*. ii. 26.

men's minds, at least, for many centuries. Perhaps, too, the explanation given by the author of the "Constitutions" may help us to understand the mystery of Mr. Home. Nor is the statement that Simon's miracles were used as credentials of a false religion altogether unworthy of consideration. The story is supposed to be related by the Apostle Peter, who is represented as thus speaking.

"Now when he came to Rome, he greatly harassed the Church by subverting many persons, and winning them over to his own party. And he astonished the Gentiles by a display of magic and the operation of demons, insomuch that once he came forward in the middle of the day, and, bidding the people drag me also into their theatre, promised that he would then fly through the air. But, while all the multitude was in a state of suspense at this bold offer, I kept secretly praying. And verily he was raised up by demons, and began to fly aloft into the air, crying out, as he rose higher, that he was returning to the heavens, and would bestow blessings upon them from thence. Then, while the people were glorifying him as a god, I lifted up my hands toward heaven with my heart, and entreated God, that, for the sake of Jesus our Lord, He would cast down the injurious deceiver, and cut short the power of the demons, since they had used it to mislead and ruin men; that He would smite Simon to the ground, and yet not kill, but only bruise, him. And so, fixing my eyes upon him, I said in answer to his words;—'If I be a man of God, a true Apostle of Jesus Christ, a teacher of piety, and no deceiver such as thou art, Simon, I command the wicked powers of the apostate from piety, by whom Simon the magician is now being supported and borne along, to let go their hold, that he may be thrown down from on high, and be exposed to the ridicule of those whom he has beguiled.' As soon as I had thus spoken, Simon was deprived of his powers, and cast down with a great noise. And, being dashed violently upon the ground, he had his hip and the flats of his feet broken. Then the multitude cried out, saying, 'There is one God Whom Peter justly declares to be in very truth the only One.' And many of Simon's disciples left him: but some, who were deserving of perdition with him, continued in his evil doctrine. And in this manner the most atheistical sect of the Simonites was first introduced at Rome, and the Devil went on working by means of the rest of the false apostles." *

The Neoplatonists were Spiritualists. Extracts from Kingsley.

If we examine the writings of the Alexandrian Neoplatonists, whose important School was founded, in the early part of the third century, upon doctrines derived from the ancient sages of the East, we discover that they were pronounced Spiritualists, or, perhaps we should say, Theosophists. Ammonius Sacchas, Plotinus, Iamblicus, and others, were powerful adepts famed for their mesmeric healings, and general magic. But since we have not time to prove this, and can only give a concise assertion of the fact, we will do so in the words of another whose opinion will be less suspected of bias than our own. The following extracts are taken from the late Canon Kingsley's "Alexandria and her Schools."

"So they set to work to perform wonders; and succeeded, I suppose, more or less. For now one

* *Apost. Const.* vi. 9.

enters into a whole fairyland of those very phenomena which are puzzling us so nowadays—ecstasy, clairvoyance, insensibility to pain, cures produced by the effects of what we now call mesmerism. They are all there, these modern puzzles, in those old books of the long bygone seekers for wisdom. It makes us love them, while it saddens us to see that their difficulties were the same as ours, and that there is nothing new under the sun."

"But again. These ecstasies, cures, and so forth, brought them rapidly back to the old priestcrafts. The Egyptian priests, the Babylonian and Jewish sorcerers, had practised all this as a trade for ages, and reduced it to an art. It was by sleeping in the temples of the deities, after due mesmeric manipulations, that cures were even then effected. Surely the old priests were the people to whom to go for information. The old philosophers of Greece were venerable. How much more those of the East, in comparison with whom the Greeks were children? Besides, if these demons and deities were so near them, might it not be possible to behold them? They seemed to have given up caring much for the world and its course—

"'Effugerant adytis templisque relictis
Dî quibus imperium steterat.'

"The old priests used to make them appear—perhaps they might do it again."

These remarks strikingly illustrate the tendency of Spiritualism to induce idolatry. And how could it do otherwise, seeing that it is an establishment of intelligent communication with the very demons which have ever been worshipped by the Pagan world. However, in the case of the Neoplatonists, the influence of Christianity had waxed too strong to admit of a return to avowed Heathenism. If the worship of countless demons, the magnetic cures, the esctasies, and the apparitions, were to be continued, this could only be effected by a profession of Christianity and the adoption of a Christian nomenclature. So the wolves put on sheep's clothing, and in course of time the Papal system was developed.

Remarkable allusions to Spiritualism in the *Apology* of Tertullian.

Let us now consider a passage in the *Apology* of Tertullian, which may be thus rendered. "Moreover, if even magicians produce apparitions, and bring into evil repute the spirits of men who are now dead; if they mesmerise boys to obtain an oracular response; * if they perform many wonders in sport by their conjuring illusions; if they even send dreams by the aiding power of angels and demons whom they have once for all summoned to their assistance, through whose influence also goats and

* How common this practice was may be seen by the subjoined extract from the *Defence* of Apuleius. That distinguished orator, romancer, and philosopher, had been accused of sorcery, and the proof first adduced was that he had a habit of purchasing various kinds of fish presumably for magical purposes. This charge he disposes of as altogether novel and absurd, and then, after affirming that his accusers were well aware that it must break down, proceeds as follows;—

"They found it necessary to concoct a more plausible charge in connection with things which are better known and are already matters of ordinary belief. And so, in accordance with generally received opinions and common report, they invented the story that, with a little altar and lamp, and in a sequestered spot from which spectators had been removed, I had with magic spells bewitched a certain boy; and that, a few witnesses being privy to it, the boy had, when bewitched, fallen to the ground, and had afterwards awakened in such a condition that he did not know himself. They have not, however, dared to go further than this in their lying fabrication. For, to complete the tale, they should have added that the boy became prescient and uttered many predictions, inasmuch as that is the advantage which we obtain from the use

tables have been made to divine; how much more will that Satanic power be zealous to do with all its strength, of its own will, and for its own purposes, that which it does to serve the ends of others."*

Now there is no reason why the apparitions here mentioned should not have been produced in precisely the same way as the spirit-forms of our own days. Nor need we feel any astonishment at the next clause, which evidently refers to necromancers resembling modern mediums. For it appears that spirits of the dead were evoked, and that either they themselves, if they obeyed the summons, or, otherwise, the demons which personated them, were guilty of unworthy and disgraceful utterances.

In the succeeding sentence there are two readings. The first is elidunt: that is, they "strangle" boys, put them to death, either as a sacrifice, or to take omens from their motions or entrails. But the second, eliciunt, is much more probable, and will give the sense of

of spells. Nor is this wonderful power of boys certified merely by the opinion of the multitude, but also by the authority of the learned. I remember that in the books of Varro the philosopher—a most accurate and polished scholar—I read, among other things of the same kind, the following account. When the inhabitants of Tralles were making inquiries by a magical process in regard to the issue of the Mithridatic war, a boy, who was gazing upon the reflection of a statue of Mercury in the water, uttered a prophecy of the future in a hundred and sixty rythmical lines. Varro also relates that Fabius having lost five hundred denarii went to consult Nigridius about it. The latter so inspired boys by his spells that they pointed out the spot in which the purse had been buried together with part of the money, and intimated that the remainder of it had been distributed, nay, even that one denarius had come into the possession of Cato the philosopher And Cato afterwards admitted that he had received the coin from an attendant as a contribution for Apollo."—Apul., *De Magia*, xlii.

* Tert., *Apol.* xxiii.

drawing out the spirit by mesmerism, putting the patient into a clairvoyant state, so that he is able to utter oracular responses.* The "many wonders" could scarcely be more numerous than those of which we are now continually hearing, and to the genuineness of which competent persons bear their testimony.

What we are to understand by "goats and tables" has always been a mystery: but we would suggest the following as a solution. We have already mentioned the *seirim*, and explained that, while usually signifying "goats," the word also denoted "satyrs," or some order of demons. May not Tertullian, for lack of a distinctive term, have rendered the Hebrew by its literal equivalent in Latin? And, in this case, the divination by demons and tables, that is, by tables which demons

* "And yet I agree with Plato that there are certain divine powers—intermediate both in their nature and locality—stationed between the gods and men, and that these powers preside over all kinds of divination and the wonders which are exhibited by magicians. Moreover, I consider that a human mind, and especially the artless mind of a boy, can, either by the allurement of spells or by the soothing influence of odours, be lulled to sleep and calmed into a forgetfulness of the things before it; and that, becoming for a little time unconscious of the body, it can be restored and return to its own nature, which is undoubtedly immortal and divine; and so, that it is able, while apparently in a kind of trance, to perceive beforehand what is about to happen. But—be this as it may—if we are to give any credit to such matters, the boy who is to foresee ought, so far as I understand, to be selected for the beauty and soundness of his body, the intelligence of his mind, and the fluency of his speech; so that either the divine power may becomingly lodge in him as in a fitting habitation—if indeed it ever is inclosed in the body of a boy—or that his mind itself, as soon as it has been awakened, may be quickly restored to its own power of divination, which, being so implanted in it as to be readily called forth, and being neither injured nor dulled by forgetfulness, can thus be easily resumed. For, as Pythagoras used to say, one ought not to carve a Mercury out of any log of wood."—Apul., *De Magia*, xliii.

cause to move, will find its exact counterpart in modern table-rapping.

Instance of spirit-communication by the aid of the alphabet related by Ammianus Marcellinus.

And that such is the meaning of the African apologist a strange story from the history of Ammianus Marcellinus will go far to prove. For that writer tells us that, in the reign of Valens, certain Spiritualists were arrested at Antioch upon the charge of having endeavoured to ascertain the name of the emperor's successor by means of magical arts. The table which they had used was brought into court, and placed before the judges: and after two of the accused, Hilarius and Patricius, had been subjected to the torture, Hilarius made the following confession.

"Under dire auspices we did, most noble judges, construct of laurel twigs, and according to the pattern of the Delphic tripod, this ill-omened little table which is now before you. Then, after we had consecrated it in due form by invocations of mystic spells and by many and protracted manipulations, we at length succeeded in getting it to move.

"And, whenever we were wishing to obtain answers respecting things unknown, the process of making it move was as follows. It was placed in the middle of a house which had been ceremonially purged on all sides with Arabian incense; and upon it was set a plain round dish, composed of various metallic substances. On the circular rim of this dish the twenty-four letters of the alphabet had been cut with great skill, and were separated by carefully measured intervals.

"Now after the deity who gives the responses has been propitiated by means of prescribed invocations, according to the laws of ceremonial science, a person clad in white linen, shod likewise with slippers of the same material, with a turban twisted about his head, and the boughs of an auspicious tree in his hand, stands over the tripod and balances a ring suspended by a very fine piece of Carpathian thread. The ring, which has been previously subjected to an initiation of mystic rites, darts forth at distinct intervals, and strikes upon each particular letter which attracts it. In this manner it spells out heroic verses, which return a suitable answer to the questions proposed, and are quite perfect as regards number and rhythm, being similar, indeed, to those which are uttered by the Pythoness or at the oracle of Branchidæ.

"In this house, then, at the time referred to, we were inquiring who should be the successor of the present emperor—a question which was suggested by a prior announcement that he would be in all points a finished character. The ring darted to the rim of the dish, and had already touched the two syllables THEO with the final addition of the letter D, when one of those present exclaimed that Theodorus was indicated by the decree of fate. Nor did we make further inquiry into the matter, since it was sufficiently clear to all of us that Theodorus was the man for whom we were asking."*

Hilarius generously added that Theodorus himself knew nothing of this *séance*: but the latter was, nevertheless, quickly seized and despatched. Nor did his death suffice to allay the suspicions of Valens: many innocent persons were afterwards executed solely because they had the misfortune to bear names commencing with the fatal syllables THEOD. But the

* Amm. Marc., xxix. 1, 29.

prediction of the ring and table was not falsified: for upon the death of Valens, after his defeat by the Goths at Hadrianople, the celebrated Theodosius was proclaimed emperor of the East.

This remarkable story seems to prove that the tripod so often mentioned in classical writers was not merely connected with divination, but, in certain cases at least, with divination of a kind similar to that which is now in vogue: for it appears to have been necessary to impregnate the table with something which communicated motion before consultations could be held. And this motion was in all probability produced much in the same manner as by modern Spiritualists. From the details of the subsequent proceedings we may learn that the use of the alphabet for spirit-communication, which is generally supposed to be of so recent a date, was well known to the initiated fifteen centuries ago. Lastly; the issue of the story, in the succession of Theodosius, is another instance of the marvellous, though unreliable, foreknowledge of demons.

Opinions of Augustine.

Passing by about half a century of the world's annals we come to Augustine, by whom the inspiration of the Roman oracles and soothsayers, nay, the very administration of their government, is again and again ascribed to demons. The numerous gods he treats as evil spirits, and powerfully exposes the utterly corrupting influence of their well-known history and of the lewd ceremonies of their public worship, although they did hypocritically put forth certain obscure teachings of morality.* He recounts with indignation, that demons

* *De Civit. Dei*, ii. 26.

had predicted success to the monster Sylla, accompanying their predictions with miraculous signs; but had never cried, Forbear thy villanies, Sylla!* He descants upon the declaration of Hermes Trismegistus, "that visible and tangible images are, as it were, only the bodies of the gods, and that there dwell in them certain spirits which have been invited to come into them, and which have power to inflict harm, or to fulfil the desires of those by whom divine honours and services are rendered to them."† He believes these evil spirits to be capable of producing appearances and visions at will, and concludes his story of the sacred bull of the Egyptians with the remark;—"For what men can do with real colours and substances, the demons can very easily effect by showing unreal forms."‡

Further illustration is forbidden by the limit and object of this work.

But it is needless to spend longer time in proving a fact so obvious as the continual intercourse between the spirits of evil and the sons of men. The instances we have adduced are amply sufficient for our purpose, and have already exceeded their proper limits. We must, therefore, pass by the magicians, enchanters, astrologers, wizards, and witches, of medieval times;§

* *Ibid.*, ii. 24. † *Ibid.*, viii. 23. ‡ *Ibid.*, xviii. 5.

§ But the following extract from Ramusio's edition of "Marco Polo" is interesting, showing, as it does, the prevalence of Spiritualistic practices at the court of the mightiest monarch of the East in the latter half of the thirteenth century.

"Now the Great Kaan (Cublay) let it be seen well enough that he held the Christian faith to be the truest and best—for, as he says, it commands nothing that is not perfectly good and holy. But he will not allow the Christians to carry the cross before them, because on it was scourged and put to death a Person so great and exalted as Christ.

"Some one may say;—'Since he holds the Christian faith to

the levitations, apparitions, and miraculous cures, of Popery; the demon-stories of the East; the *obi* men of Africa, who seem even to have retained the Hebrew name; and the vast multitude of persons and incidents which would have claimed notice had we undertaken an exhaustive history of demon-intercourse.

Table-turning practised by German Jews a century and a half ago.

Too curious, however, to be omitted is the following extract from a Jewish writer of the early part of the seventeenth century, quoted by Delitzsch in his "Biblical Psychology."

"We make the table turn in playful times by magic, and whisper into one another's ears, Schemoth, Schel, Schedim (names of demons), and then the table springs up, even when laden with many hundred-weight."

In the year 1615 Zalman Zebi defended this table-

be best, why does he not attach himself to it, and become a Christian?' Well, this is the reason that he gave to Messer Nicolo and Messer Maffeo, when he sent them as his envoys to the Pope, and when they sometimes took occasion to speak to him about the faith of Christ. He said;—'How would you have me to become a Christian? You see that the Christians of these parts are so ignorant that they achieve nothing, whilst you see the idolaters can do anything they please, insomuch that when I sit at table the cups from the middle of the hall come to me full of wine or other liquor without being touched by anybody, and I drink from them. They control storms, causing them to pass in whatever direction they please, and do many other marvels; whilst, as you know, their idols speak, and give them predictions on whatever subjects they choose. But if I were to turn to the faith of Christ and become a Christian, then my barons and others who are not converted would say;—'What has moved you to be baptized and to take up the faith of Christ? What powers or miracles have you witnessed on His part?' (You know the idolaters here say that their wonders are performed by the sanctity and power of their idols.) Well, I should not know what answer to make; so they would only be confirmed in their errors, and the idolaters, who are adepts in such surprising arts, would easily compass my death.'"—YULE'S "Marco Polo."

turning as being effected, not by means of magic, but by the power of God. The ground of his argument is that they sang excellent songs while manipulating, as, for instance, "The Lord of the world be exalted." There could not, he urges, be any work of the Devil going on when God is remembered. This is very like the reasoning of certain modern table-turners: but history will supply an endless array of proofs that men are ever profaning the name of God by thrusting it into connection with nefarious deeds. Nor is it always clear who they mean when they invoke God: for they cannot be appealing to Him Who made the heavens and the earth if they are asking for help that they may break His laws. And there are yet two Lords of the world, though the reign of one of them is all but ended.

Spiritualism is well known beyond the boundaries of Christendom.

We have merely to add that the accounts of modern travellers prove Spiritualism, and especially the cultus of demons supposed to be the spirits of ancestors or relations, to be almost universal among Pagans and barbarous tribes, whether in the heart of Africa,* in the remote countries of Asia, or among the Indians of America.

* Ample proof of this may be found in the works of recent travellers, such as Livingstone and Schweinfurth. The following extract is taken from Livingstone's "Last Journals."

"Suleiman-bin-Juma lived on the mainland, Mosessamé, opposite Zanzibar. It is impossible to deny his power of foresight, except by rejecting all evidence, for he frequently foretold the deaths of great men among the Arabs, and he was pre-eminently a good man, upright and sincere—'Thirti'; none like him now for goodness and skill. He said that two middle-sized white men, with straight noses and flowing hair down to the girdle behind, came at times and told him things to come. He died twelve years ago, and left no successor; he foretold his own decease, three days beforehand, by cholera."

A few years ago such ideas were nearly confined to the more unenlightened parts of the earth: but now the tide of Demonism has again set in, and is rapidly overflowing Christendom. The evil spirit is returning with seven others worse than himself, and the result will be a far darker Heathenism than the world has yet experienced, seeing that it will be Heathenism received back after a trial and deliberate rejection of the Lord Jesus Christ. And "if we sin wilfully after that we have received the knowledge of the truth, there remaineth no more sacrifice for sins, but a certain fearful looking for of judgment and fiery indignation, which shall devour the adversaries."

SPIRITUALISM. PART III.

THE MODERN OUTBURST.

CHAPTER XIII.

SPIRITUALISM. PART III.

THE MODERN OUTBURST.

Scriptural intimations. Exposition of Paul's prophecy in the First Epistle to Timothy.

THE Scriptures contain many prophetic intimations that in the latter days demoniacal influence will mightily increase, and at last culminate in an open manifestation of Satanic power. One of these predictions, perhaps the most remarkable of all, we propose now to consider. It occurs in the First Epistle to Timothy, and has been usually applied by Protestant interpreters to the Papal heresy, which, however, bad as it has been, cannot as yet be said to have fulfilled the requirements of this prophecy. We will first give a literal translation of the passage, following the most simple and natural construction of the Greek, and then endeavour to ascertain its import.

"And confessedly great is the Mystery of godliness; Who was manifested in flesh, justified in spirit, seen of angels, preached among nations, believed on in the world, received up in glory. Nevertheless the Spirit expressly declares that in latter times some shall fall away from the faith, giving heed to deceiving spirits and teachings of demons, who speak lies in hypocrisy, though they have been branded in their own conscience, forbid to marry, *and command* to abstain from meats, which God created for them that believe and have full knowledge of the truth to partake of with thanksgiving. For every creature of God is good, and nothing is to be refused, if it be received with thanksgiving; for it is sanctified by the word of God and supplication."*

The verb translated "fall away" must be noticed: for from it is derived the noun which expresses "the falling away"—there is a definite article in the original—mentioned in the second chapter of the Second Epistle to the Thessalonians. Both passages evidently refer to the same event, and from the latter we learn that out of this apostacy will be developed the Man of Sin, the Lawless One. Its first symptom was to be a decline of faith in the great Mystery of godliness; that is, in the Mystery the apprehension of which is at once the source and support of all real godliness. And this is explained to be the Lord Jesus, manifested in flesh, justified in spirit, seen of angels, preached among nations, believed on in the world, and received up in glory.

The apostacy was, therefore, to commence with a waning of faith in Christ, not necessarily amounting to a total denial of Him, but beginning with incredulity in regard to the miraculous circumstances of His past advent, and so gradually obscuring the only source and centre of every godly aspiration.

The word rendered "deceiving" is more commonly used in the signification of wandering or roaming, a sense very suitable to this passage. We may compare Satan's account of himself as going to and fro in

* 1 Tim. iii. 16—iv. 5.

the earth, and walking up and down in it;* his name Beelzebub given to him as Prince of the Demons,† and probably meaning "the Lord of Unrest"; and Christ's description of the ejected spirit wandering in dry places, and vainly seeking rest.‡

The succeeding clauses probably refer to the demons, and not to those whom they deceive: for this is certainly the simplest construction of the original.

What, then, is the plain meaning of the prophecy? That in the latter days there should be a great defection of faith in the fundamental truths connected with the incarnation of Christ. That this defection should be brought about by the direct teaching of unclean spirits or demons, who, though bearing a brand on their own conscience—that is, having their own inward nature defaced by sin as indelibly as a criminal is disfigured by branding—would nevertheless pretend to goodness and sanctity that they might gain credence for the lies which they would seek to propagate. And finally; that two prominent features of their doctrine would be a prohibition of marriage, and a commandment to abstain from certain kinds of food.

This prophecy has never yet been fulfilled in the Papal apostacy.

From these last particulars many have endeavoured to fasten the prophecy upon the Church of Rome, in that she forbids her priests to marry, and has set apart days for fasting. But the utterance of Paul seems to require that those of whom he speaks should openly and avowedly receive their doctrines from wandering spirits, which is not the case with Papists. Nor does the forced celibacy of the Roman clergy by any means

* Job i. 7; ii. 2. † Matt. xii. 24. ‡ Matt. xii. 43.

satisfy the words, "forbidding to marry," which evidently point to something far more general, nothing less, indeed, than an entire repudiation of God's first ordinance. So, too, the command with regard to meats does not appear to refer to particular fast-days, but to a total abstinence from certain kinds of food.

But its conditions are beginning to appear in Spiritualism. Origin of this apostacy in its modern form.

There is, however, a delusion now rapidly spreading in the midst of us which bids fair to fulfil all the conditions of the prophecy, and to become its undoubted mate in history. And that delusion is Spiritualism, the strange origin of which, in its modern phase, dates only from the forty-eighth year of the present century. Then, while the storm of democracy was beating fiercely upon the thrones of Europe, and the demons of anarchy were breaking their chains, an apparently trivial occurrence was commencing a mighty revolution in America.

On the night of the thirty-first of March, some seventy or eighty persons were assembled in the house of one Fox, a farmer of Hydesville in the state of New York. They had come together for the purpose of investigating certain unaccountable rappings and disturbances which were alleged to take place in the sleeping room of Margaret and Kate Fox, girls of twelve and nine years of age. These children had devised a means of intelligent communication with the author of the noises, who would reply by a correct number of raps to numerical questions, and would answer other interrogations by a rap for an affirmative and silence for a negative. The younger Fox had also discovered that she could obtain a response to dumb signs; so that the spirit could see as well as hear.

Proceeding upon this experience the crowd of neighbours elicited the following communication. That the mysterious existence was the spirit of a pedlar who had been murdered in the house some five years previously by the tenant of that time, a blacksmith named Bell; and that his bodily remains might be found, where they were buried, in the middle of the cellar, ten feet below the surface. With some difficulty an excavation was subsequently made in the place indicated, and, after passing through a plank at a depth of five feet, the investigators found pieces of crockery, charcoal, quicklime, and, finally, some human hair and bones.

This result stimulated curiosity, and, every effort to detect imposture having failed, many became interested; committees of inquiry were formed; the manifestations were no longer confined to rappings: "and it soon became evident that an organized attempt was being made by the denizens of the spirit-world to establish a method of communication with mankind." * On one occasion it was proposed that the alphabet should be called over, and the unseen intelligences invited to respond to the necessary letters, and so to spell out a sentence. The suggestion was greeted with a shower of raps, which was supposed to indicate an enthusiastic assent: the experiment succeeded, and those who were present received, with some degree of awe, the first message:—"We are all your dear friends and relations." The spirits were then asked by what sign they would in future intimate their wish to avail

* "How to Investigate Spiritualism." A Pamphlet by J. S. Farmer, on the cover of which is the announcement, "First issue of 100,000 copies."

themselves of this mode of communication, and they responded by making five distinct raps. Whenever, therefore, this was repeated in subsequent *séances*, it was understood to be a call for the alphabet; and thus an intelligible code of signals was instituted.

Unparalleled rapidity of its dissemination. Its literature and organs.

As soon as it had been made clear that the power of mediumship was not confined to the Foxes, and that other spirits were ready to communicate as well as that of the pedlar, the excitement became intense, and the new faith spread through the United States with so potent an influence, that in 1871 the number of its supporters was variously reckoned at from eight to eleven millions. Nor could the waves of the Atlantic set bounds to its progress. It was not long before its apostles were active on the other side of the main, where they preached its doctrines, and exhibited its wonders, with such effect that it already reckons its adherents by myriads in England and on the Continent. It has also gained a firm footing in most of the colonies and dependencies of the British Empire.

But Hindustan, and some other parts of Asia, are regarded by its votaries as the ancient abodes which it has never relinquished, and in which the great adepts of its higher mysteries are still to be found. Indeed, its appearance in America and Europe—accompanied, as it has been, by Eastern lore from the Vedas, mostly conveyed through the medium of German philosophy, and followed by doctrines of evolution and re-incarnation, and by all but avowed Buddhism—would seem to be heralding the close of a great cycle, and to signify that the old religion of the Aryan race is overtaking, and again enfolding within its meshes, those recreant tribes which, in remote ages, escaped from its influence to the lands of the West

The literature of Spiritualism is extensive and varied, and the volumes, which follow each other in quick succession, and are frequently handsome and costly, seem to find a ready sale. A recent catalogue of the Psychological Press Association—which owns one of the three or four shops established in London for the dissemination of Spiritualistic books—presents a list of some four or five hundred works, among which may be found vigorous attacks upon the Christian faith from almost every conceivable quarter. The greatest number of assailants seem, however, to be either Buddhists or Agnostics. Politics—but only those of the party to which all communicating spirits appear to be attached—are also admitted; for the descriptive title of the catalogue includes "Liberal and Reform Subjects."

But the sale of these and similar books is by no means confined to the shops which are exclusively devoted to it. Not long ago the writer observed a Theosophic treatise in two volumes in the window of a well-known bookseller in Piccadilly. Upon entering the shop he noticed one or two copies lying on the counter, while others were piled upon the floor. An inspection of the title page revealed the fact that the book was then in its fifth edition; and yet the published price was two guineas!

In regard to regular organs, a Spiritualistic tract, issued some years ago, asserted that the new faith was at the time represented on the Continent and in some parts of Africa and South America by no fewer than forty-six periodicals. In the United States there are many, the best known in this country being two long-established weekly papers — *The Banner of Light* (Boston), and *The Religio-Philosophical Journal* (Chicago). A magazine published at Boston is styled, *The Voice of Angels, A Semi-Monthly Paper, Edited and Managed by Spirits.*

In England, the most important organs are, *The Psychological Review*, *Light*, *The Medium*, *The Herald of Progress*, and *The Spiritual Record.* The last-mentioned has been recently denounced by one of its contemporaries for a manifest leaning towards the Church of Rome. *The Theosophist*, specially devoted to Occultism and the religion of Buddha, is published in Bombay, but appears to have a considerable circulation in England. *The Harbinger of Light*, a Melbourne paper, has been established for several years, and also finds its way into this country.

Setting aside for the present the general contents of these papers, one can scarcely look through the lists of associations and meeting places, the notices of forthcoming lectures trance-addresses and *séances*, and the advertisements of mediums and clairvoyants of every kind, wonder-working, prophetic, detective, and medical, without conceding that the new religion has indeed extended itself widely, and is already wielding considerable influence. And while the learning and philosophy, which is now beginning to be developed in its higher branches, will satisfy the educated and intellectual, its careless free thought, and the strongly Radical and Communistic tendency of all its doctrines, will gain much favour for it as soon as it begins to percolate more freely through the middle into the lower strata of society. It is certainly no longer possible to regard it as a mere vulgar imposture, and the confidence and expectations of its supporters are well illustrated in the following remarks of Gerald Massey :—

"I cannot help laughing to myself at times as I think of what this much-maligned and despised Spiritualism is about to accomplish. Here are our clergy asserting Sunday after Sunday, in the name of God, any number of things which any number of listeners do not believe, only they have heard them repeated till past all power of impugning—things which they themselves do not believe, if they ever come to question their own souls. And here is this new thing in our midst that is destined to put a new soul into belief, and usher in a resurrection day. It is like watching the grim black thunder-clouds mounting the dead calm sky with a deliberate haste that makes you hold your breath till they touch the sharp edge of each other."

There is, then, little doubt as to the rapidity with which Spiritualism is spreading, and the claim which it, consequently, has upon our most serious thought. We propose, therefore, to investigate its miraculous phenomena and its doctrines, drawing our information from books and papers accredited by the leaders of the movement. We will then briefly consider the kindred system of Theosophy, and its Eastern form, the religion of Buddha, which has of late been exercising a powerful influence in Christendom, and is by its quiet spells attracting to itself many of the educated and refined. Finally, we will give a few reasons for our inference, that the revolution which is now taking place in religious thought portends the closing scenes of the age.

Mr. Wallace's summary of the physical and mental manifestations of Spiritualism.

Now, in regard to the first point, to give a comprehensive view of the miraculous phenomena, we cannot do better than quote "a summary of the more important manifestations, physical and mental," from the very able and remarkable articles on Spiritualism contained in the *Fortnightly Review* for the May and June of 1874, and subsequently published in a separate volume. These were written by the well-known naturalist and author, Mr. A. R. Wallace, and seem to give a fair and reliable account of Spiritualism in its present phase.

The following is the summary, beginning with physical phenomena.

1. Simple Physical Phenomena.—Producing sounds of all kinds, from a delicate tick to blows like that of a heavy sledge-hammer. Altering the weight of bodies. Moving bodies without human agency. Raising bodies into the air. Conveying bodies to a distance out of and into closed rooms. Releasing mediums from every description of bonds, even from welded iron rings, as has happened in America.

2. Chemical.—Preserving from the effects of fire.

3. Direct Writing and Drawing.—Producing writing or drawing on marked papers placed in such positions that no human hand (or foot) can touch them. Sometimes, visibly to the spectators, a pencil rising up and writing or drawing apparently by itself. Some of the drawings in many colours have been produced on marked paper in from ten to twenty seconds, and the colours found wet. (See Mr. Coleman's evidence in *Dialectical Report*, p. 143, confirmed by Lord Borthwick, p. 150.) Communications are often obtained

in the following manner:—A bit of slate pencil, an eighth of an inch long, is laid on a table; a clean slate is laid over this, in a well-lighted room; the sound of writing is then heard, and in a few minutes a communication of considerable length is found distinctly written. Some of these communications are philosophical discussions on the nature of spirit and matter, supporting the usual spiritual theory on this subject.

4. Musical Phenomena.—Musical instruments, of various kinds, played without human agency, from a hand-bell to a closed piano. With some mediums, and where the conditions are favourable, original musical compositions of a very high character are produced.

5. Spiritual Forms.—These are either luminous appearances, sparks, stars, globes of light, luminous clouds, etc.; or hands, faces, or entire human figures, generally covered with flowing drapery, except a portion of the face and hands. The human forms are often capable of moving solid objects, and are both visible and tangible to all present. In other cases they are only visible to seers, but when this is the case it sometimes happens that the seer describes the figure as lifting a flower or a pen, and others present see the flower or the pen apparently moving by itself. In some cases they speak distinctly; in others, the noise is heard by all, the form only seen by the medium. The flowing robes of these forms have in some cases been examined and pieces cut off, which have in a short time melted away. Flowers are also brought, some of which fade away and vanish; others are real, and can be kept indefinitely. It must not be concluded that any of these forms are actual spirits; they are probably only temporary forms produced by spirits for purposes of test,

or of recognition by their friends. This is the account invariably given of them by communications obtained in various ways; so that the objection once thought to be so crushing—that there can be no "ghosts" of clothes, armour, or walking-sticks—ceases to have any weight.

6. Spiritual Photographs.—These demonstrate by a purely physical experiment the trustworthiness of the preceding class of observations.*

We now come to the mental phenomena of which the following are the chief:—

1. Automatic Writing.—The medium writes involuntarily; often matter which he is not thinking about, does not expect, and does not like. Occasionally definite and correct information is given of facts of which the medium has not, nor ever had, any knowledge. Sometimes future events are accurately predicted. The writing takes place either by the hand or through a planchette. Often the handwriting changes. Some-

* In the March of 1872 Mrs. Guppy, a well-known medium, sat for her portrait, and when the picture was developed there appeared also a spirit-form upon the plate. Curiosity was aroused, many experiments were made, especially by Mr. Hudson, of London, and Mr. Beattie, of Clifton, and it is now asserted that, if a powerful medium be present, recognisable portraits of dead friends may be readily obtained. The subjoined is an extract from a letter of Mr. William Howitt published in the *Spiritual Magazine* for October 1872.

"During my recent short and hurried visit to London, I and my daughter paid a visit to Mr. Hudson's studio, and through the mediumship of Mr. Herne—and, perhaps, of Mr. Hudson himself—obtained two photographs, perfect and unmistakable, of sons of mine, who passed into the spirit-world years ago. They had promised to thus show themselves, if possible.

"These portraits were obtained under circumstances which did not admit of deception. Neither Mr. Hudson nor Mr. Herne knew who we were. Mr. Herne I never saw before. I shut him up in the recess at the back of the studio, and secured the door

times it is written backwards; sometimes in languages the medium does not understand.

2. Seeing, or Clairvoyance, and Clairaudience.—This is of various kinds. Some mediums see the forms of deceased persons unknown to them, and describe their peculiarities so minutely that their friends at once recognise them. They often hear voices, through which they obtain names, dates, and places, connected with the individuals so described. Others read sealed letters in any language, and write appropriate answers.

3. Trance-speaking.—The medium goes into a more or less unconscious state, and then speaks, often on matters and in a style far beyond his own capacities. Thus Serjeant Cox—no mean judge in a matter of literary style—says, "I have heard an uneducated barman, when in a state of trance, maintain a dialogue with a party of philosophers on Reason and Foreknowledge, Will and Fate, and hold his own against them. I have put to him the most difficult questions

on the outside, so that he did not—and could not—appear on the scene. Mr. Benjamin Coleman, who was with us, and myself took the plates at haphazard from a dusty heap of such; and Mr. Coleman went into the dark chamber with the photographer, and took every precaution that no tricks were played there. But the greatest security was, that, not knowing us, and our visit being without any previous announcement or arrangement, the photographer could by no means know what or whom we might be expecting. Mr. Coleman himself did not know of the existence of one of these children. Still further, there was no existing likeness of one of them.

"On sending these photographs to Mrs. Howitt in Rome, she instantly and with the greatest delight recognised the truth of the portraits. The same was the case with a lady who had known these boys most intimately for years. A celebrated and most reliable lady-medium, whom they had spiritually visited many times, at once recognised them perfectly, and as resembling a spirit-sister, whom they told her had died in infancy long before themselves, and which is a fact."

in psychology, and received answers always thoughtful, often full of wisdom, and invariably conveyed in choice and elegant language. Nevertheless, a quarter of an hour afterwards, when released from the trance, he was unable to answer the simplest query on a philosophical subject, and was even at a loss for sufficient language to express a commonplace idea" ("What am I?" Vol. ii., p. 242). That this is not overstated I can myself testify from repeated observation of the same medium. And from other trance speakers—such as Mrs. Hardinge, Mrs. Tappan,* and Mr. Peebles—I have heard discourses which, for high and sustained eloquence, noble thoughts, and high moral purpose, surpassed the best efforts of any preacher or lecturer within my experience.

4. Impersonation.—This occurs during trance. The medium seems taken possession of by another being; speaks, looks, and acts, the character in a most marvellous manner; in some cases speaks foreign languages never even heard in the normal state; as in the case of Miss Edmonds already given. When the influence is violent or painful, the effects are such as have been in all ages imputed to possession by evil spirits.

5. Healing.—There are various forms of this. Sometimes by mere laying on of hands, an exalted form of simple mesmeric healing. Sometimes, in the trance state, the medium at once discovers the hidden malady,

* To this lady's power Martin F. Tupper, who is not a Spiritualist, bears the following testimony :—

"At the Brighton Pavilion I gave her, for a theme to be versified on the spot, my own heraldic motto, "L'espoir est ma force," and, to my astonishment, in a burst of rhymed eloquence she rolled off at least a dozen stanzas on Hope and its spiritual power" (*Light*, January 6th, 1883).

and prescribes for it, often describing very accurately the morbid appearance of internal organs.

Such, then, are the miraculous phenomena at present exhibited by Spiritualism. And those who are intimately acquainted with the subject will feel compelled to admit the truth of Mr. Wallace's conclusion ;—"My position, therefore, is, that the phenomena of Spiritualism in their entirety do not require further confirmation. They are proved quite as well as any facts are proved in other sciences." *

Instances of the appearance of tangible spirit-forms.

Since, however, the fifth class of physical phenomena, the appearance of tangible spiritual forms, is important to one side of our argument, some illustration is in this case necessary. We will, therefore, quote, from another part of Mr. Wallace's essay, his notice of the séances of Miss Fox with Mr. Livermore, a well-known New York banker, and an utter sceptic before commencing the experiments.

"These sittings were more than three hundred in number, extending over five years. They took place in four different houses—Mr. Livermore's and the medium's being both changed during this period—

* Lest any one should suppose that no other man of science or intellect would have spoken so strongly, we subjoin a few quotations, which might be indefinitely multiplied.

"In short," says Professor Challis, "the testimony has been so abundant and consentaneous, that either the facts must be admitted to be such as are reported, or the possibility of certifying facts by human testimony must be given up."

Camille Flammarion, the French astronomer, thus expresses himself;—"I do not hesitate to affirm my conviction, based on personal examination of the subject, that any scientific man who declares the phenomena denominated 'magnetic,' 'somnambulic,' 'mediumic,' and others not yet explained by science, to be impossible, is one who speaks without knowing what he is

under tests of the most rigid description. The chief phenomenon was the appearance of a tangible visible and audible figure of Mr. Livermore's deceased wife, sometimes accompanied by a male figure purporting to be Dr. Franklin. The former figure was often most distinct and absolutely lifelike. It moved various objects in the room. It wrote messages on cards. It was sometimes formed out of a luminous cloud, and again vanished before the eyes of the witnesses. It allowed a portion of its dress to be cut off, which, though at first of strong and apparently material gauzy texture, yet in a short time melted away and became invisible. Flowers which melted away were also given."

Mr. Wallace likewise mentions the production in London of a visible tangible and audible female figure, just after his first article had gone to the press. This spirit-form, clad in white robes, was walking and talking with the company for more than an hour, and suffered itself to be clasped by Mr. Crookes, who found it to be, apparently, a real living woman. The experiment was frequently repeated in Mr. Crookes' own house, and the efforts made by himself and Mr. Varley to detect imposture simply confirmed the belief of those scientific

talking about. . . . I have acquired, through my own observation, the absolute certainty of the reality of these phenomena."

The philosopher J. H. Fichte was moved by his experiences to write a pamphlet in his eighty-third year, giving the following reason for so doing. "Notwithstanding my age, and my exemption from the controversies of the day, I feel it my duty to bear testimony to the great fact of Spiritualism. No one should keep silence."

And lastly, the hard and rugged mind of Lord Brougham so yielded to the evidence placed before him, that, in his preface to "The Book of Nature," he remarked;—"Even in the most cloudless skies of scepticism I see a rain-cloud, if it be no bigger than a man's hand: it is modern Spiritualism."

gentlemen in the reality and superhuman nature of the appearance.*

During the last few years such materializations appear to have become matters of common experience, and many strange narratives, often attested by respectable names, may be found in the Spiritualistic periodicals. As a specimen, we may mention an account given by Dr. T. L. Nichols, late of Malvern, of a séance held through the mediumship of Mr. Bastian. After several female forms had presented themselves, a tall male figure, with a long full beard, floated out of the cabinet. One of the company expressed a wish to see him dematerialized: the medium's familiar assented to the request, and directed that the shade should be taken off the lamp, in order that the light might be stronger. The tall figure then moved just in front of those who were present, and, in that position, became gradually shorter, until his head was close to the carpet, when it soon disappeared, as did also a little white mass which seemed to be the remains of his drapery. The process occupied about thirty seconds.

"In half a minute more," continues Dr. Nichols, "we saw a white spot on the carpet, which grew like a little cloud, and from it emerged the head, then the body, then, little by little, the full form of the tall bearded figure which had disappeared.

"This was in a small carpeted room in my own house, in the presence of seven persons not likely to be deceived, and with conditions that made any such deception impossible."

* This extraordinary series of experiments, carried on at intervals during six months, is described in "The Phenomena of Spiritualism," by W. Crookes, F.R.S.

In the course of the same séance, a female figure appeared with a baby in her arms, and was immediately recognized by a gentleman present as the wife whom he had lost some years before, together with the child whose premature birth had been the cause of her death. The child was identified by a conspicuous malformation.*

We will add one other case, in which the medium was a Miss Showers,† of Teignmouth, and the narrator a Mr. Charles Blackburn, of Parkfield, Manchester, whose letter appears in the *Spiritual Magazine* for October 1874. On the occasion referred to, three experiments were made; spirit-voices being produced in the first, and spirit-faces in the second. The third is thus described.

"The same little dressing-room and curtained door was used, but the curtain was nailed to the top of the moulding of the door to shut out all light, and a couch was placed inside. Now in this important test I took her left earring out, and passed a threaded needle through the aperture, with five yards of thread. Miss Showers lay down on the couch, and I threaded the two ends of the string through where the door hinges, and fastened them to a nail driven by a gentleman into the door casing, and visible to all; thus she had a single

* *Light*, November 25th, 1882.

† This lady, "the daughter of a general officer of the Bengal Staff Corps," suddenly ceased her manifestations. In reply to inquiries her mother published a letter in *Light* (January 28th, 1882), from which we extract the following statement:—

"The spirit-manifestations, which commenced when Miss Showers was only sixteen years old, nearly cost her life, and she will probably never entirely recover from their effects. For more than six months she lost the use of her limbs, and lay in a partially cataleptic state of utter helplessness, but with the awful and unspeakable reality of Spiritualism ever before her."

thread through her ear in her dark room, and we had the two ends in the light room. She was quickly entranced, and very shortly a spirit named 'Lenore' came forth amongst us, perfectly destitute of any thread fastening. We all felt her ears; she had no boring whatever through her ears, and the lobes were very thin and far smaller than Miss Showers's. She had only one large toe to each foot; the other four toes were ossifications, and not toes at all. We all examined her very small feet with our own hands and eyes; nor are we in the slightest degree mistaken. She told us her feet would have been perfected had there been more power. When this figure retired, we all went into the cabinet with faint light, and awoke Miss Showers. She had the thread through her ear just as when she first lay down on the couch. We cut the thread close to her ear, and traced it directly to the nail without a knot or piecing in it. Miss Showers's feet, I scarcely need say, are perfect, and were examined."

These instances will serve as specimens of what is now going on in many private families, as well as at the séances of professed mediums.

Explanation of the appearance of spirit-hands.

In a book entitled "An Angel's Message"—of which we shall have more to say presently—the appearance of spirit-hands is thus explained. The "angel" affirms that a spirit can "take of the effluvia from the person of the medium, or from the various members of the circle present, and, by condensing it, can form a temporary covering for his spirit-hand, which shall be quite solid and tangible, so that it can be grasped by you, and can convey external objects from one part of the room to another. These hands can take hold of anything just as well as you can; but if you retain them long in your hand, they will melt or dissolve away. They can be seen by all present. It does not require any spiritual preparation to see them, for they are quite material during the time of their existence."

If this be true of spirit-hands, it will naturally follow that the entire forms exhibited by spirits are simply material coverings manufactured for themselves by these disembodied rebels.* Perchance invention and progress are not confined to our world: it may be that, just as men have sought out many devices for alleviating the sorrows of the curse, so demons have at length discovered a means of temporary relief to the cravings of their bodiless spirits, or, at least, a way by which they may increase their influence over mankind. Perhaps, however, they have had the knowledge before, but, save in a few instances, lacked the impious daring to use it.

Complete figures are probably formed in the same way.

The death-like trance of the mediums seems no unnatural concomitant of their large contribution to the spirit-form. Their weariness and exhaustion when restored to consciousness is often described.

If material forms ever appear without the aid of a medium, these cannot be demons, but must be angels of Satan, who, as we have before shown, are not unclothed spirits, but possess spiritual bodies which they can render visible and tangible at will.

The reader will now have a better comprehension of Mr. Wallace's fifth class of physical phenomena. But

* Theosophists, however, insist that no spirits can materialize themselves except the lower grades, or goblins, which they term Elementals, or Elementaries. But they admit that higher spirits can sometimes control these Elementaries, and make them assume appearances to suit their own purpose.

a grave reflection presents itself: for if lost spirits are thus openly active in the midst of us, to what times of confusion do we seem to be helplessly drifting! Who can wonder at the general excitement which is already beginning to unsettle the world; the rapid and unexpected succession of events; the threatening growth of armies and fleets; the vastly increased mental activity of men; the strange philosophies and creeds which are springing up on every side; the spread of discontent, insubordination, and lawlessness; the selfishness, dishonesty, unscrupulousness, immorality, and other signs of evil energy, which are daily multiplying around us!

The miraculous phenomena are put forth by demons as credentials authorising their teachings.

But these exhibitions of supernatural power, wild as they sometimes are—for séances are often described as scenes of truly demoniacal riot—have a definite aim in view. They are intended to disturb the minds of men, and to bring them back from scepticism to superstition; to shake their faith in old creeds; and so, by reducing all diversities of opinion to one dead level, to forward a more rapid propagation of the teachings which the Prince of this World would now specially press upon his human subjects. And lastly; the signs and wonders are made to serve as credentials to these teachings.

Examination of Spiritualistic doctrine. Intercourse with the dead is absolutely forbidden by the Scriptures.

We now pass on to the second division of our subject,* and proceed to examine the doctrines which are avowedly put forth as "teachings of demons."

And first; we notice that the very

* Our limits will not allow us to speak of Planchette, which is, however, by no means a modern invention. "To this day," says

foundation of the new faith is laid in direct defiance of the law of God. For the Scriptures emphatically forbid all inquiry of the spirits of the dead, and every kind of intercourse with them. "But whereas," pleads Isaiah, "they will say unto you, Inquire of them that have familiar spirits and of the wizards that chirp and mutter: should not a people inquire of their God? For the living should they inquire of the dead?"* And had an Israelite asked what harm there could possibly be in the latter course, the prophet would, perhaps, have replied in the terrible words of the law;—"The soul that turneth after such as have familiar spirits, and after wizards, to go a whoring after them, I will even set My face against that soul, and will cut him off from among his people."† The great abomination of Spiritualism, whether ancient or modern, is that it is based upon an idolatrous substitution of spirits of the dead for the Everlasting God.

Hence nothing could be stronger than the Biblical repudiation of the whole system. The Old Testament, as we have already seen, commands that wizards, witches, dealers with familiar spirits, necromancers, and sorcerers, of every kind, should be inexorably destroyed. Nor is a milder fate assigned to them in the New: for "the fearful, and unbelieving, and the abominable, and murderers, and whoremongers, and sorcerers, and idolaters, and all liars, shall have their

Mr. Lillie, "the Buddhist temple is the home of marvels; and, in China, there is in front of many statues of Buddha a table on which an apparatus similar to a planchette is used for ghostly communications. This planchette has been known for many hundred years" ("Buddha and Early Buddhism," p. 39).

* Isa. viii. 19.

† Lev. xx. 6.

part in the lake which burneth with fire and brimstone: which is the second death."

A strange attempt has indeed been made to show that our Lord abrogated the statute against seeking to the dead when He spoke with Moses and Elijah on the Mount of Transfiguration. It has been said that He broke the law before the very face of the lawgiver, "and by His example taught His disciples, the future proclaimers of His new law to the world, to do the same." Moreover, that "the disciples, admitted to a convocation which would have brought the penalty of death upon their ancestors, found it so good for them, that they desired to build tabernacles, and remain with those illustrious dead."*

Christ did not set aside this prohibition on the Mount of Transfiguration.

This argument is much used by Spiritualists, who seem to regard it as conclusive. It is, however, put forth without the least regard either to the context of the narrative and other passages which refer to it, or even to the plain facts of history. Attention to these points will show that the Transfiguration cannot in any way be associated with necromancy, but was designed to effect the following purposes.

First; to fulfil the Lord's promise, that He would reveal Himself in the glory of His kingdom to some of the disciples while they were yet in the flesh.

And secondly; to teach that He was exalted far above Moses and Elijah, the representatives of the Law and the Prophets; that they were but servants, while He was the beloved Son.

So John, in a manifest reference to the scene, says; —"And we beheld His glory, the glory as of the only

* Howitt's "History of the Supernatural," Vol i., 197.

Begotten of the Father." And Peter proves that he had not followed cunningly-devised fables by declaring that he had been an eye-witness of the majesty of the Lord Jesus when he was with Him on the Holy Mount, and had heard the voice of the Father acknowledging Him as His beloved Son.

But the disciples, it is urged, found it so good to be in the company of the "illustrious dead" that they wished to remain with them. It is true that Peter may have had feelings akin to those of modern Spiritualists when he said, "Master, it is good for us to be here: and let us make three tabernacles; one for Thee, and one for Moses, and one for Elias." But what was the answer to his proposal? In a moment the glorious vision was swept from his sight by a cloud, out of which there pealed the cry, "This is My beloved Son in Whom I am well pleased: hear ye Him." And when he looked up to see Who was thus indicated, he saw no man, save Jesus only. Could there be a plainer warning against seeking to any other than the Son of God?

Lastly; the expression, "illustrious dead," is altogether inappropriate; for it does not appear that any unclothed spirit was present at the Transfiguration. Certainly Elijah was not one; since he had never died: and in all probability Moses also was in the body. Or wherefore was his corpse wrested from Satan by the archangel Michael? Why was not he who had the power of death permitted to reduce it to corruption, and to deal with it as he did with all other bodies? Is it not likely that God preserved it for this very occasion? And thus the Lord did indeed exhibit the fashion of His kingdom: for Moses and

Elijah represented His raised and changed saints, while both of them were clad in glorified bodies like unto His own.

Many evil agencies are mentioned in Scripture, but all good spiritual influence is ascribed to the Spirit of God alone.

It is, then, impossible to find in Scripture any sanction for the consultation of the dead. And let the following statement be well weighed by those who are still open to conviction. We hear of the unlawful association of men with demons in the Old Testament: we have miserable beings possessed with unclean spirits, and the Philippian damsel inspired by a Pythonic spirit, in the New: we are told of the spirit that now worketh in the children of disobedience, of wandering spirits and demons that teach lies in hypocrisy, and of the three unclean spirits like frogs, the spirits of demons, which shall hereafter go forth and incite the haters of God to their last great effort. But throughout the whole Bible there is no instance of a spirit influencing men for good save the Spirit of God alone. This significant fact must be carefully remembered: for Spiritualists are wont to confuse the minds of the unwary by ignoring it, and to argue that Scripture sanctions demoniacal manifestations, because it records operations of the Holy Spirit and speaks of angelic messengers. But the point at issue is the lawfulness of communication with spirits of the dead, and that question can neither be solved, nor in any way affected, by revelations concerning the Spirit of God and the missions of angels.

Utterly irrelevant, therefore, are the frequently quoted words of David, in reference to the building of the temple;—"All this, even all the works of the pattern has He taught by writing from the hand of

Jehovah which came upon me."* For though it is sufficiently clear that the plans of the temple were communicated to David in some supernatural way, and though the mode of communication may possibly have resembled that of modern spirit-writing, yet the influence is expressly said to have come from Jehovah Himself, and not from spirits of the dead.

The case of the writing which came to Jehoram from Elijah the Tishbite also falls without the limits of this controversy. For even if we admit the assumption that Elijah had previously departed from earth, and that he had not left the writing behind him, but had returned to communicate it, there remains, nevertheless, the fact that he had never passed the threshold of death. It would, therefore, be absurd to draw any inference as to the condition of the dead from what is recorded of a translated prophet.†

We may, therefore, assert that the peremptory law against seeking to the dead was never cancelled or even suspended.

Angels are, indeed, frequently mentioned; but they are not spirits of the dead.

Of the ministry of angels Scripture frequently speaks; but these, as we have before seen, are not disembodied spirits. Nor are they the glorified forms of any who have lived in the flesh during our age. For the Lord Himself marks them out as a distinct creation, and tells us plainly that we cannot be like them until the

* 1 Chron. xxviii. 19.

† But it is probable that Elijah was still living upon earth at the time when the writing came to Jehoram. For the date of his translation cannot be fixed, and the incident which is supposed to prove that it must have taken place before the expedition of the Israelitish Jehoram against Moab is hardly conclusive. The servant of the king of Israel did indeed say, "Here is Elisha the son of Shaphat which poured water on the hands of Elijah":

first resurrection, which is to take place upon His return to the precincts of our world.*

Spiritualists do indeed strive to evade this difficulty by teaching, in defiance of Scripture, that the resurrection takes place at death, and is, therefore, accomplished in the case of all the dead. But we can only reply by including them in the same category as Hymenæus and Philetus, of whom Paul affirmed that they erred concerning the truth in saying that the resurrection is past already, and were overthrowing the faith of some.†

Nor do their messages in any way resemble the communications of demons.

And yet again; angels bring messages of God, infallible words, which must be received implicitly as absolute truth. But how different is this from the confessedly uncertain utterances of demons at a séance: for Spiritualists admit that their familiars can, as a rule, only give opinions. One of their canons is, "That communications from the spirit-world, whether by mental impression, inspiration, or any other mode of transmission, are not necessarily infallible truth; but, on the contrary, partake unavoidably of the imperfections of the minds from which they emanate, and of the channels through which they come, and are, moreover, liable to misrepresentation by those to whom they are addressed."‡

but it does not necessarily follow that he meant to speak of Elijah as no longer on earth. It may be that he was merely thinking of some past occasion—perhaps an appearance of the prophet at court—on which he had seen Elisha ministering to him.

* Luke xx. 35, 36.

† 2 Tim. ii. 17, 18.

‡ We add a further illustration of this uncertainty from the pen of the well-known inspirational writer T. L. Harris. "There is no dependence to be placed on the mere verbal statements of spirits as to their real belief. One class deceives purposely; they are simply flowing into your general thought, and coinciding with

And, since Spiritualists tell us that the writers of the Bible were much the same as modern mediums, it is easy to see that their doctrine of uncertainty not merely proves the worthlessness of their own oracles, but also undermines the authority of Scripture. Thus it unites its supporters with rationalists and infidel philosophers, tending, as it does, to refer everything to the discretion of human reason.

We may now push our argument still further: for, if we except the case of Samuel, who was sent up in God's anger, there is not in Scripture a single hint of the possibility of communication between the departed in the Lord and those who still remain on earth. Nay, the whole weight of evidence is opposed to such an idea. "When a few years are come," exclaims Job, "then I shall go the way whence I shall not return."* "I shall go to him, but he shall not return to me," said David of his lost son.† And Paul consoles the Thessalonians in their bereavement, not by suggesting communications with disembodied spirits, but by

Scripture testimony is against the possibility of communication with the blessed dead.

your most devout convictions, for the purpose of obtaining a supreme and ruinous dominion over your mind and body. Another class are simply parasites, negatives, drawn into the personal sphere of the medium, and seeking to sun themselves in its light and heat by absorbing the vital forces, on which they feed, and by means of which they, for a time, revive their faded intelligence and apathetic sense. To the Mohammedan they confirm the Koran; to the Pantheist they deify nature; to the believer in the Divine Humanity they glorify the Word. Fighting, as every upward growing man is, to obtain deliverance from the self-hood, with its dead obstructions, its faltering limitations, it is most dangerous to become interlocked with the deadly self-hoods of sects, of inversine human society, or of clans, hordes, tribes, and wandering banditti, of the Spiritual world."—*The Spiritualist*, June 25th, 1875.

* Job xvi. 22.

† 2 Sam. xii. 23.

bidding them look forward to the return of their Lord and the resurrection, when dead and living shall be again united never more to part.*

The usual objections to a resurrection of the body are altogether unfounded.

Nor need Spiritualists expatiate on the difficulty involved in a belief of the resurrection, and on the inextricable mixture of atoms, any one of which may have helped to form the material portion of many men and animals. Did the difficulty exist, it would be sufficient for those who believe in God—that is, in a real God, and not a mere deification of their finite selves—it would be sufficient for such to know that He had undertaken the solution. But the Scriptures never affirm that we shall rise in the actual flesh in which we lived: and to him who suggests such a resurrection Paul replies with asperity;—"Thou fool, that which thou thyself sowest is not quickened, except it die: and that which thou sowest, thou sowest not that body that shall be, but a bare grain, it may chance of wheat, or of some other grain; but God giveth it a body as it hath pleased Him, and to every seed its own body." †

So will each of God's people receive his own body on the great day: a body, not identical with that in which he lived on earth, but connected with it as the stalk of wheat is with the decayed grain out of which it sprang. And of flesh and bones will our immortal dwelling be composed, even as our Lord's resurrection-body, by which, as His own mouth declared,‡ He was distinguished from an unclothed spirit, from that which He had Himself been during His intermediate state, when, being put to death in the flesh but quickened in the spirit, He had descended to the darkness of Hades.

* Thess. iv. 13-18. † 1 Cor. xv. 36-38. ‡ Luke xxiv. 39.

Meaning of John's direction to "try the spirits."

We must not, however, pass by a frequently quoted verse which is supposed to imply communication with disembodied spirits. "Beloved," says John, "believe not every spirit, but try the spirits whether they are of God." * It is argued that such a precept not only proves the existence of Spiritualism in the early Church, but even gives positive apostolic sanction to intercourse with the dead in Christ.

Now from the way in which John speaks we can see that he is referring to the exercise of some familiar and lawful gift, of which we may, therefore, justly expect to find notice in other parts of the New Testament. And such notice we do find: for the apostle is clearly legislating for those cases of prophetic utterance and speaking with tongues which were then common in the church, and of which Paul treats at length in the First Epistle to the Corinthians.

But by what power were these manifestations produced? Not by spirits of the dead, but by the direct action of the Spirit of God. Paul is at great pains to set forth this fact in his preliminary enumeration of spiritual gifts, and not content with having *six times* mentioned it, he concludes with the emphatic words, "But all these worketh that one and the selfsame Spirit, dividing to every man severally as He will." † In perfect accord, too, is the narrative of the day of Pentecost, which states that the disciples "were all filled with the Holy Spirit, and began to speak with other tongues, as the Spirit gave them utterance." ‡

Since, then, there is but one Spirit working in the

* 1 John iv. 1. † 1 Cor. xii. 11.
‡ Acts ii. 4.

children of God, it is evident that the command to try the spirits refers, not to the inspiring cause, but to the spirits of those who claimed to be prompted by the Holy Ghost, the plural being used as it is by Paul when he affirms that "the spirits of the prophets are subject to the prophets." * And this interpretation will be found to suit the whole context.

Nor was the apostolic warning superfluous: for, as might have been anticipated, Satan quickly began to counterfeit the manifestations of the Spirit by introducing false and demon-inspired prophets among the true believers. Unmistakable traces of this mischief may be detected in Paul's affectionate entreaty to the Thessalonians, "That ye be not soon shaken in mind, or be troubled, neither *by spirit*, nor by word, nor by letter as from us, as that the day of Christ is present." † The demon-teachers were already abroad; the Mystery of Lawlessness was even then working.

Therefore the duty inculcated by John is that of testing the spirits of prophets, to discover whether they are influenced by the Spirit of God or by demons. And the Ephesians seem to have obeyed the precept when they tried those who said they were apostles, but were not, and found them liars.‡ Had, however, any one presented himself as an avowed dealer with spirits of the dead, he would have been at once rejected without any trial: for the apostles recognized only the influence of "that one and the selfsame Spirit" on the Lord's side, and knew that every necromancer was an abomination to Him.

Finally; the Bible gives us no reason to suppose

* 1 Cor. xiv. 32.

† 2 Thess. ii. 2.

‡ Rev. ii. 2.

that departed saints can even see what is going on in this world. Indeed in one instance it seems to be assumed that they cannot. For the good Shepherd, after finding the lost sheep, calls His friends and neighbours, tells them that He has recovered His own, and bids them rejoice with Him.* Now His neighbours are probably the angels, for they dwell where He is: and is it not likely that the spirits in Paradise are His friends? "Henceforth," He said to His disciples, "I call you not servants: for the servant knoweth not what his lord doeth: but I have called you friends; for all things that I have heard of My Father I have made known unto you."† It would seem, then, that, whenever any poor wanderer is brought back to the fold, the Lord calls the spirits of his relations and friends who have already entered into rest, tells them that the lost is found, and rejoices with them in the knowledge that His beloved and theirs is reconciled to the Father, and will soon join their happy and never-ending fellowship. But if it be necessary for Christ to announce this good news to the blessed spirits, it is clear that they cannot be watching their friends who are still in the flesh.

The spirits of the dead in Christ are probably unable even to see what is taking place on earth.

There is, however, a passage in the Epistle to the Hebrews which is often explained as implying that they are so employed. "Wherefore," says Paul, "seeing we also are compassed about with so great a cloud of witnesses, let us lay aside every weight, and the sin which doth so easily beset us, and let us run with patience the race that is set before us, looking unto Jesus the Author and Finisher of our faith."‡

The "cloud of witnesses" is, probably, to be understood of testifiers, and not of spectators.

* Luke xv. 6. † John xv. 15. ‡ Heb. xii. 1.

Now even if we admit that the spirits of those who died in faith are here represented as beholding our actions upon earth, there is, nevertheless, no hint of either lawful or possible communication with them, much less of any help to be obtained from them. To Jesus alone are we directed to look: the dead can but testify by the record of their past lives to His power and love. If, therefore, Spiritualists be allowed to interpret the passage in their own way, they can find no support for their fundamental doctrine. But such an explanation, although it sets a perfect metaphor before us, does not appear to suit the context.

For in the treatise upon faith, of which this verse commences the practical application, the verb of the same root as the word translated "witnesses" is used five times, occurring finally, indeed, in the very sentence preceding the one under our consideration.* In each case it has the sense of "testifying to," and not of "witnessing" a spectacle: nor does it seem likely that Paul in drawing an inference from his argument would suddenly change the meaning of so important a word.

In all probability, therefore, the witnesses are not spectators of our faith; but witnesses to faith in the abstract, to what could be accomplished by it even before the unfolding of that love of God, which, being now known, should act as a far more powerful stimulant upon us. Such a sense both falls in with the line of thought, and removes the necessity of finding in this place a doctrine which cannot be elsewhere discovered in Scripture.

The case of the wicked may be different. Coming

* Heb. xi. 39.

by death more completely under the sway of him that hath the power of death, it may be that in certain circumstances they have the range of his principality of the Air. And if so, it is by no means improbable that they communicate at times with congenial spirits still in the flesh. But even this cannot be proved, and indeed seems unlikely. For the rich man in Hades, when troubled in regard to his brothers, speaks of them as far away, feels his own inability to help them, and hoping that the condition of the blessed may be different, entreats that Lazarus may be sent to them. What follows is striking, and again casts the dark shadow of God's reprobation over the whole system of Spiritualism. Abraham answers that they have Moses and the prophets, and should hear them. And when the rich man, with the sentiment of a modern Spiritualist, urges that if one could but go to them from the dead they would repent, he is finally told that the God of mercy has devised a message to fallen men containing all that can be really effectual in turning them from their sins, and that, if they are hardened against His words, nothing will save them, not even the return of one from the dead.

The spirits of the lost may possibly have the power of communicating with earth; but even this is uncertain.

If, therefore, the spirits of the lost who have lived in our world are able to communicate with their friends at all, it can only be in exceptional cases: unless indeed the Powers of Darkness are already hastening the end by breaking down the barriers within which God would have them confined. It is probable, however, as we have before pointed out, that the beings who inspire mediums, and work wonders to establish a lie, are the blasted relics of some former world.

Thus the whole weight of Biblical evidence pronounces against communication with the dead, even if it admits its possibility. But the demons retaliate: for their teachings are openly and daringly subversive of all the doctrines of revelation, and will, if they prevail, quickly obliterate the very names of Father, Son, and Holy Spirit, substituting a worship of deified humanity. And this we will now endeavour to prove by exhibiting the opinions of some Spiritualists of mark upon the great fundamental truths of Christianity.

Spiritualism subverts all the teachings of revelation.

First, then, we would ask, What think they of Christ? Very little, apparently: for, even by those writers who still profess to regard Him as the Son of God, He is either explained away as a mere Divine efflux, or almost lost amid a cloud of benevolent demons. But the majority of Spiritualists regard Him simply as a powerful medium, and compare Him as a teacher with Buddha, Confucius, or Zoroaster. Others, again, adopt a kind of Unitarianism, similar to that of Swedenborg, making Christ and the Father the same Person, and, in some cases, adding an explanation of the Trinity which is simply appalling in its blasphemy.

Its doctrines concerning Christ.

Amongst those who speak reverently is Mrs. De Morgan: but what can we say of the following exposition in her book entitled "From Matter to Spirit"?

Christ represented as a mere efflux.

"The Word of God, then, is the phrase used in Scripture to express the outpouring efflux from our heavenly Father in its creating, life-giving, and inspiring energy, and in its redeeming and sanctifying power; and the Bible is the history of the Word in all its degrees of action and modes of manifestation, from the simple processes of magnetic healing and clairvoyance to its full and perfect manifestation in the person of the Saviour, the Word made flesh."

Christ regarded as a medium of extraordinary power.

The prevailing doctrine is, however, that which regards Christ as nothing more than a powerful medium: and great stress is laid upon the verse, "He that believeth on Me, the works that I do he shall do also: and greater works than these shall he do."* The remainder of the sentence, "because I go unto My Father," is usually suppressed; since it too strongly urges the fact that the works can only be done in and through Christ. Nor is it found expedient to quote the promise which follows: for in what way could the Lord more emphatically proclaim Himself to be God than by the words, "Whatsoever ye shall ask in My name, that will I do, that the Father may be glorified in the Son. If ye shall ask anything in My name, I will do it"?†

Yet the first part of this passage is most unfairly adduced as a proof that the miracles of Christ were no miracles at all, but simply the results of a natural law of which His mediumistic power enabled Him to avail Himself: and that it is, therefore, open to modern mediums to display similar marvels. Thus the gulf which separates Spiritualists from the modern phase of infidelity called Positivism is spanned, and there is no difficulty in accounting for the favour with which the London Dialectical Society has recently regarded Spiritualism. For the Positivist never objects to recognise wonders if he can be convinced that they are the result of natural laws. And the new religion will even

* John xiv. 12.

† John xiv. 13, 14.

enable him to profess a belief in the miracles of Christ without at all giving up his fundamental doctrine, that, "since the fathers fell asleep, all things continue as they were from the beginning of the creation."*

Inspirational address of Mrs. Cora Tappan.

In his "Heterodox London," Dr. Maurice Davies reports an inspirational address by Mrs. Cora Tappan, a well-known trance-speaker. The subject was chosen by a committee of five, selected from the audience after the commencement of the meeting, and including three non-spiritualists. It was, "What Great Teacher has produced the most Potent Effect upon Society, and Why?" In a speech of considerable power, in the course of which she threw much doubt upon the miraculous circumstances of our Lord's birth, the speaker contended that the palm was due to Him in preference to Buddha, Zoroaster, Confucius, Socrates, or Aristotle.

When she had finished her oration, she offered, being still under the influence of the demon, to answer any questions put to her by the audience, and was immediately asked, "Do you regard Christ as really God, or merely as a human teacher?" To which she evasively replied, "We were not asked for our theological views; we were only requested to state what great teacher had had the greatest influence upon human society."

Another person expressed his surprise that she had not assigned Christ's superior power to the fact that He was God. Upon which she made the following remarks. "For ourselves, we believe that all truth is of God, and that Christ embodied in His form as much of Deity as the truth He expressed; that He was the Son of God, and that He represented the possible of

* 2 Peter iii. 4.

man, inasmuch as He promised the same gifts to others that He Himself possessed. But we certainly decline entering into any discussion on the creed of the Trinitarian or Unitarian, or any form of theological controversy. Christ's words when He says, 'I and My Father are One,' did not mean that He was God; if He and His Father were One, it merely signified that they were One in spirit; and the promise given to earth's children, the same as to Christ, is a proof that Christ could not have been a greater embodiment of Deity than the Divine and perfect humanity He represented."

Opinions of Gerald Massey and "M.A. Oxon."

Comment would be superfluous: for the voice of the dragon is easily detected in this answer. Since, however, the point is important, we will quote the opinions of two other leaders of the movement.

"I do not find," says Gerald Massey, "that Christ claimed for Himself more than He held out as possible for others. When He identified Himself with the Father, it was in the oneness of mediumship—He was the great Medium or Mediator." *

And the controlling spirit of "M.A. Oxon." exhorts him to "discriminate between God's truth and man's glosses;" and to know that the Divinity of the Lord Jesus is "a fiction, which He would disown, and which man has forced upon His name." †

Identification of Christ with the Father, and blasphemous exposition of the Trinity.

Another heresy in regard to Christ is that which speaks of Him as the Father, ignoring the other Persons of the Trinity as revealed in Scripture.

"Jesus, God-Messiah, Who
Is Mediator, Father too,"

---

* "Concerning Spiritualism," p. 65.
† "Spirit Teachings," p. 90.

says the inspirational poem *A Lyric of the Martyr Age.* And the author afterwards reveals what he terms the true doctrine of the Trinity, that Jesus is the Father, and that man and woman in the everlasting condition of marriage are the Son and Spirit. This poem contains many grand and beautiful passages, but the blasphemy of its sentiments is most offensive. On the page fronting its commencement are the lines ;—

> " It bears no date of place or time,
> This poem from the Spirit-clime ;
> Nor may the outward reader claim
> To know the fountain whence it came."

If, however, the reader believe and trust it, he may hereafter meet the author stripped of all disguise, and start back with worse affright than did the victim of Khorassan's veiled prophet, when at length she caught a glimpse of the visage she had so long desired.

A dual nature assigned to Christ. Séance at Hackney. "Behold, He is in the secret chambers."

Space will permit us to mention but one other idea respecting Christ, the reckless doctrine which assigns to Him a dual nature, and so forms one of the connecting links between Spiritualism and Theosophy. It is put forward with special emphasis by the sect of T. L. Harris, whose head-quarters are at San Francisco, but who includes some respectable English names among his followers. In the visions of this seer, Christ, when He appears to give revelations, is described as evolving from Himself a female form, named Yessa, which stands beside Him! And among English Spiritualists revelations have been circulated announcing the speedy epiphany of a female Messiah, "the second Eve and the Mother of all living." * Indeed the dual Messiah,

* See Appendix B.

though at present manifested only to a favoured few, is supposed to have already returned to earth, as may be seen by the strange account which follows.

Not long ago an "Inner Circle of the Mystery of the Divine Presence" was formed, in connection with the "Christian Spiritualist Mission," in Hackney. At its first séance—October 13th, 1882—one, calling himself "the Messenger" commissioned to declare the actual return of Christ to our earth, read the first portion of "The New Revelation," which is to explain the Mystery of God as being the feminine element in the Deity. He "was listened to with enraptured attention by the circle, as the mystery was unfolded and shadowed forth in the rites, ceremonies, and visions by priest people patriarch and king, of the Old Testament."*

"On the finishing of the delivery of the Revelation, the Lord appeared standing at the back of the revelator, with the celestial feminine personality, one on each side—by their glorious presence, both to support their Messenger and to corroborate the Revelation. A long vista of innumerable angels and bright spirits, attendants and spectators of the scene, stretched away in the distance, herein fulfilling again the Scripture concerning the second coming. The words shone out in letters of light, 'Be not afraid; for I am with you!' and the influence of the presence was shed upon all." †

The impious daring of this and other attempts to introduce a feminine element into the Godhead, in direct opposition to the express terms of Scripture, will be exposed in the next chapter. And the reported appearances—for this is not a solitary instance—of the

* *Herald of Progress*, October 20th, 1882.
† *Ibid.*, October 27th, 1882.

Lord to a select few, in closed rooms, are also a grave sign of the times: for they probably furnish the clue to His meaning when He uttered the warning words;—"Wherefore, if they shall say unto you . . . Behold, He is in the secret chambers; believe it not." *

Doctrines concerning the Holy Spirit.

Such, then, are some of the various modes by which the demon-teachers seek to obliterate, or, at least, to disfigure, the glorious form of the Only Begotten Son of the Father; nor are their doctrines in regard to the Holy Spirit less dangerous. Perhaps the most prevalent error is the blasphemous fable that He is the feminine element in the Trinity; † but this belongs rather to Theosophy than Spiritualism.

The most common doctrine of the latter creed is that which Owen puts forth in his "Debatable Land,"

* Matt. xxiv. 26.

† This idea has long been working, and will presently revive the worship of the Babylonian Queen of Heaven, and, perchance, bring about an ultimate fulfilment of Rev xvii. 3-6, which we had little suspected. It is now some years since the well-known A. J. Davis gave utterance, in the fifth volume of his "Great Harmonia," to the following sentiments respecting Ann Lee:—

"She unfolded a principle, an idea, which no man, not even Jesus, had announced, or, perhaps, even surmised. That principle, in brief, is this:—*God is dual—'He and She'—Father and Mother!* Hindu teachers obtained a golden glimpse of this impersonal truth. Forming and destroying principles, male and female energies and laws, were perceived and taught by the early inhabitants. But not one person, from God Brahma to President Buchanan, has done what Ann Lee did for this world-revolutionising idea. She centrifugated it in a thousand forms of expression. It took wings in her spirit. Better than the Virgin Mary's saintly position in the ethical temple, is the simple announcement that God is as much woman as man."

They that be Christ's have in truth need to pray;—"Hallowed be Thy Name: Thy kingdom come."

when he suggests that "Holy Ghost" signifies "Holy Breath," and affirms that our Lord meant no more when He spoke of the "Spirit of Truth." *

If this be so, why, in the passage quoted by Mr. Owen, does our Lord emphatically continue, "He —ἐκεῖνος—shall guide you into all truth," * although the word for Spirit—τὸ πνεῦμα—is of the neuter gender? But Gerald Massey goes even further.

"We talk of believing in the communion of the Holy Spirit, in a vague general way, but what communion could be holier than that betwixt the child on earth and the spirit of the parent gone before? What form more natural than that could be assumed by the Holy Spirit of God Himself? 'I will send you the Comforter,' said Jesus Christ, and why should not the promise be realized by the bereaved mother through the spirit of that child which she thinks lost to her, because she lost sight of the beloved face as it entered the cloud?"

Communicating spirits, supposed to be those of the dead, are thus substituted for the Holy Spirit. It is painful to quote these teachings of demons: but multitudes, who have at present no idea of denying either the Son or the Spirit, are trifling with Spiritualism, and what can we do but sound a note of alarm?

Tendency of Spiritualism to set natural affection in the place of love to God

A very little reading will show that the majority of Spiritualistic writers agree with the sentiment in the last extract respecting natural affection. They seem ever to regard it as the most holy thing, while God occupies, at best, but the second place in their thoughts. Thus they completely reverse the

* John xvi. 13.

Scriptural order, which sets the Creator before us as the great Centre. For, although the Bible does indeed enjoin the tenderest love to our kinsmen and friends, it, nevertheless, teaches that the spring of our affection should be the fact that God has united the loved ones to us, and that Christ died for them.

It seems to be gradually obscuring the very idea of God. Figuier's explanation of conscience.

But there are not wanting indications that Spiritualists are pressing on to a denial of the Father Himself, as well as the Son and Spirit, and to an open ascription of everything to their demons. Is there not a strong tendency to this in the following remarks of the great naturalist Louis Figuier?

"In our belief conscience is the impression transmitted to us by a beloved being, snatched from us by death. It is a relative, a friend, who has left the earth, and who deigns to reveal himself to us, that he may guide us in our actions, trace out the path of safety for us, and labour for our good. Cowardly, perverse, base, and lying men exist, of whom we say that they have no conscience. They do not know how to distinguish good from evil; they are entirely wanting in moral sense. It is because they have never loved any one, and their souls, base and vile, are not worthy to be visited by any of those superior beings, who only manifest themselves to men who resemble them, or who have loved them. A man without a conscience is, then one who is rendered unworthy, by the vicious essence of his soul, of the lofty counsels and the protection of those who are no more."

So is one great witness to the presence and power of God in our midst taken away. Conscience is to be regarded, no longer as the fear of the Almighty and of

His judgment to come, but as an impression transmitted to us by some dead friend!

His theory of procuring aid and advice from the dead.

Nor is this all. We are told that disembodied spirits can also give us advice and guidance, provided we "keep up the cultus of their memory"; and to them we are directed to look in every perplexity. In support of this doctrine, Figuier, in his "Day after Death," adduces the following cases, for the authenticity of which he vouches.

"Dr. V—, a professed materialist, one who, according to the popular phrase, believes in nothing, believes, nevertheless, in his mother. He lost her early, and has never ceased to feel her presence. He told us that he is more frequently with his mother, now that she is dead, than he used to be when she was living. This professed apostle of medical materialism has, without being aware of it, conversations with an emancipated soul.

"A celebrated journalist, M. R—, lost a son, twenty years of age, a charming gentle youth, a writer, and a poet. Every day M. R— has an intimate conversation with his son. A quarter of an hour of solitary recollection admits him to direct communication with the beloved being snatched away from his love.

"M. L—, a barrister, maintains constant relations with a sister who, when living, possessed, according to him, every human perfection, and who never fails to guide her brother in every difficulty of his life, great or small.

"Another consideration suggests itself in support of the idea which occupies us at present. It has been remarked that artists, writers, and thinkers, after the loss of one beloved, have found their faculties, talents, and inspirations, increased. We might surmise that the intellectual faculties of those whom they have loved have been added to their own. I know a financier who is remarkable for his business capacities. When he finds himself in a difficulty, he stops, without troubling himself to seek for its solution. He waits, knowing that the missing idea will come to him spontaneously, and, sometimes after days, sometimes after hours, the idea comes, just as he has expected. This happy and successful man has experienced one of the deepest sorrows the heart can know; he has lost an only son, aged eighteen years, and endowed with all the qualities of maturity, combined with the graces of youth. Our readers may draw the conclusion for themselves."

Can these instances be described as anything but that seeking to the dead which the Lord hates? And if blessings are thus obtained from the spirits of lost friends, to what purpose do we worship God? Among those who believe in it, will not the cultus of the dead speedily absorb every other kind of devotion?

Mr. Wallace's explanation of the efficacy of George Müller's prayers.

But in Mr. Wallace's essay on modern Spiritualism we find a statement yet more startling, since it seems to imply that even those prayers which are presented to the Most High in the name of the Lord Jesus depend, sometimes at least, for their answer upon the good will of the spirits of the air.

"Prayer may be often answered, though not directly by the Deity. Nor does the answer depend wholly on the morality or the religion of the petitioner; but as men, who are both moral and religious, and are firm believers in a Divine response to prayer, will pray more frequently, more earnestly, and more disinterestedly, they will attract towards them a number of spiritual beings who sympathise with them, and who, when the necessary mediumistic power is present, will be able, as they are often willing, to answer the prayer. A striking case is that of Mr. George Müller of Bristol, who has now for forty years depended wholly for his own support and that of his wonderful charities on answers to prayer. . . . The Spiritualist explains all this as a personal influence. The perfect simplicity, faith, boundless charity, and goodness, of George Müller, have enlisted in his cause beings of a like nature; and his mediumistic powers have enabled them to work for him by influencing others to send him money, food, clothes, etc., all arriving, as we should say, just in the 'nick of time.'"

"It is not necessary," says an inspirational book, "for a man to pray before he can be helped, but it is advisable; because, although his spirit friends can read his thoughts and understand his wants, he loses the aid of many others who cannot read his thoughts, but who would be attracted to him by his prayers, and would help him if they knew he wanted help. Prayer is, therefore, something like advertising your wants in the newspapers." *

Open denial of the existence of God.

Those who can receive teachings such as we have quoted must soon lose the last remnant of their vague belief in God. And, indeed, a Spiritualistic writer in the *Westminster Review* † does not hesitate to express himself as follows;—

* "Life Beyond the Grave," pp. 140-1.
† October 1875.

"Furthermore, the conception of the Reign of Law harmonises with the mental fabric of the age, whereas that which it supplants does not. We have ceased to embody the conception of the State in a person, and it is time that we should cease similarly to embody the conception of the universe. Loyalty to a personal ruler is an anachronism in the nineteenth century, but the sentiment which inspired it may find ample satisfaction in disinterested devotion to the welfare of the community.

"In like manner loyalty to a Divine Person will some day become extinct as a manifestation of the feeling which ought to sway us in our relations to that whole whereof we form so insignificant a part, but its place will be taken by a conscious and cheerful accordance with the laws which make for the well-being of the universe. We shall transfer to the commonwealth of things that loving allegiance which we were wont to render to the Great King."

"This is the Antichrist," says John, "who denieth the Father and the Son." And certainly Spiritualism seems to be training men for the teachings of that terrible being.

Demon-teachings are defiant of God in their descriptions of the state after death.

We must now devote a few moments to the general subject of spirit-communications. A great part of these are either absolute nonsense or such common-places as we may easily hear in our own world. When, however, they affect to be didactic, they often propound views bearing a striking resemblance to certain rationalistic theories, but are also frequently descriptive of the spirit-land, and of the state after death.

And here again we detect the utterance of rebels: for God has altogether withheld this kind of knowledge. The Bible never enters into particulars of the intermediate state: it does not, like the Koran, group together all that is pleasing to the gross earthly senses, and hold up the picture as the prize for him that overcometh: it does not unfold the nature of that which is provided for us between death and resurrection: nay, it even seems, as we shall presently show, to give a conclusive reason for its reserve. It merely tells us that we shall have rest, comfort, and the presence of Him whom our soul loves: it only reveals that on the very day of death we shall find ourselves in Paradise, the beautiful garden of the Lord, and then its direct information ceases.

The lessons to be derived from the history of Paul's rapture into the Paradise of God.

But, though it never enters into details, it describes to us the effect produced upon the only man—so far as we know—who has been permitted to view the condition of the dead in Christ and return in full consciousness to earth; while at the same time it gives us a partial reason, at least, for the absence of further revelation. For those who were raised from the dead by our Lord and His apostles have nothing to tell us: and, since God intended from the first that they should live again in the bodies which they had left, it may be that their spirits were held in a state of unconsciousness. Or, if they did for a while tarry in the abode of the departed, impenetrable forgetfulness fell upon them when they returned to this life, and the great secret was still preserved.

But Paul knew something of it: for he was caught up alive into the Third Heaven, and into Paradise.* Yet instead of satisfying our curiosity, he tells us that

* 2 Cor. xii. 1-7

it would be impossible to do so, for that he heard unspeakable words which *it is not lawful for a man to utter*. We are thus positively forbidden to pry into the matter: but we are at least permitted to infer that what Paul saw was transcendently beautiful, full of such ravishing joy as we cannot now conceive. For, when he returned to earth, he was so elated by what he had experienced, so thoroughly unstrung for this lower life by his short taste of that which is to come, that he would have been incapacitated for further service in this world had not God brought him down to his former level by a painful affliction, a thorn in the flesh, a messenger of Satan sent to buffet him. It was, therefore, no Purgatory which Paul saw—he would not have needed a thorn in the flesh to keep him from elation after such a sight as that—but a Paradise of beauty and joy far beyond the comprehension of man.

Two reasons for the mention of this vision seem obvious. And first; from Paul's experience we may at least feel sure that we should even now, while still in the flesh, heartily appreciate what God has in store for us could we but see and understand it.

Secondly; we may learn why we must be satisfied with generalities for the present. A full knowledge of the bliss which will soon be ours would so occupy our mind, and unfit us for our daily duties, that God would be compelled to visit us with far more heavy and painful affliction than is necessary now. In mercy, then, this knowledge is withheld from us. And into which of the great Father's arrangements can we ever penetrate far without discovering that He is love?

But those communications which God has denied, and through Paul pronounced unlawful, demons are ever willing to impart. And hence, if we look upon the Bible as a revelation of the mind of the Almighty, we have another proof that the wisdom of Spiritualists is not that which comes down from above.

Specimens of demon-teachings in regard to the state after death.

The forbidden teachings are usually given by demons professing to be spirits of the departed who are commissioned to describe their experiences to their friends. They often commence by giving an account of their own death and their feelings immediately after dissolution: but the bliss they enjoy seems to be invariably ascribed, not to the atoning sacrifice of Christ, but to their own works and virtues. In "Glimpses of a Brighter Land," an inspirational book, a spirit gives the following as the words addressed to her by an angel after her emancipation from the body;—

"The threads that connected you with the frail clay were easily severed. God hath ever dwelt in your mind; sincerely did you seek to do His will and pleasure while yet on earth; tenderly did you give a cup of cold water to the thirsty, and bind up the wounds of the sick; gladly did you pour balm and oil into troubled minds, and now will you reap your reward. Happiness is in store for you far greater than any of which you have ever conceived. Pure as a lily, such shall be your spirit-name. Pearls are the fit emblem of your spirit-mind."

The descriptions of the realm of air consist of fairy landscapes, rich foliage, gorgeous temples, and stately private mansions; they are such, indeed, as might be ascribed to the shade of De Quincey, or that of the author of the "Arabian Nights." The forms of the inhabitants float about, clad in loose robes of the purest white or the most brilliant colours, with girdles of gems and crowns of glory; and conversations are often given in which the spirits of the great dead* are sometimes prominent. The following, from "Glimpses of a Brighter Land," may serve as a specimen of the scenes presented.

"Here I found other companions, who kindly welcomed me to a more beautiful mansion and garden. The flowers were more brilliant, their perfume more delicious, and the trees and shrubs more luxuriant. The mansion in which I now dwelt was spacious, and I could entertain and receive my friends therein. We often met together, and endeavoured in sweet converse to instruct one another by imparting all the knowledge we had each separately attained. Sometimes one of our guardian angels would invite us to a feast of wisdom. We then met in a spacious temple, the walls of which were of crystal, pure and transparent, emblematic of the purity of heavenly wisdom and truth, the dome was of pure gold, and the pillars that supported it. The pavement was white with a pattern in crimson upon it. Our seats were around the building. In the centre was a slightly raised platform, on which our instructors stood when they imparted knowledge to us. Ever and anon, while they spoke, light played above and around them. Roseate clouds filled the edifice, and from time to time words of divine love and wisdom would appear, as if written in letters of fire, around the building."

A well-known pamphlet, called "Heaven Opened," con-

* It is, however, admitted that the lower grades of spirits frequently assume the names of illustrious men for the purpose of adding weight to their own communications.

sists of a series of messages alleged to have come from the spirits of young members of the author's family, including some who had died in infancy. These describe their new existence, and the children's sphere in spirit-land. One of them, a girl of sixteen, found herself immediately after death on a "couch of flowery essence," and "the most beautiful horse, with a bright shining star over his eyes," presented himself to carry her through the surrounding gardens. The little spirits sit on the flowers: "the big clever spirits" form all sorts of couches and carriages of the flowers, and carry the little ones about in them. Lastly; when the air moves the flowers sing, while the little birds take the prayers of the spirits upon their wings. An aunt is described as having several mansions, one in the City of Zion, another a beautiful retreat in the country, and so on.

The demons who personate these children also urge that they are constantly present with their friends in the flesh, and are their natural advisers and protectors. The influence which results is of course enormous: nor will those who have established it fail to take full advantage of their power.

Spiritualism teaches that, even if men neglect their salvation in this life, they may, nevertheless, repair the mischief in the life to come. The seven spheres.

But such puerilities are by no means the most serious of demon-deceptions. For, the Bible doctrine that now is the accepted time, and the only day of salvation, is entirely set aside by these false messengers. Our Lord's warning that even in the intermediate state the destiny of man is fixed, and that he is either in the Paradise of God awaiting the resurrection of the just, or in the prisons of the lost dreading the judgment of the Great White Throne, is altogether rejected. The demons remove this terror of the Lord, which has been the beginning of wisdom to so many, and substitute the old Babylonian doctrine of the seven spheres. But since we prefer that Spiritualists should expound their own creed, we subjoin Miss Houghton's statement on this point.

"The spirits dwell in various regions. The unhappy spirits in places of darkness and misery beyond the power of man's imagination to conceive. There they remain, until repentance for sin begins to awaken; they then desire light, which is immediately vouchsafed to them, and the blackness with which they are surrounded becomes rather less dense. Spirits of a higher grade may then be listened to when they strive by teaching to strengthen the repentant feelings; but alas! their companions in misery are often unwilling to witness an improvement in which they are not inclined to share, and endeavour to detain them from an upward progress. Many are the trials to which they must be subjected as they rise through the different degrees into the next sphere, there being seven spheres, and seven degrees in each. . . . Those spirits who still remain in the lower spheres have but little power of locomotion, but in the higher ones they can travel through infinite space, the limits being only according to their own onward progress; for as they become more etherealized by their own ever increasing sense of happiness in their advance through the various degrees of the different spheres, they can rise to more rarefied regions, so as ever to be approaching nearer to the perfect light of heaven itself. A radiancy surrounds each spirit, of more or less brilliancy, according to the sphere they have reached. This radiance is of certain hues for each sphere, gradually increasing in size, and altering somewhat in form for each degree. Spirits in the two lower spheres have no radiance, the only difference being in rather less of blackness. In the third and fourth it may scarcely be called such, but it is, at any rate, a kind of light: thus in the third it is brown, gradually becoming lighter, and in the fourth it is grey. In the fifth the green hue of hope is seen, in the sixth violet; and in the entrance to the seventh a bright blue light, gradually acquiring vivid rainbow tints, which then fade off to a light so vivid that scarcely any colour is to be seen, all being so gloriously mingled."

In many communications spirits representing themselves as denizens of the higher spheres narrate their descents into the lower to awaken and help the irrepentant. The Gospel which they preach is not, however, that of the Lord Jesus; but, so far as we have read, consists merely of admonitions to the sinful to repent, to look to God, in which case they will be drawn upwards to Him, and to do what they can for those around them. We have never met with a single reported instance of a spirit entering the lower spheres with the glad tidings, "Believe on the Lord Jesus Christ, and thou shalt be saved."

Utterance of the familiar of "M.A. Oxon."

On the contrary, among Spiritualists, as with Theosophists and Buddhists, sin can be expiated only by personal suffering; and this dogma is often enforced with a fierceness such as might be expected from the reckless envy and anger of those fallen beings whose nature the Lord did not take upon Himself, and whose testimony He would not receive. "Sin," shrieks the familiar of "M.A. Oxon," "is remediable by repentance and atonement and reparation personally wrought out in pain and shame, not by coward cries for mercy, and by feigned assent to statements which ought to create a shudder."*

We give thanks to the God of all comfort that He does not contemn cries for mercy, nor despise the sighing of a broken and a contrite heart. And as we listen to Imperator's † frank avowal that the Messengers, or Messiahs, whom he recommends would not spare the sinner, but "let the lash be laid on,"‡ we are moved with unspeakable gratitude to Him Who took upon Himself the chastisement which should bring us peace, and endured cruel stripes that we might be healed.

As to "feigned assent," it is a very old trick of lying rhetoric to set up an image of its own fashioning, in order to produce an effect by striking it down. But our Scriptures never promise salvation to him who feigns to believe in Christ. On the contrary, they declare that the hope of the hypocrite shall perish; and

* "Spirit Teachings," p. 78. We add two other specimens of this kind of doctrine. In a weird Occultist narrative, called "Ghost Land" (p. 43), the "flying soul" of a murderer is interrogated, and relates the following;—"There, too, I saw the still living and radiantly glorious soul of my old pastor, Michael H. Sternly, but sorrowfully, he told me I had committed a great and irreparable crime; that all crime was unpardonable, and could only be wiped out by personal, and not by vicarious atonement, *as he had falsely taught whilst on earth*; that my only means of atonement was suffering, and that in kind, or in connection with my dreadful crime."

And Mrs. Hardinge Britten, in her "Nineteenth Century Miracles," quotes a strange story involving the same doctrine, the narrator of which exclaims;—"Great Heavens! If this be indeed a true picture of the life hereafter, should it not make us afraid of doing wrong! But, above all, what a wicked and soul-destroying delusion has been the clerical farce of salvation by a vicarious atonement!"

† The name assumed by the communicating demon.

‡ "Spirit Teachings," p. 159.

are careful to point out that, although we are indeed saved through faith alone, yet that faith cannot be existing in us unless it presently discovers itself in works.

Tendency of Spiritualism to amalgamate with Popery and absorb all other false religions and philosophies.

In place, however, of the Gospel, we find foolish stories of the appearance to the repentant of lights which gradually take the shape of crosses: and instructing angels are sometimes introduced with flaming crosses in their hands. In the pamphlet "Heaven Opened," referred to above, some of the communications are interspersed with crosses, upon which the writer thus remarks:—"I have been told by my spirit-guides that the crosses as given in the messages are a sign of the truth of the message and the holiness of the spirit. An evil spirit cannot give the sign of the cross." Truly this last sentence contains a wonderful piece of information, but one which it is difficult to reconcile with the world's history.

We have, however, in the use of the emblem of the cross an indication—and there are many such—of a tendency in the new faith to coalesce with Romanism. Doubtless, too, the reader will have observed that the doctrine of the seven spheres is all but identical with that of Purgatory. And since Spiritualism is merely a revival of the influence which first produced Paganism, while Popery is nothing but Paganism under a changed name, and covered with a gauzy veil of Christianity, it seems likely that these two systems will presently find no serious obstacle to their amalgamation.

The striking agreement of Spiritualism with the method of Positivism we have already noticed: nor is there much difficulty in discerning its points of affinity with other creeds, and especially with Buddhism. In fine, it appears to be preparing the way for that universal religion which has already been suggested in some of our papers and periodicals. That this is the design of its members we may see from Mr. Herbert Noyes' enumeration of the missions of Spiritualism, the seventeenth of which he declares to be ;—"To winnow the wheat of truth from the chaff of theology, and reconcile antagonistic creeds by eliminating their errors, and making manifest the spiritual truths which underlie all systems of religious belief in the world."

Specimen of the method by which Spiritualism is undermining all that opposes it in other creeds.

A remarkable passage in Mr. Wallace's essay aptly illustrates the destructive power which Spiritualism is already exercising upon other creeds, and the method by which it seems to be reducing the various religions to that dead level which must be effected before the great apostacy can tower without a rival over Christendom and the world.

"The mediums have,.almost all, been brought up in some of the usual orthodox beliefs. How is it, then, that the usual orthodox notions of heaven are never confirmed through them? In the scores of volumes and pamphlets of spiritual literature I have read, I have found no statement of a spirit describing 'winged angels,' or 'golden harps,' or 'the throne of God'—to which the humblest orthodox Christian thinks he will be introduced if he goes to heaven at all. There is no more startling and radical opposition to be found between the most diverse religious creeds, than that between the beliefs in which the majority of mediums have been brought up and the doctrines as to a future life that are delivered through them; there is nothing more marvellous in the history of the human mind than the fact that, whether in the backwoods of America or in country towns in England, ignorant men and women having been almost all brought up in the usual sectarian notions of heaven and hell, should, the moment they become seized by the strange power of mediumship, give forth teachings on this subject which are philosophical rather than religious, and which differ wholly from what had been so deeply ingrained into their minds. And this statement is not affected by the fact that communications purport to come from Catholic or Protestant, Mahometan or Hindu spirits. Because, while such communications maintain special dogmas and doctrines, yet they confirm the very facts which really constitute the spiritual theory, and which in themselves contradict the theory of the sectarian spirits. The Roman Catholic spirit, for instance, does not describe himself as being in either the orthodox purgatory, heaven, or hell; the Evangelical Dissenter who died in the firm conviction that he should certainly "go to Jesus" never describes himself as being with Christ, or as ever having seen Him, and so on throughout. Nothing is more common than for religious people at séances to ask questions about God and Christ. In reply they never get more than opinions, or more frequently the statement that they, the spirits, have no more actual knowledge of these subjects than they had while on earth."

The general tendency of this paragraph is manifest. In regard to particulars, we may remark that a change in the opinions of those who have just been possessed by demons is by no means marvellous: the alleged cause is quite sufficient to explain the effect. And seeing that mediums are influenced by organised spirit-bands from the kingdom of Satan—in which, though love be wanting, there is no lack of unity—we should reasonably expect the teachings of all to point in the same direction.

The fact that demons present themselves as Protestants, Papists, Mahometans, Hindus, and so on, merely proves that the order of Jesuits is not the only society which finds advantage in professing the creed of others for the purpose of propagating its own. That none of the communicating spirits speak of being near the Throne of God seems anything but strange to us: in regard to Christ, however, the rule laid down by Mr. Wallace has very many exceptions. In "Heaven Opened," for instance, there is a description of Christ, and He is represented as nursing the infant spirits!

Lastly; if demons can only give opinions, or are compelled to confess that they know no more than we do, of what use is it to waste time in consulting them? And if it be urged that they have information upon other points, and are only deficient in that which concerns God and His redemption of mankind, we reply that we more than suspect those who would substitute vain philosophies for the positive assertions of Scripture, and for the glorious and free salvation purchased by the blood of Christ.

Conclusion of general remarks on Spiritualism.

We must now bring our remarks on the general subject of demon-teaching to a close. So far as they go, we believe that the quotations given above form a fair statement of the doctrinal development of Spiritualism. Of course want of space compels us to omit many other points which demonstrate its extreme antagonism to Scripture:

but surely what has been said is sufficient to set the most unwary Christian on his guard, to show that the great falling away may have commenced, that the deceiving spirits are, perhaps, already engaged in their final mission of delusion.

The two specially mentioned doctrines of the apostacy. A prohibition of certain kinds of food.

But two prominent features of the last apostacy were to be a forbidding to marry, and a commanding to abstain from meats, that is, from certain kinds of food—what kinds we are not told.

Now the latter of these prohibitions, if we take it as applying to flesh, is well known to have been recognised in every age as an indispensable condition of great mediumistic power: it must, therefore, naturally become a law among those who would have much direct communication with demons. Indeed, it is not impossible that the permission to eat flesh, given as it was immediately after the angel-transgression, may have been intended to render man less capable of conscious and intelligent intercourse with supernatural beings, and, consequently, less exposed to their wiles. And if so, the desire on the part of the demons to withdraw it is easily understood.*

However, be the cause what it may, this predicted sign of the final apostacy is certainly manifesting itself among Spiritualists; while, as we shall see in the next chapter, it forms a fundamental law of Theosophy.

* The following passage from "Oahspe, the New Bible," seems to confirm this view;—"Verily, I say unto you: ye have not fulfilled the first law, which is to make clean your own corporeal bodies. Because ye have stuffed yourselves with carnal food, my holy angels cannot approach you" (*Book of Judgment*, xviii. 11). The context shows that we are to understand "carnal food," in its literal sense, of flesh.

On the very first page of "Oahspe, the New Bible," we read the following ;—

"But the Beast said: Think not I am come to send peace on the earth; I come not to send peace, but a sword. I come to set man at variance against his father; and a daughter against her mother. Whatsoever thou findest to eat, be it fish or flesh, eat thou thereof, taking no thought of to-morrow.

"And man ate fish and flesh, becoming carnivorous, and darkness came upon him, and he no more heard the voice of Jehovah, or believed in Him. This was the fifth era."

There is little need to remark upon this profane passage. The reader will notice the distortion of two of our Lord's sayings, the origin assigned to them, and the way in which they are used to throw discredit upon the Noachian Covenant.

A few pages further on, we are told that the spirit of man takes its place in the first heaven "according to his *diet* and desires and behaviour."* And in the *Book of Judgment* the following verses occur ;—"All men profess to desire resurrection; they like to ascend to exalted heavenly spheres. Yet many will not even strive to exalt themselves. He saith in one breath: To not eat the flesh of anything created alive is the highest. But straightway he filleth his belly with flesh."†

During the last few years, however, a second reason for abstinence from flesh has been rising into prominence. Theories at first confined to physical evolution have been applied to the soul with the result that transmigration has become a common doctrine among

* "Oahspe," p. 7. † "Oahspe," p. 784.

the more intellectual Spiritualists. Thus the great barrier between Buddhism and Western ideas is swept away, and a horror induced of any food that involves a sacrifice of life. For what man would devour the body of an existence destined, perhaps, ere long to be his own child? Or who would violently strip the spirit of a peccant and retrogressive ancestor?

Figuier's theory of Transmigration.

But this doctrine belongs rather to Theosophy: we will, therefore, postpone its consideration, merely subjoining a passage from Figuier's "Day after Death," which the reader may compare with the more elaborate Occultist theory to be presently described.

"Let us think of the emanations from souls dwelling in the sun descending upon the earth in solar rays. Light gives existence to plants, and produces vegetable life, accompanied by sensibility. Plants, having received this sensible germ from the sun, communicate it, aided by heat likewise emanating from the sun, to animals. Let us think of the germs of souls, placed in the breasts of animals, developing themselves, becoming perfected by degrees, from one animal to another, and finishing by becoming incarnate in a human body. Let us think, then, of the superhuman being succeeding to man, springing up into the vast plains of ether, and beginning the series of numerous transmigrations which, from one step to another, will lead him to the summit of the scale of spiritual perfection, from which every material substance has been eliminated, and where the soul, thus exalted to the purest degree of its essence, penetrates into the supreme abode of happiness, and of intellectual and moral power—the sun.

"Such may be this endless circle, such this unbroken chain, binding together all beings in nature, and passing from the visible to the invisible world."

The second specially predicted doctrine of spirit-teaching, a forbidding to marry, has been gaining strength for some years, and is propagated in two ways, both of which, as we shall presently see, lead to the same goal, a repetition of the Antediluvian crime.

The second specially predicted doctrine of the apostacy. Direct prohibition of marriage.

The first way is that of direct prohibition. Continence is often taught among Spiritualists; and in some of their sects, such as the "Brotherhood of the New Life," and the "Millennial Church," it seems to be regarded as, at least, an ultimately indispensable condition of membership. So in the "New Bible" celibacy is significantly set forth as the higher condition; while among Theosophists it is affirmed to be absolutely necessary to perfection, and, therefore, a state to which all must attain either in the present or in some future earth-life. For, urges Dr. Wild, if woman as a form be worshipped in the place of spirit, the essential, this leads to the idolatry of matter. And "thus the love towards the woman is the substitution of external for internal delights, and calls forth the jealousy of the 'Divine Sophia,' with whom those who, with profound reverence, worship God as a Spirit, and thus evoke their spiritual centre and find the Logos, are united. These know that there is a spiritual marriage incompatible with that of the flesh."*

The last sentence seems to afford a clue to the meaning of this continence: those who practise it are reserving themselves for aerial visitants. "I do not

* "Theosophy and the Higher Life," pp. 8, 9.

believe," says T. L. Harris, "that sexlessness characterizes man in his higher and final evolution." Upon such a subject we would, of course, wish to say and quote as little as possible, but must, at least, summarize so much as is necessary to be known.

The doctrine of the Two-in-one.

Following the teachings of Jacob Böhme—whose doctrines appear to have been, partly at least, derived from those of the ancient Mysteries—many Spiritualists have been wont to distinguish, as different events, the creation of man mentioned in the first chapter of Genesis, and that which is described in the second. In the former, they understand the words, "In the image of God created He him; male and female created He them," to signify that man was originally an Hermaphrodite, "two-in-one, the female issuing out of the side of the male, and the male issuing out of the side of the female; each at will making himself or herself objective."

The fall is supposed to have caused a separation of these two principles; so that marriage became necessary as a temporary alleviation of the separate condition. But the time has now come for a restoration of the original perfection, and "there must be a cessation of the old generative principle altogether, before there can be a regeneration after the order and pattern of the kingdom of God. We must gather up the spilled drops of the sea of life, from whence all humanity have had their existence, and conserve the life for higher formations, as shall please Him, Who has the forming power in His own hands, to construct a people for Himself, who shall neither sin nor die.*

* Similarly T. L. Harris writes;—"We think that generations must cease till the sons and daughters of God are prepared for

"That can only be accomplished by the involution of a spiritual nature from the Lord, Himself assuming humanity, here and now, among a select few, who welcome Him in their whole frame, body and soul consecrated to Him, that He may form within them the 'missing link,' which is their counterpartial life brought back to them, that they may be recreated in His image, two-in-one, as at first: not only in a transitory form—as it is seen in mediums of the present day, who can have during their trance-sleep many spirits coming out of them, or through them, as the door of exit, and this only for a short time—but when each one who has been recreated, regenerated, shall receive his counterpart, to be with him and in him, as the control is in a medium, and is able at times to make itself objective, or, in other words, materialize itself, so that others may see it and converse with it."*

The reader who has perused our ninth chapter will easily understand the drift of this teaching respecting "the glorious marriage of earth and sky." For while it seems probable that only demons, and not angels of Satan, will carry out the theory of the Two-in-one, yet

the higher generation, by evolution into structural and bi-sexual completeness, above the plane of sin, of disease, or of natural mortality."

"The doctrine of the Divine-human Two-in-one, in whose spiritual and physical likeness we seek to be re-born, is the pivot of our faith, and the directive force of our life. The ages wait for the Manifestation of the sons of God. Thus we are adventists, not in a sectarian sense, but in the sense of a Divine involution, and thence of a new degree in human evolution" ("Sermons," by T. L. Harris, p. xiii.). Mr. Harris does not profess to discover his doctrine in Scripture. "If," says he, "we find one vein of knowledge, or possibly correct surmise, in Swedenborg, we find other veins in Spinoza, or Böhme, or Compte."

* For this exposition, "from the pen of a clergyman," I am indebted to Mrs. McHardie's "Midnight Cry."

the object will be to prepare the world for the final crime. The fallen angels themselves will not be likely to take up their abode in human bodies, nor, so far as we know, will their intercourse go beyond the daughters of men. But when—by means of the power which they still retain, though only for a short time—they present themselves in apparently celestial glory, previous teachings and events will cause those who are abandoned of God to receive them as angels of light, or even—so the quotation just cited seems to suggest—as the Lord Himself.

The realization of the Two-in-one is said to have already commenced.

"This New Dispensation, or Fourth Generation," says the Countess of Caithness, "is now declared open to all who are ready to enter into the joy of their Lord." So that she is "expecting a manifestation both of the Sons and of the Daughters of God in whom the new life has already commenced, in whom the Divine Word has already become flesh." Could blasphemy go further; and if such sentiments are being openly disseminated, can we wonder at the terrific prophecies of the Apocalypse which are now awaiting their fulfilment!

According to the same lady, the year 1881 was the last of the old state of things, and 1882 commenced a new cycle, or the Spiritual Dispensation. In that case, then, the predictions, coming from so many quarters, that the age would end with the year 1881, were, after all, inspired; not indeed by the Spirit of God, but, like the oracles of old, by demons. And, if we are to believe the Countess and other Spiritualists, they were by no means falsified; so that now it is open, to those who are ready, to unite themselves with beings from another sphere.

Discussion of a text quoted in the spurious Clementine Epistle, which contains the doctrine of the Two-in-one.

From what has been already said, it will be evident that the doctrine of the Two-in-one is not new: indeed traces of it may be discovered in Plato and in many other writers. We will cite one instance only, a famous text quoted in the so-called Second Epistle of the Roman Clement, which may be rendered as follows.

"For the Lord Himself being asked by a certain person, when His kingdom should come, replied;—When the two shall be one, and that which is without as that which is within, and the male with the female, neither male nor female."

We have but to mention that "the without" is used for the man and "the within" for the woman, and the reader will at once perceive that every word in this passage refers to the doctrine which we are considering. Its meaning is, that, as soon as the human race recovers its alleged original condition, and its individual members receive their counterpartial lives from "heaven," the kingdom of Christ will have come. And it is easy to see how this text may be shortly used to glorify the kingdom of Antichrist.

For Spiritualists would have us accept it as Scripture; but its origin is scarcely satisfactory. Clement of Alexandria, who also quotes it in an extract from Julius Cassianus, the Docetic leader, informs us that the person who asked the question was Salome, and that "we do not find the saying in the four Gospels which have been handed down to us, but in the Gospel of the Egyptians."* Now the latter was a Gnostic and not a Christian work, and the particular sect which held it in the greatest esteem was that of the Encratites. Con-

* Clem. Alex. Strom. iii. 13.

cerning these, we learn from Hippolytus that they were very vainglorious, thinking themselves better than other men, because they never ate the flesh of anything that had lived, drank nothing but water, and abjured marriage. And the bishop promptly confutes their teachings by citing the prophecy in the First Epistle to Timothy.*

The doctrine, then, which was pleasing to the Encratites may reasonably be so to their modern imitators; but neither by its apparent origin and its supporters, nor by its tendency, does it commend itself to Christians.

Was the realization of the Two-in-one the great secret of the Mysteries?

Now Plato, the Gnostic leaders, and the Theurgic Neo-Platonists, were—like the majority of educated men in their centuries—initiates of the Mysteries. Since, then, they all seem to have been acquainted with the theory of the Two-in-one, is it not possible that the attainment of that state may have been the consummation of the Mysteries? The account of them given in the next chapter will be found to agree well with such a conclusion; and the book quoted there, "The Perfect Way," contains a sketch of a bas-relief in the Temple of the South, in the isle of Elephantine on the Nile, which adds a little further confirmation. The subject of this ancient work of art is an initiation scene: the candidate stands holding a cross,† with the initiating priestess

Hippol. Refut. Omn. Hær. viii. 13.

† "The vertical line being the male principle, and the horizontal the female, out of the union of the two at the intersection point is formed the cross—the oldest symbol in the Egyptian history of gods. It is the key of heaven in the rosy fingers of Neith, the celestial virgin, who opens the gate at dawn for the exit of her first begotten, the radiant sun. It is the Stauros of the Gnostics, and the philosophical cross of the high-grade

of Isis, bearing the rosary of the five wounds, on the one side, and the male representative of Hermes on the other—an obvious type of the junction of male and female. Over his head hovers a dove, intended, perhaps, for the spirit which is about to enter into and possess him, and in the background is an attendant priestess, holding a cross in one hand, and "the chalice of Existence or Incarnation," fixed upon the staff of Hermes, in the other. The apparel of either priestess consists, apparently, of a head-dress and deep collar only.

But if we may interpret this scene of the union of a demon with the initiate, according to the theory of the Two-in-one, it would seem that we may go even further.

Is it that of which Paul speaks as the Mystery of Lawlessness?

For, upon such an assumption, may not this be the particular crime to which Paul referred when he spoke of that Mystery of Lawlessness which was working secretly in his days, but would afterwards, when the hindrance should be removed, be disclosed to all, as the set time for the revelation of the Lawless One drew nigh? Such a conclusion is far from improbable: and should it be correct, it would follow that Satan's last stake is now being thrown; and that the great secret, guarded with such jealousy for many centuries, has at length been revealed to the world. It may be that the influences of the Spirit of God are even now in process of withdrawal, as He prepares for that departure from

Masons. We find this symbol ornamenting the *tee* of the umbrella-shaped oldest pagodas in Thibet, China, and India, as we find it in the hand of Isis, in the shape of the "handled cross." In one of the Chaitya caves, at Ajunta, it surmounts the three umbrellas in stone, and forms the centre of the vault" ("Isis Unveiled," vol. ii., p. 270).

earth which will leave it open for Nephilim, sevenfold worse than those who formerly dwelt in it, to enter, and for a short season to work their will upon the human race.

There is yet another point which may be illustrated by the initiation scene described above, the fact that many Spiritualists and Theosophists are looking for the advent, in some mode, of a Divine mother, or female Messiah, to preside over the new era. For, in the bas-relief, a woman is taking the place of Isis as initiator, while the representative of Hermes occupies a secondary position. By this arrangement some expectation is probably indicated which is, perhaps, accommodated to Western minds by the announcement of a female as well as a male Messiah, a second Eve to supplement the second Adam.

The advent of the Divine Mother.

But we must leave this dreadful theme, which we have treated at once, although it, perhaps, belongs more properly to the next chapter. The foundations of the world are shaking: but the Lord knoweth them that are His, and He shall deliver them from every evil work, and preserve them unto His heavenly Kingdom.

We have yet to consider the second way in which marriage is forbidden, not by direct prohibition, but by strange doctrines concerning elective affinities and spiritual alliances, which tend to an utter rejection of it as ordained by God.

Indirect prohibition of marriage.

In spite of our Lord's express declaration to the contrary, Spiritualists of the school with which we have now to deal teach that the marriage of male and female is the great institution of the next life, and that every person has an affinity who will be his or her spouse for eternity; but that in this present time there are frequent mistakes, and that, consequently, those who are not spiritual affinities being joined together are unable to agree and live in union. This they affirm to be the cause of all misfortune in wedded life.

In some of their books the victim of an unsuitable marriage is exhorted to bear his calamity, and to comfort himself with the certainty of receiving his own spouse in the next world, though hints that relief may come in the present life are occasionally given.* But, apart from its opposition to Scripture, how unlikely is such an idea to sooth the irritation of ill-assorted couples! Many Spiritualists, however, go much further, and declare that marriage should last only so long as the contracting parties may be disposed to live together: in short, that God's first ordinance, like every other restraint, is to be snapped asunder as soon as it becomes wearisome.

Mr. Herbert Noyes' sentiments in regard to marriage.

Let the reader judge what is likely to result if the subjoined opinions become prevalent. The extracts are taken from a paper on *Matrimonial Relations and Social Reforms*, read by Mr. Herbert Noyes before the London Dialectical Society.

After expressing his opinion that "divorce should be prompt and free whenever mutually desired," and obtainable under certain conditions and safeguards even when demanded by one only of the pair, Mr. Noyes remarks, that the main obstacle to such a state of things "consists of untenable ecclesiastical fallacies." He then gives utterance to the following sentiments;—

"Of all the mischievous inventions blasphemously ascribed to the Almighty, and published as His Word,

* The following is an example;—"Whether partnerships for life are to be the law of the future, time will show. We have our

I doubt if there be one more mischievous and mistaken than the text which asserts that there is no marriage in Heaven."

"I maintain that the churches are entirely in the right in affirming true marriage to be indissoluble; entirely in the wrong in asserting that their own rites are sufficient to constitute a true marriage. It is my firm conviction that affection and affinity are indispensable to an indissoluble marriage, and that animal passions temporarily excited are not reliable indications of these indispensable elements of the true matrimonial relations. I am disposed to think that in a true marriage man and wife are not so much one flesh as virtually one spirit and one soul — one in time and one for eternity; and I believe that when we begin to elevate the art of mesmerism into the status of a science —the science of soul—we shall begin to understand mysteries of which but the faintest glimmer is now dawning on our intelligence."

"The adventitious sanctity of marriage derived from ecclesiastical ceremonies is doomed to be ignored by coming generations. The true sanctity of marriage relations, based on the Divine laws of human nature, must come to be recognised in its place, when the future race are fully initiated in the mysteries of Will."

Direct opposition of these ideas to Scripture. They form a bond of union between Spiritualists and Secularists.

It would be worse than useless to multiply quotations upon so painful a subject. What we have given will suffice as a specimen of opinions which have been for some time spreading and developing. We

own opinions on that subject, which are based, not on theories, but on facts; and these all point in one direction. Be that as it may; at present, alliances are made for life" ("Life Beyond the Grave," p. 135).

will only add that American Spiritualists are even more advanced than their English brethren.

The awful opposition of such views to Bible doctrine needs no demonstration. For the law of God enacts that man and woman when joined together are one flesh, not one spirit,* and that neither of them may leave the other, save for the single cause of faithlessness,† till death severs the bond, when the survivor is free. But the whole paper from which we have quoted, and especially the clause respecting "the mysteries of Will," is gravely portentous of an approaching wave of lawlessness, which may, for the time, almost sweep the primal institution of the Creator from the face of the earth.

And in their ideas of marriage, and of the Divine right of human will, Spiritualists are strongly supported by numbers of Secularists,‡ from whose ranks they are receiving continual accessions. Strange that they who scoff at the miracles of God should give heed to those of Satan! How do the words of our Lord seem again to apply;—"I am come in My Father's name, and ye receive Me not: if another shall come in his own name, him ye will receive!"§

But, as we have before seen, Spiritualists teach that all will marry in the next world, if they do not in this; and that true marriage lasts through eternity. The natural inference is that the true spouses of some are already in the spirit-land. And to such an extent is this infer-

Marriage of those still on earth with beings in the other world.

* Gen. ii. 24.

† Matt. v. 32.

‡ The programme of the International League includes the abolition of marriage.

§ John v. 43.

ence followed out that many are reported to be receiving visits and communications from those spiritual beings with whom they are to be united for ever. An inspirational poem by T. L. Harris, entirely devoted to the subject of spirit-marriage, contains these lines ;—

> "Day passes on. The purple twilight ends,
> Each forest tree grows radiant to behold;
> A skyey Paradise above extends.
> Angels descend, their Loves below to fold
> In sweet embrace. With amethyst and gold
> Their deathless forms are clad. At last ascends
> That heavenly landscape; but 'tis Eden still,
> And the heart takes of love divine its liquid fill."

The ceremonious marriage of a woman to a demon is a thing not unknown in the United States: whether it has ever taken place in England we cannot say.

Account of a book entitled "An Angel's Message."

But there is before us a book called "An Angel's Message," and claiming to be communications from a spirit—who affirms that he has become an angel—to an English lady, his destined bride for eternity. This awfully blasphemous composition might deceive many by its apparent sanctity, and by the frequent truths with which the strange doctrine is mingled. But let us call to mind the prediction that the deceiving demons should speak lies in hypocrisy: let us remember that he who would press the poisoned cup takes care that the vehicle of his deadly drug shall be good wine. A few extracts from the communications will reveal the abyss to the brink of which the votaries of Spiritualism are apparently hastening, and will force upon us an awful inference.

The communicating demon describes himself as the spirit of a man of deep religious feeling, who, during his sojourn in the flesh, was accustomed to visit the house of the medium's father, though at that time he found no attraction in the medium herself. In course of years he died, as did also the mother of the lady. Soon after the decease of the latter her daughter began to receive communications understood to come from her, and among them the following with which we are at present concerned.

Extracts from the communications.

"I have seen how happy I have made you by all that has been written. Love and bless Him Who has shown you, dear J—, that you have some one that loves you here. Dear W— sees that you love his memory. He sees that, before I told you of his love for you, my dear child had always thought him a very high spirit, but now that I have been permitted to tell her, she will be sure to believe it is indeed true."

"I shall now tell you more about W—. I see that this opens your heart to him who loves you more than I can tell you. For he is your own W—, he is your conjugal partner, the one heaven has intended for you from all eternity. I see that you are now thankful that you never formed any connection in the world."

"I will now tell you what will give you great confidence. W— himself will write through you in his own hand."

"I see that I have given you great happiness. I have no more to say. When you begin again W— will write through you."

Henceforth the demon-lover inspired the medium, and, after a little hypocritical talk about her faults and their remedy, got rid of the difficulty of our Lord's declaration that in heaven they neither marry nor are given in marriage by remarking that the Sadducees asked their question in a natural sense, and that the Lord answered them in the same way.

"For in the world a woman may have seven husbands, and yet not one of them may be spiritually united to her. There may have been no union of the soul with any of the seven, or there may have been with one, but with one only; and she shall surely be his wife in heaven, and none other. 'They twain shall be one flesh, and let no man put them asunder.'"

The reader will not fail to notice the daring misapplication of the texts quoted, as well as the inference which is thereby suggested. So are God's barriers of morality being broken down that the flood of corruption may rush in.

"She who writes these lines is my wife more than may be thought possible by those who have not had a similar state opened in themselves. She is not so as to her natural body, but she is so as to her spiritual body. For 'there is a natural body, and there is a spiritual body.' The one is within the other as a kernel within a shell.

"But this state can come to the outward perception of those only who are open to spirit-intercourse. No others can perceive, during their life in the world of nature, that which belongs to the spirit alone. This state constitutes mediumship; for she who is mine is not only a writing medium, but she is also susceptible of very palpable impressions of my presence with her. We are one; and she has received the assurance of that truth by other means than the merely being told so in these writings."

There is much more to the same effect; but that

which we have quoted is sufficient to unveil the danger which may be threatening many. We will only further show what form manifestations often take, by extracting the subjoined account of intercourse between the medium and the demon represented to be the spirit of her mother.

"She has received the ardent caresses of her loved spirit-mother when in a state for open communion; but this was also before her writing mediumship commenced. On one occasion the visitation was preceded by the appearance of a white dove of a very brilliant aspect, sitting on an eminence and looking towards her. She calmly contemplated this vision and remarked to herself how beautiful it was; being perfectly awake—yet her bodily eyes were sealed, so that she could not open them, though earnestly desiring to do so. On the disappearance of the dove she was palpably embraced, but she saw no form; her spirit-eye could see the dove, but not the angelic being who then approached her. Well did she know it was the spirit of her she loved, for I was then unknown to her. Plainly did she perceive that ardent sphere of love; palpably did she feel the living breath; clearly did she hear the whispering voice—but could not catch the words it uttered, for her spirit-ear was not sufficiently opened—rapidly did that angel form pass over her passive frame, and she opened her eyes to the world of nature, filled with the tears of joy, for well she knew that it was an angelic visitation. She has also received kisses on her forehead, when so fully awake that she has asked if they might be repeated, and they were repeated as plainly as before; the feeling being precisely as though her brow were pressed by human lips, though none were in the room with her. She has felt drops of crystal water fall on her forehead, and has also asked if it might be repeated, which was done. These latter cases occurred when she was perfectly awake, for in the last instance she was about to rise, as the morning sun warned her it was already day."

Inference from these extracts.

What, then, shall we say to these things? There is nothing new under the sun. Are the so-called myths of Leda, of Europa, and of Ilia, actual history after all! Is it a literal fact that an evil spirit loved Sara the daughter of Raguel! Had Pope Innocent the Eighth a real insight of the truth when he fulminated his decretal against intercourse with the incubi and succubæ! And are the Nephilim again threatening a general descent upon our world and a repetition of the great sin of the days of old! Unless we are prepared to stigmatize large numbers of our fellow-creatures as deliberate impostors, we seem almost forced to such a conclusion.

Prophetic intimation that, in the last days, fallen angels will again appear among men.

In the twelfth chapter of the Apocalypse it is plainly announced that, before the development of Antichrist and the unparalleled woes of the end, Satan and his angels will be driven out of heaven, swept down from their aerial abodes, and confined to the narrow bounds of earth. Then will all the Nephilim, who are yet at liberty, be among men, and will quickly make them feel the meaning of that awful utterance, "Woe to the inhabiters of the earth and of the sea! for the Devil is come down unto you, having great wrath, because he knoweth that he hath but a short time." Then, not merely the demons, but the great Angels of Darkness, the Principalities, the Powers, and the World-rulers, maddened by the thought that they have lost their fair realms for ever, and that the Lord is at hand to complete their destruction, will in their rage break through every restraint, and recklessly gratify their own evil desires. And so, in the most appalling sense, the earth will again become corrupt and filled with violence.

Spiritualism seems to be a preparation for this event.

For this terrible inroad Spiritualism appears to be preparing the way. The army of demons has been sent forth in advance to bring about a universal apostacy from God and denial of Christ, and to establish a general communication between the Powers of Darkness and the children of disobedience. Years ago these demons predicted the future appearance upon earth of spiritual beings in material bodies: what has been their aim but to open men's hearts for the reception of the banished angels? Manifestations are continually increasing in power; appearances of tangible forms from the unseen world are matters of common occurrence; women are being taught that they are the wives of angels; the world is becoming accustomed to supernatural visitants! Surely the Prince of the Air must have heard that the legions of Michael are marching, and is hastily preparing his place of retreat.

THEOSOPHY.

CHAPTER XIV.

THEOSOPHY.

Theosophy.

DURING the last few years another strange phase of thought has appeared in the wake of Spiritualism, equally destructive of faith and boldly avowing its Pagan origin. We allude to Theosophy, now so common a subject of conversation, and which, in various forms, is ever presenting itself in the periodic and other literature of the day. And since we understand it to be the revival of a philosophy communicated by the Nephilim, and believe that the signs of the last apostacy may be detected in its teachings, we admit a claim upon our consideration which we will now endeavour to discharge.

The ancient religions were able to satisfy the cravings of intellect.

For many centuries the true nature of the early systems of religion was unsuspected by Christians. It has been usual to regard Paganism as a mere brutal worship of stocks and stones, as a gross superstition, so utterly devoid of intellectuality that, when once expelled, it could never return and again deceive an enlightened and educated world. It was carelessly assumed to have sprung from ignorance and mental incapacity; whereas its wonderful power of adapting itself to the carnal mind should rather have suggested an emanation from those Powers of the Air which effected the ruin of our first parents. And to suppose that anything which comes from such a source need be wanting in intellectual vigour and beauty, would be a folly as great as that which represents the fallen Son of the Morning under the guise of a horned monster. There is little chance of escaping his snares unless we recognise the fact that the resources of intellect are yet at the command of himself and his hosts, that still

> "There is some soul of *greatness* in things evil."

And so we might reasonably expect to find a faint reflection, at least, of this greatness in those who were inspired by fallen angels, and who learnt to own them as lords. Nor would such an expectation be disappointed; for if we investigate early Paganism by the light of recent discoveries, we soon perceive that its chief strength lay in its intellectual attractions, and that many of its priests and initiates were distinguished as philosophers and men of science.

Hence the present revival of their doctrines and practices, which were originally communicated by Nephilim.

But—still more strange!—if, after our investigation, we glance at the world of to-day, we see the men of this nineteenth century returning to the wisdom of long past ages, and modern thought sustaining its flight upon the wings of ancient lore. Nay, almost every characteristic of antiquity seems to be reappearing. Open intercourse with demons is being renewed on a vast scale in the very heart of Christendom, and even among the hitherto somewhat Sadducean Protestants: numerous circles are carrying on magical practices: attempts are being made to restore the influence of those ancient Mysteries which are said to have been always kept up by a few initiates: the old mesmeric healings are again performed: star-gazers and planet-rulers have greatly increased, while many amateur students are zealously assisting to re-establish the power of astrology over the human race: the use of the divining rod, and countless other practices of primal and mediæval times, are once more becoming common. And, impossible as it would have seemed a few years ago, all these "superstitions" are floating back to us upon the tide of "modern thought." They come no longer veiled in mystery, nor claiming to be miraculous or Divine; but, in accordance with the spirit of the age, present themselves as the fruit of science, as an evidence of the progress of knowledge in regard to the laws of the visible and invisible worlds.

"Unless we mistake the signs," says the writer of "Isis Unveiled," "the day is approaching when the world will receive the proofs that only ancient religions were in harmony with nature, and ancient science embraced all that can be known. . . . An era of disenchantment and rebuilding will soon begin—nay, has already begun. The cycle has almost run its course; a new one is about to begin, and the future pages of history may contain full evidence, and convey full proof, that

> "'If ancestry can be in aught believed,
> Descending spirits have conversed with man,
> And told him secrets of the world unknown.'" *

They may indeed: for the Apocalypse foretells a yet future sojourn of fallen angels upon earth, an event which will quickly dispel scepticism in regard to the past. But even now the evidence is ample, and may

* "Isis Unveiled," vol. i., p. 38.

be found, not merely in the Biblical account of the Nephilim, but in the myths of all nations. What significance, for example, are we to attach to the story that Ceres instructed men in agriculture? Why is music attributed to Apollo, eloquence to Mercury? Whence arose the legend of the great Titan, who, in defiance of Zeus, expounded the civilizing arts to men, taught them medicine, astronomy, and divination, and stole fire for them from heaven? Or, again, is there no basis of fact for the catalogue, contained in the mysterious book of Enoch, of arts which the Nephilim are said to have introduced among men;* no reflection of truth in the appeal of Michael and his companions, when they say;—"See, then, what Azâzâl has done; how he has taught all wickedness on earth, and has revealed the secrets of the world which were prepared in the heavens"?†

If, however, the ancient philosopher drew his earliest information from such a source, we cease to wonder at its extent. The hints of an acquaintance with the spherical form of the earth, and with the fact of its motion round the sun, alleged to be found in the Vedas, are no longer incredible. We can listen with equanimity to the astronomical revelations of the Great Pyramid. Nor are we bewildered by the assertion that many of the vaunted results of modern science were included in the instruction given to the initiates of the Hermetic, Orphic, Eleusinian, and Cabbalistic mysteries, and were familiar to Chaldean Magi, Egyptian Priests, Hindu Occultists, Essenes, Therapeutæ, Gnostics, and Theurgic Neo-Platonists.

* Book of Enoch, ii. 8.
† *Ibid.*, ii. 9.

And since we are also told that all occult societies have been affiliated, and, therefore, have in some sort carried on a continuous study, we are fain to admit, upon this assumption, that they may long ago have passed beyond the limits of modern science, seeing that the latter is the accumulated experience of comparatively few generations. Still more ought they to have advanced in metaphysics and psychology, studies which they have ever regarded as the most important.

Occult science probably transcends all merely human knowledge, and contains the germs of the philosophies and religions of the world.

"There is thus," in the words of A. P. Sinnett, "something more than a mere archæological interest in the identification of the occult system with the doctrines of the initiated organisations in all ages of the world's history, and we are presented by this identification with the key to the philosophy of religious development. Occultism is not merely an isolated discovery showing humanity to be possessed of certain powers over Nature, which the narrower study of Nature from the merely materialistic standpoint has failed to develop; it is an illumination cast over all previous spiritual speculation worth anything, of a kind which knits together some apparently divergent systems. It is to spiritual philosophy much what Sanscrit was found to be to comparative philology; it is a common stock of philosophical roots. Judaism, Christianity, Buddhism, and the Egyptian theology, are thus brought into one family of ideas."*

The last sentence is undoubtedly true, provided we remember that "Judaism" here stands for the Cabbala; and that "Christianity" does not mean the pure and

* "The Occult World," p. 6.

simple faith set forth in the New Testament, but the ecclesiastical compound of Heathenism to which the writers of "The Perfect Way" thus frankly express their obligation ;—

"For, like the Puritans, who coated with plaster and otherwise covered and hid from view the sacred images and decorations which were obnoxious to them, Orthodoxy has at least preserved through the ages the symbols which contain the truth beneath the errors with which it has overlaid them."

When the real meaning of these symbols becomes generally known, the object of the initiates in foisting them upon the Church will be very apparent. A revelation of their true nature will shatter the faith of those who rest upon them in the fond delusion that they are Christian, and make many a rough place smooth for the advance of the great apostacy.

The Asiatic Brotherhood, and its determination to communicate with the world.

Thus, by means of various secret associations, Occultism appears to have been handed down from the times of the Mysteries to our own days. The only Brotherhood at present mentioned in the outer world is one which extends its branches throughout the East, and of which the headquarters are reported to be in Thibet. It is open to any person who can prove himself fit for membership ; but the Neophyte, or Chela, must undergo a discipline of many years, and pass through terrible ordeals, before he can be completely initiated. These trials, it is affirmed, are neither arranged by caprice, nor designed to support a jealous exclusiveness ; but are necessary to the pupil himself, to prepare him for the tremendous revelation which will at last reward his successful perseverance.

But—as we are informed by those who claim authority for their statements—the advances of Modern Science, and especially the spread of evolutionary philosophy, having fitted the world for deeper teaching, the Brothers decided that the time had come to communicate with it, and openly influence its religion and philosophy. They have, however, become so etherealized by their practices that they are unable to endure contact with coarse human nature; it was, therefore, necessary to employ intermediaries.

Madame Blavatski and the Theosophical Society.

The first person known to have been chosen for this purpose was a Madame Blavatski,* a Russian gentlewoman, granddaughter of Princess Dolgorouki of the elder branch, and widow of General N. V. Blavatski, Governor, during the Crimean war and for many years, of Erivan in Armenia. This lady, after devoting herself to occult pursuits for some thirty years, repaired to a Himalayan retreat, where she spent seven years under the immediate direction of the Brothers, and was initiated and instructed for her mission. She was then dismissed to the outer world, and, having proceeded to America, and attracted there a number of sympathising minds, she organized the Theosophical Society, at New York, under the presidency of Colonel Olcott. This was in the year 1875. Then, after crossing to England and establishing the Society in this country, she returned to India, where

* Lately two Indian natives, Ramaswamy, a Government official at Tinnevelly, and Damodar, have been mentioned, and Colonel Olcott has become a *chela*. The latter is said to have seen the Brothers both in the flesh and in the astral form. "By a long series of the most astounding thaumaturgic displays, when he was first introduced to the subject in America, he was made acquainted with their powers" (*Light*, December 22nd, 1883).

her flattery of the natives and dislike to their British rulers, together with her nationality, caused her, and not without reason, to be regarded as a spy. At last, however, perceiving her mistake, she changed her mode of action, and, having obtained introductions to British officials at Simla, began to make some progress. The objects of the Society were then set forth as follows.

I. To form the nucleus of a Universal Brotherhood of Humanity.

II. To study Aryan literature, religion, and science.

III. To vindicate the importance of this inquiry.

IV. To explore the hidden mysteries of Nature, and the latent powers of man.

Subsequently a fifth object of the Society, the destruction of Christianity, was revealed. "Later it has determined to spread among the 'poor benighted Heathen' such evidences as to the practical results of Christianity as will at least give both sides of the story to the communities among which missionaries are at work. With this view it has established relations with associations and individuals throughout the East, to whom it furnishes authenticated reports of the ecclesiastical crimes and misdemeanours, schisms and heresies, controversies and litigations, doctrinal differences and Biblical criticisms and revisions, with which the press of Christian Europe and America constantly teems. Christendom has been long and minutely informed of the degradation and brutishness into which Buddhism, Brahmanism, and Confucianism have plunged their deluded votaries, and many millions have been lavished upon foreign missions under such false representations. The Theosophical Society, seeing daily exemplifications of this very state of things as the sequence of Christian teaching and example—the latter especially—thought it simple justice to make the facts known in Palestine, India, Ceylon, Cashmere, Tartary, Thibet, China, and Japan, in all of which countries it has influential correspondents. It may also in time have much to say about the conduct of the missionaries to those who contribute to their support."*

It will, therefore, be seen that this foe has made a formal declaration of war. By the autumn of 1883 there were already seventy branches of the Society in India, and "many thousands of Mahomedans, Buddhists, Hindus, Parsees, Christians, officials and non-officials, governors and governed, have been brought together by its instrumentality."† As proofs of its levelling power, the following incidents will not be without significance to those who know the peoples of India.

"In the year 1880 a mixed delegation of *Hindus and Parsees* were deputed by the Bombay Branch to assist the founders in organizing *Buddhist* Branches in Ceylon. In 1881 the *Buddhists* reciprocated by sending over delegates to Tinnevelly to assist in organizing a *Hindu* Branch, and these *Buddhists* were, together with Colonel Olcott, received with rapturous welcome *inside* a most sacred *Hindu* Temple, in the enclosure of which they planted a cocoa-nut tree in commemoration of their visit."‡

Dissemination of Theosophy in England and France.

Satisfied with these results, and with their success in other countries, the Brotherhood authorised A. P. Sinnett to reveal some portions of their philosophy to the Western world, which he did in the spring of 1883, in

* "Isis Unveiled," vol. i., pp. xli., xlii.

† "Hints on Esoteric Theosophy," No. I., p. 18.

‡ *Ibid.*, pp. 18, 19.

a volume entitled "Esoteric Buddhism." But a more remarkable book had been published in the previous year, "the inner inspirations" of which Mr. Sinnett supposes to be identical with those of his own work.* It is called "The Perfect Way, or the Finding of Christ," and its anonymous writers—for they claim inspiration, and decline to be styled authors—certainly display considerable ability; though in the case of the Hebrew and Greek Scriptures they exhibit a knowledge far less accurate than that which they claim in regard to the doctrines of the Mysteries. Sometimes also, to suit their purpose, they give strange meanings to words, without condescending to hint at the process by which they reached their conclusion.

Yet again, two or three years before the appearance of this work, "Les Quatres Evangiles expliqués en Esprit et en Verité" had been published in Paris by M. Roustaing. This gentleman affirms that he wrote from the dictation of the four evangelists and the other apostles, who were sent to make the communication to him. He is not without admirers and exponents in England, among the foremost of whom are the Countess of Caithness and Miss Anna Blackwell. His work is a further development of the philosophy of Allan Kardec, whose volumes have obtained an immense circulation throughout France.†

Now the fundamental theory of all these books, however much they may differ in comparatively unimportant details, is the doctrine of the evolution of the soul by means of repeated incarnations, or, as the

* It would seem, however, to be a production of Western rather than Eastern Occultism.

† One of these, "The Spirit's Book," was some time ago translated by Miss Anna Blackwell from the 120th thousand.

writers of "The Perfect Way" put it, "the Pre-existence and Perfectibility of the Soul." To expound this doctrine, we will take the last mentioned treatise as our text book.

Theosophy is identical with the doctrines of the Mysteries. Intuitional Memory.

Its writers, in explaining their position, declare the identity of their teaching with that which was given to the initiates in "the sacred Mysteries of antiquity." But, they continue, "now, as of old, those Mysteries comprise two classes of doctrine, of which one class only—that which, being historical and interpretative, belongs to the Lesser Mysteries—may be freely communicated. The other, known as the Greater Mysteries, is reserved for those who, in virtue of the interior unfoldment of their consciousness, contain within them the necessary witness."* "For reasons arising out of this necessary reserve" the writers can give no precise account of the origin of the inspired fragments which they frequently quote as authoritative.

What they mean by the unfoldment of the consciousness, or "the faculty of intuition," is soon made apparent. During the ages which we pass in countless embodiments, "that in us which perceives and permanently remembers is the Soul." And although, owing to the grossness of our present nature, we are beclouded and have lost the use of her treasures of memory, nevertheless "all that she has once learnt is at the service of those who duly cultivate relations with her."†

* "The Perfect Way," p. xiii.

† *Ibid.*, p. 4. Indeed, the man who successfully cultivates these relations seems to gain unbounded power. For "it is not his own memory alone that, thus endowed, he reads. The very planet of which he is the offspring, is, like himself, a Person, and is possessed of a medium of memory. And he to whom the soul lends

"The Intuition, then, is that operation of the mind whereby we are enabled to gain access to the interior and permanent region of our nature, and there to possess ourselves of the knowledge which in the long ages of her past existence the soul has made her own."* And Intuitional Memory must be "developed and otherwise assisted by the only mode of life compatible with sound philosophic aspirations," "the mode, therefore, invariably from the first followed by all candidates for initiation into the sacred mysteries of existence. It is only by living the life that man can know of the doctrine."† But if we inquire what are the rules of this life, the whole system is instantly condemned by the reply, that marriage is prohibited to the neophyte, and that he must abstain from flesh and alcohol. We at once recognise the "falling away" of which Paul wrote, and perceive that the so-called Intuitional Memory is no recovery of a knowledge which lies hidden in man, but an inspiration from demons who speak lies in hypocrisy.

Fourfold nature of man.

Affirming, then, that their information was obtained by means of Intuitional Memory, the writers proceed to teach that man is possessed of a fourfold nature, and that "the four elements which constitute him are, counting from without inwards, the material body, the fluidic perisoul or astral body,‡

her ears and eyes may have knowledge not only of his own past history, but of the past history of the planet, as beheld in the pictures imprinted in the magnetic light whereof the planet's memory consists. For there are actually ghosts of events, manes of past circumstances, shadows on the protoplasmic mirror, which can be evoked" ("The Perfect Way," pp. 8, 9).

* *Ibid.*, pp. 3, 4.

† *Ibid.*, p. 4.

‡ This is the so-called *doppelgänger*, which can be projected from the material body and made to appear at any distance.

the soul or individual, and the spirit or Divine Father and life of his system."* They then give their evolutionary theory, of which the following is a rapid sketch.

The manifestation of Substance. Spirit and Matter. The Pagan Trinity.

The interplanetary ether, known in the terminology of Occultism as the Astral Fluid, is the first manifestation of Substance, that which sub-stands all phenomena; and its ultimate expression is what we call Matter. There is but one Substance: and, therefore, Spirit and Matter are not two things, but are two states of the same thing; just as solid, palpable, incompressible ice is, under another condition, the same thing as fluid, invisible, compressible vapour.

Since, then, there is but one Substance, therefore the substance of the Soul, and therein of all things, and the substance of Deity, are one and the same. "And of this Substance the Life also is called God, Who, as Living Substance, is at once Life and Substance, one and yet twain, or two in one. And that which proceeds from these two, and is, theologically, called the Son and the Word, is necessarily the expression of both, and is, potentially, the Universe; for He creates it after His own Divine image by means of the Spirit He has received. Now the Divine Substance is, in its original condition, homogeneous. Every monad of it, therefore, possesses the potentialities of the whole. Of such a monad, in its original condition, every individual soul consists. And of the same Substance, projected into lower conditions, the material universe consists. It undergoes, however, no radical change of nature through such projection; but its manifestation—on

* "The Perfect Way," p. 5.

whatever plane occurring—is always as a Trinity in Unity; since that whereby substance becomes manifest is the evolution of its Trinity. Thus—to reckon from without inwards, and below upwards—on the plane physical, it is Force, universal Ether, and their offspring the Material World. On the plane intellectual, it is Life, Substance, and Phenomenon. On the plane spiritual—its original point of radiation—it is Will, Wisdom, and the Word. And on all planes whatever, it is, in some mode, Father, Mother, and Child."*

The last few sentences we have cited without abbreviation because of their importance. They contain a clear exposition of the false Trinity as, fundamentally, it is taught in all Pagan systems. Its irreconcilable and blasphemous opposition to Biblical revelation we will presently explain, but must now proceed with our sketch.

The process of evolution, whereby the Soul, imprisoned at first in inorganic matter, progresses until it ultimately becomes a Deity.

The monads of the Divine substance are at first incarcerated without individualisation in something material. And "there is no mode of Matter in which the potentiality of personality, and therein of man, does not subsist. For every molecule is a mode of the universal consciousness. Without consciousness is no being. For consciousness *is* being. The earliest manifestation of consciousness appears in the obedience paid to the laws of gravitation and chemical affinity, which constitute the basis of the later evolved organic laws of nutritive assimilation. And the perception, memory, and experience represented in man are the accumulations of long ages of toil and thought, gradually advancing, through the development of the

* "The Perfect Way," pp. 17-18.

consciousness, from organic combinations upward to God. Such is the secret meaning of the old mystery-story which relates how Deucalion and Pyrrha, under the direction of Themis (Wisdom), produced men and women from stones, and so peopled the renewed earth."*

Passing, then, at length from the mineral kingdom, the monad is manifested in the lowest modes of organic life, and at this point is individualised by self-generation, and becomes a soul or nucleus to the cell in which it has manifested itself. "And once formed, it is capable, on the breaking up of its cell, of passing into and informing another cell."† And so it progresses, in a series of lives, from the vegetable to the animal, and from the animal to the human. After experiencing many existences in the last mentioned state of being, the conditions of each rebirth being determined by the results, or *karma*, of the preceding life, it rises to the supernatural. And so at length it relinquishes its *existence* for the *being* from which it was originally projected; but returns with conscious individuality, and the full advantage of all its experiences. And returning it becomes reunited to the Deity; so that we must "conceive of God as a vast spiritual body constituted of many individual elements, all having but one will, and, therefore, being one. This condition of oneness with the Divine Will and Being constitutes what in Hindu mysticism is called the celestial Nirvâna. But though becoming pure spirit, or God, the individual retains his individuality. So that, instead of all being finally merged in the One, the One becomes many. Thus does God become millions. God is multitudes, and

* "The Perfect Way," p. 19.
† *Ibid.*, p. 18.

nations, and kingdoms, and tongues; and the voice of God is as the sound of many waters."*

Such is an outline of this daring attempt to deny both the Father and the Son, and to set before men, in a manner peculiarly seductive, the old temptation, "Ye shall be as God." It was one of the secrets taught to the initiates of antiquity, and several of the great sages are said to have remembered previous incarnations, especially Crishna, Pythagoras, Plato, Apollonius, and the Buddha Gautama. "This last—the Messenger, who fulfilled for the mystics of the East the part which six hundred years later was, for the mystics of the West, fulfilled by Jesus—is stated to have recovered the recollection of five hundred and fifty of his own incarnations. And the chief end of his doctrine is to induce men so to live as to shorten the number and duration of their earth-lives. 'He,' say the Hindu Scriptures, 'who in his lifetime recovers the memory of all that his soul has learnt, is already a god.'"†

Biblical texts quoted in support of the doctrine of Transmigration.

Now, since the Prince of this World apparently deems that the time has come to procure the same unanimity in his human as in his spiritual kingdom, and would, therefore, propagate this evolutionary philosophy in lands which have been long influenced by the revelation of God, testimony in its favour must needs be produced from the Christian Scriptures. We adduce a few specimens which will enable the reader to estimate the value of such a support.

In the Baptist's impassioned address to the bigoted Jews, he points to the pebbles on the shores of the Jordan, and exclaims;—"Think you that God cannot

* "The Perfect Way," p. 46. † *Ibid.*, pp. 22-3.

do without you because you are sons of Abraham! Had he need of such, His power could in a moment change every one of these innumerable stones into a child of Abraham."* And again, when our Lord would show the Pharisees that God's purposes are irresistible, He says;—"I tell you that if these shall hold their peace, the stones will cry out." These two passages are supposed to furnish clear evidence that both John and our Lord were aware of the presence in the stones of Divine monads which would be educated, by means of various embodiments, until they were able to assume the human form!

Again; Daniel receives the promise that he shall rest, and stand in his lot at the end of the days, when the resurrection which has just been revealed to him takes place. This is supposed to indicate reincarnation. The Lord says of John;—"If I will that he tarry till I come, what is that to thee?" The comment is;—"It was intimated by Jesus that he should tarry within reach of the earth-life, either for reincarnation or metempsychosis, when the appointed time should come." The Lord is described by Paul as the Captain of our salvation made perfect through suffering: such an expression "obviously implies a course of experience far in excess of anything that is predicable of a single brief career." And so the Gnostic Carpocrates was right when "he taught that the Founder of Christianity also was simply a person who, having a soul of great age and high degree of purity, had been enabled through his mode of life to recover the memory of its past." It is true that our Lord in speaking of the blind man positively denied that he was born so on account of his

* "The Perfect Way," p. 20.

sin in a former existence; but that proves nothing, since "His refusal to satisfy the curiosity of His disciples is readily intelligible on the supposition that He was unwilling to disclose the affairs of other souls."

Finally; the Countess of Caithness boldly affirms that our Lord taught the doctrine of reincarnation when He said;—"Except a man be born again, he cannot see the Kingdom of God."* Yet Nicodemus is rebuked for understanding the words in such a sense, and numerous other passages show that the rebirth takes place upon conversion, and that the initial rite of baptism expresses the man's death and burial to the old life and resurrection to the new, in which he is exhorted thenceforth to walk. Besides which, we have Paul's emphatic assertion that "it is appointed unto men once to die." †

Theosophical account of the Fall and Redemption of man.

Such, then, are some of the best arguments which Theosophists are able to produce from the Bible in support of their fundamental theory. To state them is a sufficient refutation; and we are not surprised to find that other views advanced by these philosophers are directly opposed to Divine revelation. "The Fall of man," we are told, "does not mean, as commonly supposed, the lapse, through a specific act, of particular individuals from a state of original perfection. . . . It means such an inversion of the due relations between the soul and the body of a personality already both spiritual and material, as involves a transference of the central will of the system concerned, from the soul—

* "Serious Letters to Serious Friends," p. 129.

† Heb. ix. 27. The Greek ἅπαξ is also a strong word meaning "once for all."

which is its proper seat—to the body, and the consequent subjection of the soul to the body, and liability of the individual to sin, disease, and all other evils which result from the limitations of matter."* And connected with this exposition is the following strange doctrine, leading up, as all Paganism does, to the worship of the great Goddess, the Mother and Child, and also to a reversal of God's order in Creation.

"Whatever the sex of the person, physically, each individual is a dualism consisting of exterior and interior, manifested personality and essential individuality, body and soul, which are to each other masculine and feminine, man and woman; he the without and she the within."† And, to summarize the remainder of the paragraph, just as the woman is to the man on the planes intellectual and spiritual, so is she on the planes physical and social. She is the proper head of creation: the subjection of the feminine to the masculine in the individual was the Fall; the subjection of the woman to the man in the world is the outward and visible sign of the Fall. And it is only by "the complete restoration crowning and exaltation of the woman, in all the planes, that redemption can be effected."

Now we have already seen that Theosophists describe man as consisting of four elements, two of which are the body and astral body, constituting the masculine principle, while the third is the Soul, which is feminine. The remaining part is spirit, and this, as being an emanation from God, is, therefore, God; so that every man carries God within himself!! The Soul, then, is placed between the Divine element and the Body: and

* "The Perfect Way," p. 215.
† *Ibid.*, p. 186.

"in order properly to fulfil her function in regard to the man, and attract his regards upwards to her, she must herself aspire continually to the Divine Spirit within her, the central sun of herself, as she is that of the man." * But if she fails in this, she falls, becomes wedded to the Body, and the whole man is as the first Adam, of the earth earthy. "The result, on the other hand, of the soul's steadfast aspiration towards God—the Spirit, that is, within her—and of her consequent action upon the Body, is that this also becomes so permeated and suffused by the Spirit as at last to have no will of its own, but to be in all things one with its Soul and Spirit, and to constitute with these one perfectly harmonious system, of which every element is under full control of the central Will. It is this unification occurring within the individual which constitutes the At-one-ment. And in him in whom it occurs in its fullest extent, Nature realizes the ideal to attain which she first came forth from God." † The marriage of the Spirit and Bride has taken place, and the result is the new birth, the man is born of Water and the Spirit—water being the symbol of the woman. This "man who is reborn in us of water—our own regenerate self, the Christ Jesus and Son of man, who in saving us is called the Captain of our salvation—is said to be made perfect through suffering. This suffering must be borne by each man for himself. To deprive any one of it by putting the consequences of his acts upon another, so far from aiding that one, would be to deprive him of his means of redemption." ‡

* "The Perfect Way," p. 188.

† *Ibid.*, p. 217.

‡ *Ibid.*, p. 217-8.

According to Theosophists the Acts of the Mysteries typified the Redemption of man, whereby he becomes "a Christ," and attains to the Nirvâna of the Buddhists.

"Although redemption, as a whole, is one, the process is manifold, and consists in a series of acts, spiritual and mental."* Space will not permit us to enter into a particular description of these; we can only mention that they are affirmed to have been typified by the six acts of the Lesser and Greater Mysteries. The first three of these—the Betrothal, or initiatory purification by Baptism, the Temptation or Trial, and the Passion or Renunciation—"belong to the Mysteries of the Rational Humanity as distinguished from those of the Spiritual Humanity." The particular act whereby the Passion "is consummated and demonstrated is called the Crucifixion. This Crucifixion means a complete unreserving surrender—to the death, if need be—without opposition, even in desire, on the part of the natural man." † It "is the last stage of the Lesser Mysteries," which belong to the Queen's Chamber of the Great Pyramid,‡ "and closes initiation into them. Immediately upon giving up the ghost—or renouncing altogether the lower life—the Christ enters into His kingdom, and the veil of the Temple is rent from the top to the bottom. For this veil is that which divides the covered place from the Holy of Holies; and by its rending is denoted the passage of the individual within the kingdom of God, or of the Soul—typified by the King's Chamber."

* "The Perfect Way," p. 220.

† *Ibid.*, p. 220.

‡ Occultists affirm that "the Pyramid is designed to illustrate, both in character and duration, the various stages of the soul's history, from her first emergence in Matter to her final triumphant release and return to Spirit." The building was, they say, used for the celebration of the mysteries.

"The last three acts—the Burial," for which the coffer found in the Great Pyramid was wont to be used, "the Resurrection, and the Ascension—belong to the Greater Mysteries of the Soul and Spirit, the Spirit being the central Lord, King, and Adonai, of the system, and the Spouse of the Bride or Soul." * "The seventh and concluding act of the whole process follows the accomplishment of the three stages of the Greater Mysteries of the King or Spirit, and is called the "Consummation of the Marriage of the Son of God." In this act, the King and Queen, Spirit and Bride, πνεῦμα and νύμφη, are indissolubly united; the Man becomes pure Spirit; and the Human is finally taken up into the Divine." † "This is 'the Sabbath' of the Hebrews, the 'Nirvâna' of the Buddhists, and the Transmutation of the Alchemists." ‡

The man who attains to the consummation of the Greater Mysteries is, then, not merely an adept, but "a Christ." Such a dignity, however—"though open potentially to all—is actually in the present open, if to any, but to few. And these are necessarily they only who, having passed through many transmigrations, and advanced far on their way to maturity, have sedulously turned their lives to the best account by means of the steadfast development of all the higher faculties and qualities of man; and who, while not declining the experiences of the body, have made the Spirit, and not the body, their object and aim."§ And to accomplish their end, they have submitted "to a discipline and training the most severe, at once physical, intellectual, moral, and spiritual." Such were Osiris, Mithras,

* "The Perfect Way," p. 249. † *Ibid.*, p. 250.
‡ *Ibid.*, p. 251. § *Ibid.*, pp. 226-7.

Crishna, Zoroaster, Dionysus, Buddha, and Jesus: for although there is none other name given under heaven whereby men can be saved except that of Christ, yet that name has been shared by many.*

Theosophists desire the union of corrupted Christianity with Buddhism and Mahometanism.

Such a statement prepares us for the assertion that Christianity is no rival to Buddhism, but was the direct and necessary sequel to that system, the two being parts of one continuous and harmonious whole. "Buddha completed the regeneration of the mind: and by his doctrine and practice men are prepared for the grace which comes by Jesus. Wherefore no man can be properly Christian, who is not also, and first, Buddhist."†

Hence, of course, the union of the two religions is to be desired, and Moslems also are exhorted to join the league.

"They who seek to wed Buddha to Jesus are of the celestial and upper; and they who interpose to forbid the banns are of the astral and nether. Between the two hemispheres stand the domain and faith of Islam, not to divide, but, as umbilical cord, to unite them. And nought is there in Islamism to hinder its fulfilment of this high function, and keep it from being a partaker of the blessings to result therefrom. For not only is it the one really monotheistic and non-idolatrous religion now existing; but its symbolic Star and Crescent are essentially one with the Cross of Christ, in that they also typify the elements masculine and feminine of the Divine existence, and the relation of the Soul to God. So that Islamism has but to accomplish that other stage of its natural evolution, which

* "The Perfect Way," p. 37. † *Ibid.*, p. 257.

will enable it to claim an equal place in the Brotherhood of the Elect. This is the practical recognition in 'Allah' of Mother as well as Father, by the exaltation of the woman to her rightful station on all planes of man's manifold nature. This accomplished, Esau and Ishmael will be joined together with Abraham Isaac and Jacob* in Christ. In this recognition of the Divine idea of humanity, and its ultimate results, will consist what are called the Second Advent and Millennial reign of Christ."†

Theosophy is thus leading to a second league of Babel, which will cause the return of the Lord Jesus.

Such, then, is the Theosophic system as put forth by the ablest of its exponents. So is the history of human souls traced from their alleged incarceration in stones until, having worked their way to man's estate, and afterwards progressed so as to know "the

* "The Perfect Way," pp. 262-3. Let not the reader suppose that these names are used in any ordinary sense: the Theosophic idea of them, which we subjoin, is peculiar, and a good example of the way in which the Bible is wrested to suit any theory.

"Abraham, Isaac, and Jacob, were types of Truth, ancestors of the spiritual Israel, and representatives of the several sacred Mysteries of whose 'kingdom' the Man Regenerate is always, the world regenerate will be ultimately, by adoption and grace, the inheritor" ("Perfect Way," p. 259). The writers then give an exposition which we can only summarise.

Abraham—Brahma—represents the Mysteries of India, which are those of the Spirit, sacred to the Supreme Being.

Isaac—a name identical at once with Isis and Jesus (!)—the Mysteries of Egypt, which are those of the soul, sacred to Isis, the goddess of the Intuition, and Mother of the Christ.

Jacob, the Mysteries of Greece, which are those of the body, sacred to Bacchus, whose mystic name, Iacchos, is identical with Jacob.

So that, according to these teachers, to be initiated into the Mysteries is to become a Member of the Spiritual Israel.

† In the closing words of this paragraph, the reader will notice a furtive attempt to make void the promise of the Lord's return. Sometimes, however, the onslaughts of Theosophical writers upon

truth," they will become able—whether Jews, Christians, Buddhists, or Mahommedans—to unite in a universal belief of the doctrine that sin is expiated by transmigrations, and in the worship of "the Great Goddess." The conception of a second league of Babel has been formed in the minds of Theosophists. And as surely as it progresses towards its realization, so surely may Christian believers know that ere long the Lord will again say;—"This they begin to do: and now nothing will be restrained from them which they have imagined to do. Come! Let us go down!"

At present the rapid spread of the Theosophic philosophy and—which is, perhaps, even more significant—of various ideas, which, harmless or even good as they may be in themselves, belong to, and tend to unite with, its system, is undeniable. Christians who take the trouble to reconnoitre in the darkening twilight are

this doctrine are much more direct. For instance, Madame Blavatski suggests that the early Christian Church must have been well versed in Asiatic philosophy; "otherwise it would have neither erected into an article of faith the Second Advent, nor cunningly invented the fable of Antichrist *as a precaution against future incarnations*" ("Isis Unveiled," vol. ii., p. 535). It is, however, difficult to understand how the early Christians could have "invented" Antichrist, seeing that they were acquainted with very circumstantial prophecies respecting that terrible being, which were uttered six or seven centuries before the Christian era. And the same remark may be applied with still greater force to the Second Advent.

But both Spiritualists and Theosophists have a special aversion to these doctrines, and are eager to explain away any Scripture which refers to them. They have no desire to realize the brevity of the triumph which will crown their rebellion: it is not their wish that the true character of the leader, whom they will rejoice to deify, should be exposed: nor have they any pleasure in anticipating that sudden interposition of the Omnipotent whereby the stately image of their power will be in a moment ground to dust, and the fallen Son of the Morning, who sustained it, hurled into the depths of the Abyss.

well aware that hostile forces are converging from various quarters, but with unmistakable concert, upon their camp; while that camp itself is, alas! becoming thinned by the almost daily desertions of those who cease to believe in the Bible as the *only* revelation from God, and in the Lord Jesus as the *One* Christ and Saviour, Who bare our sins in His own body on the tree, and gave His life a ransom for many. As to the particular teaching which we have been endeavouring to explain, it is so obviously opposed to the Christian Scriptures that—since we are at present addressing ourselves solely to those who believe in the latter—comment is almost superfluous. It seems merely necessary to *know* of the doctrines, and of the proposed alliance between the great religious systems of the world; that we may understand what are likely to be the tactics of the foe, and may pray for grace to hold fast that which we have until our Lord come. We shall, therefore, offer but a few brief remarks upon some important points.

In the first place, then, we are told that Occultism is the wisdom of primal ages, a revival of the only true philosophy, held by all the great Teachers of the world, and communicated to the initiates of the Mysteries. And we are admonished that Christianity, although it did contrive to displace the old religion in the West, has proved a failure; and that we must, therefore, return to that which is better, and confess to the superiority of ancient sages.

The philosophy of the Mysteries is commended neither by their apparent origin, nor by their results.

Now, so far as the origin of Theosophy is concerned, we are quite willing to admit the account given by our opponents. Of course none but initiates can speak positively on such a subject: but all that can be noticed by one outside would certainly incline him to acquiesce in this statement.

But, by comparing the Bible with old Mythologies and the opinions of modern Theosophists, we have shown that the whole system of the Mysteries was probably communicated by those fallen angels who transgressed just before and immediately after the Flood. And such a source, though undoubtedly ancient, can scarcely be expected to inspire confidence.

Moreover, the past results of this philosophy afford but little ground for boasting. Neither time nor opportunity had been lacking to it when the crisis came, and its leaders were trembling at the rapid progress of Christianity: but what was the state of the world after so long a subjection to the power and guidance of the initiates? It was a state of moral ruin; and there would be no great difficulty in selecting passages from contemporaneous writers which would furnish material for a sketch of the universal depravity of the times of the Cæsars such as would make many a modern indifferentist stand aghast. Meanwhile, Christianity has never yet had the world under her power, as the initiates had for so many centuries. Her beginnings were small and contemptible: she was not assisted by organized Lodges, whose members included almost all the educated and respectable men in nearly every town of the Empire. On the contrary, she was at first environed with cruel persecutions; and then, as soon as it became evident that neither fire, nor wild beasts, nor the tortures of the executioner, could drive her out of the world, she was stealthily seized from behind by those very initiates who are now held up to our admiration, and who, when they had made good their hold, distorted her form, disfigured her heavenly beauty with the brand of Satan, and compelled her thenceforth to walk the earth loaded with the heavy fetters of political Heathenism. Yet, after all this maltreatment, she retained sufficient force to ameliorate somewhat the condition of the whole world, and to become the power of God and the wisdom of God to those who received her in sincerity.

Declarations of Hippolytus, Bishop of Portus, in regard to the Mysteries.

Before leaving this subject we will give a specimen of the feelings with which contemporary Christians regarded the Mysteries. A curious fragment describing the tenets of certain philosophers and logicians had descended to us from antiquity: it was entitled " The Philosophumena," and was inserted in the Benedictine copy of Origen's works. However, the style was not at all that of Origen, nor did the personal allusions suit his circumstances; so that the Benedictine editor suggested that Epiphanius might have been the writer. But nothing further was known until the year 1842, when a manuscript was discovered, in a convent on Mount Athos, including seven books of the " Philosophumena, or a Refutation of all Heresies." These proved to be the greater portion of the work—originally consisting of ten books—to which the fragment mentioned above also belonged; and scholars soon found reason to conclude that the author of the whole treatise was Hippolytus, who had been Bishop of Portus in the first half of the third century.

Now, from the knowledge to which this Hippolytus lays claim, it is clear that he must have been an initiate of the Greater Mysteries: but upon his conversion he appears to have conceived the greatest horror of them, both as regards associations and teachings. In the preface to his treatise, he affirms that the secret finally imparted was "the consummation of wickednesses"; that it was only through silence and the concealment of their Mysteries that the initiated had avoided the charge of atheism; and, further, that if any person had once submitted to the purgation necessary before the secret could be communicated, there was little need to secure his silence by oath; since the shame and monstrosity of the act itself would be sufficient to close his mouth for ever.

Such, then, are some of the reasons which forbid us to rejoice at the prospect of a restoration of the Mysteries. Moreover, we cannot but observe a sinister omen. Just as the initiates were the avowed enemies and persecutors of the early Church, so a great number of Theosophical utterances are already breathing a terrible spirit of hatred against pure Christianity, which they sometimes term "Paulism," and delight to charge with all the sins of Pagan and infidel Christendom.*

No proof of the doctrine of Transmigration is offered: its reception must depend upon faith.

Turning now to the doctrines presented to us, we find that we are required to accept a system subversive of all our hopes, a cold inexorable fatalism, which knows no God of Mercy, no Son of His love; but demands that every sin and stain be burnt out of us by ages of pain and trouble, by a succession of hundreds of earth-

* See extract from "Isis Unveiled" on p. 402. Kenealy, in his "Commentary on the Apocalypse," pp. 655-6, makes the Beast of Rev. xiii. represent the British Empire, and remarks;—"The Dragon is said to have given it dominion, because the Dragon represents Atheism, or the denial of God, which Paulism is, and England has done more to extend the dominion of this baneful heresy than any other land. The Bible Society distributes

lives; many of them spent in the most extreme misery, in the worst of circumstances; some of them in one sex, some in the other. But how can we be assured of the truth of this astounding theory? That, Theosophists say, is just our strong point. Christianity is the offspring of blind faith, whereas Theosophy is founded upon personal experience, and, therefore, upon true knowledge. We fail to see this. Their own theories teach that none but adepts can gain an insight into realities—Plato's τὰ ὄντα—and how many Theosophists profess to have acquired the faculty of Intuition? According to all the authorities we have consulted, *not a single person who is accessible!* Even the writers of "The Perfect Way" must have obtained their information through the intuitional memory of some other beings, since they do not profess to be the authors of their book. Indeed, so far as we are aware, the only adepts specifically mentioned are the members of the invisible Asiatic Brotherhood, to which reference has already been made. And yet, as regards evidence, all other Theosophists must simply believe the adept; so that the faith required of them is as absolute as that of the Christian. But it is faith in those who come in their own name, and project their influence out of mystery and darkness, in place of faith in Him Who came in His Father's name, Who openly went about doing good and healing the people, and of Whose deeds and sufferings His apostle was not afraid to say boldly

millions of our corrupted Scriptures yearly." In his "Book of Enoch," the same writer remarks of Paul;—"I do not wonder that Swedenborg, who had studied his works for over forty years, thought he saw him in Hell 'connected with one of the worst of devils'; I do not feel surprised that he speaks of him as 'a nefarious character'" (p. vii.).

in the presence of both Roman and Jewish rulers of the land ;—"This thing was not done in a corner."

The conception of a feminine person of the Trinity is altogether Pagan, and is directly contradicted by Scripture.

Theosophy, again, teaches the existence of a feminine element in the Deity. So did the ancient Pagan religions : but it is one of the great distinctions between these and the Bible that the latter rigidly excludes such an idea. Its Trinity is fully unfolded in the New Testament, as Father Son and Spirit ; so that the only Person Who could represent the Mother would be the Holy Spirit. And, true to its Pagan origin, the Roman Church seizes upon this apparent opening, and elevates to the Godhead her who was never more than blessed *among* women.

But, on turning to the New Testament, we find that, whereas the Greek expression for the Spirit, *τὸ πνεῦμα*, is neuter, yet whenever, to emphasize His personality, the gender of a connected pronoun is changed, the pronoun becomes masculine.*

Again ; the adjective *παράκλητος* is sometimes used substantively, and applied to the Holy Spirit as the Comforter : in such a case it is invariably found in the masculine gender, although, grammatically, it might just as well have been made feminine.†

The significance of these facts is unmistakable ; but the Divine revelation seems to go still further. In the third Gospel we find the following momentous passage ; —"The children of this age marry, and are given in marriage : but they that are accounted worthy to attain to that age, and the resurrection out of the dead, neither marry, nor are given in marriage : *for neither can they*

* John xvi. 13, 14.
† John xiv. 16, 26 ; xv. 26 ; xvi. 7.

die any more: for they are equal to the angels; and are children of God, being children of the resurrection."* It is somewhat strange that the English Authorised Version leaves out the "for," or "because," of the clause in italics, thereby destroying the sense. Yet this word is found in all the best MSS., the only one of any importance—so far as we are aware—which omits it being the Codex Wolfii B.† Restoring, then, the rejected conjunction—which our Revisers also have been careful to do—we educe the meaning, that those who are raised to an equality with the angels do not marry, because, being no longer subject to death, they have no further need of that succession and renewal which marriage is appointed to supply.

And adding this testimony to that which is revealed to us respecting the Trinity, we may fairly infer that sex exists only in those orders of beings whose numbers are liable to diminution by death. But the Pagan conception of a Deity always subjects him more or less to human conditions, and frequently, as we may learn from the disgraceful lives of the Classic gods, to human failings also.

The doctrine that the woman is the head of the man.

The doctrine that woman is the true head of creation, and that her present subordination to man is abnormal, a sign of the Fall, and the cause of all misery, is a complete reversal of Biblical revelation, and helps to form a group of such reversals on which we shall presently

* Luke xx. 34-36.

† Usually known as Codex H. and dating from the ninth century, or later.

‡ From this we may see how emphatically the New Testament discountenances the prevalent and monstrous doctrine that the angels of God are Hermaphrodites. Into what sanctuary will

have something to remark. Of the difficulty in the second chapter of Genesis the writers of "The Perfect Way" make short work: they simply change "a help meet for him" into "a ruler for him," without condescending to offer reason or precedent for their arbitrary translation. Nor—if they be allowed to give whatever meaning pleases them to that word—do they explain how it comes to pass that the subjection of the woman is consistently taught throughout the Bible; that she is exhorted to obey, and not to rule, her husband; and is admonished that the woman was made for the man, and not the man for the woman.

The doctrine of atonement, or the unification of soul and spirit.

The so-called atonement is, of course, effected without the help of the Lord Jesus, Who becomes lost amid a crowd of "Christs," and is no longer needed as a Saviour by those who believe that they can both overcome sin, and exalt themselves to be as God, by their own unaided strength. Nor is this atonement described as a reconciliation to His Father, but as "the unification" of soul and spirit within the man. Indeed, the Personal God, if He be in any sense recognised by Theosophists, is merely mentioned to satisfy the scruples of the prejudiced, and has no real part in the great drama of transmigrations. We are reminded of Stuart Mill's assurance to his disciples that he was far from objecting to the idea of a Supreme Being, and only (!) required them to admit that, if there were a God, He never interfered with the ordinary course of things. It is

presumptuous mortals not dare to intrude? The Countess of Caithness pushes the idea so far that she explains the "Immaculate Conception" by it, affirming that our Lord's mother came into the world in angelic nature. This knowledge she declares to have been given to her by inspiration!

clear, therefore, that Theosophy will offer no opposition to Antichrist's predicted denial of the Father and the Son.

The assertion that the principal events in our Lord's life were taken from the acts of the ancient Mysteries.

Indeed, all its teachings are but too manifestly directed to the same point. As we have already seen, it would have us believe that our Lord's life in the Gospels,* though there may be some foundation for it in history, is mainly intended to represent the upward struggles of a typical man, until he at length attains to Nirvâna. And it adds that the principal events of that life are mere transcriptions into a history, or story, of the acts of the Mysteries, the object of which was "to symbolize the several acts in the Drama of Regeneration as occurring in the interior and secret recesses of man's being."†

As we before remarked, nothing can, of course, be known in regard to the Mysteries save that which the initiated may think proper to disclose: but if these acts really did correspond to the principal events in our Lord's life, we see little reason for surprise. Believing, as we do, that much of primal wisdom was communicated by fallen angels, and that those angels—even if we assume that they had no other sources of information—would, with their penetrating vision and collateral knowledge, easily decipher the plans of God from His prophecies, we cannot wonder if they used what they so discovered for their own purposes. And what more subtle scheme could they have devised than that of

* "Their object is, not to give an historical account of the physical life of any man whatever, but to exhibit the spiritual possibilities of humanity at large, as illustrated in a particular and typical example" ("The Perfect Way," p. 230).

† *Ibid.*, p. 238.

making the very utterances of the Almighty the basis of their teaching, in order that, by confusing the minds of men, they might induce them to reject the Son of God?

The twelve Theosophic Messiahs, the last of whom is even now expected.

Accordingly, just as the Roman king caused eleven shields to be made exactly similar to that which fell from heaven, in order that no one might be able to discover upon which of the twelve the fate of the Imperial City depended; so the upholders of the Mysteries speak of eleven other Messiahs besides the Lord Jesus, and affirm that they were from the first appointed to appear at intervals, one in each cyclic period termed a *Naros*, which includes six hundred years. Into the lives of many of these false Christs they have contrived to interweave stories similar to the facts of the Lord's life, especially in regard to the virgin mother, mentioned, as we have already seen, in the first of prophecies. Eleven of these "Messengers" have already appeared, and, according to Kenealy, their names are—Adam, Enoch, Fohi, Brigu, Zoroaster, Thoth, Moses, Lao-Tseu, Jesus, Mohammed, and Chenzig-Khan.

These "Messengers" for the most part affected particular nations only, and, owing to corruption and the ignorance of those who followed them, their teachings often seem contradictory. But it "would appear" "that the Twelfth Messenger's proper mission is to harmonize into one the perverted teachings of the Mighty Ones who have preceded him."* And in this way he will succeed in establishing "an Universal Religion which shall recognise the Messiahs of all nations."†

* Kenealy's "Comm. on the Apoc.," p. 685.
† *Ibid.*, p. 684.

Again; of the "Messengers" which have already appeared, Moses Mohammed and Chenzig-Khan were Cabiri, that is, Avengers, or Destroyers; while the remaining eight were properly Messiahs, or Peace-bringers. But the Twelfth is to unite the two offices in himself. We do not doubt it: he will, as Daniel predicts, first destroy "the mighty and the holy people,"* and "cast down the truth to the ground"; † and then all the world will wonder after him, and worship him, and say, "Who is like unto the Beast? Who is able to make war with him?"‡ For in this expected Twelfth Messenger we recognise the Antichrist, the Lawless One, and the Beast, of the Bible, the Parasu-Rama of the Hindus, and the Mahdi of the Mahometans, to whom power shall be given over every tribe and people and tongue and nation, and who will succeed in uniting East and West in a blasphemous worship of himself, until heaven cleaves asunder, with lightning flash, and reveals the awful majesty of the Everlasting God.

But Theosophists give one other particular applying

Behold, He is in the desert!

to the expected Twelfth Messenger which has a special interest for those who study the prophetic warnings of the Lord Jesus. It is contained in the following extract from "The Perfect Way."

"The man who seeks to be a Hierarch must not dwell in cities. He may begin his initiation in a city, but he cannot complete it there. For he must not breathe dead and burnt air—air, that is, the vitality of which is quenched. He must be a wanderer, a dweller in the plain, and the garden, and the mountains. He must commune with the starry heavens, and maintain direct

* Dan. viii. 24. † Dan. viii. 12. ‡ Rev. xiii. 3-4.

contact with the great electric currents of living air, and with the unpaved grass and earth of the planet, going bare-foot, and oft bathing his feet. It is *in unfrequented places*, in lands such as are mystically called the "East," where the abominations of "Babylon" are unknown, and where the magnetic chain between earth and heaven is strong, that the man who seeks Power, and who would achieve the "Great Work," must accomplish his initiation."*

Even so. Those were, then, no vague and speculative words to which He, for Whose return we are looking, gave utterance, when He said ;—"For there shall arise false Christs, and false prophets, and shall show great signs and wonders ; insomuch that, if it were possible, they should deceive the very elect. Behold, I have told you before. Wherefore if they shall say unto you, Behold, He is in the desert ; go not forth : Behold, He is in the secret chambers ; believe it not. For as the lightning cometh out of the East and shineth even unto the West ; so shall also the coming of the Son of Man be."†

Theosophical doctrines concerning the Devil and Satan.

There remains one doctrine of Theosophy, for which we have not hitherto found place, but which must be mentioned before we close this chapter. We have considered the subtleties whereby, Christ being done away, the hopes of the world are turned toward the coming Antichrist : it will be well to know what Theosophists have to say respecting the Prince of Darkness himself.

"There is," we are told, "no personal Devil. That which, mystically, is called the Devil, is the negation

* "The Perfect Way," pp. 229-30.
† Matt. xxiv. 24-27.

and opposite of God. And whereas God is I AM, or positive Being, the Devil is NOT."* But "the Devil is not to be confounded with 'Satan,' though they are sometimes spoken of in Scripture as if they were identical. In such cases, however, Scripture represents but the popular belief. The truth concerning Satan belongs to those greater mysteries which have always been reserved from general cognition. The ancient rule in this respect is still in force."†

Yes: but it is not likely always to remain so: the education of the world is rapidly progressing, and men will soon be ready to receive the great secret, which will probably be found to have some connection with the subject of the note on the fortieth page of this book.

There is little doubt that the culmination of the Mysteries was the worship of Satan himself: many facts point to this, and among them we may mention the system of the Gnostics, with whom the Demiurge, said to be the Creator of the present world and the inspirer of the Bible, is an inferior deity, subject to another in the far distant background. It would appear, then, that from remote ages, probably from the time when the Nephilim were upon earth, there has existed a league with the Prince of Darkness, a Society of men consciously on the side of Satan, and against the Most High. And when the feelings of reverence and godliness still retained by the human race have been sufficiently submerged by the flood of demon-influence which is now being poured upon us from the Air, the world will be invited to join the league, to

* "The Perfect Way," p. 69.
† *Ibid.*, pp. 70-1.

reject God and His Anointed, and to worship Antichrist and that old serpent, called the Devil and Satan, who will give him his power.

One of the great secrets of lawlessness has already been offered to and accepted by mankind: the spells by which spirits may be summoned from the unseen are now known to all; and those unearthly forms, which in past times were projected from the void only in the labyrinths caverns and subterranean chambers of the initiated, are now manifesting themselves in many a private drawing-room and parlour. Men have become enamoured of demons, and ere long will receive the Prince of the Demons as their God.

But then the red dawning of the Day of Wrath will begin to appear, and the Lord will arise to shake terribly the earth.

BUDDHISM.

CHAPTER XV.

BUDDHISM.

Spiritualism and Theosophy, which are exoteric and esoteric forms of the same system, are popularising Buddhism in Christendom.

WE have seen that the rise of Spiritualism, which is a return to the demon-intercourse and wonder-working of ancient times, soon resulted in a revival of Occultism, or the Pagan philosophy. These systems, therefore, though they may be at issue upon one or two unimportant points, have no real antagonism. They are but different aspects of the same faith, and will doubtless continue to exist side by side, just as they did in the old Heathen world—Theosophy becoming the creed of the educated and intellectual, while Spiritualism influences the masses of mankind.

But Theosophy identifies its teachings with those of the Mysteries, and declares that it is the system "which all the great religions of the world have, under various guises and with varying degrees of success, striven to express." Surely, then, the motive which impels the Prince of the Air to revive such a system in countries which have for three hundred years professed the name of the Lord Jesus, is sufficiently obvious. The hour of his brief triumph is at hand: he is beginning to draw men into confederation by those teachings of Nephilim which were successful in Antediluvian times and at Babel: he is organizing his forces with the intention of raising again the standard of universal rebellion against God and against His Christ. He will, therefore, commence in the very heart of Christendom that process which shall knit together the great religious bodies; so as, by their combined efforts, to overwhelm and destroy the one irreconcilable community, the Church of the Lord Jesus. Accordingly, we see both Spiritualists and Theosophists, and even Agnostics, stretching out the right hand to Buddhism,* and procuring for it so much favour in our own country that we must not conclude without a few remarks upon its origin and doctrine.

But, in the first place, the close connection subsisting between England and the East suggests that Buddhism may have had something to do with the propagation of its Western form, Theosophy.† For many years Anglo-Indians, not strongly attached to the Christian faith, have been wont, upon their return home, to express great admiration for the purity and self-denial of

* And if they offer the right hand to Buddhism, the left is at the same time extended towards Islam, as we may see in the extract on p. 417. The following words, from the preface to E. Arnold's "Pearls of the Faith," will also illustrate a widely-spread feeling on this point.

"Thereby that marvellous and gifted Teacher—Mahomet—created a vast empire of new belief and new civilization, and prepared a sixth part of humanity for the developments and reconciliations which later times will bring. For Islam must be conciliated; it cannot be thrust scornfully aside or rooted out. It shares the task of the education of the world with its sister religions, and it will contribute its eventual portion to

'that far-off divine event,
Towards which the whole creation moves.'"

† Had Theosophy appeared only in England, we might have been inclined to regard its origin as exclusively Eastern. But its prevalence on the Continent seems to countenance Madame

Buddhism. And of late a considerable impulse has been given to the study of its sacred literature, and some surprise has been excited by the discovery that its grosser forms are confined to the more uneducated classes, while its esoteric teachings are, at least, equal to the philosophies of the West. Its plan of salvation, again, does not, like Christianity, strike at the root of mortal pride; and its gradual deification of the human race is gratifying to those who will own no higher power than man.

Arnold's "Light of Asia."

In 1879 the interest already awakened in it was widely extended by the appearance of Edwin Arnold's "Light of Asia." This exquisitely beautiful poem relates the story of Sakya Muni, and describes his "gentle and far reaching doctrines," in so attractive a manner that it passed rapidly through edition after edition, and has done more than any other work to popularise Buddhism in England and America. But its levelling tendency, as regards the Christian religion, may be seen in the following extract from an American review.

"Surely it is by such messages as this poem bears that the Christians who believe too narrowly, and the sceptics who believe not at all, learn the truth of what our own Lowell sang;—

> 'God sends His teachers into every age and clime
> With revelations suited to their growth.'"

But alas! the great religion of Buddha is but a

Blavatski's hints of Secret Brotherhoods in various parts of Europe, and of adepts, who, preserving a strict incognito as to what they really were, have attracted attention as *nobles étrangers* in Paris and elsewhere, and to whose presence in the past she attributes the great French Revolution ("Isis Unveiled," vol. ii., pp. 402-3).

slightly altered form of that rebellious creed which men probably adopted before they were scattered from Babel. It is directly opposed to Divine revelation, because it teaches that sin is done away by personal suffering, and not by the expiatory sacrifice of the Son of God; and, beneath all its pretended humility, it fosters human pride by the Satanic promise, "Ye shall be as God."

Continued influx of Buddhist literature into England. Reprisals upon the Christian Missionary Societies.

In 1881 a significant event occurred. Mr. Rhys Davids, while delivering the Hibbert Lectures, announced that a society had been formed for the purpose of publishing trustworthy texts of the early Buddhist literature. This society, according to its report issued in 1883, has met with a success far surpassing the expectations of its promoters. The interest excited was so great that it has been joined by many scholars and representatives of public institutions in England, on the Continent, and in the United States. Besides which, more than seventy leading members of the Buddhist Order in Ceylon have enrolled themselves in its ranks, and the subscription list includes £200 from the King of Siam, and £20 from H.R.H. Krom Mun Devavansa Varoprakar.

But a great flood of Eastern literature and philosophy, in a more popular form, is pouring into England from other quarters: nor are the humbler modes of propagation neglected; for we have before us now the second edition of an elegantly printed booklet, sold for threepence, which undertakes to prove the superiority of Buddha to Christ. Its prefatory remarks are summed up in the words;—"Buddhism is to Christianity as is a palace of light to a fetid dungeon." The result of these efforts is already beginning to appear in our literature, and their influence is effecting a great change in public sentiment. "It is no very uncommon thing," says Mr. Massey, "to meet in society men who declare themselves, 'if anything,' Buddhists."

Contemporaneous movements and opinions favourable to Buddhism.

Meanwhile, many ideas and theories in accord with the spirit of Buddhism, and, therefore, favourable more or less to the spread of its influence, are just now prevalent; some of them, perhaps, owe their origin to it. "The learned," says a Buddhist, "have puzzled themselves stupidly over Buddhism; while the most ignorant in Sweden, at the Don, and in America, construct their happiness with it, and, in fact, its thoughts are stealing unseen through the whole West. We see its effects in the great leading lines of Western thought; in Broad-churchism, Universalism, Comtism, Secularism, and Quietism."*

Certainly the revival of Mysticism, of which we get many proofs through the press and a few from the pulpit, is opportune for its progress: and the same may be said of the popular evolutionary philosophy. Were the latter kept within its proper limits, and applied only to the changes which have really taken place, through variations in climate circumstances food and other causes, and which have doubtless multiplied species during the last six thousand years, the study would be interesting and harmless. But when, in defiance of Scripture and Geology, attempts are made to carry it further, and to prove that the six earth-tribes, which God created to form the present world, were not at first distinct types, but were evolved from each other;

* "Christ and Buddha Contrasted," pp. 92-3.

† See p. 174.

such teaching is not merely false in itself, but also prepares the way for the Buddhist dogma of transmigration, and leads very decidedly in the direction of virtual Atheism.

Again; the temperance-crusade, which is now being carried on with such ardour, is doubtless a necessity in consequence of the abuse of stimulants. But, while very many of those who take part in it are earnest Christians, there are others whose enthusiasm unconsciously exalts abstinence to the place of religion. These may presently notice that Christ has never prohibited the use of wine, but left it among the things that are lawful, though, of course, circumstances may render them inexpedient, or even dangerous; whereas Buddha, on the other hand, has forbidden it altogether.*

Lastly; most praiseworthy efforts have been for some years made to mitigate the sufferings of animals. But the writer has lately seen letters from one or two Christians engaged in the anti-vivisection movement, complaining that their society is being swamped, and their periodicals occupied, by Theosophists who have taken up the work on Buddhist principles, because they believe in transmigration. Other instances might be cited: but from these it will be evident that many causes are just now conducing to a favourable reception of Buddhism, and to the removal of prejudices which might have stood in the way of its recognition as one of the great and beneficial religions of the world.

* The following verse is taken from the "Buddhist Beatitudes," as given by Mr. Rhys Davids in his "Buddhism."

"To abhor, and cease from sin,
Abstinence from strong drink,
Not to be weary in well doing,
These are the greatest blessing."

Since, then, it appears to be rising into such unexpected prominence, it may be well to give a slight sketch of its origin.

Migration of Aryan tribes to Hindustan.

When the rebellious confederacy of the sons of Noah was broken up by the confusion of tongues, it would seem that the ancestors of the Aryan nations left the plains of Shinar in a body, and moved towards the East. They appear to have spoken a common language, and doubtless carried with them the religion and philosophy which had, perhaps, been handed down from antediluvian times by Ham, or revealed by the Nephilim themselves subsequently to the flood.* Probably they journeyed on through Asia until they reached Bactria, and at the time of their sojourn in that country seem—so far as we can discover from an examination of the roots which are common to all Aryan languages—to have made considerable advance in civilization. Then, whether from increasing numbers or other causes, they appear to have separated into several tribes, some of which wandered Westward from place to place, until they settled in Europe, and eventually became known as Greeks, Romans, Teutons, and Slavs: others moved to the table-land of Iran: a third multitude swarmed into the valley of the Indus, and made their home amid the Seven Rivers.† Upon these last, however, fresh tribes kept pressing from behind; so that at length they began to pass the boundaries of the Panjab, and to advance, driving the Drâvidians and Kolarians before them, into the Land

* In Gen. vi. 4—see pp. 209-10—they are said to have dwelt upon earth after the flood as well as before it.

† The date of this immigration is uncertain: probably it took place about 2000 B.C.

of the Ganges, where they founded the great kingdom of Magadha.

Then followed a season of comparative peace, during which the new inhabitants settled, and began to apply themselves to quiet pursuits. By force of circumstances, they soon fell apart into three distinct classes, or castes. The military nobility, or Kshatriyas, were, at the close of the long war, naturally regarded as first in rank: the Brahmans, or minstrels and priests, came next. And, lastly, there were the farmers and peasants, who tilled the soil, and did not go out to war except in times of emergency: these were called Vaisyas,* and formed the third caste. But in addition to the Aryan immigrants themselves, there was also a population of Turanians, suffered to live among their conquerors as inferiors and slaves: these, under the name of Sudras, made up a fourth caste.†

Formation of the castes, and ultimate supremacy of the Brahmans.

For some centuries the Kshatriyas retained their supremacy: but at length, by craft and compromise, the Brahmans succeeded in procuring the recognition of themselves as the first order, and from that time took every possible precaution to strengthen and perpetuate the institution of caste. Hence the rigid laws which forbade intermarriage, and inexorably confined every man to the caste in which he was born: while, as a check upon the discontent which naturally resulted, the

* The word Vaisya originally meant a tribesman, or comrade, and was applied to all Aryans to distinguish them, as the ruling people, from the subject aborigines. In course of time, however, it became the special name of the third caste.

† This fourth caste was, however, absolutely excluded in all matters of religion, and was recognised neither in the Avesta, or law of East Iran, nor in that of the Ganges.

Brahmans found a powerful aid in the doctrine of transmigration.* They affirmed that it was necessary for every being, in working his way to perfection, to pass successively through all the castes; so that in subsequent lives an exemplary Sudra would become a Vaisya, a Vaisya a Kshatriya, and so on.

The sacred books of these people were the four Vedas —the Rig-veda, the Yajur-veda, the Sama-veda, and the Atharva-veda, the contents of which prove the Brahman religion to be the most comprehensive ever instituted. Each of them consists of three parts, the Mantras, the Brahmanas, and the Upanishads, of which the Mantras are the oldest. These are hymns of prayer and praise, some of the more ancient, without doubt, the common property of the whole Aryan family, chanted, it may be, in remote ages by our own ancestors;

The Vedas.

* Spiritualists apprehend that the forces which they are helping to set in motion will render a similar check again necessary, if the world is to be preserved from anarchy. And that the minds of some of them are, consequently, turning towards Buddhism the following remarkable passage will show.

"The spectacle of our sickly faiths drooping and perishing in a hostile intellectual environment is the most dismal that a mind of any sincerity can contemplate. We seem to be approaching a time when the 'organized hypocrisy' of our churches will be as crying a scandal to human intelligence as monasticism had become to human morality three-and-a-half centuries ago. And when it comes, it will be a period of upheaval in more than one direction. The positive unbelief, which is visibly extending from the intellectual aristocracy to the multitude, will almost certainly react with destructive force upon political and social arrangements. It cannot but suggest the redress of inequalities in this world to those who have lost the shadowy hope of compensation in the next. Many a thoughtful mind must have dwelt with anxiety on this prospect, without seeing from what quarter the reconstruction of religious faith upon a permanent basis could be expected. Can it be that to 'the bloodless and innocent record of Buddhism' will be added this claim upon human gratitude and love?" (C. C. Massey, in *Light*, June 16th, 1883.)

while others were subsequently added. If recited, or sung, in due form, they were supposed to exercise a magic power which not even the gods could resist, and to this day they are used as spells, either for imprecation, or for the purpose of averting the influence of evil spirits. In verse, which sometimes rises to a lofty strain, they inculcate a worship of the powers of nature, and testify to a fear of malignant demons exactly similar to that which is expressed in the Chaldean magical spells. Their subjects are various. "The Vedas," says Lillie, "contain the root-idea of most of the dogmas and religious rites of the world." They reveal a Trinity in unity, and from the initials of one set of its names—Aditi, Varuna, Mitra—it is probable that the mystic word *Aum*, or, as it is sometimes written, *O'm*, was formed.

Most of the Mantras seem to have been in use while the Aryans still tarried in the valley of the Indus; but the Brahmanas are of a later date. They mark very decidedly the change from the religion of the prophet, or Rishi, to that of the priest, and expound the sacrificial system and ritualism of the Brahmans, developed after the immigration into the Land of the Ganges.

Lastly; the Upanishads—called the *Jnâna Kânda*, or Department of Knowledge—contain the philosophy of Brahmanism, and begin to date, apparently, only from the sixth century before Christ. These writings work out the doctrine;—"There is but one Being, no second." "That is," in the words of Monier Williams, "nothing really exists but the one Universal Spirit, and whatever appears to exist independently is identical with that Spirit." The result of the controversies arising from these Pantheistic treatises was Buddhism:

unless we should rather say that both the Upanishads and Buddhism were results of that wave of thought which was at the time passing over the civilized world. For Buddha in Hindustan was not the only great teacher of his age. In the same epoch Zoroaster would seem to have been communicating his philosophy to the Persians; while Pythagoras was instructing men in Greece, and Confucius in China.

Brahmanism superseded by Buddhism.

In the beginning of the sixth century, then, the Brahmans were at the height of their power, and men were writhing beneath the tyranny of caste, and were harassed by the necessity of endless expiatory sacrifices and purifications, a neglect of which would bring danger to liberty and present life, besides involving terrific punishments in the many hells of which their priests taught, and in future incarnations. But thoughtful minds began to reflect as they looked around on the misery of the world, and to inquire whether the doctrines which produced such bitter fruits could possibly be true: a leader was needed to inaugurate a new order of things: he appeared in the person of Buddha: caste, sacrifice, ritual, and priestcraft, were rapidly undermined and swept away: and Buddhism rose to the supremacy in Hindustan, and maintained its position for many long centuries, until at length, having become corrupted, it gradually yielded to that compound of itself with Brahmanism which may be termed Hinduism.

Propagation of Buddhism beyond the limits of Hindustan.

But its triumphs were by no means confined to Hindustan: its power was acknowledged from the Volga to the Japanese islands. It entered Africa and penetrated to Alexandria: the secret societies of the Therapeutæ and the Essenes drew their inspiration from it: the Gnostics were its children.* Nay, recent investigations have made it probable that Buddha was once the god of Northern Europe, and that his name is philologically identical with that of Woden, from which we take our appellation of the fourth day of the week. And, finally, it appears to be demonstrated that, in the fifth century, some Chinese Buddhists succeeded in reaching America, and established their faith in that remote land, more than nine hundred years before a thought of its existence entered the mind of Columbus. Even at the present time Buddhism dominates some five hundred millions of souls, or about forty per cent. of the whole human race, and stands, without a rival, the most widely extended, and, in point of numbers, most successful religion of the world.

Those who worship majorities are already beginning to adduce the facts just stated as a proof of Buddha's superiority to Christ. But students of Scripture are not troubled by such an argument. They are well aware that the characteristic of this age, as foretold by their Lord, is;—"Strait is the gate, and narrow is the way, which leadeth unto life, and *few* there be that find it"; and they remember His charge;—"I have told you before it come to pass, that, when it is come to pass, ye might believe." They know that His "little flock" must patiently wait until He returns to take the Kingdom: then everything will be reversed, and He

* The idea that Gnosticism was a kind of Christianity is one of the strangest figments of ecclesiastical history. It was rather, as Chiflet defines it, "the spirit of Asiatic antiquity endeavouring to usurp the empire over the human soul by insinuating itself into the Christian Church."

must needs at length have the supremacy in numbers as in all things.

The similarity of the legends of Buddha to the history of Christ is only superficial.

We cannot, of course, find space to discuss the story of Buddha: it is probable, however, that there is very little history in it. As regards its alleged parallelism with the life of Christ, we have already remarked that Satan must have known the prophecies of God respecting the latter. He must also have been aware that he was himself to play no inconsiderable part in its stupendous drama, and would, within certain limits, be permitted to arrange its temptations, whether in the wilderness, in the garden, or on the cross, according to his own plans. We have, then, no cause for surprise if, with a purpose which is now becoming too evident, he rehearsed some of the scenes beforehand.

But with all their similarity there is an inexpressible difference between the legends of Buddha and the history of Christ, and of this we will give one or two instances. In the Gospels, the circumstances of the conception are narrated with the dignity and reserve which become so transcendent a mystery. But Buddha comes down from heaven, and enters the womb of his mother in the shape of a white elephant, with a head the colour of cochineal, and with tusks of gold. Nor are these the only particulars given.

Again; the history of our Lord's birth, and of His cradle in the manger, because there was no room for Him in the inn, bears upon it the stamp of truth. Buddha's mother, on the other hand, was in the garden of Lumbini when he was born. Surrounded by sixty thousand beautiful cloud-nymphs, she proceeded towards a stately tree, which immediately bent down its branches to salute and overshadow her. According to the Thibetan version, as soon as the infant Buddha touched the ground a large white lotus sprang up: he seated himself upon it, and cried, "I am the chief of the world: this is my last birth," in words which rolled forth with mighty sound through all the worlds. Then two serpent-kings, Nanda and Upananda, appeared in the sky, and rained down water upon the child.

We need not pursue the subject further: it will be sufficiently evident that these Eastern stories are altogether different from the Gospels. It may, however, be replied;—But they are merely legends: why not deal with the history of Buddha? Unfortunately the historical data are of the very vaguest description, and, if we leave the legends, we must give up the miraculous conception, and all the main points of the alleged parallelism with the life of Christ. It is scarcely necessary to add that no detailed prophecies of the advent of Buddha were promulgated centuries before his appearance, as in the case of Christ.

The system of Buddha may be briefly summed up as follows:—

The teaching of Buddha.

I. There is no God, save what man can himself become.*

* Mr. Lillie has attempted to dispute this statement against the weight of authority. But one consideration seems fatal to his argument: the evolutionary system of Buddha, and "the inflexible justice of *Karma*," leave no room for the action of a Supreme Being. "The wondrously endowed representatives of occult science," says Mr. Sinnett, "never occupy themselves at all with any conception remotely resembling the God of Churches and Creeds." Buddhists are, however, able to gratify that irresistible disposition of the human mind to worship something: they can venerate their saints, those deified men,

II. The state of Nirvâna, or perfection, is reached by means of transmigrations, or a succession of earth-lives.

III. So long as a man retains any desire for earthly things he must continue to be reborn upon earth.

IV. Therefore, the shortest way to Nirvâna is by a severe asceticism, suppression of all action, abstract meditation, and a concentration of all desire upon the extinction of earth-life.

V. Animal sacrifices, and every kind of vicarious suffering, are useless, and must be done away.

VI. All men are equal: therefore, caste must be abolished.

Such are the main points of Sakya Muni's teachings: for the present our brief commentary must be no more than this. The circumstances which led to the rise of Buddhism, as described above, and its consequent doctrines, could not but bring it into favour with the iconoclastic and levelling spirit which is now abroad. Its severe asceticism is no bar to this: since in our self-indulgent age nothing is more common than to hear men warmly supporting a theory in the abstract, without any intention of submitting to it in practice. Its, at least, virtual Atheism renders it attractive to Secularists: its mysticism and introspection allure minds disposed to

like the gods of Homer, who have attained to Nirvâna; but who, powerless to interfere in the troubles of their votaries, may only take their part in turning the slow, dreary, monotonous, inexorable, and endless Wheel of Life. "Within the limits of the solar system"—we are again quoting Mr. Sinnett —"the mortal adept knows, of his own knowledge, that all things are accounted for by law, working on matter in its diverse forms, plus the guiding and modifying influence of the highest intelligences associated with the solar system, the Dhyan Chohans—or Planetary Spirits—the perfected humanity of the last preceding *manvantara*" ("Esoteric Buddhism," pp. 176-7).

Quietism. In all essentials its doctrine is esoterically identical with that of Theosophy, upon which we have already remarked. In both systems we are undoubtedly confronted with Satan's plan of salvation, communicated from the earliest times—probably by the Nephilim—to those who could bear it, and preserved in the esoteric teachings of the Rishis, the Brahmans, and the Buddhists of the East, and in the Mysteries of the West. And the plan is, that, without God or Saviour, men must wear away their own sins, and as soon as they have done so will become gods.

Connection of Buddhism and Spiritualism. Tomb-worship, relics, and images.

But if the esoteric teaching of Buddhism coincides with Theosophy, its general practice is in entire sympathy with Spiritualism. For worship—if we may so term it—among the Buddhists is largely connected with the cultus of the dead, who are believed to have the power of conferring aid and blessings upon those who seek to them. But an addition was made to this doctrine, which has been adopted by Romanists, and is beginning to show itself in the churchyard-mediums and some other features of Spiritualism. While the spirit of a deceased person was not supposed to remain in his corpse, "there was evidently a belief that a certain animal magnetism, or some occult force, made it more easy for the disembodied spirit to return and communicate with living mortals when they were in the actual presence of his corpse. This explains much in the rites of both the Brahmans and the Buddhists, the tomb-worship, relic-worship, and image-worship."*

For the doctrine was extended to any portion of

* Lillie's "Buddha and Early Buddhism," pp. 36-7.

human remains. Hence, "in the Cingalese history of the famous tooth of Buddha, the tooth is constantly represented as acting as if the remainder of Buddha's person, though invisible, joined the tooth when great miracles were necessary.* As the natural result of such an idea, "Bengal was by-and-by covered with stately topes and columns, each supposed to contain a minute fragment of Buddha's relics." And, probably, the skulls and bones worn by the Brahman Rishis who frequented the cemeteries are to be explained in the same way.

The introduction of images, again, seems to have been an advance upon corpse and relic-worship. A likeness of the departed was supposed in some way to attract his spirit to it, and hence "the solemn marble Buddhas, each seated on his throne, the four great Dhyâni Buddhas, the eighteen great disciples that figure in every temple in China, and the crowd of minor saints. Directly the crystal eyes are put into an image in China, the spirit of the departed is supposed to animate it." †

Mr. Lillie sums up his chapter on Buddhist demonology, from which the above extracts are taken, in the following words. "Buddhism was plainly an elaborate apparatus to nullify the action of evil spirits by the aid of good spirits operating at their highest potentiality through the instrumentality of the corpse, or a portion of the corpse, of the chief aiding spirit. The Buddhist temple, the Buddhist rites, the Buddhist liturgy, all seem based on this one idea that a whole, or portions of a dead body was necessary."

* Lillie's "Buddha and Early Buddhism," p. 38.
† *Ibid.*, p. 39.

There can be little doubt that the Buddhist tope is the original of the Roman Church, the great feature of which is its high altar containing beneath it some relic of the patron saint.* But the two religions have very many other things in common, among which we may mention the crozier, mitre, dalmatic, cope, and censer swinging on five chains; sacerdotal celibacy, worship of saints, fasts, processions, litanies, holy water, the tonsure, confession, relic-worship, the use of flowers lights and images on the altar, the sign of the cross, the worship of the Queen of Heaven, the aureole, the mystic fans of peacocks' feathers carried on either side of the Popes and Llamas on grand festivals, the orders of the ministry, and the architectural details of the churches.

Affinity of Buddhism and Romanism.

But if both religions are daughters of Babylon—and who can study the slabs and cylinders in the British Museum without feeling sure that they are?—the strong family likeness is no matter for wonder. And by helping to make this obvious, and bringing Buddhism into the favourable notice of Christendom, Spiritualists have removed a great obstacle to the coming religious union of the world.

With one more remark we close this necessarily brief and imperfect chapter. According to the statement of the Himalayan adepts, an ordinary being must pass through some eight hundred incarnations before he can complete his purification from sin, and attain to the rest of Nirvâna. During the weary ages of these existences he must struggle with blind

Buddha or Christ?

* Thus, if we look back to their origin, neither tope nor church is a place of worship used as a cemetery, but a cemetery utilized as a place of worship.

fate and with his own corruptions; there is no God of love and of all comfort to Whom he can look and pray: he must either, by his own painful and unaided exertions, raise himself to the gods, or retrograde, in ever increasing misery and vileness, until he drops unpitied into the bottomless abyss of annihilation.

> "Higher than Indra's ye may lift your lot,
> And sink it lower than the worm or gnat;
> The end of many myriad lives is this,
> The end of myriads that.
>
> "Only, while turns that wheel invisible,
> No pause, no peace, no staying place can be;
> Who mounts will fall, who falls may mount; the spokes
> Go round unceasingly."

It is said that the incarnations of one soul, together with the intervening periods spent in Devachan or Avitchi—Paradise or Purgatory—would occupy some seventy millions of years! There is a certain wisdom in this calculation leading us to suspect that it comes from a source wiser, at least, than any which is merely human. It exhibits some appreciation of the frightful nature of sin, and of the gigantic task set before the man who would fain be his own Saviour.

With what thankfulness should we turn to the gracious Lord Whose blood speaks better things to us; Who, looking on the sin-stricken and penitent face of the paralytic, said, "Son, be of good cheer; thy sins are forgiven," and in a moment effected that work for which Buddha demands ages; Who beholding with pitying gaze the fast-falling tears of the contrite woman at His feet, took the burden of her guilt upon Himself, and bade her depart in peace.

No melancholy, unbefriended, and almost endless

way lies before His disciples. Nay, He Himself is with them alway, even unto the end: He guides His sheep through the wilderness of life, gently leading those that are with young, and carrying the lambs in His bosom. He has not only borne the sins of His people, but will also sanctify them wholly, spirit soul and body, and present them faultless before the presence of His glory, with exceeding joy, by that mighty working whereby He is able even to subdue all things unto Himself.

Thanks be unto God for His unspeakable gift!

SIGNS OF THE END.

CHAPTER XVI.

SIGNS OF THE END.

Theory of Transmigration.

WE have finished our brief survey of the strange phases of thought now affecting the theology and philosophy of Christendom: it only remains to group together those features of the movement which, as we compare them with the ancient predictions of Scripture, almost seem to take bodily shape before our eyes, and, like heralds, to announce the near approach of Antichrist and the close of the age.

And first the reader will have observed that Salvation without a Saviour is the characteristic doctrine of the three systems at which we have been glancing; and that this doctrine rests, solely in Theosophy and Buddhism, and to an increasing extent in Spiritualism, upon the theory of reincarnations. One would have thought such a prospect sufficiently dismal; nevertheless, it appears to find favour with many, chiefly, no doubt, because it brings with it a delusive hope of that independence which unregenerate man is ever craving. And it falls in with a common fancy, that, on rare occasions, some dim memory of a former acquaintance with persons or places has been known to flash across the mind—an idea which D. G. Rossetti thus expresses ;—

> " I have been here before,
> But when, or how, I cannot tell :
> I know the grass beyond the door,
> The sweet keen smell,
> The sighing sound, the lights around the shore.
>
> " You have been mine before—
> How long I may not know :
> But just when at that swallow's soar
> Your neck turned so,
> Some veil did fall—I knew it all of yore.
>
> " Then, now—perchance again !
> O round mine eyes your tresses shake !
> Shall we not lie as we have lain
> Thus for love's sake,
> And sleep and wake, yet never break the chain ? "

These verses may have been suggested by the teaching of Buddha respecting himself and his wife Yasôdara ; at least they are an exact transcript of it. In Wordsworth's *Intimations of Immortality*, again, we find the following lines ;—

> " Our birth is but a sleep and a forgetting :
> The Soul that rises with us, our life's Star,
> Hath had elsewhere its setting,
> And cometh from afar."

And even Mrs. Hemans, in dealing with "the spirit's mysteries," says ;—

> " The power that dwelleth in sweet sounds to waken
> Vague yearnings, like the sailor's for the shore,
> And dim remembrances, whose hue seems taken
> From some bright former state, our own no more ;
> Is not all this a mystery ? Who shall say
> Whence are those thoughts, and whither tends their way ? "

Undoubtedly such imaginings strike a responsive chord in human hearts, and discourse sweetly and soothingly of a thought congenial—as its universality shows—to human minds. But we may not mould the articles of our faith from poetic musings, which have ever been the mightiest agencies for the spread of delusion. To receive ideas as truths because they come in ravishing form, and we are moved by every impulse of our fallen nature to love them, is indeed to surrender ourselves to the power of Maya. It is nothing less than, like the ostrich, to hide our head in the sand, content to revel in fond dreams for a moment, while the Rider on the pale horse scours the plain towards us, brandishing his glittering dart, and bringing Hades and Eternity in his train. For of things beyond our natural ken we can understand only what is revealed: and if we must cross the fixed boundary into forbidden lands, our expedition will simply procure for us teachings of demons, having no connection with truth, but only representing the views which the Powers of Evil are anxious to disseminate at the time.

The Transmigration theory is essentially Antichristian.

But, to return to our immediate subject, the growing popularity of the doctrine of transmigration in so-called Christian countries is an unmistakable preparation for the end. For this theory not only denies the Son, in that it does not include His atoning sacrifice, but also virtually ignores the Father, Who is by no means indispensable to its cheerless scheme.*

* We have noticed the Atheism of Buddhism: it might seem as though Hinduism were setting in the opposite direction to this doctrine of Antichrist. But the coutrary is really the case: both religions appear to be much the same esoterically. "The bloodthirsty idols and gluttonous gods" of Hinduism are for the masses: the initiated assign them all to the domain of Maya, or Illusion. The formal creeds are but gross and temporary bodies, through which those who have the eye of knowledge see the real spirit; and he who has learned to do this is not troubled with

Thus the great threefold movement which is spreading among us is beginning to develop the spirit which according to the plain statement of the Apostle John,* will culminate in Antichrist.

The systems described above are provoking judgment by defying the primal laws given to the World before the election of Israel and the Church.

Yet again; while in the case of professing Christians it is destroying the foundations of the faith, it is also raising the world in insurrection against God, as will appear from the subjoined considerations.

In the fourth chapter of the Apocalypse there is a grand description of the Almighty seated upon His throne of judgment. The crisis, as discovered by the context and other prophecies, is important: for the Church has just been removed from earth, because the time to restore the kingdom to Israel has come.† But, since that kingdom was formerly transferred to the nations in the days of Nebuchadnezzar, its surrender cannot be demanded without just cause: for which reason the Lord would seem to have come down in awful majesty, that He may hold His great controversy with the Gentiles, and, after judging their failure, close the times of their dominion.

The accessories of the throne are significant, and point to the Noachian covenant: for the rainbow encircles it, and at its base sit the Cherubim, the repre-

reference to his belief in the popular gods. On the other hand, to satisfy the cravings of the ignorant, Buddhists have been forced to invent deities, especially the Queen of Heaven, the Lily Lady, the Mother of Buddha, Marichi, or our Lady, by each of which titles this goddess is known in China. All false religions alike seem to have two sides—for the multitude, superstition; for the intellectual, Pantheism. Hence it will, perhaps, be no very difficult task for a master-mind to fuse them into one.

* 1 John ii. 22.

† See "The Great Prophecies."

sentatives of those earth-tribes to which the promises were made. But this covenant was God's final call to the world to arrange its government in accordance with Divine principles—a call which, as the rebellion of Babel and the history of the Cities of the Plain too evidently testify, was utterly disregarded. Then the plans of the Almighty were changed, and, restricting His more direct dealings, for a time, within narrower limits, He made two successive elections from the great masses of mankind. First His choice fell upon the children of Abraham, whom He placed under a special covenant: subsequently the Church was separated off, from Jew as well as Gentile, by peculiar laws, and by privileges and promises available only to such as should pass within her pale.

But the remainder of men, who are neither Israelites by natural nor members of Christ by spiritual birth, cannot, at least, avoid their responsibility to obey laws which were imposed without distinction upon the whole race of Adam, which have never been repealed, and the violation of which will, consequently, be visited with punishment at the hand of the Creator, the Lord God Almighty. Indeed, it is manifestly to judge the world for its disobedience to these laws that God sits upon the rainbow-encircled throne.

Now it is a grave fact that the advocates of modern thought array themselves against every principle of these early revelations of the Divine will. In proof of this the readers of our previous chapters will need little more than a bare enumeration of what we may call the cosmic or universal laws, which are as follows:—

I. The law of the Sabbath.* It was to the world

* Gen. ii. 3

that God declared the Seventh Day sanctified, not to the Israelites: therefore, the world is responsible. To the Israelites God merely said, "*Remember* the Sabbath day, to keep it holy,"* thus admonishing them not on their part to neglect the long established and universal ordinance.

II. The headship of the man over the woman.† This is not simply denied; attempts are actually being made to reverse it.

III. The institution of marriage, and its indissolubility during life on the ground that the man and woman become one flesh.‡ The varied antagonism to this law, resulting in part from the false teaching that the really married are one spirit rather than one flesh, has been sufficiently discussed.

IV. The law of substitution, that life must atone for life, and that without shedding of blood there is no remission, as taught in type by animal sacrifices.§ Latter-day philosophers affect the utmost horror of such a salvation, and will have none of Christ.

V. The command to use the flesh of animals as food.‖ This is rejected by many Spiritualists, and by all Theosophists and Buddhists.

VI. The decree that "whoso sheddeth man's blood by man shall his blood be shed."¶ This is opposed on the ground of its inhumanity (!), and because by the execution of a murderer "you cut him off debased, degraded, sensual, ignorant, mad with rage and hate, thirsting for vengeance on his fellows: you remove

* Exod. xx. 8.
† Gen. ii. 18-23; iii. 16; 1 Tim. ii. 11-14.
‡ Gen. ii. 24; Matt. xix. 4-9; Rom. vii. 2, 3.
§ Gen. iv. 3-5. ‖ Gen. ix. 3. ¶ Gen. ix. 6.

from him the great bar on his passions, and send him into spirit-life to work out without hindrance the devilish suggestions of his inflamed passions." * In such terms are the spirits of evil daring to withstand the counsels of the living God.

VII. The direction to multiply and replenish the earth †—a mandate which implied dispersion and the forming of those nations for which, as Moses tells us, God divided out the earth, ‡ and which are to remain until the close of the Millennium. At Babel the world resisted this ordinance, and now men are renewing their efforts to the same end by maintaining that we should be humanitarians, cosmopolitans, anything but lovers of our own country. This is, perhaps, a preparation for the reign of Antichrist "over every tribe and people and tongue and nation." Cosmopolitanism will, apparently, be as necessary to his development as it was to the primal insurrection of Nimrod.

The new phases of thought are, then, obliterating all the first principles which God laid down for the human race as the basis of its mode of life, society, and government—a fact ominous of coming judgment. And from this point of view the movement may be regarded as a revolt of the world against God.

Every particular of the prophecy in the First Epistle to Timothy is now in process of fulfilment.

But it is also, as the reader will have observed, fulfilling to the letter the important prophecy in the First Epistle to Timothy. Men are confessedly receiving instruction from demons; and if we glance at the published specimens of spirit-teachings, we have no difficulty in detecting the lies spoken in hypocrisy.

* "Spirit Teachings," p. 19.

† Gen. ix. 1.

‡ Deut. xxxii. 8.

Many are teaching abstinence from flesh: the abolition of marriage, either avowed or virtual, is being unscrupulously preached. And these signs are appearing, as Paul predicted that they would, coincidently with an apostacy, or falling away, from the great truths respecting the Godhead and incarnation of the Lord Jesus.

False Christs and false prophets.

Again, the monstrous theory of a plurality of "Christs" has been invented, and is being taught, not, we may be sure, without a plan for its application to coming events. Already signs and wonders are being shown by prophets who will, perhaps, ere long proclaim their Messiahs; already the cry has been raised, Behold, He is in the secret chambers; and, as we have seen reasons for supposing, we may probably ere long hear rumours that He is in the wilderness.

Recurrence of the characteristics of the days of Noah. Union of the two worlds and preparation for the descent of the Nephilim.

Lastly; the characteristic features of the days of Noah are reappearing, and, above all, a free communication has been established between the spirits of the air and the human race with a view, apparently, to a sojourn once more of Nephilim upon earth. Unlawful secrets, known in past times only to those few who seem to have acted as Satan's agents in directing the course of this world, are now recklessly offered to all men. The remembrance of that appalling scene, when their brethren were hurled by omnipotent lightnings into pits of darkness, would seem to be fading from the minds of the fallen angels; and the usual course of sin, most frightful of insanities, is urging them on to the brink of the precipice from the abysmal depths of which the groans of their blasted companions ascend. Meanwhile, numbers of the puny inhabitants of earth are ready, at their bidding, to essay any deeds of madness. For not a few even of the learned and wise, unable by reason of vanity to maintain the bare conception of a God, unless His awful majesty be displayed before their eyes, have resolved, either avowedly or virtually, that there is none greater than themselves, or, at least, than their possibility.

All things seem to be prepared for the fulfilment of the solemn prediction in the twelfth chapter of the Apocalypse, when Michael, leading the van of the host which will come with Christ to take the kingdom, shall drive the rebel High Ones down to earth. And in the following chapter we see the consequences of that marvellous event: the peoples of Satan's last refuge, of the only remaining portion of his once vast dominions, must be organised for the final struggle. And so, out of the troubled sea of anarchy and perplexity of nations, there arises, in greater majesty and power than it ever before possessed, the resuscitated empire of Rome under the immediate direction and government of the Wicked One.

The waiting Church will be removed before the fallen angels are driven down to earth.

But of far more intense interest to those who love the Lord Jesus, and long for His appearing, is that which is signified as taking place just previously to the expulsion of the Devil and his angels from heaven.* For without going into details, which we have considered elsewhere,† we may mention our conclusion that the birth and rapture of the man child refer to

* Rev. xii. 1-5.
† In "The Great Prophecies" (Messrs. Hodder & Stoughton).

the completion of the mystic Christ—of which the personal Christ is the Head and His Church the body—as manifested by the sudden translation of all waiting saints, whether dead or alive, to meet their Lord in the air.

It thus appears that this long expected event will precede Satan's banishment from heaven, and, therefore, also its results, the revival of the Roman empire, and the revelation of the Man of Sin. Like Enoch, the Church of Christ will be called away before earth is for a time abandoned to the Nephilim, before the fearful woes of the end.

Therefore, in all probability, the Lord is at hand.

If, then, the fallen angels appear to be already preparing for their descent; if the great apostacy, which will at last evolve the Lawless One, be even now spreading; who can be sure of a day or an hour? Who of Christ's watching people can tell, when he rises in the morning, whether he will not have left the scenes of earth before close of day? Who, when he retires to rest, knows whether he will be awakened by the returning light, or by the summons of the Master, the voice of the archangel, and the trump of God? Are we not living in solemn times: is not the air full of warnings: does it not behove every believer to arise, gird up his loins, and trim his lamp? Is it not the sound of the King's chariot which we hear: should not every sleeping servant rouse himself and prepare to meet the Lord with joy?

It may be that His voice will be heard in the morning, when the sun is high and men are hurrying to their various occupations: it may be that He will call at even, when the west is crimson with the setting sun, and the weary are seeking their homes after the toil and excitement of the day: it may be that His summons will startle the midnight air, and bring forth His own from the darkness of their chambers or their graves into the dazzling glory of His presence: it may be that at early dawn He will speak the word, and in an instant be surrounded by the myriads of His elect, countless as the dewdrops that spring from the womb of the morning and glisten in the reddening beams of the sun. "Watch, therefore, for ye know neither the day, nor the hour, wherein the Son of man cometh." *

"Surely I come quickly" † was His last message to His widowed Church: let no man think that he has the Spirit of Christ till he can fervently respond, "Amen. Even so, come, Lord Jesus."

* Matt. xxv. 13. † Rev. xxii. 20.

APPENDICES.

APPENDIX A.

We transcribe a few paragraphs from an essay on the Rationale of Spiritualism by Mr. F. F. Cook. They exhibit the views of an intelligent and able Spiritualist on some interesting points and difficulties of the movement.

"The time having arrived in the order of human progression to widen the avenue of communication between the two worlds, two methods were open to the spiritual powers—to admit only the higher class of minds at first, and let the truth in diluted and contracted form work downward; or, taking the opposite course, to start the movement at the very foundations of society, diversify it to the utmost, employ chiefly blind forces, and hedge the whole about with mystifying safeguards. The first course represents the human method of teaching; the last is the mode adopted by the more enlightened spirit-world. The difference is expressed by preaching and practising. In this lies the solution to all the mystery.

"It is charged against the movement that it is almost wholly confined to the uncultured. While the ranks of the believers contain many of the most enlightened minds of the age, I am free to admit that its potency lies, as yet, chiefly with a class untrammelled by precise definitions or exact thought—that it is these who give it substance, stamp it with their peculiarities, and represent it in the eyes of the world.

"One day mankind will rejoice that it is so—that in the

infancy of this dispensation the blunders of human wisdom were kept out of its experience, and that the guides were wholly spiritual.

"We sometimes learn most of the true side of a question by studying its false side. Let us suppose, therefore, that the spirit-world had taken the human-wisdom course in this instance, and confided its secrets first to the learned. See scientific world in the direst confusion, despairingly searching for its most cherished and now exploded premises! Behold a religious world in the throes of soul-agony, sitting haggard and distracted amid the *débris* of its shattered creeds! Religious beliefs have their roots in the heart, and when you tear them out by force, you take that which is almost dearer than life itself. The late Walter Bagehot well remarked: 'One of the greatest pains to human nature is the pain of a new idea.' No, a wise dispensation would not thus afflict the race. It would work precisely as it is working. It is stealing upon the world like a thief in the night. The change comes, but no man knows whereof. It operates as a gentle amelioration; its disintegrating force, though potent, is scarcely perceptible; fully one-fourth of the native-American element is even now converted; another fourth has become quite familiar with the idea, and is ready for acceptance without a pang; and with all this wonderful work accomplished, within less time than is allotted to a generation, the mischief done is a minimum. This shows how completely the destructive forces of the movement are hedged about."

* * * * * *

"Spiritualism is Revolution, not simply Reform. Reform works downward; it is scientific in its spirit, and, though not generally regarded so, is practically conservative. Revolution works upward; it reasons far less deeply than it feels. In rare instances the revolutionist and reformer are blended. The difficulties that attend a religious transition are enormous. Man is by nature lawless. Religion, whether expressed by Fetichism or an ethical refinement, aside from brute force and the love of kindred, is the sole influence that can keep this lawlessness under control. Now a readjustment is decided upon! what an uprooting must not take place! and while the transition is in progress, what care must not be exercised! Elements in their revolutionary or readjusting stage are always extremely destructive. Conservatism is simply another word for adjustment accomplished. In view of the trifling mischief that is doing during this most wonderful and radical of all transitions, I would call conversions to Spiritualism a process of spirit selection. It is so wisely ordered that the light is vouchsafed only under carefully guarded conditions. It seeks and blends only with such elements as are in affinity and individualized. Somewhat of notoriety is bound to attach to all things that are in their nature marvellous, but the aim is ever to minimize the excitement, as essential to a rational propagation.

"The observant student, as he passes along with the jostling crowd, will note great gaps marked 'exposures.' The presumption is that these expose mediums; but, in fact, only human ignorance—they are *safety-valves*—sacrifices to the Moloch of prejudice—meat cast to ravenous wolves. Somewhat in the line of "exposure" is always kept on the stage. But in the meantime, another work is going forward—a process of spirit selection. There is an esoteric Spiritualism into which there is no prying except by consent of the spirit-world. The crowd that clamours to be admitted is carefully scanned. Perhaps not above 25 per cent. of those who investigate at any time, be their motives never so good, are chosen. Sometimes it happens that a person is refused at one stage and admitted at another—the result depending on all the conditions, social, religious, moral, intellectual, or otherwise, which environ, or promise in the future to environ the investigator. You have all probably heard that 'conditions' are necessary to manifestations. This word has been much abused because, as related to Spiritualism, it is little understood. The 'conditions' to a successful séance are the most subtle factors that can be imagined. They are far less physical than mental, but they are both, and much beside—they are also spiritual."

* * * * * *

"What are the results sought to be accomplished? Nothing short of revolution in every department of thought! It means all this or nothing; it is either an intelligent, most potent, and wise dispensation, or the maddest freak that ever possessed the human mind. I hold it to be the first, and upon those who shall choose the last I will put this task;—Explain to me the genesis and evolution of the delusion! Where or in what are its antecedents? There is no effect without an adequate cause: now in what subjective potency lie these tremendous results, regarded as delusion? I have been at some pains to study this subject, but nowhere can I discover a parallel; for be it remembered that Spiritualism flourishes best where scepticism is most active. It works hand and hand with the materialist Literally it lives, grows, and thrives, upon what, according to all scientific prescriptions, should kill it."

* * * * * *

"Spiritualism, as I have before said, is revolutionary in its present relations to society, and requires revolutionary elements for its *personnel*. Respectability, except it have a strong dash of philosophy in it, is not revolutionary—is, the rather, eminently conservative. Now, to my way of looking at it, the longer you can keep this mass from cooling into dead formality—premising, of course, that in the meantime it be not violently destructive—the better for the world. It is not a bloody revolution; it has not and will not cost a single life—except it be too seriously interfered with. But I anticipate no trouble—the movement is provided with too many safety-valves. At any time a single, well-advertised, so-called 'exposure' converts it from a formidable bristling man-of-war, in the eyes of the world, into the most harmless of hulks, fit to receive, instead of hot-shot and shell, only the sneers and mocking jeers of its vaunting but hoodwinked adversaries."

APPENDIX B.

We subjoin two specimens of inspirational utterances in regard to the expected female Messiah. The first—an extract from the "New Revelation," delivered by "the Messenger" mentioned on p. 352—will also throw light upon the theory of the Two-in-one.

"Adam, created, stood alone upon the earth, yet not alone. One yet two! For his Dual Nature was manifested at the will and touch of his Creator: the inner spirit cleft in twain, one-half evolved into outer nature, and taking form ever from the body of the man, as woman stood beside him!

"Together they stood—Two, yet One. And God saw that it was good; for in His own image created He him: male and female created He them: a mystery to themselves: a Figure of the mystery of God: and a Type in the foreknowledge of God of the Man that was to come!

"Man, therefore, was created Dual: One being in Two expressions: One spirit cleft in Twain, manifested in Two outward forms. And as the things of this world are but the figures of the heavenly—and as man is made in the likeness of God, and God is manifested to us through Christ, 'the express Image of His Person'—and as the Second Adam, the Lord from Heaven, has stood once upon the earth—

"So also, at the time appointed by the Father, shall appear from Heaven

THE SECOND EVE,
WHO IS
THE MOTHER OF ALL LIVING."

Our second specimen is extracted from "The Perfect Way," being a vision accorded to one of the writers, and is entitled,

"A New Annunciation."

"A golden chalice, like those used in Catholic rites, but having three linings, was given to me by an Angel. These linings, he told me, signified the three degrees of the heavens —purity of life, purity of heart, and purity of doctrine.

"Immediately afterwards there appeared a great dome-covered temple, Moslem in style, and on the threshold of it a tall angel clad in linen, who, with an air of command, was directing a party of men engaged in destroying and throwing into the street numerous crucifixes, Bibles, prayer-books, altar utensils, and other sacred emblems. As I stood watching, somewhat scandalized at the apparent sacrilege, a Voice, at a great height in the air, cried with startling distinctness, 'All the idols he shall utterly destroy!' Then the same Voice, seeming to ascend still higher, cried to me, 'Come hither and see!' Immediately it appeared to me that I was lifted up by my hair and carried above the earth.

"And suddenly there arose in mid-air the apparition of a man of majestic aspect, in an antique garb, and surrounded by a throng of prostrate worshippers. At first the appearance of this figure was strange to me; but while I looked intently at it, a change came over the face and dress, and I thought I recognized Buddha —the Messiah of India. But scarcely had I convinced myself of this when a great Voice, like a thousand voices shouting in unison, cried to the worshippers: 'Stand upright on your feet: worship God only!' And again the figure changed, as though a cloud had passed before it, and now it seemed to assume the shape of Jesus. Again I saw the kneeling adorers, and again the mighty Voice cried, 'Arise! worship God only!' The sound of this Voice was like thunder, and I noted that it had seven echoes. Seven times the cry reverberated, ascending with each utterance, as though mounting from sphere to sphere. Then suddenly I fell through the air, as though a hand had been withdrawn from sustaining me, and again touching the earth, I stood within the temple I had seen in the first part of my vision. At its east end was a great altar, from above and behind which came faintly a white and beautiful light, the radiance of which was arrested and obscured by a dark curtain suspended from the dome before the altar. And the body of the temple, which, but for the curtain, would have been fully illumined, was plunged in gloom, broken only by the fitful gleams of a few half-expiring oil-lamps, hanging here and there from the vast cupola. At the right of the altar stood the same tall Angel I had before seen on the temple-threshold, holding in his hand a smoking censer. Then, observing that he was looking earnestly at me, I said to him, 'Tell me what curtain is this before the Light, and why is the temple in darkness?' And he answered, 'This veil is not One, but Three; and the Three are Blood, Idolatry, and the Curse of Eve. And to you it is given to withdraw them; be faithful and courageous; the time has come.' Now the first curtain was red, and very heavy; and with a great effort I drew it aside, and said, 'I have put away the veil of blood from before Thy face; shine, O Lord God!' But a Voice from behind the folds of the two remaining coverings answered me, 'I cannot shine because of the idols.' And lo, before me a curtain of many colours, woven about with all manner of images, crucifixes, madonnas, Old and New Testaments, prayer-books, and other religious symbols, some strange and hideous like the idols of China and Japan, some beautiful like those of the Greeks and Christians. And the weight of the curtain was like lead, for it was thick with gold and silver embroideries. But with both hands I tore it away, and cried, 'I have put away the idols from before Thy face; shine, O Lord God!' And now the Light was clearer and brighter. But yet before me hung a third veil, all of black, and upon it was traced in outline the figure of four lilies on a single stem inverted, their cups opening downwards. And from behind this veil the Voice answered me again, 'I cannot shine because of the curse of Eve.' Then I put forth all my strength, and with a great will rent away the curtain, crying, 'I have put away her curse from before Thee; shine, O Lord God!'

"And there was no more veil, but a landscape more glorious and perfect than words can paint, a garden of absolute beauty, filled with trees of palm, and olive, and fig; rivers of clear water and lawns of tender green; and distant groves and forests framed about by mountains crowned with snow; and on the brow of their shining peaks a rising Sun, whose light it was I had seen behind the veils. And about the Sun, in mid-air, hung white misty shapes of great Angels, as clouds at morning float above the place of dawn. And beneath, under a mighty tree of cedar, stood a white elephant, bearing in his golden houdah a beautiful woman, robed as a queen, and wearing a crown. But while I looked, entranced and longing to look for ever, the garden, the altar, and the temple, were carried up from me into Heaven.

"Then, as I stood gazing upwards, came again the Voice, at first high in the air, but falling earthwards as I listened. And behold, before me appeared the white pinnacle of a minaret, and around and beneath it the sky was all gold and red with the glory of the rising Sun.

"And I perceived that now the Voice was that of a solitary Muezzin standing on the minaret with uplifted hands and crying;—

"'Put away Blood from among you!
Destroy your Idols!
Restore your Queen!'

"And straightway a Voice, like that of an infinite multitude, coming as though from above and around and beneath my feet—a Voice like a wind rising upwards from caverns under the hills to their loftiest far-off heights among the stars—responded—

"'Worship God alone!'"

APPENDIX C.

From the first volume of a series intended "to bring within the reach, intellectual and pecuniary, of all classes of readers the teachings contained in the book after which it is named"—that is, "The Perfect Way"—we extract some remarks upon the new cycle mentioned on p. 378.

"Already have some of the more enthusiastic among the faithful adopted the style indicated on our title-page, by reckoning 1882 as the first year of the New Era, and calling it Anno Dominæ—the year of our Lady—1, considering that the reign of the masculine and force-element is past, and the reign of the feminine and love-element has begun, the turning point of the change being in 1881, from which hereafter will be dated the beginning of the removal of the 'Curse of Eve,' and the rehabilitation and restoration, to her true place in the divine-human system, of the Woman as representative of the soul and of the intuition" ("How the World came to an End in 1881," p. 83).